FRONTIERS OF THEOLOGY
IN LATIN AMERICA

FRONTIERS OF THEOLOGY IN LATIN AMERICA

EDITED BY ROSINO GIBELLINI

TRANSLATED BY JOHN DRURY

Gustavo Gutiérrez
Raúl Vidales
Joseph Comblin
Luis G. del Valle
Leonardo Boff
Hugo Assmann
Ronaldo Muñoz
Segundo Galilea
Enrique Dussel
Juan Carlos Scannone
Juan Luis Segundo
José Míguez Bonino
Rubem Alves

ORBIS BOOKS
Maryknoll, New York 10545

Library of Congress Cataloging in Publication Data

Main entry under title:

Frontiers of theology in Latin America.

　　Translation of La Nuova frontiera della teologia
in America Latina.
　　Bibliography: p.
　　CONTENTS:　　Gustavo Gutiérrez.—Raúl Vidales.—Joseph
Comblin.—Luis G. del Valle.—Leonardo Boff.—Hugo
Assmann. [etc.]
　　1.　Liberation theology—Addresses, essays, lectures.
2.　Theology, Doctrinal—Addresses, essays, lectures.
I.　Gibellini, Rosino.
BT83.57.N8613　　　261.8'098　　　78-9147
ISBN 0-88344-144-6 pbk.

The Catholic Foreign Mission Society of America (Maryknoll) recruits and trains
people for overseas missionary service. Through Orbis Books Maryknoll aims to
foster the international dialogue which is essential to mission. The books published, however, reflect the opinions of their authors and are not meant to represent the official position of the Society.

To Sergio Méndez Arceo
Bishop of Cuernavaca

Contents

Preface

Making use of earlier efforts at reflection and committed involvement, the 1968 Medellín Conference of Latin American bishops injected a new category into church reflection and ecclesial discourse. The new category, "liberation," became the central axis of a fresh theological approach that goes by the name of "liberation theology" or "theology of liberation."

Only the broad outlines of this new approach were indicated by the Medellín Conference. It was articulated much more fully in the now classic work by Gustavo Gutiérrez entitled *A Theology of Liberation*, which first appeared in Peru in 1971. The gradual development of his thinking is described for the reader in the brief biographical essay on him at the back of this volume. But Gutiérrez's work itself was only the tip of an iceberg. The theology of liberation slowly began to surface as a new frontier in theology and an original movement within the church.

In modern times Christian theology has been predominantly a European affair, with offshoots in North America; and it has also been predominantly an academic affair. By contrast the new theological approach surfaced in Latin America, a region on the periphery of world politics, and it was the work of theologians deeply involved in the struggle for liberation on their continent. However, these theologians were quick to point out that this was not just a "Latin American" theology. It was not as if European theology were the only theology that could be considered "the theology of the universal church." The new theology developed in Latin America was to be a summons and a challenge to the conscience of all Christians. It was to be a prophetic witness offered

to the universal church and Latin America's contribution toward
a truly "catholic" theology. What had been a colonial church was
becoming a truly autochthonous church.

   In one of the most illuminating passages to be found in contemporary theological literature, Gustavo Gutiérrez spelled out
clearly the difference between the new approach in Latin America
and the way theology poses its questions in the North Atlantic
Basin:

A goodly part of contemporary theology seems to take its start from the
challenge posed by the *nonbeliever*. The nonbeliever calls into question
our *religious world*, demanding its thoroughgoing purification and revitalization. Bonhoeffer accepted that challenge and incisively formulated the question that underlies much contemporary theological effort:
How are we to proclaim God in a world come of age [*mündig*]? In a
continent like Latin America, however, the main challenge does not come
from the nonbeliever but from the *nonhuman*—i.e., the human being who
is not recognized as such by the prevailing social order. These are the poor
and exploited people, the ones who are systematically and legally despoiled of their being human, those who scarcely know what a human
being might be. These nonhumans do not call into question our religious
world so much as they call into question our *economic, social, political,
and cultural world*. Their challenge impels us toward a revolutionary
transformation of the very bases of what is now a dehumanizing society.
The question, then, is no longer how we are to speak about God in a world
come of age; it is rather how to proclaim him Father in a world that is not
human and what the implications might be of telling nonhumans that
they are children of God.[1]

   Liberation theology is a richly variegated affair, both in its
motifs and in the personalities involved. That fact gave rise to this
volume, which seeks to provide an articulate, up-to-date, and representative sample for this new theological trend in the church
and its main spokesmen. After consulting with qualified
theologians in Latin America, I asked these spokesmen to write
an article for this volume which would spell out the main lines of
their own theological outlook.[2] The result is an anthology of thirteen articles by thirteen different Latin American theologians.
Most of the articles were written specifically for this volume;
where that is not the case, the original source is indicated in the
biographical sketches at the back of this book.

   The thirteen articles can be divided up into six main sections.
The first section contains the article by Gustavo Gutiérrez (1),
which picks up the line of thought in his major writings and can be
regarded as an overall introduction to the topic under discussion
here. The second section contains the articles by Raúl Vidales (2),

Joseph Comblin (3), and Luis del Valle (4); from different points of view it tackles issues centered around the new theological methodology. The third section comprises the articles by Leonardo Boff (5) and Hugo Assmann (6), and it is concerned mainly with the formulation of Christology within the framework of liberation theology. The fourth and fifth sections are made up of single articles on ecclesial themes: Ronaldo Muñoz (7) discusses ecclesiology, and Segundo Galilea (8) discusses spirituality and pastoral activity. The sixth and final section contains articles dealing with a variety of key issues in liberation theology. Enrique Dussel (9) discusses the historical backdrop. Juan Carlos Scannone (10) discusses popular culture as the hermeneutic locale for any liberation project. Juan Luis Segundo (11) discusses the central role of the choice to be made between a capitalist society on the one hand and a socialist society on the other. José Míguez Bonino (12) relates liberation theology to some of the classic themes of Protestant theology. Finally, Rubem Alves (13) offers an interesting piece of theological autobiography centered around the theology of captivity.

We close the volume with two appendixes that we hope will be of further benefit to the reader. Appendix I provides a combined biographical and bibliographical sketch of each contributor, outlining some of the stages in the development of his thinking. Appendix II provides an additional bibliography of other authors and anthologies dealing with the same general topic. The bibliographical work for this volume was done in collaboration with Raúl Vidales, a young Mexican theologian who is presently working in Lima. As the reader will readily see, liberation theology is not a homogeneous bloc; it contains manifold strands of thought and a variety of personal outlooks.

In more recent years these "theologians on the periphery" have begun to draw up a balance sheet of their work. Almost all the major theologians of Latin America involved in this new line of thought attended the 1975 Latin American theological conference in Mexico City. There they drew up various strategies for a theology and praxis of liberation in a basic situation of exile and captivity. At that conference Hugo Assmann pointed out that the time had come for "necessary negotiations and necessary alliances."

At the 1975 "Theology in the Americas" conference in Detroit, Latin American theologians made their first personal contact with people involved in liberation theology on other fronts. They met theologians interested in black theology of liberation and the theology of the women's liberation movement.[3]

I personally want to thank all the theologians who accepted my invitation to contribute to this volume, and whom I met at the two conferences just noted. My particular thanks go to Gustavo Gutiérrez and Segundo Galilea, who discussed this project with me on several different occasions. I also want to thank Ivan Illich, who welcomed me to Cuernavaca (Mexico) and let me have access to the CIDOC library. There I was able to fill out more details of the contributors' lives and work. Finally, I dedicate this volume to Sergio Méndez Arceo, the bishop of Cuernavaca, in memory of his warm and hospitable reception.

ROSINO GIBELLINI

NOTES

1. "Praxis de liberación, teología y anuncio," in *Concilium* 96, 1974, published by Seabury Press in the United States. The entire volume deals with Latin American theology and its emphasis on liberation praxis and Christian faith.

2. One of the most distinguished Argentinian theologians, Lucio Gera, could not participate in this project for reasons of health. Some of his main writings are listed in Appendix II of this volume.

3. See *Theology in the Americas*, ed. Sergio Torres and John Eagleson (Maryknoll, New York: Orbis Books, 1976).

1

Liberation Praxis and Christian Faith

Gustavo Gutiérrez (Lima, Peru)

The most recent years of Latin American history have been characterized by the discovery of the real-life world of "the other," of the poor and exploited and their compelling needs. In a social order fashioned economically, politically, and ideologically by a few for their own benefit, the "other" side has begun to make its voice heard. The lower classes of the populace, forced to live on the margins of society and oppressed since time immemorial, are beginning to speak for themselves more and more rather than relying on intermediaries. They have discovered themselves once again, and they now want the existing system to take note of their disturbing presence. They are less and less willing to be the passive objects of demagogic manipulation and social or charitable welfare in varied disguises. They want to be the active subjects of their own history and to forge a radically different society.

This discovery is made, however, only within the context of a revolutionary struggle. That struggle is calling the existing social order into question from the roots up. It insists that the people must come to power if society is to be truly free and egalitarian. In such a society private ownership of the means of production will

1

be eliminated because it enables a few to expropriate the fruits of labor performed by the many, generates class divisions in society, and permits one class to be exploited by another. In such a reordered society the social takeover of the means of production will be accompanied by a social takeover of the reins of political power that will ensure people's liberty. Thus the way will be open to a new social awareness.

For some years now a growing number of Christians have come to participate in this revolutionary process. Through that participation they have come to discover the whole world of the exploited in Latin America. This Christian involvement and commitment constitutes the major fact in the current life of the Christian community in Latin America. It has produced a new way of being human and Christian, of pondering and living the faith, of being convoked as an *ekklesia*. It has drawn a dividing line between two stages of experience and history, of lived reality and discourse, in Latin America and hence in the church.

Christian participation in this liberation process varies in depth and form from country to country. It is expressed in groping language that moves forward by trial and error. Sometimes it gets bogged down in quagmires and sidetracked into dead ends; at other times some event or concrete experience opens up the road ahead. The radical novelty of the new road for theological reflection and the community's celebration of the faith came to light only gradually. Only slowly did people realize that they would have to comprehend and celebrate their faith from the standpoint and context of the liberative praxis through which Latin Americans are fashioning a different social order and a new way of living as human beings.

Here I shall limit myself to remarks about this liberation praxis in Latin America and the involvement of Christians in it. This will enable me to show how liberation praxis serves as the matrix for a new kind of discourse about the faith and new forms of Christian community.

LIBERATION PRAXIS AS THE MATRIX

I noted above that Christian involvement in the praxis of liberation constitutes the major fact of present-day life in the Christian community within Latin America. It marks a stage in a long process and is itself the fruit of what went before. Perhaps the best way to get inside it and see its consequences would be to follow the itinerary which many Christians in Latin America have felt compelled to follow once they took note of liberation praxis in history and its exigencies.

A Long Journey

For a long time, and still today in the case of many people, Latin American Christians displayed an almost total lack of concern for temporal tasks. They were subjected to a type of religious upbringing that viewed the "hereafter" as the locale of authentic life. The present life was seen as a stage-setting where people were put to the test so that their eternal destiny might be decided. The reality of the "hereafter" was experienced and lived in a religious domain that was viewed as the only real world. It had its own inner logic and self-consistency, and it was separate from the everyday life of human beings. It was a world with its own self-sufficient norms, behavior patterns, and cultic rituals. Outside that world, beneath it to be more precise, lay the realm of the profane, and of politics if you will. It was a fleeting, transitory world with a certain air of unreality about it. However, this air of unreality did not stop those who claimed to be living solely for the hereafter from making sure that they were solidly ensconced in the world of here and now. They needed some solid platform, it seems, from which to urge others not to become attached to things that are perishable and shortlived. Eternal life was considered to be wholly a future life. It was not thought to be actively and creatively present in our present involvement in human history as well.

Such was the restricted vision of human life that prevailed. On the surface it seemed to bear the hallmark of spiritual and religious traits, but in reality it stemmed from a seriously reductionist view of the gospel message. The good will of some of those who sought to salvage the absolute character of God's kingdom in this defective way had no impact whatsoever on objective results. The gospel message was thus rendered as innocuous as a lap dog. From such a gospel the great and powerful of this world had little to fear and much to gain. Their support and backing of it was quickly forthcoming.

At that point in time Christian categories and values were taken over or reinterpreted by the ideology of the existing social order. Thus they came to reinforce the domination of one social class over another. Today the support of the dominant groups continues to be offered, and is often accepted, for the defense of "the Christian civilization of the West." This offer of support has always been conditional. Today, thanks to certain recent events in the life of the Latin American church, it is also accompanied by a threat: i.e., if the church refuses this offer of support, it can be sure that hostility and repression are right around the corner.

The new turn of events began modestly enough. Some decades ago various groups of Christians opened their eyes to what was called "the social question." The current of Christian social doctrine and Christian social concern made its way to Latin America, playing a role in awakening social awareness among some Christians. In certain countries it still continues to play that role today. The poverty in which the vast majority of Latin Americans find themselves ceased to be viewed as a matter of historical fatalism, and the people themselves were no longer regarded as merely passive objects of charitable works. Social injustice began to surface as the fundamental cause of the general situation. How could one claim to be a Christian if one did not commit oneself to remedying that situation? The Christian individual felt challenged and summoned by the harsh reality, but at that time people did not see so clearly that it was society as a whole and its prevailing system of values that were being called into question from the roots up. They did not realize that Christians were being challenged in radically demanding and comprehensive terms. The feeling then was that a more just and Christian society could be created by making the existing society a little better, by integrating those on its outskirts and doing something about the more crying forms of injustice. Sometimes the projected goals went a bit further, but the underlying socio-economic analysis lacked a truly scientific methodology. As a result, it usually ended up in some vague and general defense of the dignity of the human person, whatever the original intention may have been.

When a more scientific grasp of reality began to surface, the language turned more aggressive, and the initiatives became more effective. The point of departure, however, remained the same: i.e., doctrinal affirmations of basic principles that were cast in completely ahistorical terms. This led to a somewhat curious result, as past and even present political experience shows. The positions taken on social issues retained a certain air of ambiguity. Originally they were rejected as subversive by the prevailing system. Because of their ambiguity, however, they could be reabsorbed by the existing social order that they purported to alter. Today we have reached the point in some countries where they furnish ideological support and political allies for the most conservative and reactionary elements.[1] Within this general context, theological reflection was tinged with social concern but remained basically the same as it had always been.

This new social outlook of a Christian cast did not have equal impact on all the countries of Latin America. In many places people soon noted the inadequacies and ambiguities of the label "Christian" when applied to political activity; this was particularly true of people associated with the lay apostolate. Involvement in partisan and party politics meant involvement in various organizations where Christians and people of other religious beliefs worked openly together. When Christians got together as Christians, they did so on a different plane. Professing one and the same faith, they formed communities in which they shared their experiences of the Christian life on the basis of differing political commitments. These people were viewed with suspicion by other Christians who felt that Christianity should form a solid politico-religious bloc, though it might differ greatly from the conservative and traditional line or context. Under the cover of "Christian humanism," this Christian bloc would eventuate in distinct political parties of Christian inspiration.

However, the first group mentioned above made gradual headway in some Latin American countries. Thanks to their vigorous efforts, Christian groups were not compelled to submit to one single political perspective or option. An opening was created for differing points of view, and more than a decade ago we saw the beginnings of a fight against certain ideological uses of Christianity.

This effort at mental hygiene was attended by a theology that stressed the plane of faith proper and differentiated it from the plane of temporal activity. It was a contribution of major importance that permitted a real step forward, but the surrounding context remained very intraecclesial. The mundane realm of history and politics was not seen as something that could call into question people's way of understanding and living the faith. However, the effort at mental hygiene would have an impact later when the process of political radicalization got under way. This process would appear first in those countries where the distinction of planes had been noted and acted upon with peculiar intensity. Moreover, thanks to the earlier effort, the adoption of a radically new political perspective would not come about primar-

ily as a polemical reaction to an immediate past dominated by
temporal institutions of a specifically Christian cast. Such institutions would leave their mark on other processes, however, and
with good reason.[2]

Whichever of these two pathways were followed, one thing is
certain. More and more we see a converging trend, initiated by
young people in particular. In ever widening circles people began
to abandon positions that did not go beyond some form of developmentalism rooted in reformist principles. The socialist revolution in Cuba opened up new political horizons. The year 1965
marked a high point in armed warfare on the continent and has-
tened the political radicalization even of people who believed that
other approaches to revolutionary action should be adopted.

The figures of Camilo Torres and Che Guevara sealed the process irrevocably and had a decisive influence on various Christian
sectors in Latin America. The repressive character of the prevailing system was accentuated in most Latin American countries. To
the "institutionalized violence" condemned by the Medellín episcopal conference was added the indiscriminate use of force (imprisonment, torture, and assassination). That is how "order" was
to be maintained in the face of popular movements and uprisings.
Brazil deserves special mention in this connection, because the
highly critical situation within the country was matched by
claims to exert hegemony over nearby countries. Acting in effect
as the agent of imperialist capitalism, Brazil began to export a
model of economic growth based on the most refined and cold-
blooded exploitation of the lower classes and the less favored
sections of the country—which was courageously denounced by
the bishops of Brazil.[3] In some nearby countries this exported
model reinforced, or brought back into power, the most conservative wing of the ruling groups.

At the same time, however, other possibilities were opening up.
Though they were in the minority, they sought to implement a
more independent policy vis-à-vis imperialism. Utilizing the pressure of popular movements, they hoped to eliminate the most
crying forms of injustice and to move toward major social reforms.
Ambiguous and reversible, these efforts and initiatives were
capable of mobilizing the taproots of political energy in the exploited classes. At times they seemed to possess this capability
despite themselves, but in any case such mobilization was indispensable for any truly revolutionary transformation.

The political radicalization of the continent was moving growing numbers of Christians toward revolutionary stances. In the first stage faith now began to appear as something offering motivation and justification for a revolutionary commitment. Stripped of every ideological element that falsified a cruel and conflict-ridden social situation, the gospel message not only had no quarrel with revolution but actually demanded one. So around 1966 we see the appearance of a new line of biblical reflection, which was made explicit and publicized as a "theology of revolution." (One of its subheadings was the "theology of violence," which, like the proverbial tree, tended to obscure the forest.) Worked out initially by theologians who were not Latin Americans, it was taken out of its original context and, with certain resonances from a particular line of German theology, transposed to Latin America.[4] In this line of thought personal commitment was much more thorough and radical, calling into question the established social order in its totality; its political analysis was also far more penetrating. In some cases its proponents also pointed up the fact of class conflict. The theology of revolution, which was an attendant feature of this more basic posture, offered support and justification for the revolutionary commitment of Christians. Its merit lay in the fact that it was a first step in tearing down the image that linked the faith with an unjust social order. In return, however, there was a danger that it might be turned into a "Christian ideology of revolution" and nothing more.

Well received by some Christian groups who were taking their first steps toward involvement in the revolutionary process, its potentially restricted character soon began to surface. Despite the intentions of its first proponents, and of its own underlying thrust, it began to be used solely to "baptize" revolution. Its theological inadequacy became evident when it was presented simply as an ad hoc discussion and justification of revolution based on a rather fundamentalist interpretation of certain biblical texts—of passages in the Old Testament in particular. Thus the point of departure, and hence the way of engaging in theological reflection, had not changed. Revolutionary activity simply became a new field for the application of theological reflection. The latter was now a bit more advanced, but it still did not call into question a particular way of understanding the faith. It was not theological reflection from within the context of the liberation process; nor was it critical reflection flowing from, and dealing with, the historical praxis of liberation and faith itself as liberation-praxis.

The World of the Other

Many Christians took the journey whose high points I have just sketched. Insofar as they did, a new possibility opened up before them. They might now go one step further and begin to enter an entirely new world—the world of the other, of the poor and exploited and oppressed classes.

Love of neighbor is an essential component of Christian life. But as long as I apply that term only to the people who cross *my* path and come asking me for help, my world will remain pretty much the same. Individual almsgiving and social reformism is a type of love that never leaves its own front porch ("If you love those who love you, what merit is there in that?") On the other hand my world will change greatly if I go out to meet other people on *their* path and consider them as my neighbor, as the good Samaritan did—if I go out to meet other people on streetcorners and byways, in factories and mines, in decaying inner cities and slums. That is precisely what is entailed in "opting for the poor," because the gospel tells us that the poor are the supreme embodiment of our neighbor. It is this option that serves as the focus for a new way of being human and Christian in today's Latin America.[5]

But the existence of the poor is not fated fact; it is not neutral on the political level or innocent of ethical implications. Poor people are by-products of the system under which we live and for which we are responsible. Poor people are ones who have been shunted to the sidelines of our socio-cultural world. Poor people are those who are oppressed and exploited, who are deprived of the fruits of their labor and stripped of their life and reality as human beings. Poor people are members of the proletarian class. That is why the poverty of the poor is not a summons to alleviate their plight with acts of generosity but rather a compelling obligation to fashion an entirely different social order.

But we must consider this option carefully and notice its precise nature. When we opt for the poor in a commitment to liberation, we are forced to realize that we cannot isolate oppressed people from the social class to which they belong. If we were to do that, we would simply be sympathizing with their own individual situations. Poor and oppressed people are members of a social class which is overtly or covertly exploited by another social class. The proletariat is simply the most belligerent and clear-cut segment of this exploited social class. To opt for the poor is to opt for one social class over against another; to take cognizance of the fact of class confrontation and side with the oppressed; to enter into the milieu of the exploited social class and its associated cultural categories and values; to unite in fellowship with its interests, concerns, and struggles.

Various Christian sectors are now swiftly doing precisely that. Some segments of the common people are becoming more and more aware of their own class interests; other segments of the populace are joining in fellowship with those interests and the battles that must be fought to defend them. This solidarity finds expression in numerous texts published by various groups both before and after the Medellín Conference, which establish the immediate context and point up its urgency. But it finds its primary expression in various sorts of real-life commitment undertaken throughout the continent.

At bottom we are confronted with a real process of evangelical conversion, of coming out of one's self and opening up to God and other people. More and more Christians in Latin America are going through this experience, be they lay people, religious, priests, or bishops. It is not a private, idealistic conversion confined to the inner life of the individual, however. This particular process of conversion is conditioned by the surrounding socioeconomic, political, cultural, and human milieu. It is in that milieu that the conversion process takes place, with the ultimate aim of transforming it in turn. We must break with our mental categories, our cultural milieu, our social class, our old way of relating to other people, and our old way of identifying ourselves with the Lord. In short, we must break with anything and everything that hinders real and effective solidarity with those who are suffering from a situation of injustice and spoliation; we must break with anything that precludes a real meeting with Christ in and through alienated and oppressed human beings.

A New Understanding of the Political Realm

This same option entails a different way of approaching the political realm and taking a stand on political matters. It comes down to taking a socialist and revolutionary stand, thereby shouldering the task of politics from a very different perspective. This new perspective is much more all-embracing, scientific, and conflict-ridden than one might suspect at first in making a commitment to politics.

For a long time the political sector seemed to be just one more special sector of human life alongside family life, professional work, and leisure activities. Political activity was something a person took on in his or her spare moments; and politics as such was the special task of certain people who took on this responsibility as their own peculiar vocation.

Today, however, those who have opted for a personal commitment to liberation see politics as a dimension that embraces and conditions every area of human life and activity. It is the comprehensive conditioning factor and the collective battleground in the struggle for human fulfillment. Only when we start from this basic revolutionary standpoint and see the comprehensive role of politics can we then go on to properly define politics in the more restricted sense—i.e., as the desire and effort to win political power.

Every human activity, then, has a political dimension. To talk about the political dimension is not to disregard the multidimensional nature of human beings but rather to take it into account. It is to reject all narrow specialization that is socially unfruitful precisely because it distracts our attention from the concrete conditions in which human life unfolds. Within this freshly conceived context of politics, people emerge as free and responsible beings, as beings related to nature and other human beings, as ones who take the reins of destiny in their own hands and transform history.

Because of an upbringing that was ahistorical and focused on abstract principles, Christians were generally insensitive, if not actually hostile, to any line of scientific reasoning applied to the political realm. But those who got involved in the struggle to fashion a different sort of society felt an urgent need to acquire a precise and rigorously accurate knowledge of the mechanisms of capitalist society, which is centered around private profit and private ownership for the sake of profit. Only such knowledge could ensure effective action.

Lyrical but vague statements in defense of the dignity of the human person are completely ineffective insofar as they do not take account of the causative factors underlying the existing social order or the concrete conditions that must be met in fashioning a just society. Such statements can only deceive oneself and other people. A scientific line of reasoning is absolutely necessary, no matter how demanding it may prove to be; and it is a very real possibility, though it may still be far from worked out. Thanks to its appearance in the realm of history and societal life, people today have begun to take cognizance of the socio-cultural and economic factors that condition their lives; and they have also begun to glimpse the underlying causes of the situation that characterizes those countries that are poorest and most plundered.

It has and still does cost a great deal for Christians to enter into this new outlook. Thanks to it, however, they are moving away from the half-truths that have been so much in circulation. One such half-truth, commonly heard in Christian circles, asserted that it did little or no good to alter social structures if the heart of human beings did not undergo any change. And this was a half-truth because it ignored the fact that "hearts" can also be transformed by altering socio-cultural structures. Both aspects, in other words, are interdependent and complementary because they are grounded on a common unity. The view that a structural transformation will automatically produce different human beings is no more and no less "mechanistic" than the view that a "personal change of heart" will automatically lead to a transformation of society. Any such mechanistic views are naive and unrealistic.

But it is probably another aspect that is most shocking to Christians when they decide to side with the poor and exploited and to commit themselves to the struggle being waged by the proletariat. In such a context their social praxis takes on a very conflictive character. The realm of politics today entails confrontations between different human groups, between social classes with opposing interests; and these confrontations are marked by varying levels of violence. The desire to be an "artisan of peace" not only does not excuse one from taking part in these conflicts; it actually compels one to take part in them if one wants to tackle them at their roots and get beyond them. It forces one to realize that there can be no peace without justice. This is a harsh insight, and it disturbs people who would prefer to overlook conflict-ridden situations and settle for half-measures. It also disturbs people who, with the best of good will, confuse or identify universal love with some fictitious harmony.

But what does the gospel message command us to do? It tells us to love our enemies. In the framework of the Latin American political context this means that we must recognize the fact that

there is conflict between various social classes, that we do have
class enemies, and that those enemies must be combatted. The
gospel does not say that we are not to have enemies; it says that
we are not to exclude our enemies from our love. But we Christians are not much accustomed to thinking in historical terms
with all the conflict entailed. We prefer irenic conciliation over
antagonism, an evasive eternity over the provisional realities of
history. We must learn how to ponder and live peace in conflict and
the transhistorical in time.

Poverty and Solidarity

Liberation praxis is becoming more mature and questioning.
Henceforth it is in the framework of politics that Christians committed to the poor and the liberation of the exploited classes will
ponder and live out their faith. They will spontaneously turn their
thoughts toward a basic evangelical exigency as their guiding
star: i.e., poverty. This they must do if they wish to identify with
Christ, who came to preach the good news to the poor and to set
free the oppressed. They will be very much surprised by what they
find.[6]

As lived and thought about within the church, poverty tended to
be imprisoned within the context and limits of the religious life. It
was confined to one particular lifestyle based on a vow of poverty.
Above and beyond the realm of pure and noble intentions, poverty
seemed to be the private property of a certain group of Christians
who often seemed to flaunt it as if it were their particular form of
wealth. The average Christian, it was said, had no vocation to
poverty. In small doses it was advisable for all, and all could
benefit from a life of moderation and sobriety; but poverty was not
a precept that strictly defined the nature of Christian living.

It was not a bad division of labor insofar as Christians were
concerned. Those who lived by the solemn vow of poverty were
considered to be on a higher level of Christian perfection because
they had renounced worldly goods and pleasures. Other Christians could enjoy such wordly advantages; but in return they had
to settle for a lower level of status and perfection on the Christian
scale of values. At the same time, however, their life in the world
enabled them to sustain the more perfect Christians through
their almsgiving. Everyone gained something, everyone bene-
fited—except the gospel message itself, and the poor and exploited of this world.

For something more serious and subtle was also at work here. Poverty itself was proclaimed as a Christian ideal. But because this affirmation stayed on the level of vague generality, it was open to all sorts of ambiguity and equivocation. First of all, the Bible itself tells us that material poverty is a subhuman situation, a result of injustice and sinfulness; so a situation characterized by poverty cannot be a Christian ideal. To aspire to such a situation would be to aspire to something that denigrates people. If such were a Christian ideal, then the exigencies of the gospel message would run directly counter to the deepest aspirations of human beings. For people want to free themselves from subjection to nature, to eliminate exploitation, and to create better living conditions for all. No less serious is the fact that such an ideal would wittingly or unwittingly justify the unjust and exploitative situation that is the fundamental cause of poverty, of the concrete poverty suffered by the vast majority of Latin Americans.

In recent years concrete witness to poverty and theological reflection on it began to undergo a real change. It began with various religious communities whose spirituality was centered around a life of poverty and contemplation. This two-edged style of life was not accidental to the process, and the two faces continue to be operative today in a different context. Gradually the new exigencies of poverty began to have their impact on other segments of religious within the church. They felt compelled to trace the notion back to its roots and to give it a deeper meaningfulness. Soon, however, these exigencies spread beyond the boundaries of the religious life. Broad segments of the Christian flock now feel that they must give radical witness to poverty in their own lives because such real and radical witness was essential to any life that was to be truly in conformity with the gospel message. Thus they came to call the whole church into question, aggressively criticizing any testimony that ran counter to the demands of a truly Christian notion of poverty.

What was involved here was not simply an extension of the basic evangelical summons to a life of poverty, much less a mechanical transposition of poverty as lived by religious orders to other segments of the Christian population. The basic way of thinking about poverty and living it underwent a change, and that process is still going on. Solidarity with the poor, commitment to the liberation of the exploited classes, and renewed involvement in politics led to a rereading of the gospel message. Indeed only a process of criticism flowing out of liberation praxis would enable people to denounce the ideological function served by various ways of interpreting poverty and would thus lead them to a reinterpretation of the gospel message. The Medellín Conference of 1968 was framed within this process of rereading and reinterpretation which in turn resulted from the new experiences of various Christian groups.

Evangelical poverty now began to be lived as an act of love and liberation in solidarity with the poor of this world and as a protest against the poverty in which they were forced to live. It was seen as a way of identifying oneself with the interests of the oppressed classes and challenging the exploitation that victimized them. If egoism is the ultimate underlying cause of exploitation and alienation, then the ultimate underlying reason for voluntary poverty is love of neighbor. Viewed as the result of social injustice which is ultimately rooted in sin, poverty is now taken on insofar as it is a way of bearing witness against the evil it embodies; it is not taken on insofar as it represents some ideal lifestyle. In this respect it is assumed for much the same reasons that Christ took on the sinful human condition and all its consequences. He certainly did not do it to idealize sin; he did it in a spirit of love and fellowship in order to redeem human beings from their sins; in order to combat human egotism and abolish the injustice and divisiveness existing between human beings; in order to erase anything that produces a situation where there are rich people and poor people, exploiters and exploited. When it is lived in authentic imitation of Christ, the witness of poverty does not alienate us from the world at all. Instead it places us in the middle of oppression and spoliation, so that from that situation we may proclaim liberation and full communion with the Lord. Immersed in that situation, we proclaim and live spiritual poverty as a total openness to God.

Life in the Spirit

All this means entering a very different world. It gives rise to a new and unheard-of type of Christian experience, fraught with possibilities and promise but also with potential impasses and blind alleys. There is no easy road to triumph in living the life of faith. More than a few people are subject to serious tension when they become absorbed in the political demands occasioned by a commitment to liberation. On the one hand they seek to live in fellowship with the exploited; on the other hand they belong to a church, many members of which are closely tied to the existing social order. Their faith seems to lose its dynamism, and they feel anxiety when they note the dichotomy between their political activity on the one hand and their life as Christians on the other. Even more cruel and difficult is the case of those people who see their love of God fade out in favor of the very thing it supposedly instigates and nurtures: love of other people. Their love seems incapable of maintaining the unity that the gospel calls for, and it tends to overlook the fullness intrinsic to it.

Such instances exist, and elementary honesty forces us to acknowledge that fact. If one takes a stand on the new frontiers of life in the Christian community, if one goes out to where the commitment to revolution is being lived most intensely, one is fishing in troubled waters. Clear-eyed analysis with close attention to shadings and details is an absolute necessity. A host of factors are involved in the process. Christians committed to liberation are subject to all sorts of pressure, and they are not exempt from the impact of romanticism, emotional tension, and ambiguous doctrinal bases. All this can quickly lead to hasty breaks and various feelings of exasperation. At the same time, however, it is easy enough to see the responsibility that must be acknowledged by those Christians who take refuge in convenient "orthodoxies," who maintain their feelings of security by staying out of the picture altogether and raising an accusing finger every now and then.

So the difficulty is real enough, and the only way to find solutions is to work from within the very heart of the problem. Protective measures merely veil the real situation and postpone a fruitful response. They also suggest that people have forgotten the seriousness and urgency of the reasons calling for personal commitment to those who are being exploited by a cruel and inhuman system. In the last analysis they imply a lack of belief in the power of the gospel message and the faith. It is there where the proclamation of the gospel seems to immerse itself in the purely historical realm that theological reflection, spirituality, and preaching should now arise. For only in that soil can we preach a Christian message that is incarnated in our here and now. To evangelize, said Chenu, is to incarnate the gospel in time. Our present time is confusing and gloomy only for those who lack hope, who do not realize or are hesitant to believe that the Lord is present in it.

The fact is that for many Christians a commitment to liberation does come down to being an authentic spiritual experience in the original and biblical sense of that term. It means living in and by the Spirit, who helps us to see that we are and can be free and creative children of our father in heaven and brothers and sisters of each other (Gal. 4:6). Only through concrete acts of love and solidarity can we effectively realize our encounter with the poor and the exploited and, through them, with Jesus Christ. To give to them is to say yes to Christ; to refuse them is to reject Christ (Matt. 25:31–46).

The poor human being, the "other," now steps forward as the one who reveals the totally "Other." To live a life in the Spirit is to live in the presence of the Lord in the very midst of political activity, recognizing all its elements of conflict and the need for a scientific line of reasoning. To paraphrase a well known expression, we must be contemplatives in the very midst of our political activity.

We are not used to doing that. Spiritual life and experience is something we are used to viewing as apart, far removed from such impure human realities as politics. But we must now move in a different direction. Instead of looking for an encounter with the Lord through contact with poor individuals in isolation, with "nice" poor people, we must seek that encounter through contact with the oppressed, with all the members of a particular social class who are fighting valiantly for their most basic rights and for an altered society in which they can live as human beings. History is the locale where God reveals the mystery of his person. His word will reach us to the extent that we immerse ourselves in the ongoing process of history, and that history is riddled with conflict. It is filled with confrontations between opposing interests, with bitter struggles for justice, with human alienation and exploitation, and with yearnings for liberation. We turn this history into one of authentic communion when we opt for the poor and exploited classes, identify ourselves with their plight, and share their fate. There is no other way to accept the gratuitous gift of sonship. We must opt for the cross of Christ and have hope in his resurrection.

A NEW THEOLOGICAL DISCOURSE

Commitment to liberation, with all its attendant political exigencies, situates us in a different world. It leads us to a novel spiritual experience in the very midst of liberation praxis, which becomes the matrix of a new type of theological reflection in which we seek to comprehend the gratuitous gift of God's word as it breaks into human existence and transforms it.

A Different World

All the factors mentioned above—opting for the poor, exploited classes and the Latin American proletariat; seeing politics as a dimension that embraces all of human life, entails conflict, and demands a scientific line of reasoning; and rediscovering evangelical poverty as fellowship with the poor and a protest against their poverty—lead us to a wholly different way of perceiving ourselves as human beings and Christians.

To begin with, we come to a radical questioning of the prevailing social order. The poverty and injustice experienced in Latin America are too deeply rooted to allow for half-measures. That is why people now talk about social revolution rather than reform, about liberation rather than developmentalism, and about socialism rather than modernization of the existing system. "Realists" view such affirmations as romantic and utopian, and it is easy enough to see why. For the new affirmations are part of a line of reasoning that is completely alien to them, that proposes a historical project that denounces a society fashioned for the benefit of the few and announces a very different sort of society designed to benefit the poor and oppressed.

The new project is now being worked out. It is based on studies that are as rigorously scientific as possible. These studies start out from the fact that the vast majority of Latin Americans are being exploited by the ruling classes, and that our continent is economically, socially, politically, and culturally dependent on outside power centers located in the affluent countries of the world. External dependence and internal domination characterize the social structures of Latin America.

That is why only a class-based analysis will enable us to see what is really involved in the opposition between oppressed countries on the one hand and dominant peoples on the other. If we focus solely on the confrontation between different nations, we will falsify the real situation and mitigate its harshness. The theory of dependence will lead us astray if its analysis is not framed in the context of the class struggles that are developing on a worldwide scale. Only such an analysis will enable us to grasp the social setup of Latin America as a dependent form of capitalism, and hence to figure out the strategy required to escape from that basic situation.

Only by getting beyond a society divided into classes, only by establishing a form of political power designed to serve the vast

majority of our people, and only by eliminating private ownership
of the wealth created by human labor will we be able to lay the
foundations for a more just society. That is why efforts to project a
new society in Latin America are moving more and more toward
socialism. In doing this people are not ignoring the defects of
many actual embodiments of socialism on the world scene. They
are trying to get away from prefabricated notions and schemas, to
act creatively and follow their own path.

This projected attempt to fashion a very different society also
entails the creation of new human beings, ones who will be increasingly free from every sort of bondage that prevents them
from being active agents of their own destiny in history. This leads
people to question all the prevailing ideologies—which contain
certain religious elements—that now mold people in our society.
But the construction of a different society and a new person will
not be authentic unless it is undertaken by the oppressed themselves; hence it must start from their own values. It is from the
oppressed that the whole process of questioning the present social
order must begin, leading eventually to the abolition of the current oppressive culture.

We will not appreciate the scope of this radical questioning,
however, unless we take a second step. We must take cognizance
of the great change that has taken place in the way that people
come to know truth and relate it to their practice in history. Since
the rise of experimental science people have been acquiring a
more active role in the process of knowledge. They are no longer
restricted to admiring nature and classifying their observations.
They now question nature and provoke it, discovering its laws and
dominating it through technology. The rise of the social and
psychological sciences extended this type of knowledge in some
way to fields that had been reserved for philosophical reflection
only. On a certain level such philosophical considerations retain
their meaningfulness, but henceforth they will have to coexist
with other efforts in what are now called the human sciences.
These are still in their early stages, still trying to find their own
proper approach. They are opening up new human dimensions to
us, but ones that cannot be assimilated to the natural sciences in
any simple way.

All this helps us to see something that may be regarded as a
fundamental trait of contemporary awareness: Knowledge is
bound up with transformation. We do not come to know history,
which is an indissoluble mixture of nature and society, except in

the process of transforming it and ourselves. As Vico put it long ago, we really know only what we ourselves do. For people today truth is what we make true, what we *"veri-fy."* Knowledge of reality that does not lead to a modification of it is really an unverified interpretation, an interpretation that is not transformed into truth. In his penetrating and finely chiselled *Theses on Feuerbach*, Marx starts from that perspective to lay the epistemological bases of his own contribution to a scientific understanding of history. Historical reality thus ceases to be the field for the application of abstract truths and idealistic interpretations; instead it becomes the privileged locale from which the process of knowledge starts and to which it eventually returns. Praxis that transforms history is not the degraded embodiment of some pure, well conceived theory; instead it is the very matrix of all authentic knowledge, and the decisive proof of that knowledge's value. It is the point where people re-create their world and forge their own reality, where they come to know reality and discover their own selves.

A New Understanding of the Faith

The word of the Lord accepted in faith will be pondered and lived today by human beings who operate in terms of these new cultural categories, just as people were once molded by Greek thought. Those who cling to the old ways of thinking, who resist the new approach and accuse its proponents of distorting the faith, remind us of those who once opposed the use of Aristotle's philosophy in theology. And like the latter, they really have no future, though they may succeed for the moment with their sporadic condemnations and unfounded alarms. The future lies with a kind of faith and ecclesial communion that is not afraid of advances in human thinking and social praxis, that is open to questioning by them and ready to challenge them in turn, that is willing to be enriched but is not uncritical, that knows its own conditioning factors but also its own proper exigencies.

It is a complicated task in which we must appeal to many specialized fields. It calls for solid knowledge of all the different facets of contemporary thought, both philosophical and scientific. Without them we cannot elaborate a theological discourse today. This task of trying to comprehend the faith can be undertaken only from the starting point of real-life praxis in history, where human beings fight in order to live as human beings. It is a task animated by our hope in the One who, in revealing himself, reveals to us all the plenitude that lies within us: the Lord of history, in whom all were made and saved.

Commitment to the process of liberation ushers Christians into an unfamiliar world and forces them to take a qualitative leap. Christians must now engage in radical questioning of the social order and its ideology, breaking with their old ways of thinking and knowing in the process. For this reason a type of theological reflection fashioned in a very different cultural context will not tell them very much. To be sure, it does convey to them the awareness of faith that preceding generations of Christians had; and its expressions are points of reference. But that older language still leaves them theological orphans because it does not speak the clear and incisive and forceful language that would accord with the human and Christian experience they are actually living.

At the same time, however, the seeds of a new way of understanding the faith are sprouting within these very experiences. In and through these real-life experiences they have learned how to comprehend, link, and transform theory and praxis. They are forced into a re-reading of the gospel message. There they find something solidly and authentically traditional which, perhaps for that very reason has been overlooked or forgotten by more recent "traditions." They find that evangelical truth, truth as the gospel sees it, is something that is done. John the Evangelist tells us that we must "do" the truth, and that this truth is Love. To live love is to say yes to God. Believing in God is not restricted to affirming God's existence. Believing in God means committing one's life to him and to all people. To have faith is to come out of oneself and give oneself to God and others. As Paul puts it, faith works through charity.

I am not talking here about any mechanical correspondence between this evangelical view of truth and present-day insistence on the connection between knowing reality and transforming the world. But the cultural world in which we live at present does provide us with a newly discovered horizon and point of departure in which our theological reflection can be framed. In this general context it can make a fresh start, though of course it must also go back to its own proper wellsprings.[7]

More and more, then, faith surfaces as a liberation praxis. Insofar as faith is the acceptance of the Father's love and a response to it, it goes right to the root of social injustice. The root of social injustice is sin, which ruptures our friendship with God and our brotherhood with other human beings. But the praxis of faith cannot bypass the mediating realities of history or avoid socio-political analyses of them. For sinfulness occurs in the negation of human beings as brothers and sisters, in oppressive structures created for the benefit of only a few, and in the plundering of nations, races, cultures, and social classes. Sin is the fundamental alienation which, for that very reason, cannot be grasped in itself. It is found only in concrete historical situations and specific embodiments of alienation. It is impossible for us to comprehend the one without the other.

Sin demands a radical liberation, which necessarily includes liberation of a political nature. Only by participating aggressively and effectively in the historical process of liberation can we point a finger at the basic alienation that underlies every partial form of alienation. The radical liberation called for by sin is a gift from Christ. Through his death and resurrection he redeemed us from sin and all its consequences. As the Medellín Conference put it: "It is the same God who, in the fullness of time, sends his Son in the flesh, so that He might come to liberate all men from the slavery to which sin has subjected them: hunger, misery, oppression and ignorance—in a word, that injustice and hatred which have their origin in human selfishness."[8]

But as I have already stressed above, political activity has its own exigencies and laws. Recalling the profound sense it has for a Christian is a far cry from taking a big step backward into some earlier stage of history when people were not yet in a position to appreciate the internal mechanisms of an oppressive society, and when political activity was still at an immature point. We may talk about accepting the gift of divine sonship and making all people our brothers and sisters. But if we do not live that acceptance from day to day in the conflict-ridden reality of history, than we are merely engaging in talk and allowing ourselves to indulge in the self-satisfaction of a noble ideal. This ideal must be translated into real-life identification with the interests of those human beings who actually are being subjected to oppression by other human beings. It must lead to identification with the struggles of the exploited classes. It must enrich political processes from within through its creativity and criticism, for those processes tend to close in upon themselves and mutilate authentic dimensions of the human person. If our action is to be effective, we must use the tools provided by the human sciences so that we may become acquainted with the social realities which negate the justice and brotherhood we are seeking.

Framed in this context, theology will be critical reflection on historical praxis, flowing out of that praxis and a confrontation with the word of the Lord that is accepted and lived by faith. That faith itself comes down to us through a whole series of varied historical mediations which are sometimes ambiguous, but we ourselves rework it from day to day. Theology, then, will be reflection on faith as liberation praxis, reflection inspired by this very faith. It becomes a process of understanding the faith that is based on a previous option.[9] We seek to understand the faith on the basis of our real and effective solidarity with the exploited classes of Latin America, and we do so from within their world. Our reflection, then, is rooted in a commitment to create a just and communal society; and it in turn should help to make this commitment more radical and complete. Thus our theological discourse will be turned into truth, will be veri-fied, in and through its real-life insertion into the process of liberation.

Reflecting on faith as liberation praxis means reflecting on a truth that is not just affirmed but concretely fashioned. In the last analysis the real exegesis of God's word, to which theology seeks to make a contribution, takes place in deeds. It is in deeds, not simply in affirmations, that we salvage our understanding of the faith from all forms of idealism.

The Particular Perspective of Liberation Theology

It is this that differentiates the theology of liberation from other brands of theology with which it is sometimes linked and even mistakenly identified.[10] It differs from these other brands of theology not only in its way of analyzing reality, based on more radical and all-embracing options, but also in its way of theologizing. Liberation theology does not attempt to offer any Christian justification for stances already taken; it does not purport to be a Christian ideology of revolution. It is a process of reflection which starts out from historical praxis. It attempts to ponder the faith from the standpoint of this historical praxis and the way that faith is actually lived in a commitment to liberation.[11] Thus its themes are the great themes of all authentic theology but its focus, its way of approaching them, is different. Its relationship to historical praxis is distinct.

When I say that it does not purport to be a Christian ideology of revolution, I do not mean to suggest that it ignores the process of revolution. On the contrary, its starting point is its insertion in that process. Liberation theology wants to help that process to become more self-critical, and hence more comprehensive and radical. This is done by framing the political commitment to liberation within the context of Christ's gratuitous gift of total liberation.

Christ's liberation is not restricted to political liberation, but it occurs in historical happenings and liberative political actions. We cannot bypass these mediating factors. By the same token, however, political liberation is not some form of religious messianism. It has its own laws and its own proper autonomy; it presupposes very specific social analyses and well defined political options. But when we view human history as one in which Christ's liberation is at work, we enlarge the whole perspective and give full depth and meaning to what is involved in political commitment. Thus we are not engaging in facile but denigratory equations, distortions, or simplistic forms of reductionism; instead we are shedding light on both sides and showing how their exigencies complement and fructify one another.

The theology of liberation is a theology of salvation in the light of the concrete historical and political conditions of the present day. These mediating factors of present-day history and politics, appraised and valued in their own right, change the way we ponder and live the mystery hidden from eternity and now revealed: the mystery of our heavenly Father's love, of human brotherhood, and of salvation. It is that which the term "liberation" seeks to render present.

Theological reflection framed in the perspective of liberation starts off from the perception that this particular context forces us to rethink completely our way of being Christians and our way of being a church. This particular brand of reflection on the divine word that we accept through faith will have recourse to all the different embodiments of human reasoning today, to the human sciences as well as to philosophy. Above all, however, it will have recourse to historical praxis in a very novel way. This is how it differs from every attempt to add a tinge of "social concern" or liberation terminology to age-old pastoral and theological postures. It has become somewhat fashionable to do precisely that in order to move an old line of merchandise that is beginning to lose its appeal. Another effort along the same lines is the one that offers a "spiritualist" interpretation of everything relating to Christ's liberative work. All the human and historical implications of that liberative work are thereby stripped away. It can be accepted by the existing political and ecclesiastical system precisely because it does not call anything into question. It does not render the "other" present on the scene but keeps him safely locked away in a closet. That is why I call it a "spiritualist" interpretation—because it is not "spiritual" in the deeper and fuller sense of the term.[12]

As I have said already, liberation theology as we understand it here involves a direct and specific relationship with historical praxis; and historical praxis is a liberation praxis. It implies identification with oppressed human beings and social classes and solidarity with their interest and struggles. It involves immersion in the political process of revolution, so that from there we may proclaim and live Christ's gratuitous and liberative love. That love goes to the very root of all exploitation and injustice: the breakup of friendship with God and other people. That love enables human beings to see themselves as children of their Father and brothers and sisters to each other.

Yet in the last analysis we will not have an authentic theology of liberation unless and until the oppressed are able to express themselves freely and creatively in society and within the people of God. The sketchy outlines of such a theology that we possess today are merely a start. So far liberation theology has formulated important problems concerning theological methodology that are still to be worked out. It calls upon us to go more deeply into questions dealing with biblical hermeneutics, so that we may clarify its foundations in the Old and New Testaments. It offers us a new perspective within which to contemplate the relationship between faith and political action; and it raises radical questions about ecclesiology. Much work remains to be done, however, if this line of theological thought is to be clarified and if its questioning is to be brought to a fine edge. All sorts of improvements are possible. It could devote more attention to fresh biblical themes or burrow its roots more deeply into the tradition of the church. It could face up to other aspects of contemporary thought, other currents in present-day theology, and other strains of Christian experience. All that would be very useful, and perhaps even imperative, but it would not be enough.

The fact is that so far this critical reflection on liberation praxis has come from sectors in which the popular classes are not present in important or decisive numbers. We must realize that there will be no qualitative leap forward to a different theological outlook until the alienated and exploited become the artisans of their own liberation and make their voice heard directly. More and more they must report on their own experience with the Lord in and through their efforts to liberate themselves. Operating with their own values, they must give an account of their own hope in Christ's total liberation; for in this matter they are the spokespeople for all humankind.

We will get a new and distinctive theological perspective only when our starting point is the social praxis of the real population of Latin America, of those whose roots are buried deep in the geographical, historical, and cultural soil of our region but who now stand mute.[13] It is from that source that we will get a new reading and interpretation of the gospel message as well as a fresh expression of the experiences it has occasioned throughout history and their meaning.

All that implies a historical process of enormous dimensions. If our present theology of liberation, with all its limitations, helps to further that process and thereby open the way for a new understanding of the faith, then it will have fulfilled its role as a transitional step. Like every brand of theology, it is simply the embodiment of a particular process of advertence. It shows us what results when a given generation of Christians, living within the community of the church, take cognizance of their faith at a given moment in history. The particular generation in question here has just begun to break with the prevailing system and to discover the "other" in the world where it still lives. It has just begun to discover the presence of the Lord in the heart of Latin American history.

TOWARD A CHURCH OF THE PEOPLE

Personal involvement in the process of liberation constitutes a profound and decisive spiritual experience at the very heart of active political commitment. As we have already seen, it is the matrix of a new way of theologizing. It is not a matter of applying age-old theological notions to new fields. Instead we are faced with the inducement and the obligation to ponder and live our faith within different socio-cultural categories. That has happened more than once before in the history of the Christian community, of course, and it has always produced disquietude and upset. But we are spurred on to do this by the urgency of expressing the word of the Lord in our own everyday language.

What is involved here is precisely that: a re-reading of the gospel message from within the context of liberation praxis. Here theological discourse operates as a mediator between a new way of living the faith and the communication of that experience. For if theology is a re-reading of the gospel message, that re-reading is done precisely with a view to proclaiming it.[14]

An Ecclesial Experience of Sonship and Brotherhood

Knowing that the Lord loves us and accepting his freely proffered gift of love is the underlying source of the joy that pervades one who lives by God's word. To evangelize is to communicate and share that joy with others, to tell them the good news of God's love for us and the change it has wrought in our lives. In a certain sense that proclamation itself is gratuitous, even as the love that produced it. It is a real-life experience of the Lord that underlies and prompts the task of evangelization. Evangelization flows out of an experience in which we concretely live the Father's love that makes us his children and transforms us as human beings. Through it we become more fully human and more truly brothers and sisters to others.

To proclaim the gospel is to proclaim the mystery of divine adoption and brotherhood that lay hidden from all eternity and was eventually revealed in Jesus Christ. That is why proclaiming the gospel means convening a "church," coming together as an assembled group. Only in community can we live our faith in the spirit of love. Only in community can we celebrate and deepen it. Only in community can we live it as a single and unique gesture of fidelity to the Lord and solidarity with all human beings. Accepting God's word means turning toward the Other in and through the other people with whom we live out this divine word. Faith cannot be lived on the private level of a purely interior life, for faith is the rejection of any turning in upon oneself. The dynamism and inner thrust of the good news, the news which reveals us to be children of our heavenly Father and brothers and sisters of others, leads to the creation of a community that serves as a sign of Christ's liberation to our fellows.

Evangelization Based on Solidarity with the Exploited Classes

This gospel proclamation that convenes a church flows out of a decision to side with the interests and struggles of the poor and exploited classes in a real and active way. The decision to take one's stand in that "locale" represents a radical break with today's way of pondering, living, and communicating the faith in the church. It entails a conversion to the world of the other, a new kind of understanding of the faith, and ultimately a radical reformulation of the message.

What was once regarded as the political dimension of the gospel and its implications now shows up in a very different cast. It now becomes more obvious that we are not dealing with something annexed to the gospel from outside because of debatable pressures in a given age. Instead we are dealing with an aspect that is a necessary consequence of the gospel message itself. Moreover, this aspect or dimension is now shouldered openly and without subterfuges. To be sure, its precise scope remains to be spelled out and oversimplistic perspectives must be avoided. But no alleged apoliticism can continue to hide an obvious reality and to undermine a conviction that is increasingly wholehearted and untainted.

The gift of divine sonship is lived out in history. By making all people our brothers and sisters we accept this gift in deed rather than in word. We live and bear witness to our Father's love by fighting against all injustice and exploitation and actively involving ourselves in the creation of a more humane and fraternal society. The proclamation of a God who loves all people equally must be fleshed out in history, must become history. And that will entail challenge and conflict insofar as we proclaim that love in a society deeply marked by inequality and injustice, by the exploitation of one social class for the benefit of another.

That is why I indicated that the political dimension is part of the intrinsic dynamism of God's word insofar as it seeks to become incarnate in history. The demands of the gospel are incompatible with the social situation in which we live here in Latin America. They are incompatible with the present form of human relationships here, and with the structure in which those relationships are framed. But it is not a matter of rejecting one or another case of individual injustice. We are faced with the urgent task of fashioning a completely different social order. Only a certain level of political maturity will enable us to truly comprehend the political dimension of the gospel and to avoid reducing it to some form of social assistance or a simplistic ideal of "human betterment."

Authentic proclamation of God's love, human brotherhood, and total equality of everyone to the exploited people of our continent will make it clear to them that their situation is contrary to the gospel message; it will help them to take full cognizance of the profound injustice in the present state of affairs. The oppressed classes will acquire a clear-cut political awareness only by participating directly in the struggles of the common people. At the same time, however, the ideological struggle is an important part of the overall political process involved in breaking down the oppressive social order and producing a classless society.

Right now, unfortunately, the "Christian" element plays a different role in Latin America. It is integrated into the prevailing ideology of domination, so that it lends support and cohesiveness to a capitalist society divided into classes. All too frequently conservative sectors appeal to Christian notions to justify the social order that serves their interests and maintains their privileged position. Here we have one of the great falsehoods perpetrated in and on our Latin American society. And that is why the communication of the Christian message, insofar as it is re-read from within the context of the other side and their world, will serve the function of unmasking every attempt to put the gospel to ideological use so that it may justify a situation which is contrary to its own most elementary demands.

Evangelization for Liberation

Are we, then, talking about reducing the gospel to purely political terms? Are we advocating a "political reductionism"? Yes, in the case of those who use it to serve the interests of those in power; no, in the case of those who denounce that usage on the basis of its message of liberation and gratuitous divine love. Yes, in the case of those who place themselves and the gospel in the hands of the mighty of this world; no, in the case of those who identify themselves with the poor Christ and seek to establish solidarity with the dispossessed on this continent. Yes, in the case of those who keep it shackled to an ideology that serves the capitalist system; no, in the case of those who have been set free by the gospel message and then seek to liberate it from that same captivity. Yes, in the case of those who wish to neutralize Christ's liberation by restricting or reducing it to a purely spiritual plane that has nothing to do with the concrete world of human beings; no, in the case of those who believe that Christ's salvation is so total and radical that nothing escapes it. For the latter, evangelization is liberative because it proclaims a total liberation in Christ that includes a transformation of concrete historical and political conditions on the one hand but also conducts that history above and beyond itself to a fulfillment that is not within the reach of human foresight or any human effort.

But the human beings to whom we proclaim the gospel are not abstract, apolitical beings; they are members of a society marked by injustice and human exploitation. The bulk of these people in Latin America belong to the Christian community in one way or another, and that community is not an ahistorical reality. Its past and its present have been intimately bound up with the history of Latin American people—right from the very start, in fact. In the absence of a sound historical perspective we cannot possibly appreciate what it really means to evangelize the people of Latin America today; for the gospel has already been preached to them, so that it is already a part of their lives in one way or another.[15] By the same token, we cannot appreciate the liberative character and implications of evangelization today unless we realize the situation of the church up to now; in terms of the majority of its members, it has always been closely bound up with the social order that now prevails in Latin America.

These historical and political conditionings must be analyzed and spelled out in detail if our new focus is to be made concrete. We wish to proclaim the gospel message in the context of the real-life Latin American situation. We wish to proclaim it in a context where we live the faith in and through political action. We wish to spell out more clearly the relationship between any traditional form of theology and our effort to understand the faith from the context of revolutionary praxis. That will help us to avoid idealistic and pseudo-theoretical formulations that do not come to grips with reality.

We already have had some real incarnation of the gospel message in the past and present history of Latin America. It gives some indication of the limits and prospects of proclaiming the gospel today. It enables us to foresee the conflicts that we will have to face. To mention but a few of the more recent and well known cases, I can cite the names of Henrique Pereira Neto, Néstor Paz, and Héctor Gallego. Other people, still alive, are calumniated and tortured in the name of the "Christian civilization of the West." These and many others attempted to bear witness to their faith in ways that were off the beaten path and that were not sanctioned by the mighty of Latin America. All dissent is castigated by those in power, and that castigation is often upheld vigorously by people who call themselves "Christians." It is here, in fact, that we lay tangible hold of the process that is just begin-ning and that we are trying to describe. It is a process which, as I noted earlier, draws a dividing line between two stages of experi-ence and history, of lived reality and discourse, in Latin America and the life of the church.

The Exploited Classes and the People of God

Proclamation of the gospel based on identification with the poor convenes a church that is in solidarity with the classes to which the common people of Latin America belong. It joins them in their aspirations and struggles to be actively present in Latin Ameri-can history, in the work of abolishing a society built for the benefit of the few and building a more just and human social order for all.

All that leads to radical breaks with the past and new orienta-tions insofar as today's church is concerned.[16] But they will not be fruitful if they merely express various forms of personal anxiety, identity crisis, emotional reaction, and impatience—however legitimate they may be. If we travel that route we will encounter nothing but defensive attitudes, blind authoritarian measures, and gestures prompted by fear or a quest for security; we will get caught up in an endless spiral of intramural struggles and con-flicts within the church. If the breaks with the past and the new orientations are to be radical, they must go to the root of the matter; and the root of the matter lies outside the strictly ec-clesiastical sphere. It lies in our way of being human and Chris-tian in the present real-life situation of Latin America. Today we must identify with the oppressed classes of this continent called Latin America, which is marked by injustice and spoliation on the one hand and hope-filled yearnings for liberation on the other.

This presupposes new types of experience in carrying out the task of evangelization and in coming together as a "church." It means different ways of being present in the world of the common people, ways that get beyond all institutional rigidity. It means knowing how to listen to a voice that is very different from the ones we are used to hearing and heeding in the church. It means taking a critical look at the social and cultural categories that now shackle our manner of proclaiming and living the gospel, so that as a result we are worlds apart from the life of the exploited classes if not in actual opposition to their deepest desires for liberation.[17] It means an authentic search for the Lord in and through this encounter with the poor, and also a lucid exposition of what this spiritual experience signifies.

Viewed in this perspective, what is involved is the creation of Christian communities in which private owners of the goods of this world cease to be the owners of the gospel. A few years ago they were referred to as "rebel communities."[18] To that premonitory definition we would now add the notion that in them the dispossessed could effect a *social appropriation of the gospel.* Such groups would prophetically proclaim a different church, a church wholly in the service of those human beings fighting to be truly human, a church creatively and critically trying to help those who wish to be human in a very different way. These aspirations could hardly be comprehended at all from within the old context in which God's word has been pondered, proclaimed, and lived. The people of God must strike roots in the exploited and alienated classes. In fact it must rise out of those classes, out of their interests and aspirations and struggles and cultural categories. Only then will the people of God be a church of the people, a sign of the liberation brought by the Lord of history conveying the gospel message to all people.

None of this would make any sense, nor could we even dream of it happening, if it were not for the fact that we can see actual attempts in this direction. However sketchy and timid they may be, they are there to be seen in different areas of our continent. A growing number of Christians from every walk of life are involving themselves in the liberation process—laborers, professionals, peasants, bishops, students, priests, and so forth. This involvement is still in its initial stages, and it will have to go much deeper. Much clarification and refinement is in order. The process will compel people to take a free and critical stand within any political approach that is oversimplistic and does not take due account of all human dimensions. It must also grow and mature in such a way that the voice of the common people and populist Christian sectors can be heard speaking in its own accents. This process of involvement and commitment is a difficult one. It must sometimes move over barren stretches of ground, always encountering resistance and opposition from those who are attached to the old order— whether they be Christians or not. Yet it is also a very real and concrete process, one that has already begun to reveal its fruitfulness and effectiveness insofar as the revolutionary option and the reinterpretation of the gospel message are concerned.

The times do not allow for euphoria. The existing system has demonstrated its tenacity and its ability to repress or domesticate the forces of reform and renewal. Even in Christian sectors we can clearly glimpse the thick web of resistance that must be overcome if the gospel's disturbing message of liberation is to be brought out into the open. The concrete experience gained by popular movements in their determined efforts to fashion a different society is good grounds for continued vigilance and action. By the same token, however, this commitment is opening the way for a revitalized fidelity to the Lord of history. More and more Christians are coming to realize that only by making human beings our brothers and sisters do we truly accept God's gratuitous gift of sonship, and that this brotherhood can be created only in and through the actual historical and political conditions of our continent—from the vantage point of the poor and exploited classes.

And of course hope itself belongs to every age. Our present situation in Latin America may help us to realize once again what Paul meant when he said that we must "hope against all hope." And it may also help us to live that dictum in a new and revitalized way.

NOTES

1. This was the role played by the Christian Democratic Party in Chile during the reign of Allende's Popular Unity government. Today some segments of that political party seem to be moving some distance away from the government of General Pinochet, but in the beginning they certainly gave strong backing to the fascist coup in Chile.

2. Here again Chile is the most typical instance. Some years ago the Christian Democratic Party captured the political concern and interest that was awakening in Christian groups. But the same is true of other countries in Latin America.

3. See the document issued by the bishops of Northeast Brazil, "I Have Heard the Cries of My People," in the anthology *Signos de liberación* (Lima: CEP, 1973).

4. See the anthology edited by E. Feil and R. Weth, *Diskussion zur Theologie der Revolution* (Mainz and Munich: Kaiser and Matthias Grünewald, 1969).

5. See statements by Christian groups in the anthology entitled *Signos de liberación*. Also see the study by R. Muñoz, *Nueva conciencia de la Iglesia en América Latina* (Santiago, Chile: Nueva Universidad, 1973); and the anthology *Signos de renovación* (Lima: Universitaria, 1969); Eng. trans.: *Between Honesty and Hope* (Maryknoll, New York: Maryknoll Publications, 1970).

6. I discussed evangelical poverty more fully in my book entitled *Teología de la liberación, Perspectivas* (Lima: CEP, 1971); Eng. trans.: *A Theology of Liberation* (Maryknoll, New York: Orbis, 1973), Chap. 13.

7. In this context we might do well to go back to the reflections of Duns Scotus (c. 1266–1308) on praxis (not just action) and on theology as a practical science. See also Frans v.d. Oudenrijn, *Kritische Theologie als Kritik der Theologie* (Mainz and Munich: Kaiser-Grünewald, 1972); and W. Pannenberg, *Epistemologia e teologia*, Italian trans. (Brescia: Queriniana, 1974, original published in 1972).

8. *Justice*, no. 3, Medellín Documents, 2: 58. See Anthologies in Appendix II at the back of this volume.

9. This means that theologians themselves must be persons involved in the process of liberation. This is a necessary precondition if their work is to be concrete and scientific.

10. See G. Gutiérrez, *Hacia una teología de la liberación* (Montevideo: MIEC-JECI, 1969), text of a conference given in July 1968; idem, "Notes on Theology of Liberation," paper presented at a congress organized by Sodepax in 1969 and reproduced in the volume, *In Search of a Theology of Development* (Lausanne: Sodepax, 1970); E. Pironio, *La Iglesia, pueblo de Dios* and *La Iglesia que nace entre nosotros*, both published in Bogotá in 1970; H. Assmann, *Opresión-liberación, desafío a los cristianos* (Montevideo: Tierra Nueva, 1971); J.C. Scannone, "La teología de la liberación," in *Revista del Centro de Investigaciones y Acción Social*, no. 221, Buenos Aires, April 1973; L. Gera, "Teología de la liberación," in *Perspectivas para el Diálogo*, no. 72, Montevideo, May 1973; J. Santana, *Introduction to Theological Reflection on Domination and Dependence*, privately issued by the World Council of Churches, Geneva, 1974; Pablo Richard, *Reflexión teológica desde la lucha del pueblo* (Santiago de Chile: ISAL, 1973); R. Muñoz, see note 5 above; Raúl Vidales, "Sacramentos y liberación," in *Servir* 10 (1974): 67–76; J. Míguez Bonino, *Doing Theology in a Revolutionary Situation* (Philadelphia: Fortress Press, 1975).

11. Theology is an *actus secundus*, a second step of critical reflection which follows after the praxis of faith. This view of theology was one of the first insights glimpsed by liberation theology. See G. Gutiérrez, *La pastoral en la Iglesia latinoamericana, análisis teológico* (Montevideo: MIEC-JECI, 1968); idem, "Notes on a Theology of Liberation"; idem, *A Theology of Liberation*, p. 11.

12. At present much effort is being made to domesticate liberation theology. People are using its terminology but emptying it of any real meaning. They are also talking about pluralism, which really comes down to non-commitment.

13. It is obvious, for example, that the native peoples and cultures of Latin America are not sufficiently taken into account in our present efforts at theological reflection.

14. Yves Congar, a theologian whose thrust is deeply ecclesial and pastoral, has often stressed the connection between theology and proclamation. See, for example, his work entitled *Situation et tâches de la théologie* (Paris: Cerf, 1967).

15. See the work of Enrique Dussel, *Historia de la Iglesia en América Latina* (Barcelona: Nova Terra, 1972).

16. See the penetrating and courageous observations of K. Rahner on how we might envision a church of the future in *Cambio estructural de la Iglesia*, Spanish trans. (Madrid: Ed. Cristiandad, 1974).

17. If a grassroots ecclesial community does not adopt this basic perspective, there is a danger that it will try to evade a history riddled with conflict.

18. See Gonzalo Arroyo, "Rebeldía cristiana y compromiso comunitarion," in *Mensaje*, no. 167 (1968), pp. 78–83. This article stimulated much fresh reflection and new forms of concrete experience in Latin America.

2

Methodological Issues in Liberation Theology

Raúl Vidales (Lima, Peru)

Everyone is aware of the fact that Latin American theology must confront the whole problem of its methodology and that this problem is acquiring a more pointed urgency every day. Real-life priorities and problems are predominant in its discussions, to be sure. But when these themes are to be turned into organized reflection, there reappears the whole problem of the "reflective approach" and the analytical set of instruments that can give systematic justification for this brand of theologizing.

At bottom it is the whole problem of faith and its foundations. We are faced with the challenge of being able to talk about God, not to a world come of age but to a world of diminished and belittled human beings, not to nonbelievers but to people rendered less than human. Right off we can say that the desire to overcome those difficulties, as well as the conviction that it is possible to do so, finds its pristine base in Christian experience itself as a liberation praxis. It is from that soil that the first

34

theological word sprouts. But on another level theology is offered a second possibility of doing this. This second level is the path of reflection on the truth of faith in all its lived reality. It is a path that "comes after," a *methodos*. We can use this path to move toward our goal, to penetrate further into the reality we are living. Thus theology must consider the very possibility of having a methodology, of being able to explore its faith on the path of reflection. The issue becomes more urgent every day.

We know very well that theology cannot claim a methodology that is strictly equivalent to the scientific methodology that has evolved in the exact sciences. We also know that we cannot derive some theological end-result simply by applying the various methods of other disciplines in some mechanical fashion. We cannot simply take over the methods of historical criticism, the humanities, or the various sciences of the human spirit. If we did that, we would simply end up losing both theology and its methodology. By the same token, however, we cannot theologize in a whimsical or arbitrary way, paying no attention to the methodology as we do so.

Insofar as Latin American theology itself is concerned, we know right from the start that it is free of any "dogmatic" pretension akin to that of baroque scholasticism. At the same time, however, it does come under the general thrust of the new theology that has made its appearance with Vatican II. This new line of theology is very history-oriented and committed. Latin American theology is also akin to the recent "political theology" that has arisen in Europe, though of course the former is not without an original character of its own.

LATIN AMERICAN THEOLOGY AND WORLDWIDE THEOLOGY: METHODOLOGICAL PARALLELS

When I refer to "Latin American theology" here, I am referring specifically to the theology that is being elaborated under the general focus of "liberation." Granting its own peculiar boundaries and its original features, we can say that this new theology is located within the general tradition of world theology and its recent development. It is not so much a case of there being a "new theology" here; what we have, rather, is a new way of carrying out the same basic theological task. Here, then, I would like to point up some of the relevant relationships between liberation theology and worldwide theology, relationships that are clearly and consciously assumed on the methodological level.

Basic Shifts in Emphasis

Since Vatican II we know that theology has been paying more
clear-cut attention to the place of historical thinking within its
own field, thereby recovering one of its own most important and
essential dimensions. Though the conciliar documents themselves make only cautious beginnings in this direction, they do
explicitly leave room for the possibility of pluralism in theology. In
short, they allow for a plurality of theologies. Granting that fact, I
would still prefer to talk about different ways of carrying out the
unique but multiform task of understanding the faith. I would
prefer to talk about different emphases and perspectives rather
than about different "theologies."

Now liberation theology explicitly accepts and gives priority to
historico-critical thinking as such; and it also reclaims the dimension of history for theology, along with theology's critical function.
When a history-minded theology speaks, it speaks as a committed
and critical theology. So it is not simply a task of recovering
tradition and framing *auctoritas* in its proper dimensions; theology must also conduct a hermeneutic process regarding the present from within the context of the present, ever remaining open to
the future as it does so.

It is also a fact that the traditional "ecclesialization" of theology
ultimately degenerated into a dogmatic positivism on the part of
the magisterium. The new vision of the church glimpsed by Vatican II clearly marked a positive advance over the older perspective. The Council saw the church of Christ as a wayfaring project
in history, as a promise already initiated but not yet completely
fulfilled, and so forth. This new outlook restored the primacy of
Scripture and tradition as the "proximate norms" of faith,
thereby restoring value and status to patristic tradition as well.

Now the church is no longer viewed as a "proximate norm" of
faith; rather, the church is viewed as the servant of faith and its
authentic sources. Insofar as it is a formulation of the faith, dogma is a historical and relative dimension of that faith, possess-
ing only functional significance. Dogma is functional, in other
words, only insofar as it is of service to the word of God and is
oriented around that word. It is also relative because it performs
its function of service in a given age and in terms of the problems
peculiar to that age; it helps believers to comprehend the gospel
message correctly in a specific and concrete set of circumstances.

In this sense, then, theology returns to doing its work within a context of truth that is being realized at every moment. It must constantly reformulate its views at each concrete historical moment, for it must serve faith as it is lived by people in the concrete circumstances of history.

Seen from this perspective, the task of theology becomes an enormous hermeneutic process of translation. It starts out with exegesis and, through its own inner dynamism, gradually moves on to missionary proclamation.

Accepting this basic projection, Latin American theology must then accept the problems and challenges it entails. What is it to make of this process of exegesis and hermeneutics? How is it to carry it out?

We cannot overlook or deny the fact that in our milieu the practice and teaching of theology continues in the same old way. We are still trained by the *lectio*, the *quaestio*, and the *disputatio* in dogmatic theology. First the doctrine of the church is put forth, then it is proved on the basis of Scripture and tradition, and then we go into more speculative debates and discussions.

More recently, however, theology has been salvaging those two original elements that serve as the eyes of theology itself: i.e., "faith" and "reason." Once again theology is becoming a reflective hearing and perceiving of the faith, designed to justify faith's hope before the world (1 Pet. 3:15). Once again it is becoming a scientifically trained *intellectus fidei*, a *fides quarens intellectum* —to use the words of St. Anselm.

Thus Scripture is once again becoming the vital and formal principle and wellspring of theology; and the interpretation of Scripture is being oriented around the missionary task in its concrete historical context.

Prospects and Tasks of a History-Minded Theology

If theology wishes to remain true to the dimension of history, then it cannot be wholly preoccupied with maintaining the purity of its doctrine within the narrow confines of its own private domain of truth—apart from the conflicts and vicissitudes of history in the world at large. It must take pains to see to it that its interpretation and proclamation of the divine message is oriented toward involvement with concrete human beings and their problems.

The "orthodoxy" of the Christian message has been reduced

traditionally to its theoretical formulations or to the purity of its oral proclamation. Now we can no longer restrict the meaning of the term "orthodoxy" to "right thinking" or "right speaking." We must recover the full dimensions and connotations of the term, and its basic meaning of "right doing." While theology's starting point is the original, pristine witness of Scripture, we must reread and ponder this witness with our eyes on the current problems facing concrete human beings.

From the standpoint of the new ecclesiology, theology begins to be truly "ecclesial" only when it goes beyond its own proper limits and establishes fellowship, not just with the *communio fidelium*, but also with all those who directly or indirectly view themselves as nonbelievers. To be truly ecclesial, it must stop worrying about preserving its own purity from contamination. Instead it must accept the radical challenges, ambiguities, and sources of conflict on the frontiers. Only then will it be able to maintain its critical function.

A theology with a sound historical dimension realizes that "theory" and "praxis" can be separated only for pedagogical and methodological purposes, that in reality they are two dialectical moments in one and the same dynamic, all-encompassing process. The practical application is a structural feature and phase of truth itself. In the modern view of truth it is not simply a matter of interpreting the world but of changing it as well.

Hence an enormous task remains to be carried out by theology insofar as it is part of our faith. We must courageously tackle our theological concepts and re-examine them from the ground up—even such fundamental concepts as God, grace, and salvation. We must reconsider them in their vital relationship to reality and their meaningfulness for our concrete fleshing out of the faith. Alas, many of the central pronouncements of theology have been reduced to having no efficacy in history itself.

The biblical concept of truth is characterized by the fact that truth is not simply something that can be known or talked about but something that must also be acted upon and realized in deeds. Thus truth and fidelity are intimately united in the Bible. Promise and fulfillment are the two components of the truth that divine revelation proclaims to us. Something is true if it is promised and then carried out, so that it thereby acquires duration and solidity. God is truthful because he does what he promises, thus giving credence to our confidence and adherence. The dynamic historical pageant of truth, as proclaimed in the Bible, is played out between the two poles of promise and fulfillment. It is grace and it is justice, and hence it can be verified only in historical terms. Christ is the promise of the Father and also its fulfillment. He is the Truth which becomes history in fulfillment of a divine promise, thereby leaving everything open to the final consummation and driven on toward it.

Thus biblical truth is characterized by the fact that it is projected into history, and that this historical projection is a concrete dimension of the eschatological promise. Biblical truth is related to the history, not only by virtue of its formal structure but also by virtue of its content. It involves a historical promise and a historical fulfillment. Theology, then, is an understanding of this faith that is accepted and lived out; it is a process of integrating the multiform aspects and concrete embodiments of faith into the unique, all-embracing eschatological *Mysterium Dei* that is being realized in history.

Biblical truth entails a close and intimate relationship between its own existence as time and time as lived being. Thus liberty, time, and history constitute the broad horizon in which we come to comprehend the truth according to Jesus Christ.

Methodological Components for Liberation Theology

As I noted at the start, liberation theology is called to account not so much by the world of nonbelievers as by the world of the nonhumans—i.e., those oppressed peoples who have not attained even the bare minimum of human dignity. A radical option for, and real commitment to, this exploited class means that liberation theology must embark on a path of reflection that is quite peculiar and distinctive to it. To begin with, it must accept the mediation of a new type of scientific rationality to which it has not been accustomed. This new line of scientific reasoning is a contribution of the human sciences, of the social sciences specifically.

Insofar as the study of Latin American realities is concerned, the analysis of the social sciences leads us toward a very specific perspective. It forces us to view Latin America in terms of overall structures, historical processes, all-embracing factors, and conflict-ridden relationships. The reality which is Latin America cannot be explained as a totality resulting naturally from its own inner evolution in history; nor can internal problems be viewed in isolation from the overall reality as a whole.

Latin America is not the product of a continuous or discontinu-

ous process of inner growth alone; it is not the end result of a
society that has evolved economically, politically, and culturally
in complete isolation and autonomy. On the contrary, the oppression and dependence that now characterize it are part of an overall process which has produced the great metropolitan centers
around the world. Development and dependence are two sides of
the same coin, two faces of the same process. They form two
different structures in one system, and they are mutually interdependent. The relationship between them is riddled with conflict, and the overall dynamic process is structured on violence.

Toward the center of this reality, a wholly politicized totality,
we find the experience of faith as a liberation praxis in favor of the
oppressed. This experience, then, is wholly framed within a structured whole marked by injustice and violence. Its hallmark is
class divisiveness, for there we find classes operating dynamically
on the basis of conflict and mutual opposition. But if we wish to
live out faith in history, we must operate through such mediating
realities.

The overcoming of all dualism is of paramount importance in
the work of theology. It is no longer simply a matter of shedding
light on reality from the outside with the help of faith, or of looking
at concrete situations in the light of God's word. Right from the
start we must realize that human history, the one and only history that exists, is not only the circumstantial locale of salvation
but also salvation itself—as yet unfinished but moving toward its
final fulfillment. For the believer, in other words, human history
is the manifestation of the Christ-fact. The construction of human
history itself is the construction of the kingdom, though the two
cannot be simply equated. Seen from this perspective, God's activity is manifested in effective human efforts to create a more just
and fraternal society in line with his promise.

This same perspective obliges the theologian to re-read the
Bible from the context of the other "Bible" known as human
history. It is one dialectical activity, not two separate, parallel
tasks. On the one hand theologians are constantly referred back to
the original happening embodied in Jesus and his message because they must be able to explore and understand the fact of
history from the standpoint of the Christ-happening. On the other
hand theologians are immersed wholly in the process of concrete
history because they are obliged to appreciate the pulse of the
Word that has been sown into the ground of history. It is useless

and meaningless to do one part of the job and neglect the other. Both phases are part and parcel of one operative totality.

What relationship exists between the word of God and human history? How are the word of God and Christian praxis related? How do both operate historically? How can we interpret and structure the two so that neither essential pole is sacrificed? These are some of the basic questions facing Latin American theology as it tackles the task of hermeneutics and interpretation. And although the answer is not yet completely given, it is being worked out now. That is the important thing.

The key starting-point, then, is the discovery of Jesus' salvation in history and its concrete processes. But the concrete process of history is a global happening, and so every specific focus and all our conceptual elaborations will be profoundly affected by such categories as "totality," "universality," "historicity," and "conflict." Theological activity itself must find its place and meaning, its validity and its limitations, within the overall process of history. To be sure, the "theological product" does have a historical process of its own; it arises, evolves, finds structure, and systematization within a specific context. At the same time, however, this is not an independent process that can be explained without reference to the overall process of history. Theology cannot be reduced to being merely the embodiment of a given culture or ideology. But since it is a human product designed to serve historical human destiny, it must operate through the mediation of various cultures and different kinds of scientific reasoning.

For all these reasons, then, liberation theology seeks to be a way of understanding the faith that takes full account of the distinctive culture of our peoples, of its overall idiom, its semantic content, and its set of symbols.

Liberation theology presupposes the voice of the human sciences, of the social sciences in particular, as its first or preliminary theological word. But just as a theology would be naive to ignore the contribution of these sciences, so it would be naive to accept that contribution uncritically.

The basic contribution of the human sciences is to provide theology with a more clear-eyed view of history, a more critical approach, and a set of analytical instruments. This is particularly true at the present juncture in Latin American history. By providing basic pronouncements about reality, these sciences offer theology diagnostic tools, reveal underlying causes, highlight structural processes and dynamisms, and indicate how systems tend to function. This corpus of data clarifies the situation of people here and now, particularly the situation of those who have been deprived and impoverished for centuries.

Accepting the modern hypothesis that no science is "neutral," Latin American theology cannot view the sciences with indifference as if each and every one of them could provide the same help. It will opt for those analyses, postulates, and diagnoses that are more closely in line with the goal of discerning and achieving a social order in which human beings can live as true adults, as "new persons" after the ideal of Jesus Christ. For the very same reason it will be thoroughly critical of those scientific and ideological systems that explicitly or implicitly run counter to that ideal.

Enough has been said already of the relevance of method to scientific work. The important point is that this carefully structured approach not end up as a dry, mechanical, repetitive activity. From the days of antiquity, method has been regarded as something more than a peripheral activity of a purely extrinsic nature. This view has been reaffirmed in modern times by such people as Hegel and Heidegger. The method used in arriving at the truth is itself a forward step within the bounds of truth. Our methodological approach, then, is the truth as it is being unveiled.

This means that methodological activity itself has an intrinsic dialectical relationship with the scientific discipline in which one is engaged. That being the case, method cannot be neutral. Every methodology presupposes some theoretical framework and some ideological option. The present-day sociology of knowledge has thoroughly explored this relationship between the objective and subjective elements in the knowledge process.

Now when we talk about the "definition" of theology here, we are not talking about some classroom definition. We are talking about the "non-indifference" of theology, about the basic stance it adopts in itself and its methodology. If this non-indifference is a certainty from the methodological viewpoint, it is equally certain and obligatory from the standpoint of the divine message and faith as a lived reality. Lived out as a "liberation praxis," that message clearly entails taking a basic stand. Faced with the historical situation of Latin America and the basic element of hostility in it, theology tries to recover the subversive elements of the divine message and incorporate them into its own pronouncements. The elements are there, both in Scripture and in the lives of committed Christians today. Theology takes them and tries to project them into its mission and project in history.

Finally we must realize that every fact or event must be framed within some horizon of understanding if it is to be understood. Every science has such a horizon, and so do all individuals in their day-to-day lives. People find horizons in their cultural, pedagogical, or social traditions; the sciences find them in their postulates, criteria, and underlying hypotheses. For the theologian, this horizon of understanding is the faith.

No investigator and no reflecting person can prescind from this situational objectivity. Theologians, then, are well aware that their consideration and interpretation of the faith is "situated," which is to say, framed within their perspective, their angle of vision, their level of understanding, their resources and conditioning factors. Like all human beings, theologians cannot help but be conditioned by their social and historical situation, by their own involvement and defining factors. Each factor represents one more element conditioning the horizon of faith. This horizon necessarily operates in and through the surrounding sociocultural horizon.

But if this situational objectivity is inescapable, it is also possible to maintain and exercise a transcendental subjectivity. And this is done precisely in and through the path of reflection called the methodological process.

THE METHODOLOGICAL PROCESS
IN LATIN AMERICAN THEOLOGY

The above elements had to be spelled out before we could consider the actual methodological approach of Latin American theology with its focus on liberation. There is no doubt that much refinement and problem-solving remains to be done, but by now we can indicate the broad outlines of its reflexive approach. Three main stages are to be noted.

First Stage: Praxis as the Starting Point

Liberation theology begins with concrete experience of the faith as a liberation praxis. It is from that source that the path of reflection starts out in its attempt to understand the faith as a lived reality. At this very first stage the dialectical relationship between the word of God and Christian experience appears as a single historical category. The proclamations of salvation take on new contextual significance, and concrete reality adds the dimension of a more complicated truth than any purely conceptional notion might. Thus right from the start concrete experience of the faith is framed in the dialectic interplay between ongoing concrete history and incarnation of the divine message.

The concrete experiences of commitment to liberation become theologically significant, both on the individual and community level. These two dimensions are inseparably related, and one cannot be fully comprehended without the other. While "prophet" and "community" are not reducible to one another, they are basically interrelated. Only in the context of this twofold dimension does the basic Christian happening necessarily become a *locus theologicus* with topmost priority, signifying the living acceptance of faith. It is not simply Scripture and its pre-eminence as such that initiates our theologizing; what inititates our theological thinking is Scripture insofar as it is accepted and fleshed out by believers in a concrete historical experience. It is when we start off by recovering and maintaining the historical dimension of Scripture that we can legitimately utilize and exercise its critical and subversive dimension, applying it to our own lives as believers, to our religious system, to the social structure, and to society in general. If right at the start we can get beyond all dualism and see the happening of faith as the meeting point of salvation and history (the law of Incarnation), then we are in a position to maintain the animating and transforming force of divine revelation in history.

Critical-minded discovery of the world of the oppressed, which has resulted from the adoption of a new and more scientific line of reasoning, has gradually been leading people to a thorough reconsideration and reformulation of how our faith is to be understood, lived, and proclaimed. How are we to live as believers on a continent ravaged by violence, domination, exploitation, and dependence? How are we to live the faith in this conflict-ridden milieu so that our faith-based response to it will serve to animate and mobilize people's energies for the construction of a more just and fraternal society? The response now being offered by some Christian communities in Latin America is to be found along the pathways of "the historical praxis of liberation." This is the concrete version of liberative love. Their concrete praxis serves as the point of departure for a revitalized way of comprehending faith in Jesus Christ.

Insofar as it is "liberation praxis," faith entails a discovery of the world of the "other" in the light of the new scientific line of reasoning, and also an option for their cause. It implies a new understanding of the poor (both as individuals and as an exploited social class enmeshed in conflict), of poverty itself, and of the political dimension. It means that the believer has made the basic option of entering into the conflict-ridden world of the exploited as his or her concrete way of living in the Spirit in a new way.

In this experience is verified a new way of linking the mystical dimension of the Christian faith on the one hand and its political dimension on the other. It seeks to make clear how political liberation can be a sign of eschatological liberation.

Christian commitment is now clearly occupied with the concern to recover the historical meaning of Jesus and his salvation, particularly insofar as salvation is destined for the most disadvantaged people. With this concrete commitment Christians plunge into the complex and conflict-ridden world of the poor, regarding their choice as a fundamental option stemming from their faith in the Lord.

This new way of living the faith initiates a particular style of spirituality and opens up new horizons for Christian mysticism. The spirituality of liberation takes shape in the dialectical interplay between fidelity to Jesus on the one hand and concrete commitment to the poor on the other. If works are the real idiom of faith, then in the present Latin American context that idiom is to be found in the praxis of liberation. Commitment to liberation is the concrete fruit and result of living in the Spirit.

Christian conversion means breaking with all the egotism of the "old person" and entering the world of the "other" as a "new person" seeking to transform that world. It finds concrete expression, then, in real exercise of liberative love. It embodies a whole new way of identifying with Christ and living the Christian life. It is a new and unheard-of way of living that life, filled with promising signs and possibilities but also fraught with challenges and difficulties. There is no question of denying other dimensions of Christian spiritual experience that are more traditional and still worthwhile. The aim is rather to recover and integrate dimensions of Christian spirituality that have been somewhat overlooked: the biblical dimension, the historical dimension, and the dimension of personal commitment and involvement.

This new mystical experience takes in two dimensions of one and the same basic happening and links them together inextricably. These two basic dimensions are our personal encounter with

Christ on the one hand and Christ's presence in our fellow human beings on the other—in particular, his presence in "the least" of our brethren. It is not a matter of placing spirituality in the service of liberation. It is a matter of unleashing all the potential force of our spirituality—its historical dimension of commitment in this particular case. To speak in these terms is to situate the socio-political dimension at the very heart of Christian mystical experience as one of its basic and constitutive elements. To encounter Christ we must go through our fellow human being who is stripped and left abandoned on the side of the road.

This concrete experience of making a commitment to the liberation of the exploited classes takes place above and beyond the frontiers of any and all institutional churches. Commitment to liberation and the new conception of ecclesiology mentioned earlier prompt a new opening of theology itself to frontier areas. New, unsuspected questions suddenly arise, and the problems grow much more complex; but this is one of the challenges that Latin American theology has deliberately and consciously faced.

As we noted above, the method that leads toward the truth is itself a reflective journey within the bosom of the truth that we are fashioning as we proceed. And in this case it is a truth that is being worked out far beyond sectarian frontiers. Liberation theology is aware that it is not meant to serve only small groups of committed Christians, or the "communion of the faithful" in Latin America, or even the universal church alone. Like every theology, it must be open to serving all human beings because that is part of its ecclesial essence. In particular it should serve all those on its outer frontiers who believe in truth and love for others, and who are working for those goals.

It is obviously this openness to all human history that permits theology to claim a critical function, not only vis-à-vis ecclesial praxis but also vis-à-vis society and all systems that seek to become absolute. When any system attempts to do that, it becomes exploitative; that is true of religious systems also.

Second Stage: A Different Understanding of the Faith

From this seedbed there sprouts a very specific and distinctive understanding of the faith. We find a new pattern of theological discourse in which the critical function is clearly evident. In short, we get a very specific and distinctive way of theologizing. This theological effort takes place in the area that intervenes between concrete experience of the faith on the one hand and missionary proclamation on the other: It is there that its validity and its limits are properly defined. Viewed in those terms, liberation theology does not mean to be of service solely to the church in Latin America; instead its questioning and its insights are meant to benefit the whole church and to open us up to all human beings.

As we noted above, it was the discovery of the world of the "other" that led committed Christians to a new way of living the faith in and through revolutionary involvement. This, in turn, inaugurates a whole new way of engaging in theological discourse. Framed in a new and distinctive context, theological discourse and its understanding of the faith become distinctively different. Theory and practice now are seen to be indissolubly united as embodiments of one and the same reality. Our understanding of the faith must operate through the mediating realities and circumstances in which Christian living is immersed: i.e., history, politics, and socio-economic conditions.

Insofar as theology arises out of a specific, concrete praxis, the whole process of understanding the faith necessarily entails critical reflection and review of the concrete experience that has generated it. Theology now becomes critical of itself and its own foundations, not only because it is ever exposed to the danger of being manipulated and turned to ideological uses but also because a basically critical outlook is required in operating through the mediating factors of history. It becomes critical of committed Christian groups and their ongoing risks, and also of the social, cultural, economic, and political situation that conditions the realization of God's promise. As the theoretical embodiment of a specific line of praxis, it is critical of both the church and society. On the one hand it detects and spells out the concrete experiences of liberation going on around it; at the same time, however, it maintains a critical outlook in order to offer provocation, in order to keep prodding us on toward the final consummation.

But how can theology manage to maintain its critical function so that it will subvert and relativize would-be absolutes? It can only do so insofar as it continues to refer back to its vital underlying source and principle: the word of God. Thus theological reflection is and must be a critique of society and the church insofar as the two are convened and accosted by the word of God. It is a critical-minded theory operating in the light of God's word as accepted by faith and motivated by a practical intention; hence it is inextricably linked up with historical praxis as well.

This biblical perspective places liberation theology within the most solid and sound tradition of Christian theology. The pre-eminent function of Scripture is indisputable, as is the functional character of the church and the magisterium and their service role. Once again Scripture becomes the soul of theology, as it is meant to be. At the same time, however, theology from the stand-point of liberation is particularly concerned to recover the histori-cal dimension of God's message, to move that message away from all abstract universalism, ahistoricism, and atemporal concep-tualizations.

The historical dimension of the message stems both from the fact that it arose in a specific historical milieu and from the fact that it is essentially related to human history. Only by salvaging this historical dimension can we maintain its prophetic character and function, its subversive undertones, and its provocative Christian originality: Only thus can we preserve the only field wherein God's message retains its validity for reflection and ac-tion.

This also accounts for the critical function performed by theol-ogy. It exercises this function by moving back and forth between the original Bible containing God's word and the other "Bible" known as history.

Though still in its initial stages, liberation theology is already breaking new ground in hermeneutics. It is obvious that we need a different "hermeneutic key," one which will enable us to deal with other "texts" and to keep pace with the complex, dynamic process of a truth that is gradually being fashioned in history. We need a hermeneutics that will pay heed to the voice of the sciences, not only the sciences that help us better to understand the world of the Bible but also the sciences that help us better to understand the present-day world. Insofar as we Latin Americans are con-cerned specifically, we need a hermeneutics that is open and sen-sitive to the history of our peoples, the geography of hunger, the culture of violence, the language of the voiceless masses, the world of oppression, and the structures of an unjust social order that is badly in need of God's message of freedom.

This certainly does not mean that we are to go back and propose facile paradigmatic foundations, mechanical equations, fixist comparisons, inconsistent accommodations, and acritical paral-lels. It does mean we must try to work out a hermeneutic process that will enable us to establish the dialectical interrelationship between the historical reality of Jesus and his message on the one hand and present-day historical experience on the other. We cannot rest content with a theological effort that is merely concerned with interpreting God's salvific gesture or deed. We must proceed further to the actual work of relating it to an original and unassailable effort at historical collaboration. It is there that the much vaunted joint work of theology and exegesis takes on flesh and bones.

There has been much talk of an "existential" hermeneutics, a "revolutionary" hermeneutics, and a "political" hermeneutics. Here I should prefer to talk about a hermeneutics "from the standpoint of liberation." Such a hermeneutics would envision a transformation of concrete realities within its own area of competence and effectiveness. Its methodological process would be designed to enable us to move forward through the concrete truth that is gradually being verified in the facticity of history—our ultimate goal being the final consummation envisioned by faith. Since Latin American theology has stressed its own "critical function," the hermeneutic process that provides access to God's word of liberty should enable us to seek and fight for the Truth that makes us free.

From this basic standpoint the Bible is not to be read as a Magna Carta but rather as a creative and provocative witness to our mission in the world. This focus will do a great deal to keep us from abstract interpretations that simply try to comprehend the past in terms of the present. It will force us to keep trying to comprehend the temporal dimension of the biblical word which finds its incarnation in the present, its trans-temporal and metahistorical dimension in the future, and the dynamic interrelationship between the two. That is the challenge posed by the new "hermeneutic key." The gospel message is deeply immersed in history; at one and the same time it displays a contemporary and a noncontemporary dimension.

But it is not simply a matter of seeing the written word of the Bible inscribed in real life. This new hermeneutics must also comprehend all the historical embodiments of life in a political context. This is the method whereby faith is realized by a community living a life of liberation in the changing vicissitudes of the present and its conditions of poverty.

By the same token this hermeneutic effort will give privileged status to elements that are given second place in other outlooks. It will pay close attention to all the various aspects of Latin American life, be they historical, anthropological, political, cultural, economic, or social. It will tend to be critical rather than dogmatic, process-minded rather than formalistic, social rather than personalist, populist rather than elitist. More pointed and concrete, it will embrace both the past and the future in the solid consistency of the present; and it will also stress "orthopraxis" over "orthodoxy."

The hermeneutic synthesis is not so much a datum as a person: Jesus Christ. More specifically here, it is Christ in the person of our lowliest fellow human beings. If we are to be able to detect the Christ-happening pulsating within every human project, we must have an attitude of hope and "vigilance," and we must be constantly undergoing a process of paschal conversion. To opt for the poor and commit oneself to their struggle is to immerse oneself in a historical activity aimed at liberation; in other words, it is to undertake a liberation praxis as a praxis of love for others and of fidelity to God. For God himself chose to become history, and his love is made manifest in history; and the privileged manifestation of that love is to be found in the praxis of total liberation.

In this praxis, which is complex, all-embracing, and conflict-ridden, Latin American theology sees the convergence of God's word and human history. Faith is positive only insofar as it is a human act. Only when it is a human act, only when it is accepted and understood by a human being, is it a font and wellspring of theology. The "faith" and "reason" of theological tradition in its purest form find their dialectical unity in this love-inspired praxis of liberation. Hence this praxis constitutes an essential element of the hermeneutic process itself when viewed from the perspective of liberation.

Liberation praxis is the exercise of faith as a mixture of promise and fulfillment and as an openness to full consummation in the future. Promise and fulfillment are the dynamic elements of faith as a historical praxis of liberation; at the very same time they constitute the primordial field or locus of liberation hermeneutics.

It is concrete experience that has been providing the key intuitions and themes of liberation theology. From that locale there begins a process of abstraction that attempts to bring out or work out the theoretical categories that will combine interpretative pronouncements and hypotheses in an integrated way. A basically critical outlook on praxis enables people to discover inner relationships between apparently disconnected phenomena. Thus underlying any theoretical pronouncement is praxis itself, but this living praxis has already been analyzed and somewhat systematized in a critical way.

The methodological process does not end there, however. The most important step is to structure and systematize the whole. If we are to comprehend the religious experience in all its complexity, we must open it up to further interrelationships with a broader structure, the latter in turn having a specific function to play within a global system. This broadening process is nothing else but the critical praxis of theology; it is from there that its prophetism arises. The contradictions between what is and what ought to be in theory constitute so many elements for denunciation and so many occasions for proclamation.

Our living of the faith is not viewed in ahistorical terms. It is seen to be inserted in a concrete historical structure. Theology examines its concrete functions and roles within a given social phenomenon. Thus theology appears at one and the same time as a "service" and as a "commitment." Liberation theologians must travel this route of humiliation and *kenosis;* they must be "grassroots" theologians.

Third Stage: Proclaiming Jesus Christ Today

We noted above that all theological interpretation is essentially geared toward missionary proclamation. Here we undoubtedly come to the root problem, both insofar as methodology and praxis are concerned. How are we to proclaim Jesus Christ here and now?

For the New Testament, the basis of any discussion about God's word is the fact that God himself in his Word "became flesh." By contrast with the many and varied words we hear, the Son is the unique, definitive Word that was uttered in our midst as a real happening. God's word finds expression in this happening and calls for a response from human beings by directing their attention to that happening. Paul's outlook is based on a similar view. For him Christ, who is preached in Christian kerygma, is the fulfillment of all God's promises; and through Christ we address our "Amen" to God (2 Cor. 1:19ff.).

Thus it is the Christ-happening that occasions Christian preaching, and in turn the latter paves the way for acceptance of the faith. The word uttered in Christian proclamation takes concrete shape as the Word of God; it is the luminous self-revelation of Jesus Christ embodied in the apostolic message. God's Word is always concretized in a human and historical word, which thereby becomes God's word.

Scripture always depicts the apostle as a "servant" of the Word. From the standpoint of liberation this will oblige us to show sound judgment and to undergo a real process of conversion. It is not a matter of planning careful strategies for the task of evangelization. It is a matter of letting Jesus Christ speak of himself, of letting his Spirit be heard in the processes of history and in the heart of the individual. It is Jesus Christ who speaks through his Spirit, revealing himself and operating through a "total language." Hence the most profound type of evangelization is to be found in a certain kind of "silence" which pervades our praxis and which enables us to sense the novel presence of Christ in human history. Evangelization, then, has something to do with Christian contemplation.

Christ is the nucleus of the Christian kerygma. Kerygma retains some of his qualities as features of its own; it is not only *logos* ("word") but also *pneuma* ("spirit") and *dynamis* ("power"). As Paul puts it: "My message [*logos*] and my preaching [*kerygma*] had none of the persuasive force of 'wise' argumentation, but the convincing power [*dynamis*] of the Spirit" (1 Cor. 2:4). Thus one could not possibly picture the service of evangelization as some wholly extrinsic process in which the divine message is read in ahistorical terms and interpreted apart from human history. It must be concretely verified in and through the exigencies of a given historical moment. In and of itself the word of God contains a dimension of service and proclamation through which it goes out to meet human beings. Encounter with Christ necessarily leads to communication of that event in history.

The outlook of any evangelization process geared toward liberation is fundamentally framed within a critical approach toward our understanding of the faith. At every moment it seeks to avoid doing what the false prophets of old did: "They led my people astray, saying 'Peace!' when there was no peace" (Ezek. 13:10). The necessary precondition for any Christian prophecy is immersion in concrete reality; only in the conflict-ridden web of history does it take on meaning, validity, and force.

We cannot simply proclaim the gospel to "man." No such universal "man" really exists; what exists really are concrete human beings. The gospel message cannot be presented in universal, neutral, indefinite, and antiseptic terms; its universality does not lie in anything of that sort. The gospel message cannot be held equally by the exploiter and the exploited. That is why it is so dangerous to reduce the gospel's range of action to the purely spiritual realm, to concentrate exclusively on the salvation of the human soul. On that level it is easy enough to say that people are equal and to turn one's back on the contradictions that exist in societal life.

Liberative evangelization explicitly attempts to recover the dimension of Christian prophetism. Prophets are people of the word, which means that they must provide clear, intelligible, and logical expression. Far from being lost in the clouds, prophets have their feet firmly planted on earth. They are not messengers of some vague general truth of a metaphysical cast. Their message always has to do with God's sovereignty, and this sovereignty must be made manifest here and now in all the sectors of history and all areas of people's lives. Thus evangelization geared toward liberation is permanently caught up in the dialectics of "denunciation" on the one hand and "annunciation" on the other.

Once we reach this point in our elaboration of theology, the basic Christian categories of salvation become sufficiently clear. Neither grace nor sin is wholly individual and interior; nor is the transition from sin to grace, a process which we call conversion, something ahistorical and transtemporal.

The problem is how we are to accept God's bold message and render it present when we are confronted with sin that has hardened into structures, institutions, and systems; and also how we are to proclaim a grace that has something to do with effective action in history to transform an unjust social order. It is not a matter of reducing salvation to these historical exigencies of a social character but rather of recovering this dimension that has been spurned in the past.

The Christian message is not simply a word whispered to individuals in their isolated lives as lone persons. It is also a public proclamation to society, uttered in the face of its concrete structures and the prevailing system. This proclamation is and must be dialectical at all times. On the one hand the salvation proclaimed and promised by the gospel is not meant to compete with people's own efforts at liberation; on the other hand the gospel message will and should give this effort a certain turn as it proceeds. At the very least we can say that it ought to become more humane and fraternal. For Christian values to be authentic, they must at least begin to be verified in history.

BASIC FEATURES OF A LIBERATIVE EVANGELIZATION

It would be pretentious to claim that we have finished the task of determining what a liberative evangelization would entail. On the other hand we can point out certain basic features of such an evangelization process that will have to be clarified and supplemented as time goes on.

1. It will be based on solidarity with the exploited classes. All too often the language used in the process of evangelization is so purist, hieratic, and universal that one gets the impression that evangelization itself is completely indifferent to the "structural evil" in society. The proclamation of God's message seems to be concerned solely with the "individuals" arrayed in the contending camps. Liberative evangelization, by contrast, stems from solidarity with the exploited classes, from a decision to take their side actively in the struggles of life. As others have pointed out, this option represents a radical break with the way people think through, live out, and communicate the faith today inside the church.

Opting for the poor, Christ then went on to proclaim his universal message and to give himself up lovingly for all human beings. Hence we must avoid any kind of pharisaical universality that would have us collaborate with anti-evangelical actions or attitudes. Seen in this light, the political dimension of the gospel message surfaces in a new light. It is no longer a mere addendum on the periphery of the message but a projection of its essential summons to sonship and brotherhood.

2. It will proclaim the joy of being children and brothers and sisters. The original revelation offered to us by Jesus is his revelation of the heavenly Father, and the gift of divine filiation is fleshed out and lived in history. By working for human brotherhood we accept and make manifest this grace in deed rather than in mere words. The primordial content of any proclamation about liberty is the radical fact that God's liberation is being verified and realized in the very heart of history. We proclaim the joy of discovering and experiencing the fact that we are loved by God (in and through our adoption as his children); and we also proclaim the joy of verifying that fact in history by displaying love for all human beings (in and through brotherhood).

This comes down to saying that our fight against injustice and exploitation of every sort is the manifestation of this faith. If and when the gospel proclamation of sonship and fraternity is turned into real history, it must be so through the element of conflict that is to be found in the relationships of dependence and oppression between one country and another, one social class and another, and one individual and another. The demands imposed by divine sonship and human brotherhood are incompatible with the situation in which the exploited peoples of the world now live. To work for the effective construction of a more fraternal society is to bear witness of our hope before the world and show that we are witnesses to Jesus Christ.

3. It will operate in the very midst of a conflict-ridden totality. The task of evangelization is carried out within a global and unique process through which people liberate themselves and are liberated. It is an activity that embraces not only the socio-economic and political dimensions but also the totality of human beings in all their varied dimensions. A critical outlook will preserve the divine message from distortion, maintaining its original thrust at every moment. At the same time, however, we must realize the price we must pay if we wish to hope and fight for the new person of Jesus Christ. We must be willing to involve ourselves in the concrete struggles through which people wittingly or unwittingly seek to attain ever more adult stature.

Proclamation based on solidarity with the exploited classes necessarily has a political dimension and must take a conflict-ridden path. The conflicts in this case are those produced by a society that is structured and built on oppression and violence. God's message contributes a dimension of its own to this conflict-ridden world in the specific area of critical awareness. The process of developing historical awareness is essentially bound up with concrete tensions and struggles; it is within these that God's message proclaims its own typical dimensions of fulfillment on the one hand and critical-mindedness on the other, dimensions which it alone can provide.

4. It will operate from the horizon of faith, making use of the new scientific line of reasoning. The gospel message is the word of God. The initiative comes from God, and hence this word is a two-edged sword which comes slashing down vertically on every human juncture. Proclamation of this word cannot be done in a naive fashion. It will be truly critical and prophetic to the extent that we are capable of rereading God's message in the light of concrete historical exigencies. Thus we need the help of a new scientific line of reasoning to see into the genesis, development, and structured systematization of various problems.

If we face up to this challenge with a clear eye, we will have to accept another dimension as an integral part of our task. From the very start we must be willing to accept conflict, repression, and death in its varied forms as a dialectical moment in the journey toward the new person of Jesus Christ.

CONCLUSION: CHRIST, THE CENTRAL HAPPENING

The *locus theologicus* or central reference point for all reflection on the faith is the historical and salvific happening that God granted us in an absolute and completely gratuitous way. It is also the central idea for a theology concerned with the mutual relationships between the church and the world. Jesus' being man is the objective expression of the fact that God does communicate himself and his grace to us and that this man, who is the Son of God, does respond freely to the Father with his life.

All this has brought to the light new and unsuspected human possibilities, but these new vistas of human potential can only be explored in the light of Christ. Thanks to the Christ-happening, our human condition has come to be the possibility for the self-manifestation of the life of faith. Jesus Christ shows us that all history is encircled by God's love. This does not mean that history becomes "pneumatized" or "divinized," but it does mean that history is in the process of being sanctified through human work of justice and transformation.

Christianity sheds light on the meaning of human existence when it proclaims that the mystery on which our life is grounded has approached us in absolute terms in Christ—not only in mystical interiority but also in the tangible reality and work of history. By the law of the Incarnation, the whole cosmic and historical process has been penetrated by the Christ-happening. The Word grows within a history that itself is hopefully awaiting liberation from the fate of death. Once faith is understood in those terms, it confers a special theological significance on the reality that we call the historical process. For though this remains free and autonomous in its own realm, through Christ it, too, is brought into intimacy with God's gratuitous and liberating love.

In a liberation perspective concrete events are regarded not so much as a methodological point of departure as the path to full integration within the overall historical process. That process, in the eyes of a believing theologian, is a salvific one. History is not just the arena of salvation; it itself is revealed and realized as salvation. Grace is grace, to be sure, and human history is not an adequate font of salvation in and of itself. By the same token, however, it must be noted that human undertakings are not simply material conditions for, or occasions extrinsic to, the life of grace on the individual or collective level. Such things as the conquest of nature, the growing awareness of peoples, the cultivation of human spirits, and the education of human hearts are already grace in themselves, grace moving toward even greater fulfillment.

The mystery of historical salvation is realized fully in the risen Jesus Christ. All growth and progress in thought and action is therefore comprehended within the total truth of Jesus and his message. It is not a matter of mere repetition or eternal return within some closed totality. It is rather a matter of further emancipation and opening up to the world of one's many brothers and sisters. In the dialectical flow of history every reality, every value, every truth, and every struggle is recapitulated in Christ, whatever be its provenience; and he brings full liberation wherever authentic humanization is verified. Within Christianity salvation is turned into truth in the unfolding course of history.

When the Christian faith does not hide its own essence from itself, it finds that it cannot help but be involved with history at every moment. It is always caught up in the historical present of the moment, for it sees that as the only way to fully incorporate itself into the texture of the global process. Christians live this reality as fidelity to the divine message and fidelity to history. In the present they take on the past and already comprehend a future. In the here and now they are granted eschatological hope in the final consummation.

3

What Sort of Service
Might Theology Render?

Joseph Comblin (Talca, Chile)

My generation was brought up and trained while a certain conception of theology prevailed. That conception found its fullest expression in the German departments of theology during the course of the nineteenth century. Latin-language countries did not accept this conception until the twentieth century, and even then they had some reservations about it. Louvain and Le Saulchoir spearheaded the drive for this particular view. Despite its Germanic and Protestant origins, the newer model of academic theology eventually prevailed. Even the Gregorian University gave in around the time of the Second Vatican Council, to be followed by the University of Salamanca and other theological faculties in Italy, Latin America, and elsewhere. Yet at the very moment when this academic theology was proving to be triumphant, it was already going into a decline and losing its self-confidence.

Academic theology is a disinterested activity which finds its justification in itself and feels no need to find reasons for its existence. It considers itself to be just as universal as the train of thought in which it believes. It is contemplative, believing in the value of thought as such. In this respect it tends to look for its models in the humanists of the Renaissance and ultimately in the great Greek philosophers. History and historical criticism are the tools that enable it to entertain the illusion that it is disengaging itself from all contingent factors and operating from some absolute point of view—i.e., that of critical thinking.

In the case of Catholics these critical pretensions are interwoven with the romantic illusion of neo-Thomism. Here we have a curious theological romanticism that managed to last until the middle of the twentieth century. It was an intellectual realm living on the margins of world history, anachronistically reconstructing some total form of learning, and resurrecting a medieval world in the very midst of a technological and scientific society.

But that dream has faded away. No medieval fortress, no old-fashioned humanism, no antiquarian academism exist any longer except insofar as force of habit and institutional inertia continue to have their impact on programs of study. Roused from our dreamy state, we blink our eyes and look around us. What use are theologians, then? Of what possible use might they be from here on?

We are left with the fact that theology is a mass of words, and that theologians are people who have learned how to handle and wield certain words about God. But what purpose do these words serve, and how might we make them serviceable?

Now it does seem that words are forces, and that the art of handling them can be dangerous as well as useful. It is never gratuitous. Words do play a role in the history of peoples and nations, and in Christianity too. The word of God triggers human words. In both society and the people of God there can be a place for those who specialize in sacred words.

Theology talks about God, and Christian theology talks about Jesus Christ. But what exactly is this discourse? Why doesn't the apostolic proclamation suffice? And what can theological words really add to the eloquent silence of charity?

WEAKNESS AND STRENGTH OF THEOLOGY

Ancient theology and various romantic reconstructions of it (e.g., neo-Thomism) appear to be summas of a super-science that is safe and secure from the vicissitudes of the various human sciences. They point to the immutability of divine knowledge in order to show that they themselves are just as eternal as it is. They

appeal to the immutability of thought in order to excuse themselves from the obligation of adapting to modern times. Their
concepts now seem to have escaped from time altogether, though
at some point they certainly were borrowed from a particular
philosophy and a particular civilization. When theology took them
to its bosom, they were somehow ennobled and snatched from the
clutches of time.

This is a vain pretense, still cherished only by theologians who
have delayed too long in waking from their dream. Theology is but
a beggarly discourse that does not have the courage to admit its
poverty, a clumsy and awkward discourse that should not continue to vaunt a shrewdness it does not possess.

Theology is now learning that it is only a human discourse after
all. God does not even need it to communicate himself to human
beings. Theology is not what mediates the faith, and it is not the
theory of Christian practice. Manipulating or using the words of
which God made use in the Bible for our own discourse does not
confer the qualities of God's word on our human discourse; our
speech is not divine speech.

As human utterance, theology belongs to this world. It is wholly
conditioned by the portion of the world in which it itself is immersed. Far from trying to protect itself from all analysis by the
human sciences, it should be completely open to such analysis.
Theology should let itself be scrutinized from top to bottom, so
that there is nothing left to hide. Like every sort of human discourse, theology should submit to examination by anthropology,
sociology, ethnology, linguistics, and so forth. It is the expression
of a certain group, of a society, of certain personalities who are in
no way exceptional.

When and if theology does submit to such analysis, we shall find
that it is ever a highly anomalous and badly organized ensemble
of words and treatises stemming from different sources, though
the art of composition can serve as a corrective to some extent. It
has a long history, and it has preserved relics from each succeeding age—linguistic odds and ends that bear the stamp of their age.
It has its treasury of archaisms and anachronisms, of rigid concepts and solemn words that were defined once for all time and
never again called into question, of fragments borrowed from
various philosophical systems and arguments reiterated over the
centuries even after their source had been forgotten.

When theology does borrow words or concepts from the contemporary world, we always find that they are poorly assimilated,

rough-hewn, and taken out of context. Far from being a super-science or a higher synthesis as the people of the Middle Ages thought, and as some people continued to think in recent times, theology is an infra-science; it is always behind the disciplines whose elements it borrows in such clumsy fashion.

Theology does not possess the simplicity that marks the faith of the poor. It does not possess the correctness and rigorousness that mark the scientific knowledge of the rich. It is always lame and halting. The people of the Middle Ages saw theologians as dwarfs perched on the shoulders of giants. The theologians could see further than the pagan philosophers and sages of old because they stood on their shoulders. Now, however, theologians are more like dwarfs trying to peek through the legs of giants.

What is more, theology is never disinterested. The poor can be disinterested and unselfish, but not theologians. Theologians must eat before doing theology. They see the world through the eyes of those who guarantee them their daily bread. It is very difficult indeed for them to entrust that whole concern to God alone; they are too rich for that. There is no sense in trying to hide the fact. Though we may try to cloak them under the trappings of apostolic garb, the enslaving bonds of social position and prestige have their impact on our use of words. We know very well that not every sort of word will please people, that indiscriminate utterance may prove to be most inconvenient for us. We have discovered that even the police are interested in theology. In fact we have figured out that when the police did not show any interest in theology, it was because theologians themselves took over the task of making sure that they stayed within acceptable limits and did not arouse any suspicion.

As chance would have it, there are some theologians whose treatises always are reassuring to the police. But is it really a matter of chance, after all? Are there not unconscious mechanisms that automatically adapt their discourse to the convenience of the moment? When theology talks about God, it does so to serve him undoubtedly—but also to delude him.

At best theology will never be more than a very rough approach to God. It can never be taken literally. It intermingles with God too much that is not God, too many elements of ignorance and self-interest cloaked in the immaculate garb of devotion.

And yet theology does not founder in insignificance. There is a real problem of truth involved here. There is a true theology on the one hand and a false theology on the other. Indeed in a sense there is a true theology only because there is a false theology. Truth is recovered from error. There would be no reason for doing theology if there were no truth to be salvaged. It is certain, of course, that truth cannot be captured in formulas or defined in inexorable terms. While we may well be able to define formulas of faith, we cannot define a train of thought. The truth of Christianity is not to be found in intellectual understanding but in charity; it is a lived truth. That is why a true or authentic theology is a theology in the service of active, lived charity. It is not a theology that claims to be of service but a theology that truly is of service.

Theological truths are always partial and partisan. History will be obliged to enumerate theology's errors until the end of time. Every theology enunciates a host of errors, and the whole span of human history would not suffice to enumerate them all. But on the other hand we must realize this: At a given moment in history one particular theology was truer than another theology. And that is the point. One particular theology was in the service of charity. When we have two contradictory propositions, one is always truer than the other even though both are replete with errors.

When people today analyze the various theologies of liberation, they can readily find a plethora of mistakes in them: lack of serious analysis on the level of the human sciences, lack of serious exegesis, faulty historical knowledge, and so forth. But when you compare these theologies with others, you can readily see where the truth lies and where it does not. You can tell which will last and which will perish, which is of some use and which is of no use at all.

Theological effort is part of a vast struggle, and most of the time the enemy remains hidden. The real fight is not so much to defeat an opposing theology as it is to break the silence. Silence is the real enemy, and the error of false prophets is to keep silence when one should speak. The error of any theology is to talk vaguely about insignificant things so that time will pass, and the danger along with it. Truth consists in uttering the words that must be uttered precisely when they must be uttered. Thus in its own modest way theology is immersed in the great struggle of God's word against silence. The word of God breaks down the lying web of silence, and theology breaks the silence also. It is true, of course, that theological discourse is never fully matured and properly prepared. It is not the word of God; it is simply a human word fraught with inaccuracies. And yet there are times when this human word can be elevated to the dignity of a sacrament, when it can incarnate the word of God and its cutting edge.

THE TASK OF THEOLOGY

If we try to turn theology into the very language of divine revelation, then we are simply establishing and justifying the privileges of an elite class of clerical mandarins and scribes. We are trying to imprison God in a realm of technicalities so the technicians who know the jargon become indispensable intermediaries. This tack is not new to the Christian church, and theology did much to support the privileged position of the clergy as the "first estate" in the social setup of the old order. Wasn't "cleric" synonymous with "literate" ? The peasants lived a life of popular devotion because only the clergy held the key to knowledge and learning. For a long time the right to get up and speak in the church was reserved to clergymen, and theology was designed not to be understood by the faithful. It was a coded language. Its very mysteriousness seemed to be a sign of the sacred, when in fact it was only a way of hoodwinking God.

Then theology turned into apologetics. Language was now to be of service in the defense of the church against attacks from all sides. But does not the true defense of the church lie in its weakness and frailty? What exactly can and do we defend with the weapons of culture and education? Do we defend the church of Jesus Christ or merely the last vestiges of a Christian social order that refuses to die of its own accord? Are the scholarly sciences to be brought into service in defense of the faith, as if Christ himself appealed to the scribes to defend him when he stood before Caiaphas and Pilate? Apologetics has never convinced anyone, but it is of use to theologians and clergy. It enables them to engage in self-deception and self-justification. Theological apologetics is a form of solipsism; theologians simply convince themselves. They are really not talking about anything at all except themselves and their desire to salvage what they call their faith—which in reality is their lack of faith.

The real task of theology is to liberate the church from false theologies. It is in this sense, and on this secondary but valid level, that theology helps the church to undergo conversion and return to being what it really is. Theology is a methodology to restore the use of speech and God's word to the people of God. Various pagan or pharisaical theologies, reintroduced surreptitiously in the church, end up depriving them of that use. The church will get back to being its true self only when the people get back to using the word of God on familiar terms. Christian language and biblical language must be stripped of all the technical jargon surrounding it so that the Christian people can rediscover the simple words and straightforward language of God. The Bible was the book of simple, unlettered people, but it has become the book of clergymen and specialists. In this way the people were deprived of their most basic language, and words like "love," "liberty," truth," "community," and "kingdom of God" lost all meaning. Christian language thus was turned into a secret language having nothing to do with the simple things of life and existence. It became a type of mystification, working hand in glove with a society that was depriving the poor of their means of expression.

A theology is Christian only if it lets the poor speak their piece. It is not Christian if it presumes to speak in their name. A Christian theology will convert the church to the point where the poor rediscover the use of speech, to the point where its own language becomes that of Jesus Christ. Thus a truly Christian theology ends up being a sort of anti-theology.

The real question at stake for theology is whether people do or do not possess the language of God and its use. It must see to it that God's language ceases to be the private property of certain privileged classes, that the common people rise out of their shameful state once again. We cannot idealize the people as much populist thinking purports to do. The fact is that the Christian people are immersed in all sorts of paganism, superstition, fetishism, and animism. Deprived of the language of God, they are prey to the stammering accents of paganism that have not yet been stilled. Or else they resort to new forms of paganism for lack of discernment. Using that sort of language, the poor cannot make their voice heard or their meaning clear; and they know it. They must be helped to rediscover the simple language of the Bible, to regain the basic and straightforward words that spell out the essential realities of the human condition.

It is true, of course, that in the last analysis it is charity, not language, that really matters. But language can either shore up or dissolve the bonds that link the people of God together.

A THEOLOGY FOR WHOM?

Right off we realize that theology should not merely talk to itself. It is not an end in itself, and it should not be the purely gratuitous work of a particular class of Christian humanists. Once upon a time the sciences were just that, and theology could be satisfied with imitating them. But that day has passed, both for the sciences and theology. We no longer believe that the distinction between learned and unlearned people is a natural necessity, so much so that it should win out over Paul's view proclaiming the demise of that distinction. Theology has a social role to play.

Theology itself, however, is not addressed directly to the people of God as such. The poor and lowly could never read it. Theology must go so far as to efface itself, giving way to the straightforward enunciation of God's message. This is what the poor will really understand. Theology lies on a preliminary stage and has a preparatory role. Its role is to unravel the complicated web of past formulas in which the faith is entangled, so that the faithful may rediscover and make contact with the simplicity of the message. Theology itself, however, will never be simple and straightforward enough to reach that point. It is a process of simplification, but it itself is not the ultimate simplicity desired.

Theology cannot be in the service of the clergy. They are too polarized by their preoccupations with orthodoxy and by their overprotective paternalism. It is hard for the clergy to ponder the gospel of Jesus Christ disinterestedly. They tend to operate in a protective and paternalistic way, figuring out how they might use certain themes to do apologetics or to admonish people.

Theology cannot simply serve as the handmaid of the magisterium either. Many theologians assume this role, which is undoubtedly necessary and acceptable; but Christian thought is something related to the whole people of God, so theology must be framed within the overall process of thinking and exchanging ideas that takes place among the Christian people as a whole.

Since theology is part of a process in which the church turns back in on itself, it is addressed to minorities who feel they are somehow involved in this process. All theology is a form of wealth, signifying involvement in the world of the wealthy and solidarity with it. What gives theology legitimacy, however, is the process of getting rid of this wealth in order to distribute it to the poor. It is scarcely a matter of laying hold of some ready-made or finished science which belongs to the rich, which can be found only in books to which only the rich have access. The process is really much more complicated. A complex science must be transformed into a simple science so that it can eventually be expressed in a simple, straightforward message. The Christian intelligence does not lay hold of the word of God by relying on subtle distinctions, complicated language, and technical terms. It does so insofar as the complexities are dissolved and the word of God is reduced to its essential outlines, insofar as the message ceases to be a form of wealth reserved to a privileged class. Theology becomes authentic when it divests itself of all false trappings of prestige, or when it is at least moving in that direction.

Some groups in the church today are working wholeheartedly to bring about the resurgence of the whole Christian people within the church, to help God's poor to regain the place that rightfully belongs to them. Theology is true and authentic when it abets that effort. It is false and inauthentic when it serves as an alibi for those who would be mandarins, who wittingly or unwittingly try to have the church serve themselves.

SEARCHING FOR MEANINGFULNESS

Theology has an abiding tendency to become a purely mental construct in which logical coherence gets the better of meaningfulness. Who exactly is God? The creator of the universe, says theology. And what is the universe? That which was created by God, says theology. Who is Jesus Christ? The saviour of the world, says theology. And what is salvation? That which Jesus Christ brings us, says theology. What is original sin? The privation of grace, says theology. And what is grace? The remission of sins, says theology. And so it goes.

The words go round in circles. Each term is defined by its place in the whole circle, but one never gets outside the circle of words itself. The logic is impeccable, of course, because the concepts mutually define each other. Such a system naturally gives the mind a great feeling of calmness and security. The feeling of trueness is due to the force of the logical argument and its consistency. It all holds together so well that it must be true! In this framework the problem of theology comes down to relating any new element to the already established logical structure. When each new element or word is fitted into its proper place in the structure, then the mind is satisfied. One has thereby found the truth of the matter.

Thanks to this system, the word of God and Jesus Christ become a mental structure guaranteeing security. Jesus Christ is an ensemble of words and concepts that are brought together around a certain figure; the whole ensemble can be examined piece by piece. Theological innovation consists in bringing out new results by making new and unexpected associations between the elements. It does not take much to realize, however, that there is nothing novel or new here at all because one always stays right in the very same structure. Thus scholastic theology has locked up the word of God in a structure whose selling point is that it offers people reassurance and security, excuses them from the task of thinking, and replaces that task with mere word-association.

When this structure becomes some sort of orthodoxy, then the impression of security is further intensified. For now the associations assume a social function. Dogma must be protected, so the logical structure becomes the great defender of God's message. If you can imagine, it is going to protect the word of God! Its spokesmen denounce the "dangers" facing the word of God. It cannot be "reduced" to this or that. As soon as you try to relate biblical themes with some concrete historical situation, the guardian theologians call you up short: "The word of God cannot be reduced or equated with that. Jesus Christ is lots of other things, too, so he cannot be reduced to one particular form of activity."

The result is that theologians have created a system of words and concepts that contain no allusion whatsoever to any situation in history. They have managed to define a Christ *in se* and a Christianity *in se*, both wholly independent of any reference to the concrete. Christianity thus becomes a system of atemporal salvation, and hence incorruptible. It is rendered completely aseptic, and it is no longer in danger of being reduced to an ideology. On the other hand, it is now so well protected that it has lost all meaning. It no longer says anything to anyone because it is now pure message, removed from every context that might give it some specific meaning. We end up with a pure message that says nothing to anyone. As soon as any theology is completely detached from every ideology, it ceases to say anything. As a pure structure, it still continues to play a role of course. But now its role is to abet personality integration or social integration, not to serve as revelation.

What might the meaning of Christianity be? Either it has a specific and particular meaning, or there is no meaning at all. The real sense of the word of God is charity in action. Its meaningfulness always involves some actualization of charity. The themes of the Bible take on meaning when they are brought back to live in some new action. Does the Exodus have some meaning in itself? Does the wisdom of God revealed in Jesus Christ have some meaning in itself? The meaning that Christ's passion might have had for God is hidden from us; its meaning for us can be revealed only through some action that brings it back to life once again. There is really no sense in talking about it at all until we arrive at a moment when it must be relived once again. To talk about the passion without any reference to action is to evoke some mental structure that floats in a vacuum. That is why no theology makes sense in a church where nothing is going on. Its whole purpose is to tell us what is happening.

To be sure, what is really going on usually lies hidden from view. Real charity remains unknown and unrecognized. That is why it is hard for theology to find its real meaning. It inevitably is caught up in what is happening on the surface, even though it may make every effort to get underneath surface appearances and probe the depths. The meaningfulness of theology lies with those movements and processes that agitate the upper levels of conscious life in the church. Indeed the real task is to provide some sort of discernment so that the church can shift its concern from surface appearances to the underlying reality, from abstract, rhetorical, verbal charity to charity that is truly lived. The focus should be on preserving the substance of the church embodied in the activity of the unknown poor, not on preserving the conscious, visible, social life of the church.

Theology finds meaning when the word of God is referred to some form of specific action in the church and the world. Or, to put it better, it finds meaning when the word of God is related to some specific action of the church in the world. This action is not given in advance. It is not a matter of applying some meaning to an action already performed and finished. Quite the contrary is the case. The human sciences and the structures of society, however, tend to discourage all forms of action, pointing to their practical impossibility. Since the Roman Synod of 1971 people have been saying that the church is committed to the liberation of human beings. But what line of action concretely represents this liberation? What can one really do, and what line of action would merit the name of liberation? The sciences would quickly point out that there really is no place for such a question because the concept does not designate anything practical. The fact is that it is impossible for us to implement any line of conduct that would fully merit the name of liberation. Here Christians must move ahead gropingly, operating by trial and error. They move forward with Christian terms, seeking to give them meaning.

We have a message of liberation, but what can we really do

about it? "What are we to make of the Medellín documents now? " asked one bishop whose country had just succumbed to a military coup. We are always faced with the problem of what we are to make of Jesus Christ and his gospel. There is no pre-established line of action.

And yet we must act. There will always be room for relating the word of God to concrete situations and vice-versa. If God's word served as a theory, the task would be easy enough; but it does not have the value of a theory. Our concrete action never derives neatly from God's word. The work of theology lies precisely in discovering the connection between word and action, not in the abstract but in concrete situations.

The meaning never fully corresponds with the action in this process. Theology always proves to be an ideology. When in church history has theology not been ideological? It is not a matter of fashioning some theology for all time; that would be a blasphemous enterprise. The point is to link up word with action in the present moment. We ought to give up the idea of trying to fashion a theology that will survive us. Instead we must try to further its disappearance from the scene at the same moment that we ourselves disappear. Our theology should not weigh down on the generations that come after us. We must try to leave the ground clear when we ourselves depart. What we need now is a highly provisional theology fashioned to meet a very particular situation. The dream of Greek philosophy should not have any attraction for us. There is no sense at all in theology trying to construct any sort of Christian philosophy. That is a task for philosophers.

The current age is creating its own myths just as every age has done. The enslaving pressure of our technological and industrial society, which seems all-powerful, has given rise to the myth of the guerrilla. Myths also have a historical inscription, and thus we have such names as Vietnam and Algeria. The inscription, however, is relatively peripheral. The truth of the matter is that humanity is experiencing society in its most elemental and primitive forms. Latin America, for example, is concretely experiencing certain elementary realities which for some time had been shrouded in the trappings of an imaginary language. Those realities are fear, the need to eat, lack of security, the reign of brute force, the arbitrary exercise of power, and the triumph of the rich. They were never hidden from the eyes of the masses, who experienced them every day; but a thin veil of civilization did hide them from the intermediate strata of society, from which

theologians are recruited and for which they in turn do their
writing. A new kind of experience is bringing the ecclesiastical
public and the masses together for the first time. It has to do with
fear of the police and fear of denunciation, with *homo homini
lupus.*

It is in this experience that the gospel echoes and re-echoes.
Myth itself is not a response but a dream. Today the guerrilla is
that myth and that dream. But there is the life of every day to be
lived, and the human being must be refashioned from head to toe.
Where can liberty be lived in this world? Where can people find
their humanity again? What sort of dangers must be faced?
Caught between fear and hope, how and where can we find a way
out?

TALK ABOUT GOD

The fundamental theological question is not whether God exists
but what sort of God we believe in. It would be better to be an
atheist than to believe in some versions of God. Atheism is not the
opposite of faith in God, but rather of faith in a false god. Strictly
speaking, atheism can represent an attitude of tolerance and love;
obviously enough it bespeaks a certain timidity in the face of being
and existence. Atheism is not the evil. Nowhere in the Bible do we
find it presented as such. When God talks about atheists, he says
that they are fools but he does not see them as his enemies. His
enemies are the false gods. More tragic than atheism is faith in a
false god; and the tragedy is all the greater when that faith is
strong, partisan, and emotionally convincing.

The problem of theology is one of discernment. Countless poor
people are obsessed by the image of a false god with which others
threaten them. They must be freed from this obsession.

There is a certain monotheistic god who serves as the foundation and support of all kinds of domination: that of the father, the
teacher, the master, the owner, the state, and the army. This god
is a god of power, and he sacralizes all power. He is the god of the
ego, the god which the ego discovers within as the source of a more
expansive and bloated social ego or as the projection of an oppressive superego. There is a god whose transcendence is merely the
projection of the lonely, isolated ego. He is the great egotist, the
image and justification of every kind of individualism. In an individualistic society this god finds it easy to move around. He can be
condescending to those who are victimized in the struggle for life,

but he is also the god who initiates the whole struggle and rewards the victor. Military dictatorship likes to invoke God, but what god might it be? Faced with such a god, must we not admit that atheism is the first step in the road to faith?

Such a god has no need to be demonstrated by logical arguments. Every law and every form of domination in the world bears perduring witness to him. He need only be ascertained in the universe and in society. Order is his attribute, and the order of mere force is the best argument for his existence; he satisfies both the mind and the emotions. Such a god is reassuring. He divides the world up neatly into two segments, his friends and his enemies. His friends are those who invoke his name and who submit to his order. His enemies are those who refuse to invoke his name and thereby foment a spirit of rebelliousness. If one wants to be pious and religious, one must protect this god's friends and combat his enemies.

Now a Christian theology should bring out the authentic transcendence of God, i.e., the radical difference between God and his creatures. This transcendence is not to be found in the realm of quantity but in a radical and total novelty. Instead of grounding human attributes in God's attributes, the gospel message obliges us to make a sharp separation between the two. We are not to give the name or title of "father" to any human being, for example.

The true God is not revealed by any turning in of the ego on itself. He makes his presence felt in the other person. First and foremost this other person is Jesus Christ, and then all those with whom Jesus identifies (see Matt. 25). God is in the other person who goes unnoticed and unheralded. He is the creator of covenant relationships. He is not looking for mystical communion with the ego but for communion between human beings. In covenant, love of neighbor, the pardoning of offenses, and the mission to the Gentiles we simultaneously find a conception of God, a conception of the person, a conception of society, and a vision of the relationship between God, the person, and society. Communication between God and human beings does not come about through mysticism, work, wealth, or power (the fundamental experiences of traditional human religion), nor even through sexuality: It comes about through the assembly, the communion between human beings, which is the church. Every religion has tended to establish certain privileged relationships with God, or even to base certain privileges on that particular relationship. It is indeed a new God that reveals himself in the suppression of privileges.

REAL KNOWLEDGE OF JESUS CHRIST

In the strictest sense we can say that Christian theology is a Christology. Its unique and proper object is Jesus Christ. In him God and humanity meet each other and establish ties based on truth. Theology is a discourse about this relationship between God and humanity in Jesus Christ. There can be no denying that our current Christology is in sad shape. Contemporary theology talks very little about Jesus Christ; and when it does, it speaks more or less like an historian would. This paradoxical situation is the measure of the task that still lies ahead of us.

There is practically no contact at all between popular Christology and academic Christology. We know very little about the meaning of Jesus Christ as it is lived by the Christian masses. Our preaching, then, is blind; it is not surprising that it is also ineffective, and yet this ineffectiveness is something of a miracle. It is hard to believe that so many words could be spoken by so many people with such meager results. Our knowledge of the faith as actually lived by the Christian people is hazy. For all practical purposes we do not really know the nature of their belief. A fund of devotion is transmitted from one generation to the next, but we do not know its substance and religious sociology has hardly ever explored the subject.

Academic Christology, which is studied by the experts and enshrined in their manuals and treatises, is frozen in formulas whose original meaning is now lost to us. They are reiterated faithfully with little danger of distortion because now they are no more than mere formulas. Our official Christology is a frozen crystal. At the same time our devotion has turned Jesus into an object of cultic devotion. This process of turning the Son of God into an icon projects an intensely religious sense onto him, turning him into a means for satisfying certain religious needs and necessities. But it also deprives him of the possibility of being a revelation and a real teaching. It is on the plane of Christology, therefore, that the task facing theology shows up in its most urgent form. How are we to get beyond the present division between a rather blind popular devotion on the one hand and on the other an official doctrine that has been deprived of almost any vital sense and reduced to mere orthodoxy?

We readily sense that Christ is the locale of theology where myths should crop up in abundance. The age-old myths, now fixed in stereotyped formulas, are now in competition with modern myths. The salvation myth of various Oriental gnosticisms is now in conflict with the modern myth of the guerrilla. Besides that we find another heritage in those churches that go back to the medievalism of the West. It is the Franciscan heritage, which has never really been elaborated by theology but to which we owe almost all those types of Catholic devotion that have been developed. What are we to do with that heritage? What meaning does it really have? What are we to make of its various features: e.g., Christmas practices, Holy Week, devotion to Christ's passion, and devotion to the events and objects associated with his life in general?

It comes down to the whole question of Jesus Christ in relationship to an industrial and technological civilization. Clearly it is no easy matter to find a place for him in it. But does that mean we must relegate him to desert areas, to the remaining outposts of primitive society, to hippie colonies or abandoned parishes where hardly anyone goes any more? Must we fit him out in clothes that will suit a civilized and highly developed society? The fact is we scarcely know how or where to begin.

THE SPIRIT OF GOD AND HUMANITY

In a materialistic world the church itself is gauged in terms of its material strength. It is respected or flattered or feared on the basis of the force and power it represents. Is there not a danger that it will fall into the trap set for it by the world? Aren't power plays and such the natural concomitant of bureaucratic structures? Is ecclesiastical authority immune to the false prestige of power? Faced with materialism, it will not get far by issuing condemnations based on principle. How can one invoke the spirit when there is none to be found?

Christianity is a faith in the spirit—in the Spirit of God and in the consciousness and freedom of human beings. These are intangible, and they seem to be belied by both science and everyday experience. The existence of the church is not grounded in the force or power of its institutions but in the spirit of its members. When people are used to availing themselves of the power of material resources, culture, and authority, it is very difficult to measure the real sense of an appeal to the spirit. We are sorely tempted to associate the Spirit of God with matter and see him in material things. We still lack a theology of the Spirit.

HUMANITY

Human beings do not really exist except under an eschatological form. There is a reality buried in the heart of human beings as a hope and a promise, a hope not yet realized but ever rekindled. Human beings exist, but how are they to attain the state of real humanity? Consciousness, spirit, and liberty are not realities that one can fashion from outside or force into being. Either they develop of themselves or they do not exist at all.

At the same time, however, the spirit does not awaken to life all by itself. It awakens in and through contact with the spirit of others. The same holds true for liberty, which is not formed in solitude. What exactly is this action that brings people into being as spirit and liberty? It is both radically personal and radically social, obviously enough, but what exactly is it?

It is not the mission of theology to invent Christian action. Strictly speaking, it does not even have the mission of giving orientation and direction to that action. Its capabilities do not reach that far, but it can clear the ground and facilitate the task of those who have received the charism.

Our current theology is saturated to the point of nausea with existentialist and personalist themes: commitment, self-giving, decision, choice-making, encounter, dialogue, and so forth. That sort of talk is spouted endlessly and no longer says anything meaningful at all. One cannot attend the most innocuous meeting without being fed large doses of it. One might feel sorry for the unfortunate Christians in attendance if one did not realize that they had developed defense mechanisms to handle this force-feeding. The flood of nouns and adjectives does not really tell us what to do at all. We are told that we must act with intensity and commitment, but we are not told what we are to do. More and more Christians, however, are growing concerned about the content of their action. What exactly are they supposed to do?

The fact is that human action, moral action, always falls in line with collective models. Human beings are led by certain types of people who offer them coherent models. It is these models that give concrete definition to the concept of *homo*, which is too remote and abstract itself. They serve as a reference point in the day-to-day circumstances of life. The current perplexity of Christians stems from the fact that the age-old models are now disintegrating. They cannot use the types that provided moral support and living models to generations of Christians.

Consider two examples. The type of the cavalier and of the religious monk prevailed for a long time in the church. In one guise or another they were still around a generation or two ago. Christian morality, the morality of the gospels, was in practice identified with one or the other of these types. Moral education came down to initiating people into the practice of these models in a systematic and progressive way. No one really asked whether the life of the cavalier or the life of the monk was evangelical or not. That was taken for granted as a basic postulate and starting point by all. On a more human level, where most people lived, there was another model: the craftsman father (and his female sidekick) who taught us the joy of a job well done. That particular model was destroyed by the industrial revolution, but the problem of what to do next was not really raised at the time. The model went back to time immemorial, and now it kept operating of its own accord.

New types of human beings have arisen in our present civilization, but Christianity does not find itself in them. As we know very well, we no longer find an identification between the prevailing societal types and the various lines of Christian action. Today we find two prevailing types, each corresponding to one of the two major societies into which the world is now divided. In the capitalist world we have the VIP, the competent businessman in the broadest sense. He is a technocrat: competent, effective, punctual, objective, and scientific. He can be found in corporate enterprises, in public administration, in the university, and increasingly in the armed forces. These people constitute the new class of mandarins, and their values and worth are disseminated by the mass media. In the socialist world, on the other hand, we have the Bolshevik. He is the professional revolutionary: doctrinaire, objective, disciplined, totally dedicated to the cause he serves, and completely self-effacing for the sake of the party which is his all. He is the monk of a secularized society.

These are the two types or models which now polarize the aspirations of the majority. Of their very nature they attract elites. It is they who define the concrete norms of conduct, and society judges in their terms. People's vocations in current society are measured in terms of those models.

Now the problem facing Christians is that the church does not recognize itself in either of these two prevailing types. Hence the new moral and societal elites go their own way outside the church. If technocrats still say they are Christian, they retain the label by emptying Christianity of all human and concrete content. Christians, for their part, are attracted by one or the other type; but they have a bad conscience about it. They see readily enough that these types are luring them outside the church, that they will increasingly feel like strangers to the church as they identify with the models.

So what is going to happen? Must the church accept a minority status and a lack of any real influence in a society that is now dominated by human models that are alien to it? Can it envision its activity as an effort to modify the model from within, so that it is changed enough to allow for some identification between it and Christian action? Is that what happened a long time ago? Was the cavalier perhaps a bandit who was civilized a bit by the monks and accepted as a Christian type, with people closing their eyes to certain incorrigible traits (dueling, the point of honor, idleness, exploitation of the peasants, etc.)? And what about Christian artisans or peasants? Were they perhaps the old neolithic peasants who simply agreed to replace their idols with images of the saints? Was the transformation any more profound than that? Can we envision a point in the future when the Bolshevik and the technocrat will be altered enough to be recognized as Christian types and proposed for emulation by young people? Or should we wait until these models collapse under their own weight, being content to hide in the shadows of civilization and give up any idea of exerting influence on it?

One thing does seem certain. It seems unrealistic to envision the creation of a purely Christian type. Such a type has never existed. Christianity does not have the power to create new or novel types; it can simply react to the types that impose themselves. But react in what sense?

If the reaction is one of identification, then Christianity is ideologized in some way or another. In capitalist society we see the church trying to emulate the technocratic model. We get such things as cursillos, Opus Dei, and the Serra Club. (It is nowhere more evident than in the book entitled *Caminos*, which charts a process of christianization based on the technocratic model.) Insofar as the other model is concerned, identification with the Bolshevik leads toward a materialistic ideology that rejects the church and its institutions. We find obvious traces of this in various revolutionary movements on our continent: e.g., *Ação popular* and MAPU.

If our reaction is one of opposition, then we find that these elites move away from us. The church becomes the retreat of all the anachronistic segments of society, the haven of all that has been left behind by modern industrial society.

So while we may agree that we must react to existing models and try to change them, we do not know what our reaction should be. We have not yet discovered any method or approach.

We can gain some time by undertaking the task on an easier level. The fact is that we do find subtypes which are less effective and dynamic but which also exert a power of their own in the ranks of minority movements. There is a type known as "the militant," and we have also had our "Christian militants." The militant operates in social movements which do not go so far as to embrace total radicalism, and which are not effective for that very reason. Bolshevik revolutionaries always end up winning out over the militants because their effort is more consistent, disciplined, and radical in both its demands and its desire for efficacy. More recently we have the *animadores,* the guiding spirits of the small *comunidades de base.* But they can readily become tools of the technocrats or the Bolsheviks. They are not really in control of the discipline they practice. We find such guiding spirits behind the various Christian grassroots communities. Up to now, however, this type remains vague and unsure of itself because the grassroots communities are not sure of themselves or their role.

We must not imagine that the present identity crisis of Christians will be resolved easily. Rather we must ask ourselves what it means. Perhaps Christians have no special identity of their own. Like Jesus, the Christian may simply be a "son of man"; Christians may get their identity by adopting a model that a given civilization provides and by making it their own. Certainly no one can rest content with simply being a human being without any identifying feature or particularity. Like everyone else, Christians must lay hold of something and try to be something. They must adopt some mask in order to be someone. But exactly how do we get the mask and our life to tie in to each other?

We certainly can adopt existentialist or personalist terms and talk about the Christian who is pure faith, pure commitment, and pure love. But such talk remains on the level of pure rhetoric. The problem reappears as soon as we start to talk about real life. The inflated language of existentialism ends up by leading us astray and discouraging us. We must see the world and life as they really are.

Can we live without any model type? Can we invent our activity from moment to moment? How are we to relate our active efforts and our passive sufferings? What is the connection between the sin from which we liberate ourselves and the sin to which we submit?

The peoples of the Third World are discovering the problems of existing in a technical and industrial civilization as new and novel problems. The impact is extraordinary. The shock produced by the contact between social reality on the one hand and theological idealism on the other is producing a dramatic crisis involving millions of human beings. What is to be done? How are we to do it? Theology will not figure out the answer to those questions, but it can and should help the sciences not to obscure the voice of the church altogether. Anonymous voices will provide the ultimate response, but we must clear the air so that they can be heard when the time comes.

The church says that it is engaged in the liberation of peoples. But what must it do to that end? What will be liberating? There is no ready-made response at hand. Or rather, the responses at hand derive from coherent systems that are lived out by coherent human types in which the church does not recognize itself. Thus when the moment for action comes, we find hesitation and self-questioning. The action at hand is troubling. Or is it that concrete action is situated on a different level? What sort of false questions are we raising for ourselves on this whole matter?

A sound moral theology should be a critical reflection on the moral message that is really transmitted by the church, a reflection on the content of various spiritualities, on the educational approaches used in Christian institutions, and on the types or fragmented types that are emphasized in various ecclesial sectors. This task is of secondary importance of course, because we know that authentic Christian action is performed in obscurity and anonymity. But critical reflection does help to put things back in their proper place.

The lamp of truth must be set up high on the lamp stand. We know for a fact that a correct response to present-day situations is being given and is being lived; but it is not out in the open or apparent. It remains hidden, and one of the main reasons for this is that our attention is focused on false theologies. We must create an atmosphere of greater silence and attention if we want to make sure that the lamp will be taken out from under the bushel basket and placed on the lamp stand. Theology itself cannot provide the light, but it can help to remove the bushel basket.

4

Toward a Theological Outlook Starting from Concrete Events

Luis G. del Valle (Mexico City)

This consideration of a potentially different theological outlook and approach will be based on an analysis of three events that have had a profound impact on my own theological practice and that of other people in Mexico. Presented in the order of their importance, the three events are: (1) the Theology Congress held in Mexico City in November 1969; (2) the rise of the movement known as *Sacerdotes para el Pueblo* in Mexico around the same time; and (3) new approaches to the teaching of theology that have given rise to some conflict. In the final section I shall try to sum up the main features of the new theological outlook.

THE 1969 THEOLOGY CONGRESS IN MEXICO CITY

Background

In order to deal with the pastoral tasks facing the Archdiocese of Mexico, a group of people were called together and recognized as the archdiocesan Pastoral Council by the archbishop of Mexico City. This group got the idea of convening a

79

diocesan synod that would be somewhat different from the usual
type. Instead of being a legislative meeting of the diocesan bishop
and his parish priests, it would be a pastoral synod of and for the
whole diocese. All the faithful and their pastors would have a say
in it. This idea did not succeed insofar as it envisioned a diocesan
synod; but it did lay the groundwork for a far more comprehensive
sort of ecclesial gathering.

While matters stood thus, the then president of the Mexican
Theology Society approached the same group, which was still
functioning as the pastoral commission of the Archdiocese of Mexico. He thought they might join forces to hold an event that would
put life into the newly formed but rather moribund theological
society. The group responded in the affirmative, proposing that a
national theology congress be held along the lines it had envisioned for the diocesan synod which had not taken place. That is
how the Theology Congress came into being, sponsored by the
Mexican Theology Society and organized along national rather
than diocesan lines.

The Congress was planned out in terms of three successive
phases: event, prophecy, and conversion. That is how the Congress came to focus on a "theology of concrete events." To clarify
the meaning of the three phases, questions were formulated for
each and the participants were expected to respond to them as a
group.

Two basic questions were proposed for the first phase dealing
with "events": (1) What is going on? (2) How do we evaluate what
is going on? Subsidiary questions under this basic heading were:
What is the genesis and background history of what is going on?
Why has it developed in this particular way? What are the underlying historical and ideological causes? What future development
can we foresee if we do not act on it now?

The second phase, "prophecy," also considered two basic questions: What is God telling us in and through what is going on and
what we have already evaluated? How are we to correlate this
word of God with what God has told us through other means—
through Sacred Scripture and church tradition in particular?

Finally, in the third phase ("conversion") the group pondered
this question: What new attitudes must we adopt in the light of
God's word regarding the present situation?

Of great importance for the ultimate course of the Congress was
the preparation of the team of people who would serve to catalyze
its activities. It was an interdisciplinary team made up of

theologians and people familiar with various aspects of the present situation in Mexico. Nine particular issues were selected. With the help of the Jesuit Center for Investigation and Social Action (CIAS), papers were published on eight topics: education in Mexico, Mexican society, Mexican politics, the rural problem, the social communications media, the Mexican population, statistical data on the church in Mexico, and the economic situation in Mexico. One additional paper on urban reform was contributed.

This team met several times before the Congress so that it itself might start using the new approach in preliminary efforts at theological reflection. Thus it would have some experience with the methodology that was to be applied later on at the Congress, and a small nucleus of ideas from its own reflection. The team of course felt sure that the whole direction of the Congress might change when the reflection of additional people was added, and that proved to be the case. The position papers of the various subgroups dealing with particular issues were not to be the last word, presented to the participants at the Congress as final authoritative conclusions. They would simply lay out the facts as best they could, seeking to remain faithful to the chosen methodology from start to finish.

The results of the Congress were spelled out in part in a memoir that was published in two volumes.[1] The most important result was the impetus that the Congress gave to many militant groups. Some were directly affected because they participated in the Congress. Others were affected indirectly because they came into contact with people who had been involved in the Congress, or because they read about the Congress in the nation's press. Press coverage was great. Even though the Congress itself lasted only a week, the press dealt with it for almost a month.

The Resultant Theological Outlook

Though my summary of the actual events has been rather brief and sketchy, I think we can move on to draw some conclusions about the issue that concerns us here: i.e., the inculcation of a new theological outlook.

The Congress attracted *widespread attention*. Christian groups were deeply interested because many of their members attended. Public opinion was greatly interested because of what it read in the newspapers and the press. The organizers of the meeting had disagreed about the potential number of participants. The most optimistic thought it might draw four hundred people. Those who prided themselves on their realism felt that no more than two hundred would attend. The person entrusted with the task of handling all the practical details, therefore, concluded that he could safely provide documentation and accommodations for no more than five hundred participants. In fact, however, 754 people registered for the meeting and its sessions; an additional number attended the sessions without ever registering formally. This unexpectedly high attendance put a heavy strain on the Congress. Improvisation allowed it to function satisfactorily, but technical details were not handled as well as might have been desired.

Public opinion was also greatly interested in the Congress. Some people supported it, while others attacked it or issued warnings about it. Margarita González Tiscareño summarized and analyzed press treatment of the Congress in a report of her own.[2] She points out that the press showed little interest before the Congress opened, when its basic theme was still purported to be "faith and development." That changed very quickly once the Congress began and journalists realized that it was to be a reflection on the Christian faith based on the concrete events of life in Mexico. Thus eight daily papers in Mexico City published fifty-five news items about the Congress, dealt with it in five editorials, issued forty commentaries, and presented ten special reports in the course of three weeks.

This mass interest on the part of the press and participants permits us to propose the following hypothesis: Theology is a science that starts its work with a careful analysis of the concrete conditions in which a given people is living, of its yearnings and hopes as well as its struggles and failures. It fully comes under the heading of a historical science, and it must therefore subordinate itself to the social sciences which analyze the facts and events lived by human beings collectively.

It is difficult to measure *the fruits of conversion* produced by the Congress. Their magnitude and importance can be measured only by someone who is actively present in the dynamic growth and activation of the individuals and groups who participated in the Congress. Certain indications can be offered, however.

The Congress helped some Mexican bishops to see their pastoral role in a new light. Henceforth it seems certain that any episcopal document of relatively major importance will have to begin with an analysis of the concrete situation.

The Congress also had an impact on those militant Christian

groups that tend to operate more or less with the see-judge-act methodology. They came to realize more fully, or perhaps for the first time, that they cannot see, judge, and act from outside the situations of real life. They must do it from within those situations, actively committing themselves to work for the transformation of the world in which we live.

In the case of many individuals, the Congress enabled them to discover their faith. Up to that point they had conceived and lived their faith as an abstract commitment of a purely notional sort, meanwhile uncritically accepting and sharing the accepted values, rites, and norms of collective society. Now they discovered that faith is a radical commitment of the whole human being, a total obedience to God rooted in the very depths of being and life rather than in a reasoning process or even in one's self alone. Our commitment is made in the presence of God, who is actively operative in two ways. On the one hand God is there raising questions in the innermost structure of the human person who is challenged by the structure of society; on the other hand God is there raising questions in the structure of society which challenges the innermost structure of the human person.

This leads us to formulate additional notions about the character of theology: Theology both derives from and leads to conversion. Conversion is here understood as a real commitment to, and involvement in, society. Society must be changed to measure up to a faith that is both utopian and rooted in the present moment. Thus theology is critical of itself. In the light of faith it is also critical of the praxis of Christians. It drives them on to the transformation of society, not letting them rest content with mere contemplation of some revealed truth.

It should be evident, then, that there is *a close connection between a theology of events and a theology of liberation.* Most of the discussion groups at the Congress saw this clearly, and the insight was summed up in the preliminary evaluation drawn up at the end of the Congress by the organizing committee: "We planned a Congress dealing with the theme of 'faith and development.' In actual fact we find that all the talk has been about 'faith and liberation.' The fact is that liberation is the perduring condition for development. The convergence of the two themes makes it clear how Mexican Christians gathered here see development today. They see it in terms of liberation."[3]

The reality underlying that observation links the theology of events with the theology of liberation.[4] This discovery of "liberation," of the struggle it entails and the process it involves, was only natural for a Congress that took place in Latin America and used an inductive approach.

Use of an *inductive method* was explicitly proposed by the organizing committee, but a real debate arose the night before the groups began the second phase of their theme: prophecy. As I indicated near the start, one of the basic questions here was: "What is God telling us through what is going on and what we have already evaluated?" Some people on the personnel team, particularly among those who were trained or brought in late because of the extraordinary number of participants, were worried about how we might be able to channel group dialogue and reflection with this question. Some felt that we should have recourse to written documents of an authoritative sort: e.g., Scripture, the fathers of the church, past documents of the magisterium, and the documents of Vatican II in particular. There we presumably would find "God's response" to the questions that had been raised in the first phase over the course of two days. At bottom the issue was one of theological methodology and the proper role to be played by the sources of theology. It also had to do with deciding whether theology should or should not be subordinated to the human sciences insofar as it itself was a science.

The debate also had to do with the pressure being exerted on and by those in attendance. Would they be capable of discerning the voice of God in concrete events? Even if they could do that, would they be able to interpret it correctly? Is that role restricted exclusively to the hierarchy of the church? Here the debate sometimes touched upon an issue of ecclesiology. Who is a theologian in the church, and what is the theologian's relationship with the bishop?

It was a crucial night for the Congress. There was no full theoretical clarification of all these questions, but most came to realize that the organizing committee had chosen the right approach. What we really wanted now was an inductive theology ascending from the ground up. The role of the sources is not to provide principles from which we can deduce the teaching that should be held by all. All Christians who are involved in the transformation of society, and who want to be able to account for their hope to themselves and others, share in the role of the theologians in the church. So the initial question was left as it had been, and we placed our trust in the participants at the Congress.

Needless to say, we were not trying to overlook or reject an appeal to the sources. After hearing the word of God in the concrete events of today, we would compare it with the word of God that was heard in the events of a past day. In particular, we would compare it with the word of God that echoed in the supreme event: Jesus Christ, the Word made flesh.

Our initial hypotheses were gradually confirmed as the Congress proceeded: Theology is an inductive science ascending from the ground up. It does not start with basic principles and then draw conclusions from them. Instead it moves forward by proposing hypotheses that are verified, corrected, or rejected as it proceeds. Thus its affirmations are provisional in nature. They gradually become the theology of and for all insofar as they go out to meet one person after another, and one group after another.

Some bishops participated fully in the Congress. Accepting the initial formulations and ground rules, they joined with priests, religious, and laity in following the whole process through. Other bishops attended only a few of the plenary sessions of the Congress, where news and information were disseminated and the work of the various groups was coordinated. At these sessions various grassroots movements developed. They raised questions and complaints about many things: the whole organization of the Congress, bishops, and even the civil authorities. Witnessing all this without benefit of a wider context, some bishops may well have felt suspicion and resentment. In any case, after the Congress was over, the episcopate issued a formal statement in which they put a prudent distance between themselves and it:

The complicated nature of the subject and the way in which it was studied at the Congress explain the inconclusiveness and the lack of general agreement. Each individual and each group spoke for themselves. It is obvious, then, that neither the Congress as a whole nor the Mexican Theology Society, much less the Episcopal Commission on Faith and Doctrine, can assume responsibility for the statements made during the Congress. . . . Rather than pointing out the undeniable doctrinal deviations in some statements, the Mexican episcopate would like to take the opportunity offered by its annual meeting to make note of the legitimate yearnings and anxieties that were expressed at the Theology Congress. It will do all it can to make sure that they are channeled in the right direction.[5]

There is obviously some tension between the hierarchical position and that of the Congress itself. The Congress wanted to propose a provisional theology that would be constantly modified and reshaped through further reflection on concrete events. The episcopate noticed the fact that it had not arrived at definite conclusions, and was bothered by their absence. The Congress was looking for committed conversion on the part of people; the episcopate was looking for doctrinal affirmations.

Here, then, we have another feature of this new way of doing theology. It always involves a certain amount of tension with ecclesiastical authorities. This does not mean that we spurn their role as pastors. It does mean that the loyalty of Christians will be a critical-minded one; for they will gradually assume their own full share of responsibility as Christians living in the world.

SACERDOTES PARA EL PUEBLO (SPP)[6]

Background

In September 1969 a group of Jesuits got together and formulated a basic position paper. The purpose of the document, the kind of theological effort it envisioned, and our attitude toward the magisterium are spelled out in the following extracts:

> The object of this document is to try to spell out our ideological position as a group of Christians vis-à-vis the realities of Mexico today: ecclesiastical realities, Jesuit realities, and sociopolitical realities. . . .
> The provisional nature of this attempt is quite clear. We are trying to trace out the general lines of some future process of reflection that would be carried on as a group and that we hope would turn out to be our theological contribution to Christianity in today's Mexico. In all too many respects it seems to lack direction today. . . .
> It is regrettable that the church, through its official representatives, continues to maintain this dogmatism. Its approach is to continue to speak authoritatively on psychological, economic, and other questions, . . . proclaiming itself an "expert on humanity." We do not mean to suggest that faith is not a light that can illuminate human life, nor that the church is unable to contribute to the human quest. . . . Our committed involvement as Christians should come down to fighting against every form of oppression, every abuse of power, and every type of discrimination—be they economic, political, social, or even religious.[7]

This document was examined by all involved and a consensus was reached. It would be a Christian presence, not a document, that would bind us together. Our aim would be to be "a pressure group that took its starting point from faith and the gospel message in order to denounce irregularities adversely affecting the people and to support acts and initiatives conveying a message of liberation."[8] For that very reason we could not remain an isolated or self-contained group of Jesuits. So we immediately began to establish contacts with groups in other parts of the country whom we knew shared our general concerns and anxieties.

It was becoming clear to us that the movement would be one of Christians who would not form still another organization with officers and assignments, but who would take concrete steps on the basis of a thorough analysis of the Mexican situation and a commitment to the liberation of the oppressed. In its actual development this movement would involve priests specifically, but it would not be restricted to Jesuits.

Various meetings were held throughout the country. The participants were priests who shared the same spirit. At some point they began to call themselves *Sacerdotes para el Pueblo* ("Priests for the People"). Certain minimum requirements for membership were gradually worked out and eventually summarized as follows:

1. The movement would entail the participation of priests in the construction of a new (socialist) society. Each participant would do what he could in terms of his own schedule and capabilities.
2. It would entail a grassroots effort with the oppressed. Concrete initiatives would be undertaken to eliminate various injustices.
3. Instead of being a clandestine effort, it would be an open effort done with prudence and discretion.
4. There would be organized expressions of solidarity with the movement. SPP would hold meetings, seminars, and conventions. . . .[9]

SPP has had a history of concrete initiatives since it stepped out into the open on April 14, 1972. There have been two meetings a year, a total of five so far. There have been strong expressions of solidarity and fellowship, and much consciousness-raising among its members. At the same time, however, it is difficult to evaluate the vitality of the movement on the basis of its own organizational activities. Our aim is not to organize ourselves into one more organism and burden the members with an additional commitment distinct from their commitment to the oppressed. SPP seeks to be an animating spirit behind our more basic commitment to the oppressed, a spirit that is concretely manifested only now and again in formal ways.

An important step in the theological development of the movement was the SPP document issued on December 8, 1972.[10] It spelled out the following points as part of the SPP program:

1. To analyze our concrete situation, with particular attention to Mexico.
2. To opt for a socialist program as the only feasible and effective way to organize a truly humane economy that will meet the real needs of society as a whole.
3. To undertake an "evangelical" rereading of politics as a liberation praxis and also a "political" rereading of the gospel. This would come down to giving a new sense to the faith and the church. We would not deny or negate the old sense but rather go beyond it because we realize that the historical situation has changed on its own independent terms and that the Lord has been active in that process.
4. To analyze the conflicts that have and will occur in the church. Here we must face the necessary task of dialectically confronting the opposition arising in the church between Christians whose political and religious practices are different—without doing damage to the spirit of brotherhood.
5. To offer our services to others, sharing the process of reflection and praxis that led us to our own option.

The Resultant Theological Outlook

Reflection on the SPP movement, which is a historical process, confirms some of the traits ascribed to theology above and suggests others. Once again we are led to view theology as a science that begins by analyzing the concrete situations in which people live their lives; but this analysis cannot be done by us as mere outside spectators. It must entail a commitment to transform a human group in order to produce more just living conditions for all, and hence it must include real effort and struggle on the political level. Purely rational observation and analysis from the outside will falsify our understanding of the phenomenon observed because it will not enable us to penetrate the element of conflict that explains the forward course of the situation in history. And once the element of conflict is concealed, the possibility of real change is stifled. We end up with an ideology that serves to prevent any radical questioning of the historical process involved in the given situation. We never go further than improving the given situation by removing certain defects, without in any way breaking away from it.

Viewed in this light, then, theology is a type of reflection arising out of a commitment to transform radically the existing structures of society, which are seen to be unjust. This points us in the direction of a *new ecclesiology*, a practical ecclesiology that will provide us with a viable way of overcoming the church's current crisis of identity.

Theoretical considerations and various anthropological studies of peasant religious life are beginning to make it clear that the church is currently caught in the web of an internal contradiction. On the one hand it is aware that it has a calling to be universal; on the other hand its actual way of functioning, and its language and symbols in particular, tend to serve only those who dominate the cultural scene precisely because they also dominate the political and economic scene. In short, we are getting a rerun of the colonial period. The implicit assumption is that its own culture, language, and symbols as such are the appropriate vehicle for the faith in Christ that is lived in common. Other people must abandon their paganism and learn these new symbols and meanings. One reaction against this sort of colonialism is a pluralistic outlook that would give equal citizenship rights to various cultures.

Different cultures can coexist with each other. But when we come to the matter of different social classes with discordant and even opposing interests, the universality of the church exists only on the level of words and intentions. Only among those who are actually working and fighting to overcome social conflict for the benefit of all will we get language and symbols that can serve as the vehicle for the universality of the church's message of faith in Christ. Taking part in this process will make it possible for us to re-examine church tradition and the gospel message and to come up with a theology and an ecclesiology that will be truly universal in our conflict-ridden age.

That will not be done in a day, however. It will involve a long process of interaction and mutual correction between two operative factors. On the one hand there will be the ongoing struggle for a society with less alienation and more justice. On the other hand there will be the theology and ecclesiology that is worked out by those people who are active in the struggle for a better society and who share a common faith in the risen Christ. As the living historical presence of God in our own history, it is he who continues to criticize all our achievements insofar as we seek to absolutize them; for there is only one Lord. And it is also he who keeps driving us on to be perfect even as our heavenly Father is.

A practical ecclesiology of this sort assumes at the start that the church will seek to serve the poor. Its service will not be apolitical; it will seek instead to help those who are oppressed by structures to fight for their own liberation. It will provide opportunities for those among the oppressed to organize and fight systematically in the political arena for the transformation of the system that now weighs down upon us. A community formed by people who have assumed this struggle in a clear-eyed and responsible way will serve as the locale for a different type of church. Its organization, institutional forms, and modes of expression may surprise us, but they will truly tie in with the church's claim to be for all.

The reaction of mistrust evident among some bishops confirms the assumption that we had formulated on the basis of the first National Theology Congress. This current way of doing theology entails a certain amount of tension with many members of the hierarchy. It will continue to exist so long as misunderstandings and misinterpretations prevail, so long as hierarchical officials fail to realize that theologians and the SPP are trying specifically to get to work on the universality of the church and turn it into a reality. In many cases, however, it will be very difficult, if not impossible, to dispel the socio-cultural misunderstandings.[11]

CHANGES IN THE TEACHING OF THEOLOGY

When we compare the way theology is being taught in our own institute today with the way it was taught a few years ago, it is obvious that certain changes have taken place. We must analyze and evaluate these changes if we wish to lay out some path for theology in the future.

Noting Basic Changes

Even the most superficial observer can readily detect some of the changes that have taken place. Once upon a time, for example, we lived in a building complex that contained many different resources and services within its own walls: housing, classrooms, offices, recreational facilities, and a farm area providing meat, milk, and dairy products. Today the complex is half-empty because many have gone to live outside its walls; and the farm area has ceased to exist as such.

Once upon a time the actual teaching was done almost exclusively through regular classes and conferences: today small study groups abound. Once student activities were almost entirely academic in nature; today students engage in many different sorts of activities, including apostolic and non-apostolic ones. At one time class attendance was very high, and the schedule of exams, vacations, days off, and so forth was very rigid. Today students are readily excused from attending class, and the same course may differ greatly from year to year. Where once the curriculum was basically the same for all with few electives, we now find quite a bit of variety: new forms of evaluation have now appeared alongside the more traditional exams and papers. Once the status of the professor and his formal qualifications were very clear-cut; now even students may give some courses without having an academic degree, on the basis of some known or alleged expertise. New courses and disciplines have appeared in the theology curriculum which were once regarded as part of sociology or anthropology.

Once study plans were made up solely with the aim of presenting a certain body of doctrine in clear and coherent fashion; today they also take account of the attitudes to be inculcated and the methods leading to that end. The presentation once centered around some "thesis" to be demonstrated or proven—particularly in dogmatic theology. Now the presentations are much more free-wheeling and replete with "hypotheses." The aim once was to have the student accumulate a fund of knowledge about the various doctrines, so that at the end of his studies he would possess a doctrinal synthesis of all the important questions covered in all his courses. Now the import of what is being taught to him is stressed, and he is being offered a methodology that will enable him to broach new questions of a meaningful sort; thus there is less emphasis on his having to know all the questions.

Matters were once debated and discussed by small advisory bodies, and all decisions were made by those in authority. The minutes and agendas of all such meetings were a closely guarded secret. Now the range of consultation and debate is much greater. Students can participate in such meetings, and there are few secrets.

All these facts can be observed readily. Together they seem to add up to a chaotic mass of unconnected data in which anomie prevails. The juridic complex of written rules and long-standing customs has fallen apart. Sometimes the traditional norms function and prevail, but often they do not.

Explanations for the Situation

There should be some way to explain this situation, however chaotic it may seem at first glance. Certain possible explanations, however, are not really satisfactory. Broad generalizations tend to be of this sort. Some suggest that there is no respect for authority today. Young people are incapable of serious study and unfit for austere discipline. Some suggest that positivism and secularism have taken over, or that we need the old-fashioned kind of Superior who knew how to give commands. On the other side we hear people saying that imagination must now take first place. Others suggest that individual reform is not enough, that this is the time for structural change, and that those who once exercised authority must learn how to step into the background.

All such explanations really fail to come to grips with the phenomenon itself. In the last analysis they simply tend to place the blame on someone or other for the fact that things are not as they were or that they have not changed fast enough. Even if we could accurately portion out responsibility, that would not really make the phenomenon itself intelligible.

A first step in this direction is to try to find a genetic explanation, to uncover the genesis of the present situation. That is what I shall try to do here. Then I shall try to explore the meaningfulness of the phenomenon at the level of basic, underlying options.

The current state of affairs at the institute where I teach theology can be viewed more or less as the result of two opposing processes operating simultaneously in one and the same place. One process seeks to change a given situation A to a very different situation B; the other process seeks to stop that transition, to do nothing more than add improvements or corrections within the context of situation A. Both are operative in the same milieu, seeking to dominate the structure and functioning of a particular school of theology. Moreover, so far the people involved have not sought or managed to suppress the process which runs counter to the one they espouse. Indeed it seems for the most part that they have not even adverted to the fact that there are two contrary processes at work. At this level of abstraction, then, it is not surprising that the resultant situation appears to be chaotic.

We can take another step forward in trying to explain the situation if we manage to describe exactly what situation A is and what situation B is. An alumnus and teacher of our institute, Jorge Fernández Font, has tried to do precisely that, describing the two situations as two different educational and communication models.[12]

Using communication theory, we can try to explain how someone sends a message to another. To transmit a message, the sender makes use of a certain medium, codifies the message in a particular code with reference to some object of the message, and addresses it to the receiver. The latter, in turn, must possess the same medium and know how to decode the message in terms of the same code used by the sender. The basic setup can be schematized as follows:

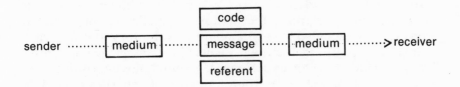

Following this basic scheme, Fernández goes on to compare the way these various elements appear in our Situation A and our Situation B. They can be schematized as follows:

Element	Situation A	Situation B
sender	professors and books	historical reality, revelation and tradition
medium	classes and written materials	first-hand contact and experience, group reflection, tutorial dialogue, conferences, written materials
message	systematic philosophy	God's plan in salvation history
code	formal logic and deductive metaphysics	transcendental epistemology, logic, anthropology, metaphysics
referent	revelation and tradition; a certain way of comprehending being	God and human beings operating in history
receiver	the students	the whole work team: students, professors, and tutors

Thus we can briefly describe the two situations in the following terms. In Situation A a group of students consults a group of professors and written books to find out what God has revealed and how being and life are to be understood. Through conferences, formal classes, and recommended bibliographies they seek a coherent, structured doctrinal synthesis of philosophy and theology that will account for God's revelation in Scripture as it has been preserved and interpreted by church tradition.

In situation B students and professors come together as a group for study and investigation of history. Specifically they want to study God as revealed in the happenings of history and the tradition that the church has held about this historical happening. Through sharing their experiences, group dialogue, conferences given by some member or other, and study of written materials, they seek to lay hold of God's plan in salvation history so that they may actively comprehend and assimilate his action in history in terms of their own lives.

Thus far we have analyzed the two Situations as communication models. We can also see them as two educational models, analyzing the function that each serves for society. An educational model fulfills three basic functions in a given society: an economic function, an academic function, and a socio-political function. Let us now consider Situation A and Situation B in terms of these functions.

Insofar as the economic function is concerned, Situation A is designed to train a labor force that will satisfy certain church needs of an intellectual sort, and that will conserve and reproduce the existing form of social coexistence in the church. Situation B, on the other hand, is designed to train a labor force that will undertake an apostolic effort designed to liberate both the church and society; thus it seeks to make the labor force creative and critical-minded with respect to the social processes in which it is living.

Insofar as the academic function is concerned, Situation A is designed to communicate theological and philosophical data as well as information about those types of social and ecclesial functioning that are required if one is to live in accordance with a church structure that is dogmatic and juridical. Situation B is designed to provide information about various ways of approaching reality and the various possibilities for reality insofar as they are based on a utopian vision of both the church and society.

Insofar as the socio-political function is concerned, Situation A is designed to inculcate a *dogmatic* approach in relating to other systems of thought, a *deductive* approach in relating to concrete praxis, and a *dependent* attitude toward decision-making groups. Situation B, on the other hand, is designed to inculcate an *interdisciplinary and tentative* approach in relating to other interpretations, an *inductive* approach in relating to concrete praxis, and a sense of *criticism and personal responsibility* vis-à-vis decision-making groups and historical processes.

The seemingly chaotic situation in current theological education is now somewhat intelligible. The seeming chaos is due to the fact that two processes are operative simultaneously and that they differ radically in many respects. This is a potential source of continuing conflict, but such conflicts are not consciously noted and dealt with as such. Needless to say, the above models are not to be regarded as exact and correct in every detail, nor can it be said that each individual fits neatly into the scheme on every point; but as a general frame of reference, the models can be taken as valid.

Meaning of the Situation

I think we can go even deeper in trying to see the meaning of this phenomenon if we explore the basic options that underlie the school personnel's espousal of a given model. At what level does their option lie? I would propose the hypothesis that people's option for model A or model B lies on a pedagogical level, or an epistemological level, or on an ideological level. Let us consider each possibility in turn.

Many of the changes in the teaching of theology described above were introduced for *pedagogical reasons*. They were proposed in those terms and accepted or tolerated on that ground. At one point, when the faculty was feeling quite uneasy about the seemingly chaotic situation, we decided to hold a seminar on modern pedagogy during a vacation period. Our basis for discussion was the book by Carl Rogers entitled *Freedom to Learn*.[13] There was much discussion, exchange of views, and decision-making. But once courses were back in session, it did not seem that our seminar had had any marked influence on our teaching. We did not even comply with the resolutions that we all had formulated and accepted at that time. This suggests several things. There is obviously diversity in our pedagogical options because that was evident in our seminar and the final resolutions we drew up there.

Moreover, this diversity of options is not restricted to the pedagogical level. Hence we have not yet found the solution for our
situation. We must look to some other level to explain why some of
us opt for model A and some for model B.

Let us consider the *epistemological level*. Our corps of professors
has engaged in countless discussions where the basic question
had to do with the nature of theology as a science, the criterion of
theological truth, and the relationship between praxis and theory.
When other matters were being discussed, we often came back to
those same issues in one form or another. It became obvious that
people were speaking two different languages and repeating the
same basic arguments. One language and line of argument was
intelligible and persuasive for some people while it left others
completely cold, and vice-versa. Our talk seemed to be moving on
two parallel lines that never met. Is theology a deductive science,
a science of principles from which conclusions are drawn and
which also uses principles and conclusions from other sciences? Or
is it a science akin to the empirical sciences, a science that takes in
data that must then be subjected to verification through hypotheses and is therefore modified in the process of becoming known?
One group of people answered those questions one way, the other
group had a very different answer. Recognizing the fact that
there were epistemological differences between us, we at the
school decided to get together and explore the issue of theological
method. Our discussions centered around Lonergan's book entitled *Method in Theology*.[14] There were long study sessions, led for
the most part by two people who had specialized in Lonergan's
thought. Curiously enough, they espoused two different tendencies. They came to their study of theological methodology with
some prior option affecting their epistemology. And so we must
move to still another level to find the deeper underlying option.

The option that I have in mind here lies on the *ideological level*.
It is the option that Claude Geffré is talking about in *Concilium*
when he contrasts current Latin American theology with that of
Europe and North America.[15] Talking about Latin American
theologians, he says:

But, more surprisingly, they criticize even more radically the various
"progressive" theologies of the western world—whether "secularization
theologies" or "political theology." They share the defect of unconsciously playing the game of western capitalist society.[16]

Given this situation, Geffré urges people to pay close attention to
the theology that is now arising on the Latin American continent:

"Whatever its limitations and technical inexactitudes, we should pay great attention to the rise of this new theology which puts in question the theology of the western world as the dominant ideology of the universal Church."[17]

Though Geffré refers to Latin American theologians in general, he is obviously talking about those who are working on liberation theology in the terms just described. They are the theologians who are relativizing what was once known as "theology" because in fact it was "European theology." They have come to see that in Latin America the message of faith must somehow be brought to the "nonhuman" rather than to the "nonbeliever."[18]

Now the point is that we find two kinds of theologians in Latin America also. One group follows the European line just indicated; the other follows the new Latin American approach. To avoid couching this along nationalistic or ethnic lines, let us say that one group accepts and elaborates the theology that has been handed down to them without criticizing it as an ideology; they may even move it forward in some way or other. The other group seeks to engage in such criticism on the basis of social praxis, however hesitant and unsure this may still be. This difference in options is what I would call an "ideological" one. And my point is that it more than anything else lies behind people's preference for one educational model over another, for one communication model over another.

SUMMARY: OPTIONS INVOLVED IN A NEW THEOLOGICAL OUTLOOK

It is time to bring together all the observations made in this article and apply them to the question of a new basic theological outlook and approach. Our analysis of three specific happenings has, I think, pointed toward a future theological outlook that would contain certain basic features. Here I should like to describe those features in terms of the three options described in the last section.

Insofar as I am concerned, theology in the future will presuppose three basic options: on the pedagogical, epistemological, and ideological level.

On the *pedagogical* level, we must take seriously the student subjects who are being trained. They must grow and develop freely and autonomously. The role of the professor will have more to do with creating a favorable atmosphere and providing the students with methods and tools that will foster theological productivity. The professors will be companions and guides rather than commanders. In all our theological work we will start off from a careful analysis of the concrete situation in which our people live.

On the *epistemological* level, we will treat theology more as an empirical science. Our presupposition will be that we know only what we transform through the use of hypotheses. And our hypotheses will be corrected, approved, or rejected in the very process of transforming the reality that underlies the phenomenal data. Theology, then, is to be fully included under the historical sciences and subordinated to the social sciences that analyze the facts of collective human life. It must also look with a critical eye on the concrete practice of Christians, viewing it in the light of faith. It will move them beyond mere contemplation of revealed truth to the active work of transforming society. Theology will be an inductive science ascending from the ground up rather than a deductive science drawing conclusions from a priori principles. It will move forward by forming hypotheses that are then subjected to verification. Its statements will be provisional, and it will become everybody's theology insofar as it goes out to meet person after person and group after group. In short, theology will be an "evangelical" rereading of politics as a liberation praxis, and a "political" rereading of the gospel.

On the *ideological* level, we must carefully analyze theologies and their message from the standpoint of a liberation praxis on behalf of the oppressed. We must unmask any elements in them that unwittingly justify one or another type of exploitation. Our future theology will be born of conversion and lead to conversion. In this instance the conversion will entail real involvement with society and a commitment to change it on the basis of a faith that is both utopian and rooted in the here and now. Our theology will be based on an option in favor of a socialist historical project as the only real viable alternative for building a humane economy that will satisfy the needs of the social body. It will try to help the oppressed to organize and fight systematically in the political arena for the transformation of the current system of oppression; and it will then analyze the faith from within the context of this shared social life. Finally, this theology will be carried out in a state of tension with the ecclesiastical hierarchy. Without disregarding their role as pastors, Christians will display a critical-minded loyalty. They will assume an increasing share of personal responsibility for their place as Christians in this world. And theology will analyze the conflicts taking place within the church.

NOTES

1. *Memoria del Primer Congreso Nacional de Teología: Fe y Desarrollo*, Sociedad Teológica Mexicana, 2 vols. (Mexico D.F.: Ed. Alianza, 1970).

2. Margarita González Tiscareño, *El Congreso de Teología en la Prensa*, issued privately by the Sociedad Teológica Mexicana.

3. *Memoria*, 1:16; 2:337, 414.

4. I pointed out this connection in a later interview conducted by R. Lahusen and published by the Center for Ecumenical Studies in Mexico City:

Lahusen: "Do you think that the theology of events and the theology of liberation are in the same line? "

Del Valle: "I think that the two do coincide at present because of the historical situation. The situation in Latin America absolutely calls for human liberation. Throughout the world, but particularly here, we have a situation where masses of people are oppressed by small minorities, but on the national and supranational level. Now if the theology of events purports to analyze concrete situations, and if the concrete situation is one of oppression, then obviously the two theologies converge at that point" (*Estudios Ecuménicos*, 11 [1971]:29).

5. Declaration of the Mexican episcopate, October 16, 1970, *Memoria*, 2:431.

6. Note that the abbreviation SPP stands for *Sacerdotes para el Pueblo*.

7. Basic draft document, September 20–21, 1969, unpublished.

8. Letter of October 24, 1970, from the group in Mexico, D.F., to the whole "Liberación" group.

9. Basic draft document of the SPP, dated October 4, 1972.

10. Document of the first SPP Congress, December 8, 1972. See *Contacto* 10 (1973): 64–72.

11. The experience of the movement in this area has varied greatly insofar as relations with the local ordinary and with the entire episcopate are concerned. One example was a process of dialogue that took place between March and June of 1973. There were five plenary sessions in which three bishops from the episcopal clergy commission took part, and four or five with the SPP coordinating committee. The tension is clear in the official proceedings, but it has to do with the situation itself, not with personalities. The atmosphere of all the meetings was very cordial, but the bishops made such remarks as these:

Do you love your socialist position more than you love the church?

Are you not forming another authoritative body, not to serve the church but to serve your ideology and your choice in favor of socialism?

I fear that membership in this movement will make priests lose confidence in their bishops.

The image you project as a movement is that of being Marxist.

12. Jorge Fernández Font, *Dos maneras de comprender la Segunda Etapa*, a mimeographed paper presented to the faculty synod of the Colegio de Cristo Rey. The "second stage" in question here is the second stage in Jesuit training in present-day Mexico. The college is a place where Jesuits receive training in philosophy and theology.

13. Carl Rogers, *Freedom to Learn* (Columbus, Ohio: Charles E. Merril, 1969).

14. Bernard Lonergan, *Method in Theology* (New York: Seabury, 1972).

15. Claude Geffré, "A Prophetic Theology," in *Concilium* 96 (New York: Herder and Herder, 1974), pp. 7–16. In talking about this particular level, the "ideological" option, I preferred to bring in the witness of a European theologian as support.

16. Ibid., p. 9.

17. Ibid., p. 12.

18. Geffré alludes to the text of Gutiérrez on the "nonhuman," which is quoted in the Preface to this present volume.

5

Christ's Liberation via Oppression: An Attempt at Theological Construction from the Standpoint of Latin America

Leonardo Boff (Petrópolis, Brazil)

THE BASIC QUESTION

The basic question here and now is how we are to proclaim the liberation brought by Jesus Christ in a way that will be meaningful to people today. Today's human being is not an abstract universal. It is people who, like us in Latin America, live in a more or less pervasive situation of captivity on the outskirts of the great decision-making centers of the world where cultural, economic, political, and religious questions are decided. It is people who are led to feel that they are marginal, concrete human beings who suffer from frustrated hopes. They look in vain for a structural change in their way of life and their relationship with worldly goods and other human beings. They must bear the full weight of the fact that their generation will not live to see the appearance of a more just and fraternal world, that it will have to put up with a

100

global system that generates rich and poor, periphery and center, violence and oppression.

These human beings cannot help but ask certain questions. Is the liberation brought by Jesus Christ only for the end of the world and the afterlife? Does it transport us beyond our conflict-ridden world, only to leave this world abandoned to the mechanism of its own peculiar laws? Is it that his liberation is not inaugurated within the conflict of this world, that it does not begin to bud amid oppression itself? Are we to believe that it is not fleshed out in those historical mediations that open the way for more freedom, more justice, more participation, more human dignity and equality, and thus for the progressive building up and establishment of what we call the "kingdom of God"? What is meant *concretely* when people make all-embracing and sometimes highly rhetorical proclamations about liberation from sin and death?

Faith is to be seen as the matrix that gives meaning to the history we live, not as some superstructure that has nothing more to say to us. In every here and now we must be ready to give an account of our hope (1 Pet. 3:15), to translate the liberative message of faith in a way that will be meaningful to ourselves and others. It is a message of faith in Jesus Christ, who died under oppression and was resurrected in glory.

The first and foremost question, then, is this: What meaning does Christ's liberation have in a context where people are yearning for liberation and suffering from oppression? We do not want to be naive from the hermeneutic standpoint. Our question is prompted by a very clear and well defined interest. We seek to detect and establish the concrete mediations that do flesh out his liberation in history. Universal statements are not enough; they must be verified in the very texture of human life. Without such mediation they are unreal and ideological, and they end up bolstering the powers that be. When we inquire about Christ's liberation and its meaningfulness in terms of the liberation process now going on in Latin America, we are already pointing the response in a certain direction and setting up a viewpoint through which we will scan the words, life, and historical journey of Jesus Christ.

It is certainly true that this is only one possible reading of that event, but it happens to be the one that forces itself on us right now. The way in which we interpret Christ's life is not a matter of indifference. The only legitimate interpretation is the one which gives fulfillment and meaning to our life, purifying it, testing it, and allowing us to experience what Christ's liberation really signifies. Every interpretation is given orientation by some existential or social interest—even those interpretations that view Christ's redemptive work as vicarious satisfaction, expiatory sacrifice, or whatever else is expressed in the New Testament and theological tradition.[1] It is only in this way that Christ finds insertion into our life and actualizes his liberation in the world.

The important thing is to make this inevitable procedure as conscious as possible. If we do not, then we will tend to fall back into ideological positions that absolutize images and interpretations deriving from a given cultural framework. The images and interpretations will be petrified and put forth as valid for all places and ages. That is how we end up with all sorts of abstract and hollow talk about redemption, death, the behavior of the historical Jesus, and the intraworldly value of his resurrection.

If we read and evaluate Christ's work of liberation in the context of our concrete situation, which bespeaks captivity and cries out for liberation, we can salvage important values in Christian tradition and shed a ray of surprisingly new light upon them. We can dare to answer a question that has been left hanging in our own reflection: Is there any chance at all of breaking the vicious circle of oppression-liberation, of captivity and exodus? Faith boldly presents Jesus Christ as the one who did precisely that by turning his own oppression into a path to liberation, and his own captivity into the definitive exodus from the prevailing human condition. He, the Suffering Servant, is fashioned and proclaimed as the Liberator. He, the weak and powerless one, is proclaimed Lord of the entire cosmos.

Christ's life was redemptive in each of its phases and moments, not just at his initial incarnation or his final death on the cross. Liberation was not some doctrine he proclaimed; it was first and foremost a concrete praxis that he inaugurated. But here we do well to remember that it is not enough to engage in a historical and descriptive reading of his novel liberative praxis. One of the major flaws in a certain brand of theology was that it tended to reduce Jesus to the category of past history. It spoke of his deeds and reiterated his words, but it made no effort to translate their import for the context in which we live. Imprisoned in the dead letter of past history, it failed to imitate the theology of the church fathers in recovering the spirit of that history so that it might vivify the present. That spirit is embodied in the words and deeds of Jesus, to be sure, but it is not exhausted there. His words and deeds are indicative of some perduring meaningfulness that is meant to be actualized in our concrete experience of the faith today. Hence our hermeneutic effort should always be concerned to break through the limiting framework of Jesus' own concrete situation and find the perduring transcendent meaning that is articulated there; for that meaning must now be turned into history in our own present-day context.[2]

Our task here, then, is to do two things. First we must show how Christ's liberation was a concrete liberation for the world with which he had to deal. That world was strikingly similar to our own Latin American world; it was a world suffering from oppression both within and without. Second, we must then try to discern in that concrete liberation a dimension that transcends that particular historical embodiment of liberation, a dimension that has to do with us in our present and different situation in history.

To put it a bit differently, the liberation achieved by Jesus Christ has a universal and transcendent reach. But its universality and transcendence are mediated and made feasible through concrete liberative actions and events. It is in human efforts at liberative change that they are fleshed out in history. Christ himself translated this universal liberation into practice by implementing a concrete approach to liberation within his particular situation. We must do the same if Christ's liberation is to become meaningful in our own lives.

JESUS' WORLD: MARKED BY INTERNAL AND EXTERNAL OPPRESSION

The socio-political situation in Jesus' day presents striking parallels to the situation that gave rise to liberation theology in Latin America. Let us consider some of the main features here.[3]

General Situation of Dependence

For centuries Palestine had been living in a general state of oppression. From 587 B.C. on it was dependent on the great empires around it: Babylonia (up to 538 B.C.), Persia (up to 331 B.C.), and Greek Macedonia afterwards (Alexander up to 323 B.C.; the Ptolemies in Egypt up to 197 B.C.; and the Seleucids in Syria up to 166 B.C.). Finally, in 64 B.C. it came under the control of the Roman

Empire. It was a small canton in the Roman province of Syria. At the time Jesus was born, it was governed by a pagan king named Herod who had Rome's support.

This dependence on an outside power center was made visible in the country itself by the presence of Roman occupation forces and by a whole class of imperial tax collectors. Roman nobles sold the job to a group of Jews; they in turn delegated it to others in Palestine itself and thus maintained a network of roving functionaries. Extortion and exaction of other payments were common. In addition there was the party known as the Sadduccees. They played Rome's game in order to maintain their own capital investments, particularly in the temple and the other monumental works in Jerusalem.

Political dependence bred cultural dependence. Herod, who was educated in Rome, constructed grandiose works that would have done justice to an Egyptian pharaoh: palaces, baths, theaters, and fortresses. The presence of Roman culture made the oppression all the more hateful and revolting because of the religious bent of the Jews.

Socio-Economic Oppression

The economy was based on agriculture and fishing. Galilean society, which was the chief scene of Jesus' activity, was made up of small cultivators and groups of fishermen. Speaking generally, we can say that there was work for everyone but the standard of living was not very high. Lacking knowledge of the savings system, people were hard hit by illness and famine. Such calamities drove them from the countryside to look for work in the local towns. Day laborers gathered in the town squares (Matt. 20:1–15) or put themselves out to hire to some large landowner until they had paid off their debts.

The growth of the salaried class was indirectly fostered by the Mosaic law, which provided that the firstborn of a family would receive twice as much of the inheritance as anyone else. The other sons often could not find work, and they swelled the ranks of job-seekers until they formed a real proletariat: unemployed, beggars, vagabonds, and thieves. The rich landowners sometimes fleeced the peasants with mortgages and other liens based on unpaid debts. The tax system was heavy and detailed. There were taxes on almost everything and everyone: on each member of a family, land, cattle, fruit-bearing plants, water, meat, salt, and the roadways. Herod's huge construction projects impoverished the general populace and even the great landowners.

Jesus' family profession was that of a *teknon*, which might mean either a "carpenter" or a "roofer." The *teknon* could eventually become a mason working on the construction of houses. In all likelihood Joseph was employed in the rebuilding of the city of Sepphoris, which lay not far beyond the hills of Nazareth and which had been completely destroyed by the Romans after it was occupied by Zealot guerrillas in 7 B.C.

The presence of an alien and pagan force represented a real religious temptation for the Jewish people. They pictured and worshipped God as the one and only Lord of the land and its people, who had promised them perpetual possession of Israel. Oppression exasperated the religious fancies of many. Almost all of them were expecting some imminent finale highlighted by God's spectacular intervention. Apocalyptic expectations bubbled everywhere, and the Gospels indicate that they were shared to some extent by Jesus himself (e.g., Mark 13). Various liberation movements, particularly that of the Zealots, sought to pave the way for God's saving intervention or even to provoke it through the use of violence and guerrilla tactics. For God's own intervention would entail the liquidation of all his enemies and the submission of all nations to Yahweh's lordship.

Religious Oppression

But the real oppression did not consist in the presence of an alien, pagan power. The real oppression lay in a legalistic interpretation of religion and the will of God. In postexilic Judaism careful cultivation of the law became the very essence of Jewish life. Something that was meant to help people in their own search for God became overburdened with sophistic interpretations and absurd traditions. It degenerated into a terrible and impossible form of bondage proclaimed in God's name (Matt. 23:4; Luke 11:46). Jesus himself vented his feelings about the situation: "You have made a fine art of setting aside God's commandments in the interests of keeping your traditions" (Mark 7:9).

Scrupulous observance of the law for the sake of winning salvation caused the Jewish people to forget God himself, the author of both the law and salvation. The Pharisees in particular were keen on observing the law down to the last letter, and they frightened the populace into maintaining the same scrupulosity. Reacting against Jesus, they claimed he had a following only among those who knew nothing about the law, "and they are lost anyway" (John 7:49). But though they were perfect in their observance of the legal code, they possessed a basic streak of malice which Jesus spotlighted: "You pay tithes . . . while neglecting the weightier matters of the law, justice and mercy and good faith" (Matt. 23:23).

Instead of fostering liberation, the law had become a golden fetter. Instead of helping human beings to relate to each other and God, it closed them off from doing so by setting up neat divisions. On one side were those whom God loved, those who were pure, and those who were one's neighbor that should be loved; on the other side were those whom God hated, those who were impure, and those who were enemies to be hated. The Pharisees had a dreary conception of God. Their God no longer spoke to human beings but had left them a law for guidance. Those who did not fit into this overall conception of the law were regarded as public sinners and social outcasts already well on their way to perdition.

In Jesus' day Judaism was also deeply tinged with an apocalyptic theology, which maintained that the world was in the hands of diabolic forces and suffering from an oppressive captivity. But it also said that God's saving intervention was imminent. The old Davidic kingdom would soon be restored and the conquered nations of the world would soon be on their way to venerate the true God in Jerusalem.

Such was the backdrop for Jesus' life and activity. What might liberation mean in such a context? That is the question we shall consider in the following sections of this article and try to apply to our own situation in the final section.

THE PRESENCE OF ABSOLUTE MEANING: CHALLENGE TO THE PRESENT

Jesus' reaction to this general situation is somewhat surprising. Unlike a man such as Bar Kochba, he does not present himself as a revolutionary dedicated to overthrowing the existing power relations. Unlike a man such as John the Baptist, he does not present himself as a preacher interested solely in the conversion of people's consciences. Instead he proclaims some ultimate, structural, and all-embracing meaningfulness that goes far above and beyond everything that can be decided or done by human beings. He proclaims some final end that calls into question all immediate interests of a social, political, or religious nature.

Jesus maintained this universal, cosmic perspective in everything he said and did. He did not immediately satisfy the concrete and limited expectations of his listeners. He called them together for the sake of some absolutely transcendent dimension that goes far beyond the facticity of this world and its history of special interests, power plays, and the survival of the fittest. Instead of proclaiming some particular kind of meaning, be it political, economic, or social, he proclaims an absolute sense that embraces but supersedes everything.

The key term used to convey this radical meaning and to embody its challenge to the present state of things is "the kingdom of God."[4] Its roots are buried deep in people's most utopian yearnings. It is there that Jesus touches and quickens the wellsprings of absolute hope that have been buried or dried up by history and its structures. He revivifies hope for total liberation from all those things that alienate people from their authentic identity. His very first public words present this utopian yearning as something that is not only promised but already real: "This is the time of fulfillment. The reign of God is at hand! Reform your lives and believe in the gospel! " (Mark 1:15).

The whole of creation, not just the restricted realm of the Jews, is to be liberated in all its dimensions. But Jesus' message is not just another prophetic or utopian pronouncement. In every age Jewish and pagan prophets had talked about the advent of a totally new and reconciled world; in that respect Jesus was hardly original. The novel feature in Jesus is that he anticipates the future and brings the utopian element right into the heart of present-day life. He does not say that the kingdom of God is coming in the future but that it is at hand now (Mark 1:15; Matt. 3:17), that it is in their very midst (Luke 17:21). With his own presence the kingdom, too, is made present: "But if it is by the finger of God that I cast out devils, then the reign of God is upon you" (Luke 11:20). His presence is the appearance of the stronger who overcomes the strong (Mark 3:27).

JESUS' TEMPTATION TO REGIONALIZE THE KINGDOM

The "kingdom of God" signifies the world's totality of meaning in God's eyes. The great temptation here is to regionalize it, to privatize it and turn it into some intraworldly embodiment of grandeur. Liberation is true liberation only if it possesses a universal and globalizing character, only if it translates and embodies the absolute meaningfulness sought by humankind. We pervert the original and pristine sense of the kingdom as meant by Jesus when and if we regionalize it and the concept of liberation by defining it in terms of some ideology of well-being or some particular religion.

The Evangelists report that Jesus was confronted with this very temptation (Matt. 4:1–11; Luke 4:1–13), and that it stayed with him throughout his life (Luke 22:28). The precise temptation here was to restrict the universal idea of God's kingdom to some kingly province of this world and political domination, to some form of religious power, or to some form of miraculous social and political sway which would satisfy people's basic needs. These three temptations, described symbolically in the gospel accounts of Jesus' temptation in the desert, fitted in with the three basic images of the Messiah and his kingdom that were in vogue at the time—i.e., the Messiah as prophet, priest, and king.

All of these images had to do with power. Throughout his public life Jesus was tempted to use the divine power at his disposal to impose a radical transformation of the world with the help of power and a touch of magic. But that would mean manipulating people's wills and excusing them from their human responsibilities. Human beings would be mere spectators and beneficiaries rather than participants. Rather than making history they would be liberated in a paternalistic way. Liberation would not be the reward of conquest and achievement.

Jesus categorically refused to inaugurate a kingdom based on power and its use. He was the servant of every human creature, not their ruler. Thus he stood as the incarnation of God's love rather than of God's power. Or, to put it better perhaps, he tangibly represented the power of God's love to inaugurate an order that does not violate people's freedom nor exempt them from the task of taking charge of their own human project. That is why it is through conversion that the kingdom begins to take concrete shape in history. That is why human beings, in accepting the novel aspects of hope for such a world, also collaborate in its construction through the mediating factors of politics, persons, religions, and social activities.

The basic attitude of Jesus remains the same in this respect. Whether he is engaged in moral disputes with the Pharisees or confronted with the temptation of power by his own disciples (Luke 9:46–48; Matt. 20:20–28), Jesus refuses to lay down particularizing norms or to encourage regionalizing hopes and solutions. He thereby took a critical stand at some distance removed from the basic structure that we noted to be the pillar of our present world: i.e., power as a force for domination. This refusal to have recourse to power caused the masses to move away from him with feelings of disappointment and disillusionment. Power and its use was all that impressed them: "Let's see him come down from that cross and then we will believe in him" (Matt. 27:42). But power as a category of religion and liberation was completely de-divinized by Jesus. In his view power, insofar as it means domination, is essentially diabolic and contrary to the mystery of God (Matt. 4:1–11; Luke 4:1–13).

But Jesus' insistence on preserving the universal and total character of the kingdom did not lead him to do nothing at all or to wait calmly and expectantly for the kingdom to burst in all of a sudden. That absolute goal and end was mediated through concrete gestures, anticipated in certain surprising behavior patterns, and made tangible in attitudes that signified that the end was already present somehow in the very midst of this life.

And so there are two aspects to the liberation brought by Jesus Christ. On the one hand it proclaims complete liberation for all history, not just for certain segments of it; on the other hand this complete liberation is anticipated in a process that takes on flesh and blood in partial liberations that ever remain open and ready for completion. On the one hand it proclaims some full and complete hope in a utopian future; on the other hand it is made viable and feasible in the present. To preach some complete and utopian end for people without anticipating it in history would be to nurture wild fantasies and innocuous dreams completely devoid of credibility; to introduce partial liberations without any view of the future or a finished totality would be to frustate the hopes that had been aroused and to fall into an incoherent immediatism.

In his own activity Jesus maintains the difficult tension of this basic dialectic. On the one hand he tells people that the kingdom is already in their midst, serving as a leaven in the old order. Yet at the same time it remains in the future, an object of hope and of joint effort by God and human beings.

JESUS' PRAXIS AS NOVEL AND LIBERATIVE

Now let us consider some of the concrete steps involved in Jesus' anticipation of the new world. Let us see what was involved in his process of liberation and redemption.[5]

Relativization of Human Self-Sufficiency

In the world faced by Jesus there were many kinds of absolutization going on, and they all tended to place human beings in bondage. Religion, tradition, and the Mosaic Law were absolutized, for example. Religion was no longer the way in which people expressed their openness to God; it had become a substantive world in itself, composed of rituals and sacrifices. Jesus refers to the prophetic tradition (Mark 7:6–8) and says that love, justice, and mercy are more important than ritual worship. The criteria of salvation operate in terms of love of neighbor rather than in terms of ritual worship. Human beings are more important than tradition and the Sabbath (Mark 2:23–26), more important and valuable than anything else (Matt. 6:26). People come before ritual service (Luke 10:30–37), sacrifice (Matt. 5:23–24; Mark 12:33), and observance of the Mosaic Law and tradition (Matt. 23:23).

Whenever Jesus talks about love of God, he talks about love of neighbor at the same time (Mark 12:31–33; Matt. 22:36–39). Salvation is decided in terms of love for one's neighbor, not in terms of love for God taken in himself (Matt. 25:31–46). When people ask Jesus what they must do to obtain salvation, he answers by alluding to the commandments on the second tablet of the law; and all of them have to do with other people (Mark 10:17–22). It is made clear that we cannot talk about God in abstract terms, prescinding from his children and love for human beings. There is a real unity between love for one's neighbor and love for God, and it is brought out superbly in the Johannine writings: "If anyone says, 'My love is fixed on God,' yet hates his brother, he is a liar. One who has no love for the brother he has seen cannot love the God he has not seen" (1 John 4:19–20).

Thus Jesus de-absolutizes the legal, cultic, and religious forms that held a monopoly on the road to salvation. Salvation really must entail love of neighbor. That is decisive. Religion is not meant to replace our neighbor but to keep us pointed in the direction of real love for other human beings where God lies hidden and incognito (Mark 6:20–21; Matt. 25:40). The work of relativization effected by Jesus extended as far as the allegedly divine power and authority of the Roman emperors. He denied their divine character (Matt. 22:21) and their alleged claim to be the last court of power and appeal: "You would have no power over me whatever unless it were given you from above" (John 19:11).

Creation of a New Kind of Solidarity

Redemption is not fleshed out simply in the relativization of laws and cultic forms but also in a new kind of solidarity between human beings. The social world of Jesus' day was highly structured. All sorts of social discrimination existed, and careful distinctions were made between the pure and the impure, Jews and non-Jews, neighbors and non-neighbors, men and women, learned observers of the law and simple people who were terrified by the fact that they could not live up to the legal interpretations of the learned. The Pharisees, for example, carefully kept their distance from the weak and suffering people who were castigated as sinners and kept on the margins of society.

Jesus, on the other hand, established fellowship with all these oppressed groups. He always took the side of the weak who were criticized and judged wrong in terms of the prevailing norms: e.g., the prostitute, the Samaritan heretic, the publican, the Roman centurion, the paralytic, the man blind from birth, the pagan Syro-Phoenician woman, and even his own apostles when they were criticized for not fasting as the disciples of John the Baptist did. His approach was to accept all of these people and let them experience first-hand that they are not outside the pale of salvation. God loves all, even the wicked and ungrateful (Luke 6:35). It is those who are sick that stand in need of a physician (Mark 2:17), and he has come "to search out and save what was lost" (Luke 19:10).

Jesus is not afraid to accept the consequences of this solidarity. He is insulted and defamed. He is called the boon companion of wicked people. He is accused of being a subversive, a heretic, a madman, and a tool of the devil. But it is through this sort of love and these mediating conditions that he senses the meaning of God's kingdom and liberation from the oppressive frameworks that create discrimination between human beings. One's neighbors are not just those who hold the same faith or belong to the same family or race; one's neighbors are all human beings insofar as I draw closer to them, whatever their ideology or religious persuasion may be (see Luke 10:30–37).

Respect for the Liberty of the Other Person

When we read the Gospels and note the way in which Jesus spoke, we immediately notice that his talk never lies on some transcendent, authoritarian plane. His vocabulary is simple. His conversation is filled with parables and examples taken from everyday life and events. He plunges into the crowd. He knows how to listen and ask people questions. He gives all people a chance to speak their own essential word. He asks one questioner what the law says. He asks his own disciples what people are saying about him. He asks one man by the roadside what he would have him do. He lets the Samaritan woman speak her piece, and he pays heed to the questions of the Pharisees. He does not present any systematic teaching, as if he were a school teacher. Instead he asks questions and answers them, letting all people define themselves and freely take a stand on those matters that are critical for their destiny. When he is asked about taxation or the political power of the Roman emperor, he does not go into any theoretical exposition. Instead he takes a coin and asks whose inscription is on it. The other person is always allowed to have his or her say. Only the rich young man failed to say his piece. Perhaps that is why we do not know his name: because he failed to define himself.

Jesus does not let other people serve him. He himself is willing to serve at table (Luke 22:27). But this is no mystification posing as humility, the sort of thing that many popes and bishops mastered so well in the course of church history. They called themselves the servants of God's servants when in fact they were using a highly refined technique to wield oppressive, anti-evangelical power over people's consciences. But when Jesus insists that power is meant to be service and that the last are to be first (Mark 10:42–44; 9:35; Matt. 23:8–12), he is trying to break the master-slave relationship and the power structure built on blind submission and privilege.

What Jesus wants is not *hierarchia* ("sacred power") but *hierodulia* ("sacred service"). He is not in favor of some autocratic and self-sufficient exercise of power and authority. What he favors insistently is service for the benefit of all, service in the interests of the community. Any center of jurisdiction, even an ecclesiastical one, that affirms its own position independently of the community of the faithful is one that cannot claim the authority of Jesus for itself.[6]

Jesus himself clearly operates with the attitude we have just been describing. His line of argument is never fanatical, demanding abject submission to what he says. He tries to persuade and convince, to appeal to common sense and sound reasoning. His affirmations are not authoritative but persuasive. He always leaves the other party free. His disciples are not trained to teach his doctrine fanatically but to respect even their enemies and persecutors. He never uses violence to ensure victory for his ideals. His appeal and his discourse is directed to people's consciences.

Within the circle of his closest disciples we find a collaborator with the occupation forces (a tax collector; Mark 2:15–17) on the one hand and a nationalist Zealot guerrilla on the other (Mark 3:18–19). They live in a state of coexistence and form part of Jesus' community despite the tensions that are apparent between the more skeptical and the more sanguine elements.

An Inexhaustible Capacity to Tolerate Differences

I have been trying to show how Jesus concretely brought liberation within a particular historical context and through a particular approach. He addressed himself to everyone without discriminating against anyone. His fundamental attitude, summed up by John, was that he would not send away anyone who came to him. His preaching of the gospel is directed first and foremost to the poor, but that term is not restricted to those suffering from economic need. As J. Jeremias puts it: "The 'poor' are those who are oppressed in quite a general sense: the oppressed who cannot defend themselves, the desperate, the hopeless."[7] This would include all those who are suffering from hunger and thirst, who are ill or imprisoned or homeless or weighed down by the burden they must bear—the sinners, the lost, simple souls.

Jesus tries to help all of them and to defend their rights. He pays particular attention to the sick, the possessed, and those who have leprosy. These people were viewed as public sinners and maligned by society. Coming to their defense, Jesus makes it clear that sickness need not be the result of any personal sin on the part of the afflicted or their kin and that it does not make the afflicted impure. At the same time he is willing to circulate among his opponents, who are rigidly fixed in their conservative legalism and sometimes greatly concerned with occupying the places of honor at a gathering (Mark 2:13–3:6). He is willing to share a meal with them (Luke 7:36ff.; 11:37ff.), but he will not share their outlook. Even as he sits at table with them he will say: "But woe to you rich, for your consolation is now" (Luke 6:24). Jesus is also willing to eat with the despised publicans and his presence among them can produce great changes in their conduct, as the story of Zaccheus indicates.

Everything in our heart and in society that can adversely affect the rights of another person is condemned by Jesus: e.g., hatred and anger (Matt. 5:21–22), envy (Matt. 5:27–28), calumny, aggression, and murder. He champions kindness and meekness, criticizing all lack of respect for the dignity of other people (Matt. 7:1–5; Luke 6:37–41). Jesus does not move at a haughty distance from the field of human conflict. He is always ready to step in when it is a matter of defending another's rights, even though the other person may be considered a heretic or pagan or alien. He communicates with anyone and everyone, calling for an end to the use of violence as a means of obtaining some objective. The way power works basically is to look for more and more power and to subjugate others to its own ideals. Thus it gives rise to feelings of fear and revenge and to a desire for complete domination, thereby destroying communication and communion between human beings. Order is fashioned in the human realm, but at great cost to society. Anything that might spark uncertainty, questioning, or social change is kept under rigorous surveillance, whether it be in civil society or in religious society. When the threat to the established order becomes truly real, then the primitive mechanisms of hate, defamation, repression, and elimination are set in motion. The enemies of order and security must be wiped out. Self-justifying reactions of that sort certainly cannot appeal to Jesus' attitudes for support because the latter favored careful reflection, frank communication between groups, and change.

His call for the renunciation of power is matched by a plea for pardon and mercy, but it implies a clear-cut perception of worldly reality. There will always be structures based on power and vengeance, but that should not lead us to grow discouraged or to accept them resignedly. It should prompt us to realize the need for pardon and mercy and to develop our capacity for enduring and living with the excesses of power. Jesus, therefore, commands us to love our enemies. We must be clear about this. Loving our enemies does not mean loving them in some romantic fashion, as if they were a different sort of friend. Loving them as enemies means realizing that they are our enemies and loving them as Jesus loved his enemies. Instead of avoiding communication with his enemies, Jesus raised questions about the attitudes that were enslaving them and making them his enemies. To renounce the pattern of hatred is not to give up one's opposition to something. Jesus was quite ready for argument, debate, and opposition, but he would not operate within the framework favoring the use of violence. Instead he would try to commit himself fully to interpersonal contact and communication. To have given up his opposition, however, would have been to add fuel to the fires of domination.

Acceptance of Mortality

In the life of Jesus we find life itself with all its contradictions. He is not a complainer who frets about the evil in the world. He does not bemoan the fact that God could have made a better world, that there is too much sin and wickedness in it and God seems to do nothing. Jesus takes life as it comes. He does not refuse the sacrifice entailed in any truly committed life. He is willing to be isolated, defamed, persecuted, and misunderstood. He accepts all life's limitations and he bears witness to all the feelings and conditions with which we are familiar: anger, joy, kindness, sadness, poverty, hunger, thirst, compassion, and melancholy. He lives a life of self-giving rather that one of self-preservation: "The Son of Man has not come to be served but to serve" (Mark 10:45). He does not seem to display any vacillation in his basic resolve to be a man-for-others.

Now to live a life of self-giving is to live life as a sacrifice and wear oneself out for others. And what about death? Let us assume that death is not just the last moment of life, that it is the very structure of mortal life because our life starts slipping away from us from the moment we are conceived. Let us also assume that this gradual slipping away is not so much a biological inevitability as an opportunity for us to freely accept our finiteness and mortality and to open up to something greater than death. Let us assume that dying means making room for something greater, emptying oneself to be able to receive a fullness that comes from the One who is greater than life. If we assume all that, then we can say that from the very start Christ's life was equivalent to embracing death with all the courage of which a human being is capable. He was completely empty of self in order to be full of others and God. He took on our mortal life and the death that was gradually being prepared within his committed life as a roving prophet and the

Messiah who had come to liberate people. It is in this basic context that we shall now reflect upon the death of Christ and its redemptive meaning.

The immanent aspect of Christ's death. We are used to interpreting the death of Jesus along the lines provided by the passion accounts. In them it is clear that his death was for our sins, that it corresponded with certain prophecies in the Old Testament, that it accomplished one phase of the divine mission entrusted to Jesus and was therefore a necessary part of God's salvific plan.[8] These interpretations do reveal the transcendent truth of Jesus' total surrender to God, but they may also give rise to a false understanding of the truly historical character of his fatal destiny.

The fact is that those interpretations in the gospel accounts are the final product of a long process of reflection on the scandal of Good Friday by the primitive Christian community. In the context of that age, the shameful death of Jesus on the cross (see Gal. 3:13) was a clear sign of abandonment by God and of the falsity of a prophet's message (see Matt. 27:39–44; Mark 15:29–32; Luke 23:35–37). Thus it represented a real problem for the primitive community. Viewing it in the light of the resurrection and further reflection on the Old Testament (see Luke 24:13–35), however, the early Christians began to make some sense out of what had seemed absurd. Through this interpretative and theological effort they began to detect a hidden meaning in the disgraceful events of the passion; and their conclusions were brought together in the gospel accounts of Jesus' passion, death, and resurrection. The Evangelists were not neutral or disinterested historians. They wrote their accounts as theologians interested in bringing out the transcendent, universal, definitive meaning of Christ's death.

Valid as that kind of interpretation may be, it may hold traps for the unwary reader and give a false image of the passion. It may suggest that the passion was a suprahistorical drama in which all the players were mere marionettes carrying out some pre-established plan; thus they are stripped of any personal responsibility. The dramatic and burdensome nature of Jesus' death disappears from view, for he too is simply carrying out some necessary plan. What is more, the necessary nature of the plan is not made clear. Christ's death is detached from the rest of his life and begins to possess a salvific meaning of its own.

In such a case the historical dimension of Jesus' death is lost for the most part. We no longer see it as the consequence of his own attitudes and the outcome of a judicial process. We do well to remember the following remarks by a noted theologian:

In fact, Jesus' passion cannot be separated from his earthly life and his message. It is his life, as well as his resurrection, that gives meaning to his death. Jesus did not die just any death. He was condemned to death, not because of some misunderstanding but because of his concrete attitude in history and day-to-day life. Any interpretation that jumps immediately from the particular details of his life and death to some "metaphysical" conflict between love and hate, or belief and nonbelief in the Son of God, evades the many mediating factors that are required for a proper understanding of it. This evasion of history has religious consequences. To give one example, I would say that meditation on the passion has not always avoided a rather suspect sadness. Instead of promoting people to put evil and death behind them, it has often produced an unhealthy fixation on mere resignation. Thus suffering and death came to be glorified in themselves.[9]

The perduring and valid meaning discovered by the Evangelists must be salvaged through the historical (rather than the theological) context of Christ's death. Only then will his death cease to be ahistorical, and hence hollow. Only then will it take on dimensions that are truly valid for our faith today as well.

Christ's death was, first and foremost, a human death. In other words, it was framed in the context of a human life and an ongoing conflict. Death was the result, but it was not imposed from without by any divine decree; it was imposed by certain specific human beings. So we can follow the course of this death historically and observe its features.

Jesus died for the same reasons that prophets in every age die. He placed the values he preached about above the preservation of his own life. He freely chose to die rather than to deny or renounce truth, justice, the ideal of universal brotherhood, and the truth about divine sonship and God's unlimited goodness. On this level Christ takes his place among the host of witnesses who have preached a message and died for it; who have called for the betterment of the world, the creation of more fraternal social ties, and a greater openness to the Absolute.[10] His death registered his challenge to firmly rooted but closed systems, his accusation against a world closed in upon itself, his dissent to its sinfulness.

His death was being prepared throughout the course of his life. Our earlier remarks have indicated how he represented a radical crisis for the Judaism of his own day. He presents himself as a prophet who proclaims a new doctrine rather than tradition

(Mark 1:27). He does not simply call for observance of the law and its traditional interpretations; instead he conducts himself as one who possesses sovereign freedom in that regard. If the law helps to foster love and people's contact with each other and God, Jesus accepts it; if it is an obstacle to all that, then he disregards that law or simply abrogates it altogether. In the eyes of the prophet from Nazareth, the will of God is not to be found solely in the classic texts of Scripture. Life itself is the place where God's salvific will for human beings is made manifest.

Liberation for people's oppressed consciousness can be sensed in all Jesus' attitudes and words. The people perceive it and are deeply stirred. The authorities grow panicky. Jesus represents a real threat to the established system and its certainties. He might well arouse the masses to take action against the Roman forces of occupation. The authority with which he speaks, the sovereign freedom with which he acts, and the superior attitudes he displays before them provoke a crisis of conscience for the guardians of the official dogma. The man from Galilee is too far removed from official orthodoxy. He does not appeal to any recognized approach to justify his teaching, his behavior, or the demands he puts forth.

We should not assume or imagine that the Jews of that day, the Pharisees, or the guardians of the religious and social order were people of sheer ill will; that they were simply vindictive, malevolent, and ill-intentioned persecutors. In reality they were faithful observers of the law and religion that had been piously handed down by generations of people who had had their martyrs and confessors. Their questioning of Jesus and their attempts to frame him in terms of established moral and dogmatic canons resulted from the crisis of conscience that his person and activity created for them. They tried to fit him back into the framework established by the law. When they could not do that, they isolated him, disparaged him, put him on trial, and eventually condemned him to crucifixion.

Christ's death resulted from a conflict that was clearly circumstantiated and defined in legal terms. It was not the result of any "sadistic machinations,"[11] or any juridical misunderstanding. To them Jesus really seemed to be a false prophet and a disturber of the religious status quo who might end up disturbing the political status quo as well. It was a combination of attitudes and peccadillos, none of them criminal in themselves perhaps, which eventually dictated the liquidation of Jesus: enclosure within one's own system of values, placed beyond challenge or questioning; an inability to open up and learn anything new; a narrowing of one's horizons and a fanatical attachment to one's own way of arranging life and religion; and feelings of self-assurance based on one's own conception of tradition and orthodoxy. Such attitudes continue to characterize defenders of the established order today. While such people may have a solid supply of good will, they are devoid of any critical sense and any sense of history.

The transcendent aspect of Christ's death. If the motives which brought Jesus to his trial and execution were banal enough, his death was not banal. In it the whole greatness of Jesus shines out. He turned oppression itself into a pathway of liberation. From a certain point in his life on (the crisis in Galilee), Jesus was sure that he would meet a violent end; at the very least he was sure that a drama was unfolding against his own life. The death of John the Baptist did not catch him unaware (Mark 6:14–29). He knew the fate reserved for prophets (Matt. 23:37; Luke 13:33–34; Acts 2:23), and he saw himself in that category. Hence he did not go naively to his death.

That does not mean, however, that he sought it or wanted it. The Evangelists reveal him going into hiding (John 11:57; 12:36; 18:2; Luke 21:37) and avoiding the Pharisees who importuned him a great deal (Mark 7:24; 8:13; Matt. 12:15; 14:13). He was more ready than any other just person to sacrifice his life in bearing witness to the truth if that should prove necessary (John 18:37). He sought out conversations with the Jews. Even when he felt alone and isolated, he did not give way to resignation or try to make compromises for the sake of his own survival. He remained faithful to his truth to the very end, even though that fidelity meant death.

Jesus chose and embraced death freely. He did not accept it as a biological fate; instead he freely sacrificed his own life in order to bear witness to his message. "No one takes it from me. I lay it down freely" (John 10:18). His death is witness, not punishment; free choice, not fate. He is not afraid of death, and his actions are not prompted by such fear. He lives and acts in spite of death, even though death may be demanded of him. The motivating force and inspiration of his life is not fear of death but commitment to his Father's will. So he accepts life and commits himself to his message of liberation for all his brothers and sisters.

The prophet and the just person, like Jesus, die for justice and truth. They denounce the evil in this world and place checks on the closed systems that claim to have a monopoly on truth and goodness. This monopolistic self-closure is the sin of the world, and Christ died because of this banal, structured sinfulness. His reaction did not fit into the framework of his enemies. He, a victim of oppression and violence, did not use violence and oppression to impose his own view: "Hatred can kill, but it cannot define the meaning that the dying person gives to his own life."[12] Christ defined the sense of his death in terms of love, self-giving, and freely proffered sacrifice for his killers and all human beings.

The prophet of Nazareth who died on the cross was the Son of God as well. This reality became clear to the eye of faith only after his resurrection. But though he was the Son of God, he did not make use of divine power, which is capable of altering every situation. Jesus did not offer the witness of power as domination, since this represents the diabolic aspect of power and produces both oppression and obstacles to communion. Jesus bore witness to the real power of God: love. It is love that liberates human beings, establishes fellowship between them, and opens them up to the authentic process of liberation. Such love rules out all violence and oppression, even for the sake of having love itself prevail. Its efficacy is not the efficacy of violence that alters situations and eliminates human beings. The apparent efficacy of violence does not in fact manage to break the spiralling process of violence.

Love has its own peculiar efficacy, which is not readily noticeable or discernable. It is the courage which prompts one to lay down one's life out of love. It is the certainty that the future lies with justice, love, and brotherhood rather than with injustice, vengeance, and oppression. It is not at all surprising that the murderers of prophets and just people become all the more violent to the extent that they can glimpse their own defeat,[13] and the testimony of history bears eloquent witness to the fact. The iniquity of injustice destroys the bonds between evil people and isolates murderers from one another. God does not do what human beings, in their freedom, do not choose to have. The kingdom of God is a process in which people are meant to participate. If they should refuse to do that, loving sacrifice rather than violence will be used to encourage them to change their minds: "And I—once I am lifted up from earth—will draw all men to myself" (John 12:32).

Quite independently of any light shed by the resurrection, the death of Christ has a meaning that is wholly consistent with the life he led. All those like Jesus who set forth demands for greater justice, love, and rights for the oppressed, and more liberty for God, must count on opposition and the threat of elimination. Death is conquered to the extent that it is no longer a scarecrow frightening us and preventing us from living and proclaiming the truth.

Death is accepted and incorporated into the project of the just person and the true prophet. They can and must count on it. The greatness of Jesus lies in the fact that he did not take the easy way out when he was faced with opposition and condemnation. Even when he felt abandoned on the cross by the very God whom he had always served, he did not give way to resignation. He pardoned his enemies, and continued to believe and hope. Amid a sudden paroxysm of defeat and failure he entrusted himself to the hands of the mysterious Father, in whom lies the ultimate meaning of the death of this innocent one with all its absurdity. In the very depths of despair and abandonment his trust in the Father and his surrender to him reached its acme. No longer did he look to himself or his own work for support. His sole support now was God, and only in God could he find repose. Such hope already transcends the limits of death itself. His work of liberation is already complete, because he has liberated himself totally from himself to be wholly God's.

THE FOUNDATION OF CHRIST'S LIBERATION: EXPERIENCE OF GOD AS A LOVING FATHER

My description above may seem to be a bit too anthropological to some. It seems to suggest that the man from Galilee brought liberation with his life and death as many others have done before and after him. On this level of reflection Christ does take his place in the ranks of all those just people and prophets who have been treated unjustly and put to death. As we shall see in the next section, it is the resurrection that elevates Jesus above and beyond all analogies and enables us to discover new dimensions in his seemingly banal death as a prophet and martyr.

But a question is in order here: What motivating force and inspiration fed his liberative life? The gospels are clear on the matter: His liberative project grew out of a profound personal experience of God as the absolute sense of all history (the kingdom of God) and as the Father of infinite goodness and love for all human beings, particularly for those who are wicked or ungrateful or lost. Jesus did not experience God as the God of the Mosaic law, a God making clear distinctions between the good and the wicked, the just and the unjust. His experience is with a good God who loves and pardons people, who goes after the lost sheep and waits anxiously for the return of the prodigal son, who rejoices more over the conversion of one sinner than over the salvation of ninety-nine just people.

The original praxis of Jesus described above is ultimately rooted in this original personal experience of God.[14] One who knows he is completely loved by God loves all without distinction, even his enemies. Knowing he is accepted and pardoned by God, he accepts and pardons others as well. Jesus incarnated the love and pardon of his Father, showing goodness and mercy to all; and he was particularly kind to those who were regarded as social or religious outcasts.

This was not humanitarianism on Jesus' part. It was his way of making the Father's love concrete in his own life. If God himself is that way toward all, why shouldn't the Son of God act likewise?

THE ACHIEVEMENT OF COMPLETE LIBERATION

The above reflections sought to point out the liberation process undertaken by Jesus in all the dimensions of his life. Insofar as it is a process, this liberation is partial in character. It is an open-ended process: Where will it end up? Of what is it an anticipation? If Christ had been restricted to this process, he would not have been proclaimed the universal liberator because his liberation would not be total. Authentic liberation, to be truly worthy of the name, should be total and universal in character.

This fullness of liberation comes with the resurrection. Thanks to the resurrection, the utopian truth of the kingdom becomes topical here and now. Thanks to the resurrection, we are given the certain assurance that the process of liberation will not remain fixed in the vicious circle of oppression versus liberation, that it will ultimately end up in complete and total liberation.

The resurrection is not a phenomenon having to do with cellular physiology and human biology. Christ was not brought back to life to lead the type of life he had before his death. The resurrection signifies the full enthronement of human reality (body and soul) in the divine realm; hence it signifies complete hominization and liberation. Thanks to it, history reached its end and goal in the person of Jesus, and it can now be viewed as complete human liberation. Death is overcome, and a new kind of human life begins. Human life is no longer ruled by the mechanisms of death and exhaustion; instead it is invigorated with the divine life itself.

In this sense, then, the resurrection is significant as a protest against the "justice" and "legal right" which condemned Jesus to death. It is a protest against a merely immanent meaning of this present world which, through its order and its laws, ended up rejecting the person whom God later confirmed through the resurrection. Thus the resurrection is the matrix for a liberative hope that goes far beyond the present world which is haunted by the specter of death. James Cone, the noted spokesman for black theology of liberation sums it up well:

His [Jesus'] resurrection is the disclosure that God is not defeated by oppression but transforms it into the possibility of freedom. For men and women who live in an oppressive society this means that they do not have to behave as if *death* is the ultimate. God in Christ has set us free from death, and we can now live without worrying about social ostracism, economic insecurity or political death. "In Christ the immortal God has tasted death and in so doing . . . destroyed death."[15]

The one who was resurrected was the crucified one. The one who brings liberation is the oppressed Suffering Servant. To live liberation from death means not to let death have the ultimate say about our life and determine what our outlook and activity shall be. The resurrection proved that living for justice and truth is not senseless, that the life manifested in Jesus Christ is reserved for the oppressed and the downtrodden. So now we can take courage and live the freedom of God's children without submitting to the inhibiting forces of death.

Taking the resurrection as their starting point, the Evangelists could re-examine the death of their prophet and martyr, Jesus of Nazareth. It was no longer a death like any other, however heroic these might have been. It was the death of God's Son and the Father's envoy. It was no longer simply a conflict between the freedom of Jesus and legalistic observance of the law: now it was also a conflict between the decadent kingdom of human beings and the kingdom of God. The cross was no longer the most shameful punishment of the day but a symbol of what people could do when they were carried away by their piety, their fanatic zeal for God, their self-enclosed dogmatism, and their conception of revelation as petrified in a written text. We must never forget that it was the pious people who condemned Jesus.

To Jesus, who always lived for God, the cross was repugnant and absurd (see Heb. 5:7). But he shouldered it nevertheless, transforming it into a symbol of liberation from the very thing that had provoked it in his case: enclosure in one's own self-sufficiency, pettiness, and the desire for revenge. The resurrection is not just an event which glorifies and justifies Jesus Christ and the truth of his attitudes; it is also a manifestation of what the kingdom of God really is in all its fulness, an epiphany of the future promised by God.

In the light of the resurrection, all of these dimensions were discovered in Christ's life and death and woven into the gospel accounts. On the one hand they recount facts and events. On the other hand they inject a deeper meaning into them which goes beyond mere factual history but is supported by that history. If we do not clearly distinguish those two levels, then the deeper sense of Christ's life and death will seem somewhat abstract and unsupported by reality.

In the light of the resurrection, the early Christians discovered that the oppressed Jesus was the liberator. This discovery prompted a highly significant interpretation of his infancy and his activity. As the Synoptic Gospels clearly indicate, the birth of Jesus embodies and expresses the identification of the oppressed liberator with the oppressed peoples of the earth: the shepherds, the innocent babies who are murdered, and the pagan kings. From the very start Jesus is seen to be an oppressed human being, without a place in which to be born (Luke 2:7). The social and economic poverty of his country is highlighted precisely through his own identification with the poor and oppressed. Meditating on the gospel accounts, the primitive Christian community would conclude that Jesus' messiahship was linked up with humiliation. The poor and humiliated of the earth could feel consolation in the fact that the Messiah was one of them. It is through such humiliation, not in spite of it, that he is the Messiah and liberator. The same point of view is developed in the gospel accounts of Jesus' public ministry and his intercourse with the marginal people of his day. Alongside the historical interest goes their theological concern to show that Jesus identified himself with the oppressed, shouldered their burden, and liberated them for a new kind of solidarity and fellowship.

In this way the whole life of Jesus from birth to death took on liberative meaning. That meaning was already present in the factual course of concrete events, but it is totally revealed only after the explosion of the resurrection. It is the resurrection that forced them to undertake a deeper reading of the same facts, to find in them a meaning that was more profound, transcendent, universal, and exemplary.

REDEMPTION ANTICIPATED AND REALIZED IN THE PROCESS OF LIBERATION

What significance does the liberation attained by Jesus have in terms of our own history and concrete conditions today? We can speak meaningfully of redemption and liberation only in terms of the opposite pole: perdition and oppression. How do the latter present themselves to us today? How can Christ's redemption and liberation be articulated in such a way that it will be faith's real and effective response to the situation in which we find ourselves?

Our Situation of Captivity

We live in a cultural epoch in which people have come to find and define the meaning of their existence in terms of a scientific and technological domination of nature that will enable them to obtain the greatest possible number of consumer goods and to live freely in the face of nature's demands. This basic technological emphasis implies more than just the utilization of a set of technical instruments, for it entails a particular view held by human beings about themselves. People see themselves as the masters of nature, who can turn nature itself into an objective object. Alongside this technological interest there exists a humanistic component. People envision and seek broader communication and understanding between human beings through the creation of more humane social structures and more universal and tolerant norms and ideals than those based on one's caste.

At the same time, however, it is painfully evident that there are profound distortions in both of these two components of our culture. On the economic front, we find enormous wealth in one small segment of the world and dire poverty in the rest of the world. On the social front, some human beings are dominating others with instruments that grow more refined and sophisticated each day; the channels of communication are thus perverted or completely destroyed as such.[16] The decision to gain control over nature has broadened into a desire to dominate human beings and nations, so that we end up with a general and pervasive regimen of captivity.

The situation of Latin America specifically is one of underdevelopment when compared with that of the affluent northern hemisphere. This backwardness is not a technological problem nor a fated historical circumstance. It is the byproduct of a socioeconomic system that favors a small minority with wealth while keeping the vast majority of humankind in a state of dependence on the margins of societal life. The majority are thus prevented from moving toward freedom, progress, and self-support. Following a purely developmental approach, we will never bridge the gap that separates the current centers of power from those on the periphery. We must look in another direction for the solution to

this problem. We must break the ties of dependency and create
new values that will allow us to structure a new form of social life
for human beings. We must stop the exploitation of some people by
others and get all people to bear their fair share of the social
burden.[17]

Operating out of this horizon of dependence that typifies the
Third World, liberation theology has articulated concerns that
have to do with liberation of this sort. Poverty and alienation on a
continental scale are not innocent or neutral phenomena. They
are morally unjust and cry to heaven for vengeance. Thus we are
faced with two basic tasks. First we must undertake a social and
analytic reading of the existing situation. Only in that way can we
make clear the structural and systematic nature of the present
state of cultural, political, and economic dependence. Second, we
must elaborate a theological interpretation of the same situation,
making clear that it does not correspond with God's designs as
seen by the eye of faith. The present situation indicates that clear
presence of sin and social injustice; it embodies a state of perdition
that cries out for salvation.

Our clearest experience of perdition today lies in our experience
of social sin and structural distortion. We can see it in the perverted forms of people's relationship to nature and other people as
well as in the various forms of discrimination that prevail between
rich and poor nations. Christ's redemption and salvation will assume a contemporary cast insofar as they are related to our liberation from the present situation or our attempt to live a meaningful life in spite of the surrounding situation. This experience will
provide us with a standpoint from which we can interpret the
liberating message of Jesus Christ. It will provide us with a point
of view from which we can pinpoint the practical steps whereby
Jesus fleshed out his liberation in the world which he lived
through denunciation and proclamation.

Socio-Political Liberation as the Presence
of Redemption in History

Clearly enough the first task facing us is to denounce and
thereby unmask the vaunted progress of modern times. This
progress, as well as the technology that permitted it, is basically
indecent because it requires too high a human cost. Besides
operating in an ecologically irresponsible way, it generates a type
of living that is anemic, egotistical, and violent. Today some peo-

ple have managed to free themselves from the ideological snares that support the status quo. Thanks to their critical awareness, we are now seeing the demise of the utopian dream of unending forward progress and development.[18] Though that illusion still pervades the models proposed by existing regimes, human intelligence is now tearing away the mask it wears. It is already being challenged in our universities, our art, our cultural life, and among our young people.

The next task is to proclaim and anticipate a whole new meaning for human society and a whole new way of using the rich set of instruments provided by science and technology. Instead of being used to generate some people's domination over others, they must be used to resolve the age-old social problems of hunger, illness, poverty, and discrimination. For any theology of liberation, the praxis of Jesus Christ himself is exemplary in this regard.

Like Jesus Christ, who proclaimed a universal and ultimate meaning (the kingdom of God), liberation theology believes in a global meaning that transcends all partial meanings and in a definitive liberation that goes beyond all partial concrete steps towards liberation. The world is not so dominated by structural and diabolic forces that it cannot be liberated. There is room to hope for a happy outcome to the human drama. This hope, framed in universal terms and pointed toward the future, is an inexhaustible source of confidence. It generates optimism in all those who seek to embody the ultimate meaning of time in concrete historical commitments.

Faith must remain permanently open to this qualitative betterment in history, to something that goes beyond our own capabilities. Only thus can faith avoid degenerating into intraworldly ideologies and losing its transcendent aspect; only thus can it remain focused on God. The kingdom of God is not merely the prolongation of this present world. The world must be altered globally and structurally if it is to become the truly human and divine human homeland.

For us this ultimate meaning (the kingdom of God) is not merely in the future, just as it was not for Jesus Christ. It is already anticipated in the present through a new sort of praxis that helps to produce the "new person." Persuasion is not enough to guarantee a new world. Persuasion is important, to be sure, because there will be no transformation if human beings do not choose it and will it; so we must keep trying to persuade people, to release people's initiative from the forces that may be blocking them. But we must also have a new praxis and a concrete effort at concrete liberation. The forms may be many and varied: i.e., creating new kinds of solidarity, performing original gestures, altering our way of dealing with persons and things, and effecting structural changes where possible. But all such concrete steps represent ways of mediating redemption here and now and thereby anticipating complete, definitive redemption.

As *Gaudium et Spes* tells us (nos. 38–39), it is here that we prepare the material for the kingdom of heaven and shape the outlines of the life to come. Eschatology does not begin with the end of the world. It is already given here in the present. It is mediated through historical happenings, and it moves through the ambiguities of our *tempus medium* (our in-between time) toward its fulfillment in God. Theologically speaking, then, we must interpret all concrete commitment in that light. Any concrete commitment to the transformation of this continent, be it by individuals, the church, or ideological groups, must be viewed as mediating and carrying forward the eschatological liberation and redemption of Jesus Christ himself. Jesus knew how to translate God's definitive liberation into the concrete terms of his own life and milieu. As we saw above, he proclaimed and embodied liberation from legalism and the spirit of vengeance as well as creative effort to establish a new kind of solidarity and human relationships.

Today the *main* scene of liberation is the socio-political realm, because it is there that we most keenly feel the stings of alienation and sin, of oppression and the lack of freedom. It is certainly true that the liberation of Christ and God is something more than just socio-political liberation. But it is *also* socio-political liberation. Any authentic theology, therefore, will be marked by two aspects. On the one hand it will be very concrete because it will see just economic and political measures as the contemporary mediations of Jesus Christ's salvation for our own day. On the other hand it will ever remain open for something more because liberation embraces more than the political and economic dimensions. Liberation goes further. It is all-inclusive and universal. Its main components are liberation from everything that vitiates human effort (i.e., sin) and the conquest of death.

In the meantime we must keep our eyes open, watching out for lines of talk that represent an obstacle to every authentically liberative force. This kind of talk may stress points that are true, and that we would not want to deny at all; but those points do not get down to the heart of our own situation. One might say, for example, that prayer and recollection are necessary; that the spiritual life must be cultivated. We would readily grant that. Without prayer, meditation, and the cross of Christ no liberation could really call itself Christian. But neither is liberation Christian if it stresses only those dimensions, if it relegates other aspects of life and liberation to the private sphere as if faith had nothing to do with them.

Someone might say that liberation also entails accepting the violence of repression and knowing how to live in spite of one's state of dependence. While that may be true, such talk can still be alienating. If we live in a historical context where faith is called upon to denounce the violence of the prevailing regime, then we may eviscerate the dissenting force of the Christian message by stressing the need for resignation. In the end we will be cooperating with the status quo, which likes nothing better than not to be questioned or attacked. There may well be situations in which there is nothing left for Christians to do but to accept repression and shoulder their crosses as Christ did. But they will not deliberately seek out that alternative. They will accept it only when it seems forced on them by the situation they are in.

The poverty of millions in Latin America certainly prompts us to view liberation as an effort to overcome the causes underlying this poverty. Lack of food is not the underlying cause. The real cause lies in a system of power and ownership that prevents millions of people from gaining access to decent work and participating in the life of their society. Our theological reflection and our praxis of the faith should stress this dimension.

Captivity as Incarnating the Cross of Christ

In the meantime we must be realistic. The overall system in force today is strong enough to balance out its inner contradictions. In all likelihood our generation will not witness the liberation of our continent from hunger and alienation nor the emergence of a more humane, open, and fraternal society. We must work liberatively within a pervasive system of captivity. Such a situation, akin to that of the Israelites in Egypt and Babylon, calls for different tasks and a different strategy than might be proper in eras of liberty and peace.

The period of gestation entails different concerns than the period of birth and growth. If conception does not occur or gestation does not proceed under a watchful and attentive eye, there may be no child or it may be premature, or stillborn, or may even abort. We today live in a situation of captivity. To believe and hope and work for liberation in such a situation, when we are fairly sure that we will not live to see the fruits of our work, is to incarnate in our own day the cross of Christ. We must establish a solid mystique of hope that goes beyond what is immediately verifiable. The suffering implied in hope can generate awesome and unexpected forces for liberation. Faith identifies the Liberator with the Suffering Servant and the Man of Sorrows. This identification gives us reason to hope and expect that the future does not lie with the criminally affluent and the heartless but with the unjustly oppressed and crucified.

Jesus himself lived a similar situation of personal captivity. At an important turning point in his life he found himself alone, abandoned, and powerless in the face of the powers that be. He had to accept the prospect of death and to live in exile from God and other human beings. But he managed to hope against hope, without giving way to cynicism or haughty stoicism. Liberation may require us to undergo liberation from our own life because the issue at stake is more important than life here and now in the historical present.

Every indication is that the present moment in world culture, and particularly in our Latin American culture, is a period of conception and gestation rather than of birth and growth in freedom. Now is a time for preparing the soil and sowing the seeds of liberation; we should not count on reaping the harvest. In one of his most recent books (*Tomorrow's Child*), Rubem Alves talks about the need for discipline in a life based on love and hope. Rather than letting our creativity go up in the smoke of the immediately tangible present, we must have the disciplined love of the prophets and commit our love to a future that we may never see. Like the seed falling into the ground, our bodies must prepare the way for the future. Or, as Nietzsche put it: "Wake and listen, you that are lonely! From the future come winds with secret wing-beats; and good tidings are proclaimed to delicate ears. You that are lonely today, you that are withdrawing, you shall one day be the people. . . . Verily, the earth shall yet become a site of recovery. And even now a new fragrance surrounds it, bringing salvation—and a new hope."[19]

NOTES

1. On this whole issue see H.W. Bartsch, "Die Ideologiekritik des Evangeliums dargestellt an der Leidensgeschichte," in *Evangelische Theologie* 34 (1974): 176–95; E. Castelli, *Demitizzazione e ideologia* (Padova: CEDAM, 1973).

2. For efforts based on the Latin American situation as a starting point see: H. Borrat, "Para una cristología de la vanguardia," in *Víspera* 17 (1970): 26–31; A. Zanteno, "Liberación social y Cristo," in *Cuadernos de liberación*, Ed. Secretariado Social Mexicano, 1971; G. Gutiérrez, *Teología de la liberación*, 1972, pp. 216–29, see entry under his name in Appendix I of this volume; Bravo-Catao-Comblin, *Cristología y pastoral en América Latina* (Santiago-Barcelona, 1965); H. Assmann, *Teología desde la praxis de la liberación* (Salamanca, 1973), see entry under his name in Appendix I of this volume; B.A. Dumas, *Los dos rostros alienados de la Iglesia una* (Buenos Aires: Latinoamerica Libros, 1971), pp. 41–79; L. Boff, *Jesus Cristo Libertador* (Petrópolis: Vozes, 1974), see entry under his name in Appendix I of this volume; L. Boff, "Salvation in Jesus Christ and the Process of Liberation," in *Concilium* 96 (New York: Herder and Herder, 1974), pp. 78–91; S. Galilea and R. Vidales, *Cristología y pastoral popular* (Bogotá: Paulinas, 1974); M.P. Galvez, "Elementos cristológicos para una teología de la liberación," in *Liberación, Diálogos en Celam* (Bogotá, 1974), pp. 323–36.

3. The literature on this topic is extensive. For an approach based on the principal ancient sources see C. Boff, "Foi Jesus revolucionário?" in *Revista Eclesiástica Brasileira* 31 (1971):87–118; L. Gonçalves, *Cristo e contestaçao política* (Petrópolis, 1974); M. Hengel, *Eigentum und Reichtum in der frühen Kirche, Aspekte einer frühchristlichen Sozialgeschichte* (Stuttgart, 1973), pp. 31–39; Eng. trans.: *Property and Riches in the Early Church* (Philadelphia: Fortress, 1974); J. Jeremias, *Jerusalem zur Zeit Jesu* (Göttingen: Vandenhoeck, 1958), 1:1–33; Eng. trans.: *Jerusalem in the Time of Jesus* (Philadelphia: Fortress, 1969); G. Dalmann, *Arbeit und Sitte in Palästina*, vol. I (Gütersloh, 1928); J. Herz, "Grossgrundbesitz in Palästina in Zeitalter Jesu," in *Palästinajahrbuch*, 24 (1928): 98–113.

4. For further bibliography on this matter see L. Boff, *Jesus Cristo Libertador*, pp. 62–75.

5. Ibid., pp. 76–112; also J. Ernst, *Anfänge der Christologie* (Stuttgart, 1972), pp. 145–58; H. Kessler, *Erlösung als Befreiung* (Düsseldorf, 1972), pp. 62–74; J. Guillet, *Jésus devant sa vie et sa mort* (Paris: Aubier, 1971), pp. 75–83, Eng. trans.: *The Consciousness of Jesus* (New York: Newman, 1972); C. Mesters, "Jesus e o povo: qual foi a libertação que ele trouxe para o povo do seu tempo?" in *Palvra de Deus na história dos homens* (Petrópolis: Vozes, 1971), 2:135–181.

6. See H. Kessler, *Erlösung als Befreiung*, p. 65.

7. J. Jeremias, *New Testament Theology*, Eng. trans. (New York: Scribner's, 1971), p. 113.

8. See A. Paul, "Pluralité des interprétations théologiques de la mort du Christ dans le Nouveau Testament," in *Lumière et Vie* 101 (1971):18–33; A. Vanhoye, "Structure et théologie des récits de la Passion dans les évangiles synoptiques," *Nouvelle Revue Théologique* 89 (1967):145–63.

9. C. Duquoc, *Christologie*, vol. 2, *Le Messie* (Paris: Cerf, 1972), p. 197.

10. See G. Crespy, "Recherche sur la signification politique de la mort du Christ," in *Lumière et Vie* 101 (1971):89–109.

11. C. Duquoc, *Christologie*, p. 197.

12. Ibid., p. 204.

13. See the apt remarks of T. Cavalcanti, "Notas sobre a mensagem central do Cristianismo," in *Revista Eclesiástica Brasileira*, 34 (1974):295–96.

14. See L. Boff, *Atualidade da experiência de Deus*, CRB 17 (Rio de Janeiro, 1974), pp. 54–66 and the associated bibliography.

15. James Cone, *A Black Theology of Liberation* (Philadelphia: Lippincott, 1970), pp. 210–11.

16. This critical analysis has been carried through most fittingly by the so-called Frankfurt School. See J. Habermas, *Technik und Wissenschaft als Ideologie* (Frankfurt: Suhrkamp, 1968); idem, *Erkenntnis und Interesse* (Frankfurt: Suhrkamp, 1968), Eng. trans.: *Knowledge and Human Interests* (Boston: Beacon, 1971); H. Marcuse, "The End of Utopia," in *Five Lectures* (Boston: Beacon, 1970); E. Fromm, *The Crisis of Psychoanalysis* (Greenwich, Conn.: Fawcett, 1970); T. Adorno, *Negative Dialektik* (Frankfurt, 1970), Eng. trans., *Negative Dialectics* (New York: Seabury, 1972).

17. There is a significant body of scientific literature dealing with the socio-economic analysis of dependence. Some significant works are: F. Cardoso and H. Faletto, *Dependencia y desarrollo en América Latina* (Santiago: ILPES, 1967); C. Furtado, *La economía latinoamericana desde la conquista ibérica hasta la revolución cubana* (Santiago: Universitaria, 1970); A. Gunder Frank, *Lumpen-burguesía: Lumpendesarrollo* (Bogotá: Oveja Negra, 1970); T. Dos Santos, *Lucha de clases y dependencia en América Latina* (Bogotá: Oveja Negra, 1970); a summary of this thinking can be found in G. Arroyo, "Pensamiento latino-americano sobre subdesarrollo y dependencia externa," in *Fe cristiana y cambio social en América Latina* (Salamanca: Sígueme 1973), pp. 305–34.

18. C. Furtado, *O fim da utopia do desenvolvimento* (Rio de Janeiro, 1974).

19. F. Nietzsche, *Thus Spoke Zarathustra*, First Part ("On the Gift-giving Virtue"), Kaufmann translation, *Viking Portable Nietzsche*, p. 189. Alves cites this passage of Nietzsche in *Tomorrow's Child*. See his entry in Appendix I for bibliographic details.

6

The Power of Christ in History: Conflicting Christologies and Discernment

Hugo Assmann (San José, Costa Rica)

"I shall come to you soon ... and find out, not what they say, but what they can do. The kingdom of God does not consist in talk but in power" (1 Cor. 4:19–20).

PRELIMINARY NOTE ON THEOLOGIZING
IN LATIN AMERICA

"Latin America" does not signify one single and well defined context. A wide diversity of situations, both in socio-political and Christian terms, is certainly one of the hallmarks of our raised consciousness in the seventies. In the decade of the sixties much thinking was orientated around basic values and background features, and it led toward a great deal of oversimplification. We saw a lot of comprehensive statements and efforts in the field of social analysis (e.g., the theory of "dependence"), Christian reflection (e.g., liberation theology), and official church pronouncements (e.g., the 1968 Medellín episcopal conference). In many instances, however, these efforts did not respond to the particular and specific nature of the context; what is needed now is a new definition of "contextuality," of what it means to relate to a given context.

Our newfound awareness of context and its implications clearly suggest that we must move beyond surface realities. Basic to any effort now is the assertion that theologies must be "inductive, pluralistic, experiential, partial, and related to their environment in order to be relevant." This assertion must be accepted, along with the methodology it entails. Basically it means that Christians cannot possibly fashion a language that meaningfully reflects their experience of the faith unless it includes in-depth social analyses and political strategies.

It is precisely on this issue that official sectors within the church are incapable of moving because they are hampered by some block. They think that the first obligation imposed by the Christian faith is a recognition and acknowledgement of certain "absolutes" concerning the meaning and thrust of history. There is no role accorded to analysis and commitment, to theory and practice, as a unified experience of interpretation and transformation. Their outlook and talk remains on the level of verbal pronouncements and denunciations.

On both the theoretical and the practical level, however, many Christian groups have come in contact with non-Christians involved in the same struggle for liberation. As a result they have seen that their Christian faith must find a deeper kind of solidity ("faith implies commitment") and new theological reference points. The conflicts rooted in every specific context have become the contextual touchstone through which God speaks to us today. The "word of God" is no longer some perduring, unchanging absolute, some eternal proposition that we accept as such before analyzing social conflicts and committing ourselves to the transformation of historical reality. God's summons to us—God's word today—arises out of communal analysis of historical data and historical happenings as praxis. The Bible and Christian tradition as a whole do not address themselves "directly" to us in our present situation; instead they stand as a basic point of reference for us, indicating how God speaks to human beings in widely divergent contexts. Thus they can help us to see how God might be speaking to us in our present context.

It is certainly true that this new type of hermeneutics can destroy the false security engendered by a divine word "uttered once for all time" and "absolute in itself." We now deny that this word can be regarded as a direct summons that we can grasp without analyzing the various obstacles placed in its way over the course of the last two thousand years. There are countless false mediations of that word in the past that have falsified and idealized it too much. In particular we might note the incorporation of the bourgeois outlook of the capitalist system within the whole scheme of biblical interpretation. All that must stop.

The basic reference points of traditional theology, the Bible and tradition (however the latter term may be understood), do not suffice for doing theology because they are not directly accessible. Our approach to these touchstones of the Christian faith is affected and conditioned by blocks set up in the past. We must take note of these blocks in our present context and try to remove them in our own analysis and praxis.

Praxis, then, becomes the basic reference point for any truly contextual theology. Never forgetting the historical implications of our faith and the need for concrete involvement, we are forced to engage in an ongoing process of self-criticism. Praxis cannot come down to some sort of spontaneous generosity. It means that our instruments of analysis must be used both to interpret historical processes below the mere surface level and to examine the political definition we formulate within the framework of clearly proposed strategic goals.

Thus there is a standing risk that the logical consequences of this new mode of theologizing will be radicalized. To overlook the role of the church and other Christians, however, would be to become completely non-contextual in our approach; such an approach would be completely abstract and impractical. A concrete "context" must take into account all the elements that play a determining role in carrying out a given praxis with and among other Christians. All the communicative aspects are of fundamental importance in the methodology that we have just described.

At times it seems that all too few of us in Latin America have been logically consistent in applying the factors required by this new methodology. It is not because the methodology itself is imprecise, in my opinion. Rather, it is because our own colonized minds have led us to keep on mouthing an *elitist* language. Grassroots Christians are far more radical in their use of the new methodology. It is really their methodology, their authentic methodology, because it is a type of Christian reflection that corresponds with their own practical experience of the faith in the context of political praxis. That is why they are more radical in doing what we theologians are trying to do; that is why their expression in grassroots language is more suited to the real-life context than our sophisticated but extra-contextual talk.

Awareness of this fact is now leading theologians toward a fresher terminology and greater sensitivity to tactics and practical relevance. Here in the seventies we are moving toward a "people's version of theology." At the same time we are turning our attention away from false polemics in the realm of the official church in order to find new ways of establishing common denominators without dodging the obligation to keep moving ahead. All this, too, is a way of being consistent with a methodology that seeks to make theologizing a critical reflection on a relevant, contextual, and feasible praxis.

CHRISTOLOGICAL DEBATE IN LATIN AMERICA

For some years now people have been talking about the christological void or gap in Latin American theology. Some complain that we need a "Christology for the avant-garde" and do not have one—the assumption being that such avant-gardes are revolutionary, of course. Moreover, the "theology of liberation" is criticized for its alleged tendency to "prescind from Christ." Granting the element of validity in such objections, we are still faced with a basic problem here. It has to do with what can be regarded as irreconcilable differences in the standpoints of those who make such objections.

In the case of some people their objection almost certainly stems from a nostalgic yearning for a body of christological doctrines that is to be kept safe and secure from change, objections, and any contact with history. History is not to play any mediating role so that this doctrine might be relevant to the Latin American situation. To such people we must reply that any attempt to prescind from history undermines meaningful talk about Christ from the very start; that it sabotages Christology in the alleged name of Christology. There is nothing new in this, of course, because we can find such sabotage of the gospel message throughout the history of Christianity and even in some of the biblical writings themselves; it is sabotage done in the name of that very message.

In the case of other people, however, their objection arises out of their basic agreement with the thrust of a liberative theology. Starting from the praxis of a Christian faith that has taken a definite stand in favor of the oppressed, they want to elaborate a theological idiom that expresses what they think and feel. When they call for more and better Christology, they are trying to immerse themselves even more deeply in the basic standpoint that is criticized by the first group.

Failure to note the basic difference in standpoint between these two groups, both of whom may object to the present gap in Christology, can have rather serious consequences. It can break important ties of solidarity between those engaged in the struggle for liberation, so that some actually end up playing into the hands of the enemy. That is what we see happening when some of the people involved with the periodical *Víspera* make common cause with people like R. Vekemans and Bishop López Trujillo in their articles and discussions.

Many examples could be cited to prove the contradictory thrust of various calls for a Latin American Christology. Take the case of L. Boff's book, *Jesus Cristo Libertador* (Petrópolis: Vozes, 1972; Eng. trans.: *Jesus Christ Liberator*, Maryknoll, New York: Orbis Books, 1978). Some episcopal spokesman saw it as a reductionist attack on Christ, an attempt to reduce him to nothing more than a historical and socio-political liberator. Other critics, most from the Spanish-speaking sector of Latin America, felt that it was a fine synthesis of the vague and scattered findings of European exegesis and theology but that it failed to go into or use any analysis of the current Latin American situation in the process. Here we would do well to realize one of the basic presuppositions held by those who made the latter criticism. They question the very possibility of resolving christological conflicts simply by going back to "sounder" or "better" exegetical sources and thereby objectively purifying or refining christological doctrine. I myself lean toward the same view. One reason is that there is so much debate on the exegetical scene that it seems unlikely that one could elaborate an exegesis of the basic christological message that would not be objected to by some exegete or another.

Another and more important reason is based on a clear sociological fact: While biblical scholars and theologians may exert some influence, they do not exercise any effective control over the various contradictory Christologies that are preached and spread broadcast. In the case of Latin America, for example, it is hard to picture "modern exegesis" having a complete and thoroughly purifying influence on the various conflicting images of Christ that are around, even if we go so far as to make the dubious assumption that such exegesis would carry us beyond a Christ garbed in the trappings of liberalism and integrated within the existing system. This is not to suggest, of course, that we can or should spurn the important contributions made by biblical scholars.

To put the point slightly differently, it seems excessively naive to think that we can fill the christological gap in Latin American theology by providing some smashing "biblical portrait" that will sweep all before it. Yet some do seem to think along these lines. Some seem to think it can be done with an ingenious blending of Marxism and existentialism: e.g., José P. Miranda, *El ser y el mesías* (Salamanca: Sígueme, 1973; Eng. trans.: *Being and the Messiah*, Maryknoll, New York: Orbis Books, 1977). Others think it can be done by juxtaposing the allegedly opposing christological message of Mark and Matthew and forcefully emphasizing the difference: e.g., Joan Leita, *El Antievangelio* (Barcelona: Ed. Laia, 1973). Ecclesiastical institutions will continue to assert that it is up to them, not to exegetes or theologians, to provide an authoritative solution for doctrinal questions. In the dialectics of societal life, meanwhile, the historical praxis of Christians will continue to be influenced by various images of Christ that are acknowledged and cultivated. And this influence will be exerted through explicit theologies on the one hand, but perhaps even more forcefully by implicit subterranean theologies on the other.

All this leads us to our first conclusion: The conflict of differing Christologies cannot be analyzed or resolved outside the dialectics of socio-political conflicts. Such conflicts have ever been the concrete conditioning factors of all Christologies. Any other approach to the problem is vitiated by its idealism.

THE CONTINUING VITALITY
OF CONFLICTING IMAGES OF CHRIST

Once we accept the fact that the conflict between differing Christologies is conditioned by historical contradictions in our societies, we can begin to appreciate a fact that does not sit well with those of us who possess the faith. The fact is that there is no immediate prospect of a solution for the conflict between Christologies. Why? Because there is no immediate prospect of a solution for the serious social contradictions in our "Christian" America.

In making this statement I am assuming that a "Christian"

historical milieu does exist here, at least in a sociological sense, and that it has been an influencing factor in the history of Latin America. If we entertained the idea of a liberation process for our people which did not take that historical milieu into account, then we would be in danger of overlooking the underlying wellsprings of social awareness that are powerfully operative in our social processes. The forces of reaction, as we know, have no thought of committing such a mistake. The forces of the "metaphysical left," whose ideological radicalism is very idealist, tend to make that mistake frequently.

In other words, the prospect for the immediate future in Latin America is that we will continue to find "Christs" on both sides of the fence, both among the revolutionaries and among the reactionaries. This situation will be aggravated by the fact that the latter, operating in terms of continuity with the past rather than in terms of a break with the past, will make appeals to Christ that are more "authorized." Thus the faith of revolutionary Christians will have to bear with the tension involved in all this. "Their" Christ will not be the only Christ invoked in the process of social dialectics. They will try in vain to "monopolize" the situation with their image of Christ the Liberator. What is more, their liberator Christ will continue to be a "lesser" Christ, who is also less authorized by the official institutions of the church even though he seems to be more solidly grounded in the Bible; and this same Christ will stand over against the Christs of the bourgeoisie. It will be quite an achievement in itself if the image of Christ the Liberator is not labelled as completely heretical, due to its solid support in the biblical fonts and the witness of history. But there will be plenty of disavowals from other sectors of the church, claiming that there is no official authorization for such a view of Christ. Indeed this right to disavow images of Christ is not new in many ecclesiastical circles; it began with their disavowal of the "liberal" Christ fashioned by one predominant strain of modern exegesis.

So we must stress the obvious fact that any faith in a liberator Christ is going to run into conflicts. Such an image of Christ will inevitably come into conflict with all the different Christs of the oppressor classes. There are plenty of such Christs around, each fashioned or brought back into vogue as the need arises.

What kind of Christs are currently being invoked in Latin America? Here there is no room for an exhaustive analysis of all the Christs being preached here. We could not even discuss all the

main images of Christ on one side or the other, much less the more
peripheral and secondary images that share certain basic features but run a broad gamut of meaning in the "Christian" devotion of our peoples and nations. Here I should simply like to call
attention to some of the fragments in the dialectical conflict between differing Christologies.

Ever since the recent military coup in Chile, pronouncements by
both church and government officials reflect the strong resurgence of Christologies that many had thought to have been
declared illegitimate during the period of Allende's rule. They
come down to two basic images of Christ. One is the Christ of
conciliatory "third-way" approaches. For him there is no irreconcilable conflict, no victors and vanquished; there is only one
happy, fraternal family living above and beyond all social conflict.
The other is the Christ of the coup. It is he who underlies the
thinking of those who try to legitimate the coup by appealing to
the need to defend "Christian" values. The shifting sands of
allegiance to one or another image of Christ have much to tell the
sociologist, but they are discouraging to any theologian or biblical
scholar who is confident that we can move history forward simply
by purifying people's ideas.

Such moments in history are very instructive. They tell us a
great deal about the conditioning influence of social contexts on
ideas. When we examine certain episcopal texts, such as the
statement by Bishop González of Temuco, we see how difficult it is
to blend together a Christ who is somewhat of the third-way bent
with a Christ who is just the slightest bit in favor of the coup. The
slightest shift in emphasis can produce a great change in one's
ideological cast. This is evident when we compare the statements
of the Cardinal and Bishop Ariztía on the one hand with those of
Bishop Tagle of Valparaíso on the other—the former taking a
"discreet distance" from the coup, the latter openly endorsing it.

Insofar as "leftist" Christologies exist at all, and they do tend to
be fragmentary, the following observations seem to be in order.
First of all, they generally do not take the form of a new doctrinal
corpus that is fully rounded and complete. Their Christ does not
tend to claim the comprehensiveness and completeness that
seems to be suggested by *the* Christ in whose name the official
churches and the rightists speak. It is another Christ; or, if you
will, Christ is this too. Their Christ does not make claim to any
exclusiveness, for people are too vividly aware of the fact that
there are other Christs around. It is the ideological aspect rather

than the Christ image in itself that rounds out the picture and injects yearnings for some full and total meaningfulness into the picture.

As this "leftist" Christ takes on traits of class consciousness, however, his antithetical character is reinforced and he comes closer to the image of an exclusivist Christ. Other than that, he tends to be a Christ acceptable to a "broad sector of the left," hence tolerant and not too sectarian. The Christ invoked by the left tends to be a paschal Christ, a Christ promising life; that is one of his most basic features. He is pointed toward the future and a better life. In this connection it is interesting to note the paschal content of the christological metaphors that are applied to revolutionaries who have died in the struggle for liberation: "Ché lives!" "Luciano lives!" "Camilo, here!" The same note of paschal promise is present in directly sacrificial metaphors. In a documentary filmed for German television, one can see and hear the children of Cuba chanting this about Ché: "He died for all the children of this world."

In general these leftist Christologies do the same thing that Engels, Kautsky, Lunacharsky, and many other Marxists have done. They tend to make a great leap above and beyond the "distorted Christs" of the history of Christianity—a procedure, be it noted in passing, that is neither very historical nor materialistic. They do this to find some alleged "original Christ" of primitive Christianity, who marches out to meet them as a "natural ally" without them having to do any heavy road-clearing work. But a theology centered around Christ the Liberator should take more account of the various Christs that have been influential in history and that attempt to mediate and obstruct our access to the Christ of the Gospels. Even the Christ of the Gospels has already passed through the mediating influence of different kerygmatic thrusts, as we noted already.

Insofar as the many Christs of the "people" and the "baptized masses" in Latin America are concerned, rather curious things are going on. In the 1970 election in Chile, when Allende came to power, approximately 70 percent of the Pentecostals voted for Allende. An authoritative source in the Pentecostal church assured me that at least part of the explanation lay in the fact that many Pentecostals tended to have anti-Catholic feelings and to be opposed to the Christian Democratic party in politics. An anti-Frei Christ?

What I want to bring out here is a characteristic widely shared by various "populist" Christs. As seen by popular devotions to them, their power and their claims to power are quite modest. Their Christ is one to whom they do not attribute dominion over all realms. Instead he is a specialist in certain specific sectors of power and authority. The remaining "areas" are entrusted to the Virgin Mary or certain saints. This fact shows up clearly in Brazilian popular devotions. The "people" do not recognize Christ as the Alpha and Omega, the principle and end of all things.

We might well ask what dialectical role can be attributed to such Christs, who do not seem to be anything more than just another saint. Their "usefulness" to messianic ideologies that seek to take in the whole of social reality would seem to be quite limited. Sometimes we find a certain "ideological respect" for Christ that prompts people not to attribute any "functions" to him. It is "better" if such functions are attributed to the Virgin Mary. The Virgin Mary of Carmel, for example, is the "Generalísima" of the Chilean Armed Forces. Seen in that light, we can appreciate the tremendous symbolic force of the new oath that is taken by the cadets of the Chilean Military Academy. Since the coup they now take an oath "in the name of Christ."

To sum up, we can say that the utilization of the Virgin Mary is more explicit and vulgar: e.g., recitations of the rosary to ward off the menace of communism, and various sorts of processions. The Christ of the right is not so free to step directly out into the open; his mission unfolds from behind the scenes.

NEED FOR THEOLOGICAL DISCERNMENT

The sociologist and the political scientist would find nothing absurd or harebrained in the above way of looking at conflicting Christologies, though they might be bothered by the broad superficial nature of the observations and their lack of scientific exactitude. To their eyes christological myths, symbols, and metaphors would seem to form a natural part of the conflict between ideologies. As they took concrete form in institutions, movements, attitudes, and concrete socio-political happenings, they would deserve attention as "meaningful elements of the power situation" in the overall context of the community's awareness.

The historian, the ethnologist, the anthropologist, and the social psychologist might take a similar interest in such topics, all examining them from their own particular point of analysis. Even the literary critic might find it interesting to detect and explore the deeper workings of the christological metaphor in literary works. Consider Gabriel García Márquez's tale, *El ahogado más hermoso del mundo*, for example. The story recounts the sudden and curious appearance of a dead man on the beach of a small fishing village. The dead man is big and handsome ("the most beautiful drowned man in the world"), and arrives dead. No one can say where he is from or why he came, but he arouses the devotional impulses of the people, of the women in particular. Buried by the villagers as their own special treasure, he generates a profound, peace-giving silence.

But what about the theologians? Can they adopt a similar outlook on all this? Is that enough for the person of faith, the person who believes in Jesus Christ? As we have already seen, there is no reason why the revolutionary Christian and the theologian of liberation should avoid this conflict between christological ideologies; in fact there is no way they can avoid it, since the conflict is very real and down to earth. They can and should give consideration to the "concrete influence" and the "dynamics of historical power" that are embodied in these varying christological ideologies. If we do not face up to them, it does not seem that we can provide a reasonable explanation for our own adhesion to Christ and our faith in his power. But precisely because faith in Christ is involved here, the revolutionary Christian and the theologian cannot rest content with taking note of the "influences" operating under the veil of varying Christologies. Their faith-inspired option for Christ obliges them to undertake an effort at discernment. If various Christs are truly in conflict with each other, their faith obliges them to opt for "one" Christ and to implement that option with deeds. This will very likely mean that they must or do take a stand against "other" Christs.

Where are we to look for criteria in making our option? As we noted above, christological conflicts cannot be readily resolved by resorting to sounder biblical information. That is of enormous help, to be sure, and we consider that step obligatory. But it would be naive to think that it will suffice. We will not have to wait long for "authorized" disavowals of the image we find in the biblical sources. Moreover, we do well to remember that the revolutionary Christian and the theologian of liberation will tend to find that adherence to "official" Christs of the churches leads them into a kind of blind alley. Why? First of all because these official Christs, besides being contradictory and numerous, are captives of authority and the law and caught within the existing system for the most part.

This point, however, should not be overstressed. However much effort may be expended in keeping the christological doctrine of the churches subject to authoritarian control, it contains essential and "salvageable" elements that cannot be kept imprisoned very easily or completely. It contains elements that escape the clutches of the official churches. These elements represent an already existing and available point of departure for any attempt to activate features of a liberative Christology within the churches themselves. Despite the opposition that may crop up, then, church Christologies continue to be potential, partial allies of a liberation Christology. This holds true on the doctrinal level, and it is even more true on the practical level. The fact is that the revolutionary Christian cannot take the liberty of going against those who adhere to the ecclesiastical Christologies when, for social and class reasons, they represent potential allies in the liberation process. The situation is different, of course, in the case of those who uphold oppression and domination in the name of Christianity. Their Christology must be shown to be illegitimate and unmasked in a stance of opposition and conflict.

But where are we to find criteria if recourse to the "sources" is not enough? Besides recourse to the biblical sources for clarification, there are several other criteria. I prefer to call them criteria of "approximation" because they too are not sufficient or definitive. Here are a couple of examples of what I mean, based on christological developments in recent decades. Prior to Vatican II, the traditional Catholic tract on Christology was predominantly apologetic (dealing with problems concerning the historical Jesus) and philosophical (dealing with the human and divine "I" of Christ). In short, they dealt essentially with the Jesus of "another time" and Christ, the Son of God; they were more or less a defense of the Council of Chalcedon. Little treatment was accorded to such burning issues as the Incarnation, the relevance of the historical Christ today, and the paschal mystery in our present-day human history. The central focus of Christology has shifted a great deal in more recent years. Our Christological tracts have moved from the individual Christ to the total Christ; from Christ *in se* to the Christ "in Christians"; and, more timidly and gradually, from the bygone Christ to a Christ and his power operating in the full dimensions of history and here and now today.

EUROPEAN POLITICAL THEOLOGY
AND LATIN AMERICAN THEOLOGY

As the last remarks suggest, theology itself has been moving more and more toward a face-to-face confrontation with a dilemma. It is the dilemma implied in the basic affirmation that Christ's power is an active, operative force in all of history, and hence in our present conflict-ridden situation. This dilemma was confronted directly by the "theology of hope" and "political theology." Let us put it in concrete terms.

If we say that Christ's power is a force in history, then we must do one of two things: Either we spell out its concrete political relevance in this world or else we make it clear, once and for all, that it is a purely eschatological, post-historical power. Of course we still find thoroughgoing eschatologists on the Christian scene today. But the two lines of theology just mentioned above deserve credit for having opted decisively in favor of the contemporary, operative relevance of Christ's power and his resurrection. They opted for one of the horns of the dilemma, rejecting a wholly individualistic notion of salvation.

But what is so new or great about that? Isn't that one of the most traditional components in what the church has always said about Christ's power? Yes, it is, at least insofar as talk is concerned; but Paul tells us it is not a matter of talk at all. The two theologies we have just mentioned above attempt to take Paul's emphasis on deeds seriously. They seek to consider Christ's power in the reality of socio-political events.

Having reached that crucial point, the "political" theologians took another big step forward. They began to dismantle the alibis that the churches have used to make the power of Christ innocuous politically. Those alibis are of an ideological cast, and they can be analyzed in terms of their political function. But *abyssus abyssum invocat*, and one dilemma gives rise to another. When we start to unmask the alibis that keep Christ's power vague and undefined, we are doing something that will entail a lot more commitment than vague general statements about his power operating in history. We are then obliged to determine "where" Christ's power is operative in the conflict-ridden context of human history, though our determination may not have to be exclusivist. Locating where his power is at work, at least for the most part, means determining who it sides with and who it sides against.

It was at this precise point, in my view, that European "political theology" began to get cold feet. Frightened by its own boldness, it began to go off into vague generalities that did not correspond with the scientific idiom and terminology that was available, however fragmentary and imperfect, to describe the conflict-ridden play of power in history. To put it plainly and simply, European theologians did not dare to go further in their analysis of the historical mediations of power at play.

It was at this point that Latin American theology did dare to take a few timid steps further. Without entertaining the delusion that it could pinpoint the location of Christ's power completely, it did change its methodology somewhat. In its theological reflection it began to introduce certain analytical tools that would enable it to come closer to determining the side that Christ was on. This "leap" forward produced some of the initial features of a liberator Christ, a Christ integrated into the one and only pageant of human history with all its contradictions and conflicts.

Christ's power is necessarily operative in a certain well-defined direction. It is on the side of the oppressed and against their oppressors. No longer is he the "great reconciler" standing outside and above the conflicts that are going on here and now, though brotherly reconciliation between human beings in history is certainly the ultimate goal of his operative power. He is not a sectarian Christ who favors narrow partisanship and fanatically espouses a single tactic. But neither does he exercise his power apart from human history, operating in some isolated history of his own; his power takes sides in and through human beings.

This burgeoning liberation Christology has not yet said anything that the churches have not maintained in the past or still maintain today in rather forceful terms. The only thing is that their espousal of this image has been of the opposite ideological cast. The new Christology is not "heretical" because it has gone overboard in trying to pinpoint and localize where the power of Christ is operative. Its efforts in this area have been modest and open-ended. The power of Christ has not been tied to any one historical movement in a narrow partisan way, so that Christ himself becomes the one definitive figure legitimating a single line of action. Instead the challenging image of Christ the Liberator keeps one step ahead of us all the time. He keeps pointing us toward the future because that is where we will encounter him. His challenge to liberate the oppressed implies an ongoing revolution, but a realistic rather than an idealistic one.

But where exactly is the scandal then? The scandal lies in those who are scandalized, and in the bold decision to stand up in opposition to the clear ideological cast of their own political option. While their option is clear, it may be something of which they are not fully aware.

PROBLEMS AND PROSPECTS
OF A LIBERATIVE CHRISTOLOGY

No one can fail to realize that the path of any liberative Christology is strewn with fresh dilemmas. The scientific tools for a true "reading of reality" are still far from perfect. This must be said by way of opposition to any kind of schematic Marxism and, if you will, for the benefit of Marxism itself. But without falling into a positivistic scientism, we must emphasize that these analytical instruments are not at point zero either. Choosing between the available variety of instruments is itself a problematic issue entailing an ethical step. And every ethical matter implies the possibility not only of error but of guilt.

Thus the new dilemmas posed by a Christology focusing on the liberative power of Christ in history are of manifold origin. Human history undoubtedly contains many aspects that our futile science will never manage to "verify" scientifically. That of course does not excuse us from using the degrees of verifiability available to us. Now when people talk about the workings of power-in-conflict within human history, they are wont to talk in economic, political, and social terms—in other words, in historical terms. But unknowns, surprising events, and shadowy zones still remain. Can we assume, for example, that the historical dialectics of Christ's liberative power at work here and now shares in the dialectics of the "economic object"? For the Christian who is also a Marxist in many respects, this is a real dilemma. For Marxism asserts that the economic factor, or the material structure of society to put it more broadly, is the determining factor in the "last instance," though this notion remains rather mysterious and unexplained.

A resurgence of "historicism" in certain brands of Marxism is paving the way for a new appreciation of the primacy of the political factor. Christians, with their proclaimed faith in human beings and their freedom, might well find this more to their taste. But with their aversion to "economicist materialism" (and what could be more "economicist" than capitalism?), they might be readily inclined to fall into the snares of a voluntaristic kind of spontaneity. By way of a jest, we might consider how easy it is to take certain christological schemas that are completely traditional and nondialectical and fit them into the fad of the moment: e.g., a deterministic emphasis on the "objective factor" on the one hand, or a subjective voluntarism of an anarchic bent on the other. Here is how we might do it:

objective redemption—Christ's power—objective conditions

subjective redemption—justification by faith—subjective conditions

Fragile and faulty as its efforts may be, liberation theology is trying to maintain the proper dialectical tension between the two elements that are essential to its methodology: recourse to the "mediations of analysis" on the one hand and the privacy of praxis as pondered critically on the other. The notion of power with which it operates, then, can never be simply a noun (i.e., something we possess or acquire); it must always be a verb as well (i.e., the actual exercise or practice of power). Hence the notion of "Christ's power" can never be reduced to some pre-existing force or some objective quality of history that is there from the very start. For it inevitably operates through our own praxis. Our own praxis, in turn, unfolds in a conflict-ridden historical situation. While it should move in the direction of a liberation dialectics, there is no point where this praxis is definitively crystallized because it must move and operate dialectically in the midst of conflicts. Praxis enjoys a dialectical freedom that cannot be defined in advance. If we explored this feature of praxis more closely, we might come closer to the theological ideal of not creating definitive images of Christ's power in history.

Our older christological faith used too many nouns and substantives when it talked about Christ and his paschal activity in history. Those nouns gave promise of turning into verbs (i.e., into a liberation praxis), but in the end their use proved to be merely adverbial. Christ touched human history only tangentially. Precisely because it was never "constructed" or "built up," his power always ended up being identified with the established authorities. Because it never took on the active dynamism of a countervailing power, of a power offering critical opposition, it always ended up serving as an auxiliary support for the "thrones and powers" that be. That is what happens when one talks about power without asking how it might be effectively channeled and put to use. Those that are effective in exercising domination appropriate it for their own use.

Some Christologies claim to be apolitical. They offer us a Christ who "has" power but does not exercise it, and who never takes sides. They are simply ways of concealing the fact that an option for one side has already been made. The newer political Christologies are ways of stripping the mask off these allegedly apolitical Christs and revealing their true countenance.

The supposedly apolitical Christologies are really theological (or better, ecclesiastical) Yalta Pacts, because they divide life and the world into "spheres of influence," and this division is profoundly political in character. They always end up promoting "peaceful coexistence." "Divide and conquer" is the watchword, so we get a divided history, a divided world, and a division of labor. Who would keep us from asking the basic question: With whom is the pact made?

The sorrowful Christs of Latin America focus all attention on the cross. They are Christs imaging the impotence that is interiorized in the oppressed: defeat, sacrifice, sorrow, the cross. Impotence is presented as an essential element accepted and digested from the start, *"mitreflektiert,"* the Germans would say. Defeat is not a possible outcome or a temporary condition that one must take for granted as such in the midst of struggle. It is an inescapable necessity, the precondition for life being possible at all. The impossibility of ever holding or wielding real, effective power is laid down as the precondition for life continuing at all. And life itself is presented as an idealized promise of power that can never be fulfilled. It is a trap from which there is no escape, a perfect alibi. But for what perfect crimes, and whose crimes? we might well ask.

On the other side stand the rather rarer glorious Christs of Latin America. There they sit on their thrones with crowns on their head, as real as the kings of Spain. And yet, curiously enough, they are not "other" Christs, distinct from the sorrowful Christs just mentioned. They are really the other side of the coin, the glorious counterparts of the sorrowful Christs. They are the side that the dominators of Latin America see.

There is no way of separating the cross and the resurrection without succumbing to alienating Christs. The Christ of oppressive Christologies really has two faces. On the one side are all the Christs of the power establishment, who do not need to fight because they already hold a position of dominance; on the other are all the Christs of established impotence, who cannot fight against the dominance to which they are subject.

When faith affirms the operative presence of Christ's power in the midst of this general situation, it is asserting the need to fight in a situation where defeat will pave the way for victory, and where victory itself will ultimately have to meet defeat if it is to continue to be victorious. It is asserting the need for a continuous, ongoing struggle for liberation that will flesh out and make present the dialectics of cross and resurrection.

7

The Historical Vocation of the Church

Ronaldo Muñoz (Santiago, Chile)

Today, more than ever before perhaps, the church in our midst gives us reason for scandal or faith, for frustration or hope. This is particularly true in the public domain, where the destiny of Chile is at stake. Living through the intense drama of our nation's contemporary history, we all have somehow managed to experience the important role played by the church. That is the plain fact, however differently we may interpret it. The importance of the church and its role is evident whether we praise its actions as legitimate or denounce them as illegitimate and neglectful. One need only allude to the many and varied movements and personalities in our country: the Christian Democratic party, Christians for Socialism, the Committee for Peace, and such figures as P. Hasbún and Cardinal Silva Henríquez. Any discussion about the church tends to be freighted with emotion, suggesting a shared awareness that the church does or should represent certain attitudes and values. These may go beyond political contingencies, but the feeling is that they should also serve as a saving leaven in our society.

Faced with this situation and the expectations it arouses, I

151

should like to suggest a few lines of reflection concerning the
historical vocation of the church. Let me start out by making clear
what I do and do not mean here by its "historical vocation." I am
not trying to suggest that the church brings any particularly
glorious history with it from the past; nor am I suggesting that its
destiny in the future is particularly "transcendental" in the jour-
nalistic sense. When I speak of its "historical vocation," I am
alluding to two points that are more straightforward and also
more profound: (1) that the church is a human reality subject to
the contingencies, limitations, and conditioning influence of the
society in which it lives (i.e., that it really is "historical"); (2) that
the church bears within itself a particular impulse and commission which goes back to its origins on the one hand and which is
designed to transform society on the other hand, thus opening
society to a future of greater peace and justice (i.e., that it has a
specific, irreplaceable vocation in and for human history).

I do not propose to "demonstrate" these two assertions in the
present article. They are the basic presuppositions underlying my
remarks here. This is not to suggest that they are obvious to
everyone. There are many Catholics who find it very hard to see
that the church is a "historical" reality in the full sense of the
word, particularly when it comes to accepting all the consequences of that assertion and putting them into practice. And
there are many non-Catholics who are such precisely because
they do not acknowledge that the church has any particular "vocation," at least in the full and strict sense of the word.

Rather than demonstrating my two basic presuppositions here,
I want to indicate how they are being recognized and im-
plemented concretely in the present-day history of the Chilean
church. I want to point out certain aspects and factors that may
help to verify my presuppositions by appealing to the personal
experiences of my readers and helping them to live their membership in the church more actively and consciously.

I shall do this by dealing with four aspects of the church. Using
quite traditional terms, I shall consider the church as a people, as
endowed with a prophetic mission, as a sacrament, and as a community. As we know, Vatican II applied these features to the
church—among others—and they have deep roots in the Bible and
theology. Here I shall not use the typical approach, however. I will
not begin by exploring the rich depths of tradition in order to shed
light on the current condition and tasks of the church afterwards.
Instead I will start from the other end, pointing up various as-

pects of our own present-day church's situation and mission as they appear in our critiques and our efforts at revitalization. Then I shall try to show how and in what sense an awareness of tradition has been part of our quest for a revitalized church, particularly in terms of the four aspects mentioned, and how that may shed light on the current tasks of the church and its responsibilities for the future.

For the Chilean church the decade of the sixties was one of *self-criticism and renewal*. That was particularly true from 1965 on. Different as their forms and connotations may be, self-criticism and renewal are complementary and mutually reinforcing. They are an inevitable result of the Council's updating and our new awareness of the church's presence in our own society. From 1968 on, general critiques and changes in the church began to take a second place to a different concern: *the polarization between conflicting tendencies*.[1] These tendencies were due to the difficulty involved in assimilating the initiatives and experiments prompted by church renewal, and also to the increasingly conscious adherence of Christian individuals and groups to one or another of the social sectors in conflict. All this took place in the more pervasive context of growing political and ideological polarization within Chile.[2] We must keep this background in mind if we want to offer an objective analysis of the four aspects of church life under consideration here.

THE CHURCH AS A PEOPLE

Perhaps the strongest and most shocking feature of the church's self-criticism in the period under review here is the assertion that it has become a church of the rich, far removed from the world of the poor who make up the majority of the population. This criticism does not overlook the fact that the church is among the poor in some way and working for them, or that the people who are poor are also within the church in some sense. It simply underlines the fact that the presence and work of the church's agents among the poor does not go so far as to identify with them and to help them grow on their own terms and initiative. Thus the presence of poor people and the laboring class in the church comes down to marginal membership. They do not really participate in its decisions or plans, and they find that its institutional interests and its official language are alien to them.

Yet this criticism is only one side of the coin. On the other side we find a more positive fact that is both a consequence of this criticism and its underlying precondition: i.e., the growing rapprochement between various segments of the church (priests, religious, and lay groups) and the poor and laboring classes. Many individuals and groups within the church, whose roots and ties were with the bourgeoisie and middle-class sectors, have begun to approach the common people in a new way. They seek to immerse themselves in village and labor circles in order to share the hopes and struggles of the general populace.

This movement of people from a middle-class church toward the common people would not have been fruitful, however, if it had not been matched by a similar movement on the part of the common people. More and more we find laborers, villagers, and peasants banding together into nuclear groups. Aware of their ties to the common people and of their mission as Christians, these groups have been establishing organic ties with the hierarchy and other segments of the church. Thanks to these two movements and their mutual impact on each other, the church has been drawing closer to the poor in a more authentic way and putting itself in a better position to serve the common people. More significantly, perhaps, it has gradually been transforming itself into the church of the poor, the church of the common populace.

Entering into this quest for renewal more or less deliberately has been the basic theme of the church as *the people of the poor*, the people that are loved by God and are working out their liberation in history. In the light of faith we can sense a line of continuity between the people in our midst who are suffering and looking for liberation and the people of Israel who were oppressed in Egypt and liberated through the intervention of Moses. We realize it is the same people whom the prophets, as men of God, championed long ago: the same poor and alienated people whom Jesus of Nazareth preferred to share his life with and who were proclaimed heirs of the kingdom of God.

Vatican II referred to the church as the people of God,[3] and it stressed the solidarity of Christ's followers with "the joys and the hopes, the griefs and the anxieties of the men of this age, especially those who are poor or in any way afflicted."[4] Here we can readily sense why this should create painful tension for all those Christians who take that solidarity seriously. For on the one hand we have the "people of God" made up of the poor and laboring classes, whether or not they are attached to the hierarchically organized church; and on the other hand we have the "people of

God" made up of church believers, whether or not they belong to the world of the poor and identify with their yearnings for liberation. It is the tension implied in the very term, "church of the poor," which was used a great deal during the conciliar debates but which connotes a program rather than any real identity. It is the same tension that can be found in a hesitant but suggestive remark made by the 1971 Synod of Bishops: "The power of the Spirit, who raised Christ from the dead, is continuously at work in the world. *The People of God is uninterruptedly present, through the Church's generous sons and daughters, in the midst of the poor and of those who suffer oppression and persecution;* it lives in its own flesh and heart the Passion of Christ and bears witness to his Resurrection."[5]

THE PROPHETIC CHURCH

The notion of bearing witness to Christ in the midst of the world's people brings us to the second point underlined by ecclesial self-criticism in the decade of the sixties. It became clear that the church had not only lost its central focus on the poor and laboring classes but also tended to serve as an opiate in the face of social injustice. There was no denying that for at least two decades official spokesmen for the Chilean church had raised their voices to denounce unjust situations (particularly in the labor field) and to champion participatory socio-economic structures. The point was that, in spite of such spokesmen, the church's hierarchy as a body had gone on providing religious justification for the established order, either out of inertia or because of pressure from those in power. The social and religious services provided by the church at the grassroots level often tended to evade issues and tranquilize consciences rather than to nurture a historically clear-eyed faith and a socially responsible charity. Among large segments of the faithful, therefore, one could see a great gap between faith and religious practice on the one hand and socio-political responsibilities on the other.

Here again, however, there was another side to the story. The function of the church with respect to society and its structures was obviously flawed. But this very realization arose out of a new way of understanding and implementing the mission of the church in society and the implications of Christian faith for societal living. The fact is that the hierarchy was gradually succeeding in the task of asserting its independence from the centers of political and economic power. It was beginning to voice its loyal criticism of those centers and to espouse the authentic interests and rights of the poor and all human beings. Moreover, on the grassroots level the pastoral agents of the church were immersing themselves more fully in the world of the common people. They were beginning to see how they might present the gospel as truly concerned with human liberation on the individual and collective level, and thereby give impetus to charity in its socio-political dimensions.

Entering into this particular aspect of renewal more or less consciously was the basic theme of the church as a *prophetic* community, as a community chosen and sent by God to speak out to the people and their leaders, to reveal to them the deeper underlying meaning of their situation in history, and thus to awaken their sense of responsibility and their hopes. It was seen that the Christian community has an obligation to carry out the mission that the ancient prophets carried out in Israel. In some way or another, as Peter proclaimed on Pentecost, it must denounce the idolatry and injustice of the powerful, enkindle the hopes of people, and awaken in them a new sense of personal responsibility toward the God of history. This is the same mission that was carried out so completely and perfectly by Jesus the Messiah. Through his message and his whole way of life he proclaimed the good news of liberation for the poor and oppressed, of the justice and reconciliation that marked the reign of God that was already here and still to come.

Vatican II spoke about the church's prophetic mission,[6] associating it not only with the pastors of the church but also with all Christians.[7] It pointed out that the church "has always had the duty of scrutinizing the signs of the times and of interpreting them in the light of the gospel."[8] As a community it must try to "decipher authentic signs of God's presence and purpose in the happenings, needs, and desires in which this People has a part along with other men of our age."[9] The 1971 Synod of Bishops bears even more concrete witness to the church's newfound prophetic awareness: *"Listening to the cry of those who suffer violence and are oppressed by unjust systems and structures*, and hearing too the appeal of a world that by its perversity contradicts the plan of its Creator, *we have taken into account the Church's vocation to be present in the midst of the world by proclaiming the Good News to the poor, freedom to the oppressed, and joy to the afflicted."*[10]

In proclaiming this prophetic vocation, the church is not trying to set up a smokescreen for opportunistic accommodation. It sees how central that vocation is: "The present world situation, seen in the light of faith, calls us back to the very essence of the Christian message, creating in us a deep awareness of its true meaning and its urgent requirements. . . . The Church has received from Christ the mission of preaching the Gospel message, which contains a call to man to turn away from sin to the love of the Father, universal brotherhood, and a consequent demand for justice in the world. This is the reason why the Church has the right—*indeed even the duty—to proclaim justice on the social, national and international level, and to denounce instances of injustice when the fundamental rights of man and his very salvation demand it.*"[11]

THE CHURCH AS SIGN OR SACRAMENT

To be comprehensible and effective, the church's prophetic message cannot get lost in the clouds. It must speak about the reality of people's lives, and then it must be illustrated and verified by committed action and a transparent way of life. That brings us to the third point brought out by recent self-criticism within the church. Its language and sensibility have been far removed from people's lives, its activities and services have been ineffective and unsuitable, and its lifestyle has been inconsistent. This criticism is primarily aimed at priests and religious insofar as they continue to live in a world apart. Their lifestyle is an alien one, their speech and interests far removed from that of other people, and their activities do not do anything to fill the void in our society. But the same criticism applies to the Christian laity at every social level insofar as they come together and operate as church groups. Even among them we often miss the taste of worship performed in the spirit of the gospel message and the consistency of a truly involved and committed faith.

Here, too, there is another side to the story. Perhaps one of the most obvious happenings in recent church life has been the breaking down of the wall separating the clergy from the laity and the Catholic world from the human world. It was a wall that had once divided one group from another in society and one area of an individual's life from other areas.[12] For some years now religious and lay people have been coming closer together, not only to exchange the "spiritual" services of the former for the "temporal" services of the latter but also to help each other to live a truly incarnate Christianity in their lives among other people. Thanks to new situations and personal experiences, they had come to appreciate that the Christian faith does not place believers in a world apart, that in reality it reveals to them the hope and meaningfulness imbedded in everyday life and human history, thereby committing them to give their best and their all for life and history.

This breaking down of old barriers through a deeper immersion of the gospel in the human world has had an important result for both believers and nonbelievers. It has made it possible for both to see that the gospel message really means something, and something radical, for their own lives. Consequently the church, through its message and its life, once again becomes the "sign" or "sacrament" injecting the gospel as a leavening agent into human life and placing Christ on the lampstand for all humankind to see. It becomes the sign and saving instrument of a God who has revealed himself to us as the God of life, the God-with-us, the God who revealed his radical humanity in Christ.

This aspect of the current renewal has been reinforced by a rediscovery of the "humanity" of the biblical God. The biblical God made human beings "in his image." God is interested in all the details of daily life, from work and marriage to the economy and dealings with one's fellows. Fidelity to God calls for personal initiative and a sense of responsibility. The God of the Bible takes joy in human growth and joy. God "blesses" human beings with the fruits of the earth so that we may enjoy them gratefully in the cordial and convivial company of friends and fellows. Thus God is a God who obliges his followers to place themselves in the service of their fellows who are suffering from poverty, loneliness, and oppression.

This human experience of God, rooted in the most ancient religious tradition of Israel and reinforced by prophets and sages throughout its history, reaches its most clear-cut and radical expression in Jesus of Nazareth. Jesus lives the life of a layman in the social and religious context of his day. He relativizes the fulfillment of religious obligations, relating it all to the salvation of concrete human beings. He shows a profound interest and concern for the details of people's lives. Thus, instead of relying on mere words or "religious" symbols to reveal the Father's love, he reveals that love directly and spells out the responsibility that people have toward God's coming kingdom. The "signs" that he performs for them are not cultic actions; they are human gestures designed to heal and save people suffering from wretchedness. He tells people to recognize his presence and that of the Father's love, not in the Temple, in religious rites, or in abstract contemplation, but in their suffering fellows and their community life as brothers and sisters.

This same Christian experience of God's humanity was taken up and given new impetus by Vatican II. The Council was convened in the name of a church that is here to serve human beings.[13] The church's very reason for being is to serve as a "sacrament" of the reconciliation of all people and as the seed of liberation for human reality as a whole.[14] As a sign, it must be reborn incarnate in every culture and among every people, so that it may speak their own language and save them from within.[15] In his closing address to the Council Fathers, Pope Paul VI pointed out that the Council's concern to address and serve people today did not represent a turning away from God but rather a turning toward God. Why? Because the Christian religion is a religion of love for others and service to them, focusing on the poor in particular. It is in them that we recognize the face of Christ, the face of God.[16]

Hence the church truly and effectively serves as the sign of the God of Jesus Christ *insofar as it is the concrete, accessible, and effective sign of brotherly love and service to the needy*. Or, as the 1971 Synod of Bishops put it: "Unless the Christian message of love and justice shows its effectiveness *through action in the cause of justice in the world*, it will only with difficulty gain credibility with the men of our times."[17]

THE CHURCH AS A COMMUNITY

Even supposing that the public message of the church were very much committed to those in need and to reconciliation, and that the services promoted by Christian individuals and organizations were timely and effective, we would have to say that would not suffice to make it an effective sign of human community. If it is to serve as such a sign for all humankind, then its own internal operations and relationships must be characterized by a sense of community and co-responsibility. That brings us to the final point brought out in the church's recent efforts at self-criticism. People have come to see that at the most basic levels the church does not adequately exemplify real community; and so it is not able to attract the adherence of individuals in a truly open and integrative way. It does not provide adequate channels for communication, dialogue, and collaborative effort. Its decisions often come down vertically from the top, and the heavy hand of authoritative pronouncements seems to disregard the concrete experience of human beings.

For this reason the adherence of most faithful continues to be a very passive one. When different movements and groups do arise within the Christian community, they often tend to develop along parallel lines. We do not find the contact and interaction that might keep them on the right track and make their search more fruitful. Many responsible Christians withdraw from the church, disappointed at seeing their initiatives frustrated by overly paternalistic authority. Even more serious is the fact that the church's own service to people, and its possible meaningfulness for them, is undermined and often annulled by its lack of organic structure and the absence of real communion in the plans and activities of Christians.

Here again there is another side to the story. In the last decade our church has taken numerous important steps toward self-transformation. The more or less anonymous setup of parish life, with a clergy under the uniform discipline of the hierarchy, has been giving way to a network of different communities composed of very real persons. Each has a vitality of its own, and they all have established lively ties with each other under the coordinated ministry of their clerical pastors. Much progress is still wanting, to be sure. These grassroots communities are not as lively as they might be, their mutual ties must be reinforced further, and there is room for greater pastoral coordination of an effective and respectful sort. But everywhere we see signs of Christians trying to break with the passivity and anonymity of the past. They really are trying to set up nuclear communities where the faith is truly shared, where brotherhood is concretely lived out, and where the responsibilities of service to the surrounding milieu are taken seriously. More and more these groups are feeling the need to establish ties with each other, though this process may be proceeding more slowly; they are trying to offer each other mutual support and to join together in confronting the broader challenges that society poses to the church. Finally, we cannot overlook the new attitude among many pastors of souls. They have learned how to share the life and concerns of the grassroots communities, how to offer themselves in the service of discernment and mutual coordination, thereby ministering the Spirit of Christ who is operative among the People of God.

This thrust toward a truly fraternal and communitarian church has undoubtedly been prompted by new living conditions and the crisis of solidarity in our society. But Christians and the church itself have also experienced it as a process of evangelical renewal, as a rediscovery of the "community of brothers and sisters" that the church was meant to be from the very start. Right from the beginning Jesus' disciples were called together to share a community style of life in which there would be no fathers, or masters, or rulers. All were to be brothers and sisters, bearing witness to one and the same Father. Showing love and service to each other, they were to bear witness to the love of Christ, who loved unto death. They would share in common their faith and their prayer, their joyfulness and their worldly goods, and the responsibility of their saving mission to all peoples. Sharing fellowship and responsibility as the members of one single body, they were to carry on the new life of the risen Lord and communicate it to the world.

Closer to our own day, Vatican II affirmed what the church's reason for being is. For believers and the rest of humankind it is meant to be the "sacrament," the sign and instrument as well as the active, concrete expresssion of *the community existing between human beings on the one hand and between them and God on the other.*[18] Its task is to promote *brotherhood, peace, and unity between human beings and peoples.*[19] Vatican II pointed out that the church, as the people of God, is meant to take in a multitude of races, cultures, tendencies, and abilities. But it is also to be a people of brothers and sisters, wholly animated and guided by the Spirit of Christ.[20]

The office of pastor in the church, noted the Council, must be exercised in a spirit of docility to that same Spirit. It must be in the service of church fellowship, providing discernment and cohesion to the community on its different levels.[21] Vatican II also stressed that it is legitimate for there to be different ideological tendencies among Christian individuals and groups. Not only must they respect each other and their different views. They must also *confront and dialogue with each other as they seek to be more faithful to the gospel message*, and thereby find a more satisfactory solution for the social injustice that now afflicts most human beings.[22]

These, in my opinion, are the main features of our church's concrete life and activity today. They represent an inevitable mixture of renewal and self-criticism, doctrine and practice, novel evangelical points and the historical factors conditioning our society. Through all this we can recognize the active initiative of Christ's Spirit at work. He "serves as the guiding force behind the growth and adaptation of the church in any given historical age, distributing charisms and graces so that loyalty and resemblance to its founder may continue to grow." At the same time our recognition of this fact entails a commitment for us. We must "build up the church along the original lines of the gospel message so that Christ, through it, may effect brotherhood and reconciliation."[23]

NOTES

1. In this connection one might find it instructive to compare the conclusions reached at the 1967 Santiago Synod with those reached at the sessions of the following year. They are contained in the two-volume work entitled *Iglesia de Santiago, ¿qué dices de ti misma?*, Santiago, vol. 1, 1967, especially pp. 92–116; vol. 2, 1968, especially p. 209ff.

2. See my article, "Tensiones en una Iglesia viva," *Mensaje*, June 1973; it is based primarily on the concrete experience of various lay movements.

3. Vatican II, *Lumen Gentium*, nos. 9 and 13.

4. Vatican II, *Gaudium et Spes*, no. 1.

5. 1971 Synod of Bishops, document entitled *Justice in the World*, Eng. trans., *The Pope Speaks* 16 (1972):377–89, emphasis added. Passages cited here are taken from that English translation.

6. Vatican II, *Lumen Gentium*, no. 12.

7. See ibid., no. 35.

8. Vatican II, *Gaudium et Spes*, no. 4.

9. Ibid., no. 11.

10. 1971 Synod of Bishops, *Justice in the World*, "Introduction," emphasis added.

11. Ibid., "Part Two," emphasis added.

12. The cassock of the clergyman and the Latin of the liturgy were not without significance in this connection. They symbolized a clergy living a segregated lifestyle and a religious idiom alien to people's daily lives.

13. Vatican II, *Message to Humanity* from the Council Fathers. See also *Gaudium et Spes*, nos. 3 and 93.

14. See Vatican II, *Lumen Gentium*, nos. 1 and 9; *Gaudium et Spes*, nos. 42, 45, and 89; *Nostra Aetate*, no. 1.

15. See Vatican II, *Ad Gentes*, nos. 5, 8, 10, and 12; *Gaudium et Spes*, nos. 44, 58, and 62.

16. Paul VI, Address on the religious value of the Council at the closing session, December 7, 1965.

17. 1971 Synod of Bishops, *Justice in the World*, Part Two, emphasis added.

18. See Vatican II, *Lumen Gentium*, nos. 1 and 9; *Sacrosanctum Concilium*, nos. 5 and 26.

19. See Vatican II, *Gaudium et Spes*, nos. 40, 42, 45, 77, 89, and 92; *Nostra Aetate*, no. 1.

20. See Vatican II, *Lumen Gentium*, nos. 9, 12–13, and 32; *Ad Gentes*, nos. 10–11.

21. See Vatican II, *Lumen Gentium*, nos. 18 and 32; *Christus Dominus*, no. 16; *Presbyterorum Ordinis*, no. 9.

22. See Vatican II, *Gaudium et Spes*, nos. 43 and 92; Paul VI, encyclical *Octogesima Adveniens*, nos. 31–37 and 50; 1971 Synod of Bishops.

23. Letter issued by the bishops and vicars of Santiago, May 17, 1974.

8

Liberation Theology and
New Tasks Facing Christians

Segundo Galilea (Medellín, Colombia)

My interest and involvement in liberation theology grew out of my concern for pastoral renewal in Latin America, a renewal that would be framed in terms of a truly indigenous theology. In the last decade, for the first time in our history, there emerged new lines of apostolic action that were framed in the concrete context of Latin American reality. To be more specific, they were based on concrete efforts at evangelization on the grassroots community level, on the level of what is called "popular Catholicism." We have chosen to call this pastoral effort a "liberative" one. It is not simply a new line of approach or activity in one isolated area; it is rather an all-encompassing dimension that takes in the whole mission of Christianity vis-à-vis human beings in Latin America. This new dimension poses new tasks and commitments of which earlier generations were not aware, and on which liberation theology sheds further light and clarification. It stimulates us to make sure that our work will truly be consistent with the gospel message.

On the basis of this pastoral effort and the social transformations to which it seeks to respond, we have come to realize that a

163

new situation has been created for the faith. New attitudes and lifestyles have come into being. All this represents a crisis situation, and in particular a crisis of our spirituality. The whole issue of liberation raises questions for us. It also offers us an opportunity to flesh out and "historify" our Christian spirituality, which all too often has been associated with unauthentic traditions or "ideologies."

I myself came to see that liberation theology provided important elements for elaborating the evangelical attitudes and historical responses of any new spirituality. Those of us who came to liberation theology through our concrete missionary preoccupations soon realized that this new Latin American theology was also bound to have some impact on other aspects of what is called "pastoral theology": e.g., on ecclesiology and sacramental doctrine. Liberation theology is a force pushing the Latin American church toward sociological reform of itself, and this impetus is intensifying as time goes on. That is why so much conflict now surrounds it, in my opinion.

My basic concern, then, is with evangelization. From this basic starting point, therefore, I would like to spell out certain points that must be considered if we are to give depth and solidity to liberation theology itself and the pastoral tasks inspired by it. In the first main section of this article I will examine the status of liberation theology, proving that it is solidly in line with the official church pronouncements of the 1968 Medellín Conference. In the second main section I shall try to point up certain tasks facing us on the level of doctrinal elaboration and praxis if Latin American Christianity is to faithfully follow its new theological line. Here I am referring primarily to cultural liberation and liberation from violence. In the third and final main section I shall consider what Christian faith must do if it is to offer an authentically liberative spirituality.

LIBERATION AT MEDELLIN AND SINCE

One of the major options taken by the bishops of Latin America at the 1968 Medellín Conference was their decision to accept the liberation process of their people and commit themselves to it. The presence of the church in Latin America thereby recovered the authentic socio-political dimension that had been obscured in earlier decades. In discovering that the people of Latin America were exploited, our pastoral activity rediscovered its prophetic aspect and its task of truly defending God's real plan for humankind.

The church's pastoral and prophetic commitment to liberation presumes a careful analysis of reality, but it is not to be identified with any one positive science or ideology. Christian commitment is based on the exigencies of a truly committed faith, not on any ideology. It presupposes a clear-eyed awareness of reality, of the exploitation, injustice, underdevelopment, and frustrated hopes that scar our continent.[1] In Christian and theological terms this fact is translated into such terms as a "sinful situation"[2] and "institutionalized violence."[3] The latter term is here used for the first time in an official church document. Social sin and social violence summon the church to establish solidarity with the poor and lowly and to work for their liberation from the social sinfulness that now oppresses them. This is the task entailed in our "commitment to liberation," one of the most important and urgent tasks facing the Latin American church.[4]

Both the term and the theme of liberation were used for the first time in an official church document at the Medellín Conference. Since then it has become the hallmark of Christian reflection and action in Latin America. In all honesty we must point out that the term "liberation" was not used extensively in the Medellín documents. It evolved more slowly, coming into full prominence in our Christian vocabulary only after the Medellín Conference.

The documents of Medellín follow more directly in the line of the encyclical *Populorum Progressio*, often alluding to "integral development."[5] That term, however, is practically synonymous with "liberation" in its Christian sense, and even in the Medellín documents we see the bishops moving more and more toward use of the latter term. The fact is that the term "liberation" does seem to be more humanist, more in line with the gospel message, and freer of the socio-economic connotations surrounding the term "integral development." But it attained full status in our vocabulary only in later years.

It was not only the term "liberation" that took root in the church through the Medellín Conference. As might have been expected, this notion of Christian commitment prompted theological reflection and led to the gradual elaboration of a liberation theology. In the decade of the seventies it would become the distinctive theology of Latin America, combining and synthesizing evangelization and social commitment. It would also attempt to combine soteriology with Latin American "political theology," thereby getting beyond dualism while still preserving the autonomy of the socio-political realm on the one hand and the transcendence of salvation on the other.

Liberation theology marks a new era in the history of the church in Latin America. Its original and distinctive feature is that it considers the present juncture in Latin American history as an intrinsic feature of its own work. Differing from European schools of theological thought in this respect, it is the first specifically Latin American theology because the distinctive situation of Latin America is part of its intrinsic content and because its methodological approach begins with an analysis of this concrete situation with the help of the social sciences.

However, neither the analysis of reality nor the social sciences constitute the specific and defining quality of liberation theology as such. Like any theology, its formal nature lies in the fact that it is reflection on the faith. The other factors are its starting point and its raw material insofar as theology, being reflection on the faith, must reflect not only on God's revelation in his verbal message but also on God's revelation in historical realities. While not denigrating the many other tasks confronting present-day theology, liberation theology stresses one task that is of the utmost urgency in Latin America, i.e., reflection on the concrete experience of faith as lived by Christian individuals and communities in today's situation in Latin America, with a view to promoting evangelization.

At present liberation theology is not a homogeneous school of thought but a developing current with varied directions and emphases. Much material has been produced in the last five years, most of it in the form of articles and documents rather than books. To identify and evaluate it properly, we must make a clear distinction between two basic types of material: the material that is properly theological in content and approach on the one hand, and the material embodying the reflection of Christians on socio-political issues on the other hand. The latter is not really liberation theology, though it often gains wide publicity because it comes from involved and committed Christians. Failure to distinguish between these two types of material has been prejudicial to liberation theology in the strict sense. It has been subjected to criticism that really applies to the other type of material.. For example, it has been accused of reducing theology to a purely political dimension without properly theological or pastoral aspects.

The various currents of liberation theology tend to focus on different Christian themes or to have their own particular emphases. Some focus more on socio-political issues and the present situation in history; others are primarily concerned with biblical and other specifically religious themes. Some see liberation as a specific application of the "theology of salvation"; others see present-day Latin America as the proper starting point, and liberation theology our specific version of "political theology." Be that as it may, any authentic liberation theology must entail a rapprochement between the salvation brought by Jesus Christ and liberation in all its forms (e.g., cultural, social, political, and religious).

Liberation theology is rooted in three assumptions that form the Christian's view of the present juncture in Latin American history: (1) The present situation is one in which the vast majority of Latin Americans live in a state of underdevelopment and unjust dependence; (2) viewed in Christian terms, this is a "sinful situation"; (3) hence it is the duty of Christians in conscience, and of the church in its pastoral activity, to commit themselves to efforts to overcome this situation.

The first assumption sees unjust dependence as one of the basic causes for the present misery and poverty of our peoples—though not the only cause. On the most obvious level this dependence is socio-economic; on a deeper and more subtle level it is political and cultural. The cultural level is of primary importance. Theology starts off by accepting the fact of dependence. It does not analyze this situation according to one specific line of thought, nor is it bound to any one particular ideological interpretation of it. It is not tied to any specific "theory of dependence," be it Marxist or not. Theology starts off with the concrete fact of dependence, not with any theory about it. This enables it to avoid becoming an "ideologized" theology, to stay on the prophetic level where Christians of differing ideological bent can truly come together. When theological formulations about liberation have started off from a specific socio-political analysis or option, they have always fallen prey to ideology and ended up justifying a partisan position.

The second step is to interpret the unjust concrete situation as a sinful situation. Like other people today seeking authentic justice, Christians see unjust situations as violations of human rights. But then they go further and also see them as offenses against God and his loving plan. The unjust situation is an attack on God himself. Here is where liberation theology makes two peculiar contributions of its own to theological reflection. First, it sees sin taking concrete shape not only in individual actions but also in unjust societal structures of all sorts. In the latter case we may not be able to blame any one individual; we must hold society itself responsible for the sinful situation. It is what might be called the sin of Latin American society embodied in history. Second, liberation theology takes the reality of "sin," which is such a traditional part of Christianity, and makes it the starting point for its own theological reflection. Its intent, therefore, is deeply apostolic because its socio-political observations are linked up with this sinful situation and the salvation brought by Jesus Christ.

That leads to the third step: an appeal to the conscience of individual Christians and the church. They are asked to undertake the process of liberation in all its aspects and to work for its success.

The major themes of liberation theology are worked out on the basis of these three underlying assumptions and their pastoral import. Traditional biblical themes pointing up God's effort to save human beings are reinterpreted in the light of Latin American realities. The basic aim here is to show that God's saving plan entails an intrinsic relationship between economic, cultural, and socio-political liberation on the one hand and Jesus Christ's eschatological salvation. The theological themes treated here include these typical ones: the relationship between creation and salvation, and hence between humanization, development, liberation, and eschatological salvation; hope as a certainty that the eschatological kingdom is coming and its features and conditions must be anticipated here and now in society; salvation history and profane history as one single history, with the resultant conclusion that salvation is being played out here and now in the historical processes of Latin America; the liberation of the poor as the privileged point where this challenge is accepted and lived; loving service to the poor and their liberation as salvific encounter with the Lord (Matt. 25:30); finally, the establishment of justice here on earth as a prophetic sign of God's promises being fulfilled and of the fact that the kingdom is already here in our midst.

The whole theological theme of a liberation that is brought by a saving God, and that is anticipated in the precarious signs of cultural and socio-political liberation, is a broad and ample one. It also needs to be explored more deeply and completely. Here again we meet pluralism. Some stress one theme, some stress another. Others prefer to focus on some global or comprehensive perspective: e.g., on the biblical theme of the Exodus and its politico-religious interpretation, which was hinted at in the Medellín Conference.[6]

Liberation theology has provoked criticism and outright opposition, both in Latin America and elsewhere. It is not easy to evaluate the criticisms, to weigh their legitimacy and their positive contributions. The reasons behind them are complex and varied, as are the objects of the criticism. Therefore certain basic distinctions are in order.

First of all, we noted earlier that liberation theology is not a uniform school of thought; it is a pluralistic current running within the basic channels we have sketched above. Some stress the religious aspects of liberation while others stress its temporal aspects. This paves the way for a confrontation which, in my opinion, is very positive and prompts us to explore all the varied forms of liberation more deeply.

Second, some criticisms of liberation theology are really aimed at views that cannot be regarded as liberation theology in any adequate sense. I mentioned earlier that we should make a clear distinction between liberation theology proper and the welter of documents published by Christians about socio-political topics. The latter cannot be regarded as representative of current Latin American theology in the strict sense. By their very nature they tend to embody people's spontaneous impressions and judgments rather than scientific analysis or scholarly study. As estimations of the moment, they are more than a little debatable. However, many critics and opponents of liberation theology lump both types of writing together in their attacks. This gives rise to a great deal of confusion, which is probably compounded in the case of those viewing Latin America from the outside. For example, some people would tend to equate the final document issued by the convention of Christians for Socialism[7] with Gutiérrez's authentically theological work entitled *A Theology of Liberation*.

Third, this confusion of levels has adverse repercussions on the very concept of liberation. We began by examining its Christian import as first brought out by the Medellín Conference. That is the meaning that it has for our theologians in their work. Many

critics, swayed mostly by the mass of pseudo-theological literature, conclude that liberation comes down to some sort of political
reductionism.

Fourth, we must realize that some forms of liberation theology
do tend to be "ideologized" for one reason or another. They may
start out by identifying themselves with one particular ideological analysis of reality or assuming one particular theory of dependence. In such a case their theology loses its "catholic" features
and serves to interpret only one particular group of revolutionary
Christians or one leftist ideology. Here criticism is in order so long
as it recognizes that it is dealing with only one brand of liberation
theology and does not include all of liberation theology in its
attack.

Fifth, one current of the "ideologized" liberation theology just
mentioned tends to rely on Marxist categories for its interpretation of liberation, dependence, politics, and liberative commitment. This current is a rather limited one, but it leads some people
to suspect liberation theology as a whole. They fear that it has
been infiltrated by Marxism and that it leads to "horizontalism,"
pure politicism, and a merely temporal humanism.

Needless to say, it is quite unfair to extend that criticism to
liberation theology as a whole. No serious theologian in Latin
America who is truly representative of our current Christian
thinking goes along with that approach. As I noted earlier, the
major lines of liberation theology go back to the Medellín Conference. They are oriented primarily around evangelization rather
than politics, and they have an essential reference to sin and the
integral salvation brought by Jesus Christ.

My feeling, then, is that much of the present opposition to liberation theology is due to faulty logical jumps and a lack of basic
information. I also think that one of the nontheological reasons
for the opposition to liberation theology is the division that has
cropped up between Christians since the Medellín Conference.
Medellín inaugurated a new era in Latin American Christianity,
but many still do not realize that. It gave impetus to a specifically
indigenous line of theological thinking and to commitment to history and liberation. Unfortunately that whole set of problems is
dividing Christians more than Vatican II did. Many see liberation
theology as an "abuse of the Medellín Conference" and a fomentor
of "radical" commitments. If we add the fact that Latin American
governments are now tending to be more repressive and less

willing to let their people take an active part in bringing about change, we can see that liberation theology faces new problems on that whole front. To many politicians and rulers it is the badge of a pushy "progressivist" church.

All that jeopardizes the profoundly pastoral and prophetic content of the Medellín Conference and the theological current that issued from it. In my opinion, it represents a graver danger to the church's mission than any potential or alleged distortions of liberation theology itself.

URGENT TASKS FACING CHRISTIANS

There are many different aspects involved in the liberation of people in Latin America today. My feeling is that the Christian contribution to this liberation would be decisive in two major areas. One has to do with cultural liberation, the other with liberation from violence.

Cultural Liberation

Cultural dependence and alienation is one of the worst consequences of economic domination and its attendant socio-political domination. This holds true for the Third World in general and for Latin America in particular, the latter being part of the cultural family of the West. Unfortunately the Medellín Conference did not pay enough attention to the problem of cultural domination, and that void is still evident in subsequent theological reflection as well as Christian concern for liberation and commitment. It is reinforced by the thrust of political ideologies, of Marxism in particular, which tend to overlook or sacrifice the cultural dimension for the sake of economic or socio-political concerns.

The growing cultural alienation of Latin America is obvious enough. The most alarming symptoms of this fact can be described more or less as follows. First of all, we see the adoption of development models that are out of line with, or even alien to, the socio-cultural reality of our people and nations. Thanks to the mass media in particular, these models are imposed on us by the "developed" countries. This proves beneficial to their own economic imperialism, generates false values that are alien to our indigenous culture, and provokes frustrating, alienating desires. A false model of development intensifies our dependence and does not allow us to grow along our own cultural lines. We are nurtured on the ideology of bourgeois capitalism in most cases, or on the ideology of Marxism in the case of Cuba.

This means that an alien cultural ideology is imposed on us along with the alien developmental model. The genius and distinctive character of our peoples and nations is not really noted or interpreted, even in what are called popular institutions. This implies a criticism of Latin American leftist movements and suggests one intrinsic reason for their failures. It also implies criticism of strategic formulations of the issue (e.g., armed subversion), and of certain serious oversights in so-called populist ideologies (e.g., the fact of popular religiosity).

The end result is that the people of Latin America are driven to inconsistent and alienating lifestyles. Their own proper values fall into disuse and are not appreciated, so that they lose their national and cultural identity. In extreme cases (e.g., the native Indians of the backlands and other minority groups) this form of dependence is leading to cultural genocide.

Faced with this situation, we must "invent" a throughly and radically Latin American approach to development and liberation. This imperative has become all the more clear in the light of more recent historical developments. Consider the crisis in politics today, specifically the crisis confronting political parties with their lost prestige. That is almost universally the case in Latin America today. In addition, there is the fact that the common people of Latin America have almost no share of political power; that their active participation in power seems to be a dead issue. Even in those instances where the government displays some social concern, government power is tending to become more and more centralized. While it may be used in the service of the people, they themselves do not enjoy any decisive share of power.

This basic political tendency is evident in both capitalist and socialist systems. Here we see a surprising convergence. In more or less subtle forms, government everywhere is tending toward a powerful centralized government based on what is now called "the military-industrial complex" and, in some instances, on a single political party. The whole problem of power and the "idolatry of power" is now a grave one in Latin America. It is a serious cultural issue, imposing the task of liberation upon us. In terms of this basic and pervasive tendency there is an amazing similarity between Brazil and Cuba, though they seem to lie at opposite ends of the ideological spectrum.

In such a situation the model for a just society on our continent remains to be invented. If this is to be done, it seems we cannot dispense with the cultural values of our peoples. They must be allowed to express those values freely, and these values in turn must be allowed to prevail at every level of popular life. In particular we must hear from those who have been silenced and oppressed. The common people created their own folklore and their own forms of popular religion. They managed to defend their own way of life in the face of every obstacle. To the extent that they win their cultural liberation, they will be able to create social and political forms ensuring a new and juster society.

Such cultural liberation may well be more difficult because it has to do with an "ethos," with a change of mentality. Nothing is more critical than that which has to do with a culture and its healthy inner development. Through its own values it must keep growing and changing, engaging in self-criticism when that is necessary. This means that people must be aware and free to express themselves, which raises the whole challenge of consciousness-raising. Unfortunately we often get a mere caricature of *"concientización"*; it becomes little more than an ideological politicization. Political impositions and cultural oppression are the ever-present dangers threatening authentic consciousness-raising. Consciousness-raising means moving from an uncritical, conformist outlook based on feelings of cultural inferiority to a creative outlook that is aware of its own identity and critical of all forms of cultural, ideological, and political alienation, however subtle they may be.

Christianity—the church—possesses the ethical substrate of any authentic consciousness-raising in the values which it transmits through the preaching of the gospel. Hence it possesses the ethical basis for any authentic cultural liberation that will prompt people to accept their own vocation in history and build a society based on their own values. The gospel message gives stimulus and support to such values. It supports the vocation which people have to unleash the creativity of their culture and build their own utopia. Because the gospel itself is not bound to any one cultural form or ideology, it can accompany any culture in its process of liberation, helping it to undergo purification without succumbing to alienation *(Gaudium et Spes,* no. 58).

Such is the case, of course, when evangelization meets the ideal. For that to happen, however, Catholicism must engage in constant self-criticism, examining its historical embodiments and the concrete effects of its message; for it is ever tempted to identify itself with the dominant culture and the prevailing ideology. When it gives in to that temptation, we get decadent forms of Christianity that are in subtle complicity with the prevailing culture or ideology and that obstruct liberation rather than fostering it. That raises the whole problem of liberative evangelization, of which the Latin American church is well aware today.

By its very nature authentic evangelization will stimulate human beings to be the active and free agents of their own Christian vocation within the framework and spirit of a given culture. Christianity brings out the dignity and value of every people and culture by highlighting its ultimate import and deeper meaning. It reveals the presence of Christ in every fellow human and the "seeds of the divine word" in every culture. By proclaiming that the salvation of human beings and of cultures takes place in history, it provides people with the ultimate reason and justification for their responsibility to history. It thus inspires them to the active work of growth and commitment. To the extent that Christianity has managed to free itself from the dominant ideologies and cultures, it will criticize them as well as the centers of power and dehumanizing models or strategies for development. In that way it will clear away the most deeply rooted obstacles to the cultural liberation of the Latin American people.

Liberation from Violence

Violence is certainly the most radical challenge facing Latin America. The current exploitation of workers, peasants, and racial minorities in Latin America bears witness to economic, political, social, and cultural oppression. This unjust situation was labelled "institutionalized violence" by the Medellín Conference.[8] It is the most deep-rooted sociological source for the resultant repressive violence on the one hand and subversive violence on the other. Both types of violence are symptoms of the established disorder. The temptation to subversive violence, in particular, is viewed as symptomatic of the existing situation. While many tend to regard it as the most obvious or even the only kind of violence, the Medellín Conference saw it in slightly different terms: "One should not abuse the patience of a people that for years has borne a situation that would not be acceptable to any one with any degree of awareness of human rights."[9]

The pervasive violence on our continent is leading to political systems that are more and more repressive. They are both a cause and effect of the pervasive situation of violence. The vicious circle created by the various symptoms and forms of this situation constitutes the worst possible oppression of human beings. We must break that circle. Liberation from violence is one of the most important tasks confronting Christianity today. This is all the more true because ideologies and sociological analyses cannot cure, cannot redeem, the roots of this pervasive violence oppressing so many of our fellow human beings. They are inadequate to the task because the various forms of human and historical injustice alone are not the underlying causes of the violence. They operate in collusion with hatred, passion, and sectarian intolerance, with all the destructive tendencies that dwell in the human heart. Violence is a collective kind of sin, or a collective temptation if you prefer, and as such it must be redeemed at its very roots. Here we have an open door for the message of Christian liberation.

There is no thoroughgoing redemption, no radical liberation, without *the cross*. The cross is the sign of Christ's suffering love, and we Christians are called to incorporate ourselves into it. Only it destroys sin, which lies at the core of violent situations. Here the church and liberation theology have a very specific and indispensable contribution to make. They tell us that violence cannot be overcome with purely human means or with other forms of violence. It must be redeemed, and there is no redemption without suffering and the cross. They tell us that through hope the suffering of people subjected to violence, as well as that of those committed to their Christian liberation, serves as the seed of salvation and liberation in justice.

Proclamation of the mystery of the cross is an essential component of evangelization. But it is not enough either. It must be accompanied by the efforts of Christians on behalf of justice and peace, which are the happy result when violence is overcome. In our present conflict-ridden situation, these efforts will often take the form of *moral pressure* exerted either by committed Christian groups or the official church. The suffering of the cross will thus be complemented by the work of prophecy.

Prophetic proclamation is not just denunciation. First and foremost it is *the proclamation of the individual's and society's vocation to brotherhood, pardon, and reconciliation.* In this respect the truth of faith corresponds with the deepest underlying tendencies of every society; it could not do otherwise. Throughout the course of history, society is racked by a twofold dialectical tension; it is the temporal expression of the dialectical tension between grace and sin in salvation history.

The first dialectical tension here is that between the master and the slave. It is the wellspring of exploitation, domination of some people by others, and violence. Marx took this particular dialectics from Hegel and applied it to economic relationships, to capitalism in particular. As we all know, it has been amply popularized and preached by Marxism, though in a wholly one-sided sense. For Marxism has forgotten, or chosen to disregard, the other dialectical tension that is also revealed by history and confirmed by faith.

The second dialectics is that of parent and child, and that between brothers. It leads to solidarity, union, and reconciliation. Thanks to Christ, this second dialectics is destined to triumph over servitude and to find expression in historical forms of solidarity and brotherhood. Christianity denounces the sin involved in the first dialectics and proclaims the certain hope that humankind can achieve the second, thereby motivating people to work toward it.

The history of humankind is stamped with the impress of this twofold dialectics. On the one hand human beings seek to exploit each other; on the other hand they yearn to be brothers and sisters. We can see this concretely in the history of our own Latin America where some exploited the native population and others tried valiantly to defend them. Liberation signifies the objective triumph of brotherhood over servitude through a long historical process. Authentic liberation is not a cloak thrown over reality by the privileged to hide injustice and maintain a state of established disorder. Christian reconciliation, the basis of brotherhood and peace, is the product of justice and people's willingness to attain it. In situations that are riddled with conflict and openly unjust, as is the case in Latin America, reconciliation presupposes a struggle for justice and the use of moral and prophetic pressure to obtain it.

That is not all, however. Reconciliation also presupposes *pardon*. It is not enough to have achieved justice or to be on the way toward achieving it. That process is inevitably marked by confrontation and conflict. People offend one another and become adversaries, making accusations and charges against each other. That does not simply disappear when some agreement is reached or objective justice is established. Vindictiveness and the desire for revenge may perdure. Christian pardon is the only thing capable of overcoming this attitude and achieving a reconciliation that is not only formal and juridical but also fraternal. Vivified by love,

Christian reconciliation is the only stable kind. Itself the result of justice and pardon, it leads to solidarity, brotherhood, and peace. Reconciling love makes the difference between a just society and a fraternal one.

Christian liberation, then, implies reconciliation; hence liberation theology implies a *theology of reconciliation*. Going beyond "ideologized" formulations, it roots in the grand evangelical attitudes to which we have been alluding: intense struggle for justice, pardon, universal brotherhood, and the cross.

A theology of reconciliation will also enable us to revivify the significance of the sacraments within a liberation context. That is particularly true of Penance and the Eucharist, which are aptly described as the "sacraments of reconciliation." In them we receive reconciliation as the victorious power of the risen Christ. In reconciling us with God, Christ injects into society and history the mystery of pardon and mercy as gratuitous gifts that cannot be attained by human effort alone. These gratuitous gifts fill up the gaps and crevices that lie on the road to the justice and solidarity sought by human beings.

TOWARD LIBERATION SPIRITUALITY

Liberation from violence and cultural liberation presuppose a new ethico-cultural content, a transformed mentality. As I noted above, Christianity can and should inspire and support those transformations to the extent that it transmits a spirituality. Such a spirituality would offer attitudes and values that are rooted in the gospel message and that are capable of being fleshed out in history through the commitments imposed by our option for the oppressed and the lowly.

Thus liberation theology and the concrete tasks imposed by it cannot help but raise the whole issue of a *liberation spirituality*. This is at the root of any change in the Catholic mentality and any complete liberation from violence. Such a spirituality is profoundly traditional, and hence ever innovative. All spirituality is essentially "evangelical" and "historical": evangelical because it is identical with the Christian way of life, which is to follow the crucified and risen Christ through his message transmitted by the church; historical because that message is heard and understood today in the light of certain emphases and exigencies that are based on the way in which salvation in history takes shape today. Today, as always, Christian commitment is the result of faith and love; but it is also the result of having "translated" and incarnated that faith and love in the concrete history that we must live. In our case, then, "liberation spirituality" might also be called "Latin American spirituality."

Emphasis on the Poor and the Sinful

The basic intuition of such a spirituality is that the liberation of the poor is an exigency posed to every Christian as the primary and privileged challenge. This spiritual exigency reveals to us the gospel content of the term "poor" (e.g., "Blessed are the poor"), which is far richer and more profound than any merely sociological definition or focus on material externals. At bottom it refers to freedom of heart, liberation at its loftiest form for the attainment of love. It has to do with "being" rather than "having." Thus the one who is uniquely blessed is Christ, and the "poor" person shares in this radical blessedness. Every day the poor person renounces all that he or she possesses in order to be Christ's disciple (Luke 14:33).

By the same token, however, a spirituality of liberation will also seek to "historify" the poor in Latin America in terms of sociological reality—without undermining the evangelical meaning of the term "poor." Otherwise we are left with angelism. When Jesus was asked by someone who his brother and neighbor was, Jesus historified and concretized the issue by translating it into the concrete situation of this day—in the parable of the Good Samaritan (Luke 10:29–37). Today we must translate the notion of the blessed poor into concrete sociological terms also. That is the contribution that liberation theology is making.

From its standpoint the poor among us are identified with social classes such as peasants and laborers. The poor include racial classes such as blacks and native Indians, and also all those alienated on the margins of society: the lower proletariat in the cities, the unemployed, and the disabled of all sorts. While that does not exhaust the Christian meaning of the term "poor," those people are the privileged subjects of liberation. They are the "least brothers" of whom Jesus speaks (Matt. 25:40). In his eyes "the poor" are all those who are somehow denigrated by the rest of society (Matt. 18:10), who depend on others and have no power over their own destiny (Matt. 10:42), who suffer from want and oppression unjustly, or perhaps even justly (Matt. 25:31 ff.). That is why even those in prison and exile are included under the term.

All these people require the privileged service of the Christian community, which nevertheless remains open to love in all its universality. It is the service stemming from a faith that enables us to see Christ in them: "As often as you did it for one of my least brothers, you did it for me" (Matt. 25:40). Such service is a real encounter with the Lord, hence a wellspring of spiritual experience and contemplative prayer. Christ's identification with the poor is not simply a juridical one, so that when we serve the poor it is "as if" we were serving him. In some mysterious way the identification is true and real, as the experience of the church's saints makes clear.

Here liberation spirituality touches upon a point that is original and of the essence of Christianity: i.e., that love for God is inseparable from love for neighbor; that personal encounter with Christ cannot help but lead us to serve other human beings and discern in them the ultimate reason for their dignity and radical liberty.

There is another category of human beings that is an equally privileged object of Christian liberation: i.e., sinners. They, too, can hope for salvation; and the proclamation of that fact and that hope is also an essential component of evangelization. As Jesus tells us: "I have not come to invite the self-righteous to a change of heart, but sinners" (Luke 5:32). Just as we must incarnate the idea of "the poor" without draining it, so we can and must do something similar with the notion of "sinner" on our continent. In liberation terms they are the exploiters and those who act unjustly. A message of liberation is addressed to them also, though in different terms. They must undergo conversion and become poor, abetting the liberation of the poor rather than hindering it. They must become poor along the lines spelled out by Jesus: "None of you can be my disciple if he does not renounce all his possessions" (Luke 14:33). The point is illustrated in the parable of the heavy-eating rich man and the poor Lazarus. Thus the "liberation of the rich" also has its place in Latin American theology and spirituality. Such liberation is possible for them insofar as they are willing to become poor. This means that the church, in its work of evangelization, must utter the summons to conversion from the basic standpoint of identification with the poor and their significance in salvation history rather than identification with the rich and their hold on power.

Ecclesiology, Contemplation, and Praxis

This brings us to another spiritual demand: evangelical and sociological poverty for Christians and the official church. This is an essential point in liberation theology, not a mere appendix. We are brought to realize that serving sinners and the lowly means more than just working on their behalf. The church must continually work to make itself a poor and lowly servant, following in Christ's footsteps.

This raises specifically *ecclesiological questions* concerning the church and liberation as well as the church and the people. They are Latin American questions in this case, including such issues as the following: the church's visible establishment among the poor as a sign of salvation; its relationship with power centers and the meaning and use of power in the church itself; evangelization as an activity flowing out of poverty and a critico-historical awareness of society; the problem of liberty in the Christian community itself; and the reform of church structures.

Latin American ecclesiology is confronted with a challenge and historic opportunity that is almost unique in the present-day world; i.e., to vest itself in the evangelical qualities of service to the poor and service to sinners. The opportunity is unique to it because only on our continent do we find two converging facts together: (1) the fact that the masses on our continent are poor and in need of liberation; (2) the fact that our church still has a great deal of social and cultural influence, so that its mission can be highly significant in the cause of justice. The possibility of the church and the poor offering each other mutual support and enrichment is uniquely present on the continent of Latin America.

Another fundamental intuition of liberation spirituality is the rehabilitation of *Christian contemplation* as a font of liberative praxis and brotherly service. If our encounter with the poor and lowly is a form of real encounter with the Lord and the transcendence of "the other," it is because the Lord himself has already been encountered in the Christian's experience of contemplative prayer. Only if we sincerely seek out Jesus as a person revealed in the signs of faith will we be able to find him revealing himself in history through other human beings. Only our contemplative experience of the divine absolute will lead us to see the absolute in our neighbor. But conversion to God does take place through conversion to other people, and particularly to the most lowly.

Liberation spirituality, then, leads us toward a historical and incarnate form of contemplation where the values of faith are verified in praxis. It is here that Christianity and its contemplative practice part ways with every other religion or ideology: i.e., insofar as its values are verified in history. Contemplation thereby becomes liberative praxis; charity thereby attains historical efficacy.

So this sprituality insists on *liberative praxis*. This is an activity that transforms individuals, groups, and society as a whole—each in their own way—for the benefit of the exploited. This Christian praxis may be pastoral, educational, social, or political, depending on the given situation. Today it represents one of the most authentic ways of living out Christian charity in the concrete. The various communities of the church, being public signs of love, must realize that life has to be effective and historical, that their contemplative faith must also be historical and committed in that direction.

In a society riddled with the dialectics of conflict and reconciliation, Christian charity assumes *solidarity*. The solidarity of a love that ever remains open to pardon and universality is a characteristic feature of a liberative spirituality. Solidarity here means solidarity with the oppressed, first of all. We must not only share their situation, in different ways of course, but also and primarily accompany them in their struggle for justice and their ascent to liberation. Amid many different situations and possibilities this charity based on solidarity will lead people to accept misunderstanding, persecution, loneliness, frustration, and other forms of suffering as ways of identifying with the redemptive cross of Christ. At this level Christians are akin to the prophets of old, and their commitment takes on the features of the *prophetic task*. They take after Moses and Elijah, contemplatives absorbed in the absolute of God who served their people at the same time. Keeping their people firm in their hope, they were able to endure humiliation because of the strength that they had received from their contemplation of the Invisible (Heb. 11:26–27). To reiterate something said earlier, the radically evangelical attitudes that go hand in hand with the painful process of Christian liberation and redemption from violence are contemplation, prophecy, and the cross.

A Spirituality Grounded on Hope

The soul of this liberative spirituality is a basic and symbolic attitude, namely, *hope*. Hope is the confidence that the history of Latin America is an integral part of the realization of God's plan, which is seen as a promise. God's whole revelation is a promise of integral salvation and of something better. The promise is gradually being fulfilled in history, with its dialectics of grace and sin. Thus it ever remains ambiguous and precarious, reaching its definitive fulfillment only in the parousia. No moment in history can fully embody it or exhaust its content.

For this reason the Christian remains ever open to the future. History means moving on from one horizon to the next, from one provisional situation to the next, toward a future that is ever new. In the eyes of Christians the gospel message never means settling down comfortably in the present realization of Christ's promise. It means an ongoing process of constant renewal and ever new promises. This openness to the future that characterizes Christian spirituality includes a certain detachment from the present and a radical criticism of any here-and-now situation that claims to be the ideal. A refusal to settle down in the present and a willingness to criticize every here-and-now situation are characteristic of a liberative spirituality.

Faithful to God's promise, the people of hope believe that things that seem impossible of realization now will be possible in the future through the power of God. They do not give up hope in Christian liberty, reconciliation, and universal brotherhood: "We do not fix our gaze on what is seen but on what is unseen" (2 Cor. 4:18; see Heb. 1:11ff.).

This provides the efforts of Christians with an inexhaustible source of inspiration and optimism, for it is rooted not only in human resources but also in the power of Christ.

Hope also means a willingness and readiness to glimpse the signs of what is coming in the future. Openly disposed toward them, Christians are willing to give a whole new direction to their lives when they come. Holding this spiritual outlook, Christians are convinced that their work on behalf of liberation and brotherhood is work toward a real goal rather than some utopia: "This hope will not leave us disappointed" (Rom. 5:4).

Here hoping means having confidence in the people of Latin America: in their culture, their region, their religiosity, and their ability to create a better society. It means confidence in their ability to become the active agents of their own liberation, to do what others before them could not or did not do, to find alternatives and approaches that had not been foreseen by any political analysis. It was not without reason that the bishops of Latin America concluded the Medellín Conference with a message of hope: "We have faith in God, in men, in the values and future of Latin America."[10]

NOTES

1. Medellín Conference documents (see entry under the anthologies in Appendix II of this volume), "Justice," nos. 1–2; "Peace," nos. 1–13.

2. Ibid., "Peace," no. 1.

3. Ibid., no. 16.

4. Ibid., "Introduction to the Final Documents," nos. 4–6; "Justice," nos. 3–5; "Peace," nos. 22–30.

5. Ibid., "Introduction to the Final Documents," nos. 4–6; "Justice," nos. 11, 15.

6. Ibid., "Introduction to the Final Documents," no. 6.

7. See anthology entitled *Christians and Socialism* in Appendix II of this volume.

8. Medellín Conference documents, "Peace," no. 16.

9. Ibid.

10. Ibid., "Message to the Peoples of Latin America," closing words.

9

Historical and Philosophical Presuppositions for Latin American Theology

Enrique D. Dussel (Mendoza, Argentina)

Liberation theology arose in Latin America out of the revolutionary praxis of numerous Christians committedly involved with the people of our continent. The following reflections start off from that praxis on both the individual and community level. They seek not only to sum up what has been achieved so far but also to indicate certain approaches that might help us to take further steps forward. In addition, the editor of this volume asked me to provide an autobiographical section that would illustrate how particular problems arose in a given concrete context. So I shall also add a few comments on personal, regional, and national experiences that might help to clarify the genesis of a theology. Europeans are so far removed from the day-to-day life of the "periphery" that there is every reason to point up the existential distance and the distinct Christian experience of Latin America. As the reader will see later, our experience is *analogically* distinct.

My treatment is divided into two main sections. The first is genetic and epistemological in character. It seeks to describe the genesis of an approach that begins from personal experience and ends with a discussion of the difference between the *univocal* universality of theology on the one hand and its *analogous* catholicity (*mundialidad* or *catolicidad*) on the other. The second main section is focused around Latin American history. Using precise categories worked out on a philosophical level, I shall propose a discourse centered around four specific issues: theology in the strict sense, pedagogy, politics, and theologal erotics. My reflections, then, seek to ponder our "peripheral" reality from the standpoint of Christian praxis in Latin America.

THE ANALOGICAL CATHOLICITY OF THEOLOGY

In a recent article for Concilium I offered a synthesis that I shall not repeat here.[1] The concluding section of that article alluded to the theme I wish to treat here. European theology is not universally valid in its univocal or dominating sense; but neither are theologies equivocal, or valid for their own region alone. We must recover the *analogical* sense of a catholic theology. The Greek term *kata holon* means "in terms of the whole or the totality"; in our context that "totality" or "whole" is eschatological, worldwide, and respectful of the inalienable exteriority of each individual, people, and region.

Conditions Making a Specific Theology Possible

The factors that have made possible the theology that is now operative in Latin America are quite varied and go back a long way. Here I shall focus on one without meaning to suggest that it is either the only factor or even the most important one. The "theme" of liberation is as old as the Judeo-Christian tradition itself (see Exod. 3:8); it is also as old as Latin America. In his testament written in 1564, Bartolomé de Las Casas (1474–1566), the Latin American prophet, had this to say: "God deigned to choose me as his minister ... to try to restore all those peoples of what we call the Indies ... to the pristine freedom of which they have been unjustly robbed, and to *liberate* them from the violent death which they are still forced to endure."[2]

The "praxis" of liberation goes back just as far in our history, if not further. It begins with that Franciscan friar, a lay brother, who arrived in the Caribbean toward the end of the fifteenth century. And though it was frustrated by ever new domination, it

was still carried on by successive waves of heroic figures: Domini-
cans inspired by Las Casas, numerous bishops and missionaries,
the Jesuit founders of the Reductions, and the holy figures who
worked among the Indians, the blacks, and the creoles. The praxis
of liberation has always been present in Latin America. Perhaps it
never shined so brightly in our colonial Christian period
(1492–1808) as it did in the case of that descendent of the Incas,
Tupac Amaru (1738–1781). His liberation praxis was at once Latin
American, populist, and Christian. His rebellion was grounded in
"our sacred Catholic religion " and was intended to "suppress
countless injustices."³ Subjected to atrocious tortures and tied to
four horses for the final trial of death, he exclaimed: "I am the only
and sole conspirator . . . because I sought to *liberate* the people
from such tyranny" (May 15, 1781).

The same traits can be found in the liberation praxis of the
curate, Father Hidalgo. Bearing the standard of the Virgin of
Guadalupe, he proclaimed the cause of his people's liberty before
an army of Indians: "The land for those who work it! " (1809). As
Octavio Paz points out: "Our populist leaders, humble priests,
. . . possess a deeper sense of reality and are better at hearing
what the people say to them in muted half-tones."⁴

Since our political emancipation, which began in 1809, there
have been many movements of a popular and grassroots sort. One
which was highly significant in terms of liberation was the 1910
revolution in Mexico: "The Mexican revolution is an event which
breaks in upon our history as an authentic *revelation of our
being.*"⁵ That same irruption of an oppressed people will find expression in the Brazil of Getulio Vargas, the Argentina of Juan
Perón, the Cuba of Fidel Castro, the 1968 revolution in Peru, and
so forth. Obviously enough the liberation praxis directed against
Spain was different from that which would be directed against
England or the United States; but it all is part of a liberation
history that never reaches completion.

I spent the first years of my own life in a small village of no more
than three thousand inhabitants. It lay near the Argentinian
Andes, about 150 kilometers from the city of Mendoza. It was
steppe terrain such as you might find on the *altiplano* of Peru or in
Israel itself. I can recall the wrinkled faces of men and women in
the fields and the wretched little huts of the Indians and mestizos.
The poverty filled my early childhood with sadness. You would
have to see some Arab village along the Mediterranean to appreciate what I am saying here. *Poverty was a primeval experience*

for me. When I was brought to the big city, Buenos Aires, I would long nostalgically for the land, the horses, and the grapevines of my village. On returning to Mendoza, the provincial capital of the interior, I experienced the internal dependence to be found in a neocolonial nation.

Catholic Action of the Italian variety was my first personal experience with Christian praxis in childhood and early youth. Founder of the *Movimiento Guías* (because Mendoza is also mountainous and guides are useful), I also took part in university movements and the Christian Democratic Party. My earning of a licentiate in philosophy and my profound experience of serious personal responsibilities in my youth would be followed by ten years in Europe and Israel. From Spain I came to know Latin America as a totality from the "outside." After winning my doctorate in philosophy in Madrid, in the midst of a completely traditional neo-Scholasticism, I left for Israel. There I engaged in two years of manual labor with Paul Gauthier. I did carpentry work in Nazareth and fished on Lake Gennesareth for the Ginnosar Kibbutz.

It was there that I began to write my book on Semitic humanism, *El humanismo semita,* which was to be the first in a study of history that would culminate with Latin America. Upon returning to Europe in 1961, I began my study of theology in Pontigny. I pursued this study at the Catholic Institute in Paris, in Mainz (where I studied church history under Lortz), and in Münster. Continuing with my philosophy, I also obtained a doctorate in history from the Sorbonne with a thesis on the Hispano-American bishops who had defended the native Indians of Latin America between 1504 and 1620.[6] This whole period was one of study, centered around the idea of uncovering and discovering the reality of Latin America and its people from the very beginnings. I wrote on hellenic humanism and on the dualism to be found in the anthropology of Christendom. The first edition of my history of the Latin American church appeared in 1969, the third revised and enlarged edition in 1974.

Upon returning to Latin America in 1966, I was invited by the Latin American Pastoral Institute (IPLA) to take charge of a course on the history of the church in Latin America. This enabled me to take frequent trips throughout our continent, to feel the impact of an infinite variety of experiences, and to begin experiencing the concrete anguish and anxiety of thousands of Christians. My involvement in my own province, at the grassroots

level and at the university, led to a serious attempt on my life that
destroyed part of my house and my library. A bomb planted by
extreme rightists on October 2, 1973, confronted me in a definitive
way with the reality of a world movement that was perfectly
orchestrated: i.e., the counter-revolution. My own option was
made once and for all.

In 1969 a meeting was held in Buenos Aires to study popular
Catholicism in Argentina, and the papers were later published. It
was on this occasion that I came to realize the new import that the
theory of socio-economic dependence might have for Christian reflection in Latin America. All my efforts and studies now turned in
that direction. Various theological articles were published at the
time, and I also gave the lectures that were issued as *Caminos de
liberación latinoamericana (I* and *II)*. I also wrote philosophical
works on the methodology of a liberation philosophy and on liberation ethics. All these efforts sought to spell out the methodological categories that might help us interpret our rich reality to some
extent.

And so we have several factors working together. History offers
its solid underpinnings to the Christian reality on our continent
while philosophy offers a clarified methodology. The praxis of
numerous Christians combines with the simple faith of the believer. All of these factors enable us to work out a theology with
deep historical roots that stays very close to everyday life. However, it is an everyday life already tinged with the blood of many
martyrs: Father Gallegos in Panama, Antonio Pereira Neto in
Brazil, and Carlos Mugica in Argentina, for example. It involves
the imprisonment of many Christian witnesses and the exercise of
many heroic options. Constant exercise turns them into habit. We
have gotten used to living close to death. Torture is always a
possibility; prison is always on the horizon. All those who choose
to enter the list with Christ can hear his words ringing in their
ears: "We must now go up to Jerusalem so that all that was
written by the prophets concerning the Son of Man may be accomplished" (Luke 18:31); "A time will come when anyone who puts
you to death will claim to be serving God" (John 16:2).

From Univocal to Catholic Discourse in Theology

On the occasion of the 1974 Synod of Bishops in Rome, there was
much talk about "pluralism in unity."[7] It came to be accepted that
there could be as many different theologies as there are conti-
nents and cultures. At the same time the universality of evangeli-

zation and its importance was also stressed. Evangelization was addressed to all human beings, there being no limitations imposed by geography, race, nation, history, or civilization. This was the "catholicity" of the Christian reality, the church, and theology.

It is our feeling, in any case, that it is possible to do some critical reflecting on a whole sector. This reflection embraces not only Latin America but also Africa and Asia (the latter in particular). Hence it is not surprising that the basic proposal begins from the concrete suggestions of Cardinal Cordeiro, the Archbishop of Karachi (Pakistan).

When we are talking about "different theologies," such terms as "unity," "plurality," "universality," and "difference" mean different things, depending on the logical discourse in which they appear. If they are used in a *univocal* discourse based on identity on the one hand and differences on the other (e.g., genus and species), then they have one meaning. If they are used in an *analogical* discourse based on participation and distinction, on the other hand, the meaning will be quite different; in this case one thing will be analogous to the other by virtue of some likeness (*similitudo*).

The whole issue of analogy was studied by such major figures as Cajetan in the sixteenth century, Santiago Ramírez of Salamanca around the turn of this century, Cornelio Fabro around the middle of this century, and Puntel in our own day. My feeling is that the whole issue of analogy is of major importance. Without getting highly technical, we can diagram a *univocal* discourse as follows:

DIAGRAM 1

The univocal signification of identity and difference

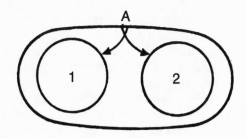

If A is the horizon of that which is identical to itself (the "being" of Hegel, for example, or "genus" in Aristotelian logic), then 1 and 2 are examples of that which is "dragged into duality" and made different (Hegel's *Dasein* and Aristotle's "species"). In such a framework the entity or the species is completely embraced within the horizon of being or genus; nothing of theirs is *exterior* to that horizon. Any plurality, then, is solely the plurality of the different entities; and the "unity" is that of the identical as a totality.

Now if we interpret the comments about "pluralism in unity" in those basic terms, we will note a curious phenomenon. It would seem to require that some *univocal* Christian experience or theology, which in fact arose in a given culture and is lived in a certain geopolitical region, has to be repeated or imitated *univocally* by every other concrete form of Christian experience or theology. If other Christians in different cultures have a particular Christian experience or theology imposed on them by way of domination, then the only thing they can properly do on their own is flesh it out with certain specific differences or individualize it with certain accidental details. In a univocal framework the genus can have different species, and a species can have different individuals. But while the differences could be of a species sort, the univocal universality would comprehend and take in the whole totality of meanings or significations (just as A includes 1 and 2 in Diagram 1).

In such a case "pluralism in unity" would be nothing more than certain specifications or individuations. In our case there cannot be specifications because each species would be essentially different from the other. Thus, in the case of Christianity we would end up with different religions. So the only other thing left would be the embodiment of difference on the *individual* level. As we know, however, difference on that level is *accidental*. It has to do with such things as differences of time, place, and relationship. It would not touch or affect the Christian experience any more deeply than that because it would be an *extrinsic* accidentality.

The opposite position, of course, would be that of equivocalness, where 1 and 2 in Diagram 1 would have nothing in common. In that case the "pluralism" would be without any unity. Rather than being differences, theological differences would really represent total ignorance of one another. They would really be *other* theologies, differing from each other in an equivocal way. That is the danger we seek to avoid. But if we do not pay close heed to the question, we may avoid equivocalness by turning full tilt toward the other extreme of univocalness. That is equally dangerous because one form of "Christendom" can usurp or claim for itself the univocal totality of Christian experience and Christian theology.

It is here that the well known doctrine of *analogy* comes to our aid, smartly bridging the gap between univocalness on the one hand and equivocality on the other insofar as Christianity and theology are concerned. We can diagram an *analogous* discourse as follows:

DIAGRAM 2

The analogous signification of participation and distinction

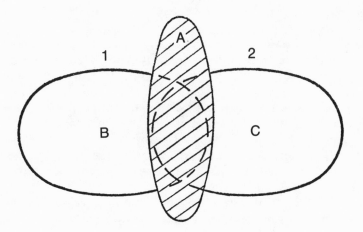

In analogy, realms 1 and 2 both share in A (Diagram 2). But they also have a distinct (not just different) moment where they are diverse and not enclosed within the univocalness of any species or genus (B and C). Moreover, while 1 and 2 "participate" in A, they do not do so identically because their starting point (B and C) for this participation is distinct. The convergence in a point of resemblance (*similitudo*) is not identical in analogate 1 and analogate 2.

To take an example, St. Basil (1) believed in Christ (A). But his

faith is not generically identical to the faith of Bartolomé de Las
Casas (2) in the same Christ (A). Christ (A) is identical in himself,
but he is shared analogically by St. Basil and Bartolomé de Las
Casas; hence he is experienced and lived by them in an analogous
way rather that in a generically identical way. There are not *two*
Christs (equivocalness), nor do both experience him identically as
species (univocalness). Rather, one and the same Christ is experienced analogically rather than differently by them.

The same holds true in theology. Every individual person, people, and culture (1 and 2) *participate* in the Christ-event in the
church and develops its theology analogously. The church *as such*
is identical in itself. In its essence it is the risen Christ present in
salvation history as a critical and redeeming divine word. Theology, however, does not possess any such generic self-identity.
Being a re-flection, it is already a reduplicative *pondering* of the
divine happening of Christ and the church from the standpoint of
a given person, culture, and point in time.

Do not mistake me here. I am not saying that there is not "one"
history and tradition that is the bearer of the "deposit." What I am
saying here is that the deposit is neither a genus nor a species,
that it is a Someone and the ways in which he has been shared by
distinct peoples and cultures at different points in time: e.g., by
Israel before the Incarnation, the primitive Christian community,
the church of the early fathers, Byzantine and Latin Christendom, the Christendom of the Indies, the churches in the modern
age, and today by people in a distinctive catholicity of its own that
must be closely examined.

Thus the faith of Basil and that of Bartolomé are not generically
identical, not only because they were two distinct persons but also
because they lived at two different moments in history. Rather
than *differentiating them individually*, however, this distin-
guishes them metaphysically.[8] At the same time we can say that
their faith bears the unity of analogy both in terms of history and
tradition.

Theology, for its part, finds its primary analogate in the beatific
or face-to-face vision of the just in the eschatological kingdom,
where faith and theology will be superseded by immediate vision.
In history, however, theology has both synchronic and diachronic
distinctiveness. Theology is practiced in diverse cultures that
coexist at a given moment in history, and it also goes through the
changing vicissitudes of history.

DIAGRAM 3

The synchronic and diachronic dimensions of analogy in theology

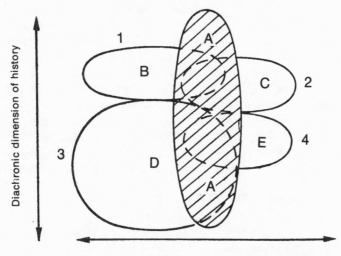

Synchronic dimension of geopolitical coexistence

Consider what this means. First of all, theology can participate or share in catholicity contemporaneously (i.e., on the synchronic level), since the Greek term *kata holon* connotes an analogical and eschatological universality rather than any sort of dominating univocalness. But this theology can also be marked by analogical "distinctions" that are characteristic of the metaphysical *innovativeness* of a given individual theologian or a given culture in all its inimitable uniqueness. In terms of our diagram, then, 1 and 2 can be contemporaneous, just as Armenian Christianity was contemporaneous with Byzantine Christianity in the fourth century and participated analogically in ecclesial catholicity. That is not all, however. We can also have participation in that same catholicity in different historical epochs, thereby forming *one and the same* tradition through time (i.e., diachronically); but the "sameness" would not be of a univocal sort. Such would be the case with 1 and 3, and 2 and 4, in our diagram. Such would be the case with the first Christian communities in Palestine on the one hand and the communities of Latin crusaders in Jerusalem in the twelfth century.

Participation in "the same thing," A (i.e., in Christ and, through him, in the Trinity), would come about from a "distinct" point of departure or access. Thus it would not be identical in the two cases, nor would it be differentiated solely on the individual level. The individual human person is not just an individual differentiated from the species-totality but a *free and unique exteriority*. The human "species" is a "historical species"—which is to say, an "analogous" species. Consider a Palestinian Christian of the first century and a Hispano-American Christian living in Lima in the late sixteenth century. The two gain access to Christ and his church from a "distinct" personal experience embodying the mystery of each's unique liberty and "otherness." Each individual human being, and hence each human culture, is not the individuation of a species—the species being something pre-existent that allows for nothing more than individual differences. Instead what we get is the *speciation of the individual* (since humanity multiplies from the first human beings on) and, even more radically, the *procreation of new history*. This point has been explained well by Xavier Zubiri, Emmanuel Lévinas, and our own Latin American "philosophy of liberation." Out of the nothingness (*ex nihilo*) of every possible system[9] we get participation and collaboration in the common history. The community involved here is one of *similitudo* ("likeness") rather than *identitas* ("identity"), however, so that the shared history is taken on by each in a novel, unique, inimitable, historical way.

If the church is indeed "universal," it is not universal in a univocal sense. Its catholicity is analogical, which is much more procreative and rich. Since it seems to me that Hegel misappropriated the term "universality" (in his *Logik*, his *Rechtsphilosophie*, and elsewhere), we must try to take the term "catholic" (*mundial*) and give it its full meaning. Hence we are not interested in the univocal universality (*universalidad*) of theology but rather in its analogical catholicity (*mundialidad*). When people talk about "Latin American theology," I want to know what they mean by the term before I will consent to its use. If they are thinking of a "different" *species*, then I reject their term. If they are thinking of a "different" *individual*, I reject their term also. But if they are thinking about an *analogical degree* of "participation" in the history of *one* theology, then I will accept it. In this case, however, we can point out that there is a real "distinction" between medieval Latin theology, modern European theology, and contemporary Latin American theology. Latin American theology is rightly called "liberation theology" because it puts the required stress on the social, geopolitical, and worldwide connotations of sin and redemption.

Keeping the above in mind, we can now assert that there should be as many distinct theologies participating in the *unity* of Christ and his church and in the "one" analogical history of theology as there are distinct cultures to be found existing synchronically or diachronically in history. We certainly find examples of this in history, though the picture may not have turned out quite as it should have. Consider Byzantine theology and medieval Latin theology. Were they not distinct within the unity or oneness of analogical participation? The problem is the excessive influence exerted by the Mediterranean world of the Byzantine and Latin churches. For centuries these two realms of Christendom embodied the dominant forms of Christian cultural experience. This led them to identify or equate their own *particular* experience with Christian experience *as such*. This surreptitious pretension and ideological manipulation *"consecrated" the theology of one culture as the "universal" theology.* Univocal in its own milieu and sharing analogically in the one analogical history of theology, this particular theology was universalized so that the other "distinct" realms and cultures of the Christian world were not allowed to have any Christian or historical validity. Their theologies were denied analogical participation in the one history of Christian theology.

This theological abuse simply reflected and extended the political, economic, and cultural abuse. The imperial Christian nations took over their colonies, exploited their markets, and presented their own imperial culture as the one and only human one. Transformed into "universality," European "particularity" leaves the concrete, valid level at which it originated and becomes an imperial abstraction imposed on Africa, Asia, and Latin America. As such, it can no longer even explain the horizon within which it arose (i.e., Europe, Russia, and the United States).

The time has come to make this clear! The time has come to criticize the *univocalness of being* as actually described by Aristotle and Hegel. The whole doctrine of the analogy of being (*esse*) brings us in line with the best tradition and thrusts us into the forefront of the revolutionary process that seeks to liberate the oppressed periphery.

Latin America is the *child* of the European conqueror and its Indian mother, Amerindia. For almost five centuries it has been prevented from explicating its own "distinctiveness," its own way of participating analogically in the catholicity of Christ's one and

only church. Univocal discourse is imperialist, war-bent, and
child-killing; it is filicide. Analogical discourse respects the distinctiveness of father and mother; hence it admits and recognizes
the originality of the child, of Latin America and its *original*
theology. Nothing endangers the unity of the church more than
neurotic, univocal uniqueness. This refuses to recognize creative
"distinctiveness," stifling or suffocating the poor for the sake of a
vaunted "universality" that is only an absolutized "particularity." Nothing enhances living, organic unity in obedience and love
more than a church that is respectful of distinctiveness in all its
mysterious fruitfulness. Such a church joyously participates and
collaborates in a catholicity fashioned by all, in a catholicity
where all can contribute *their own* distinctiveness.

Here we are dealing with practically opposite extremes. It is one
thing to force people to leave their own distinctiveness outside
and don that of another. If they can, and if they have the power,
they will turn their own abandoned distinctiveness into a contrary absolute. It is something very different, however, to try to
get people to place their distinctiveness in the common pool where
nothing will be left out and all will find rebirth in fellowship:
"Those who believed shared all things in common" (Acts 2:44).
Univocal, dominating "universality" (*universalidad*) is sterile and
bureaucratic; it demeans the "other" and forces that other into
imitation, repetition, and a perduring state of naiveté. Analogical,
liberative "catholicity" (*mundialidad*) is dialogic, participatory,
and fruitful; respecting the "other" as *other*, it teaches that other
to be innovative and creative after itself learning how to be criticized and called into question by the exteriority of its child or
pupil: "The Lord God has given me a well-trained tongue, that I
might know how to speak to the weary a word that will rouse them.
Morning after morning he opens my ear that I may hear . . . " (Isa.
50:4).

No one can be a teacher unless one is first a disciple. First one
must learn to heed and appreciate the distinctiveness of those one
seeks to evangelize—whether it be an individual, a class, a nation,
or a culture. If one tries to teach before learning of and from this
distinctiveness, then one has fallen prey to idolatry, fetishism,
imperialism, sin, filicide!

FOUR SPECIFIC ISSUES IN A THEOLOGICAL DISCOURSE

The four issues discussed here are not the only ones that might
enter into a theological discourse; indeed they may not even be the

four most important issues. They are simply four issues among many possible ones. My aim here is to come to grips with them in a methodical way.

The first issue brings us to the whole problematic question of the divine as such in our own day. That issue begins from a point that is prior to any consideration of God as Other or Creator. Moving on to the latter plan, our theological discourse then becomes trinitarian. First of all, God is Father; so we and his Word are his children; the *pedagogical* relationship is that of father and child. Secondly, God is our brother; the *political* relationship is that of brother to brother. Thirdly, God is Love as a person, the Holy Spirit; hence anthropological *eroticism* is the epiphany of God as love in the male-female relationship.

This particular discourse makes no claims to being exhaustive. It merely proposes to introduce the reader to the whole subject, indicating how we might approach it from a Latin American standpoint. It is the "distinct" experience of Latin America, which I took in from my mother's breast and my environment, which was conveyed to me by all the symbols of our convulsed society, that serves as the backdrop for what I have to say.

Unmasking a Fetishistic Theology

In this section the term "theology" simply means "thinking about the divine." Thus it includes very different types of thinking that make its use *equivocal* here. It takes in fetishism or idolatry, which is ontologically pantheistic, as well as affirmative belief in a personal God who is the Creator.

Taking that as our starting point, we must state flatly that "atheism" is a false problem. Neither in theory nor in practice has atheism ever been people's *final* position. What we get is the negation of some divinity: Creationism denies the divinity of the whole whereas pantheism denies the existence of a creator God. What most students of atheism and the "death of God" overlook, however, is that such negation *always* entails the theoretical or practical affirmation of some divinity that is not denied. If I deny the reality of a creator God, then my theory or practice will affirm fetishism or idolatry. If I say no to idolatry or pantheism, then I say yes to a creator God. There is no third possibility.

Since atheism does not exist, then, it cannot be the most serious question of our age. That distinction goes to idolatry or fetishism, as Jesus and the ancient prophets realized full well. They only spoke about atheism now and then in passing, not because they were unaware of the issue but because it has always been a secondary issue at best in the authentic theological discourse of the Judeo-Christian tradition. What we find around us are not atheists but fetishists. The cult of *latria* is simply transferred to new and different deities. Idolatry becomes dollaratry, the cult of the American buck. "In God We Trust," it says on the bill, but in what God exactly? Isn't the dollar bill itself the deity in question? Aren't wars initiated and kept up to protect certain investments? Aren't military arms sold to keep profits up? Aren't human beings exploited because people worship gold and silver?

The very fact that much importance is attached to atheism and little to fetishism indicates a great deal. Many people who claim to be Christian will readily fall in with the idea of accepting the fetish (e.g., money) as a *profane value* that is not invested with any sacred character; and they will spend *all their time* preoccupied with that object. But if the same wholehearted preoccupation with money is evident in people who refuse to worship a creator God, Christians will be inclined to say that they have erased all thought of the divine from their lives. What is really happening here is that the person who is an "atheist" with respect to the Christian God is *in practice* worshipping the fetish; and so are Christians who spend all their time trying to make money. The latter cannot possibly offer any real criticism of fetishistic practice. Instead they secularize the fetish in theory while actually worshipping it in practice as the professed non-Christian does. Of both it can be said: "The father you spring from is the devil, and willingly you carry out his wishes" (John 8:44).

DIAGRAM 4

Idolatry or Fetishism:
"Atheism" with respect to a creator God

1. Negative side: denial of otherness (atheism with respect to divine creation).
2. Positive side: affirmation of the totality or "the system" as divine (idolatry).

Idolatry or fetishism can be summarized as in Diagram 4. Its adherents are "without hope and without God in the world" (Eph. 2:12), as Paul puts it, but also surrounded by many different fetishes. Their fetishism and idolatry are evident in the fact that they want to make a god who will be their leader; so they use their gold to make a molten calf as the Hebrews in the desert did (Exod. 32:1–4). The *wishes of the devil* must be sated: "They went up to Assyria—a wild ass off on its own—Ephraim bargained for lovers" (Hos. 8:9); "they consult their piece of wood, and their wand makes pronouncements for them. For the spirit of harlotry has led them astray; they commit harlotry, forsaking their God" (Hos. 4:12).

Today European countries and the United States prostitute themselves for oil, wheat, meat, coffee, and iron. Buying and selling at unjust prices, they succumb to the idolatry of technology, comfort, eroticism, and so forth. They are idolaters, not atheists, and idolatry is a far more serious issue. Rather than secularization we are seeing the divinization of the whole system and the conversion of money into a fetish. As far back as the sixteenth century one Latin American bishop had this to say: "About four years ago, when this land was beginning to go to ruin, they discovered a veritable gate of hell. Through it each year go countless people [native Indians], driven down by the greed of the Spaniards in sacrifice to the Spaniards' god. It is a silver mine called Potosí" (letter dated July 1, 1550). Today we might say the same thing of the Russians, Europeans, and North Americans. We might well denounce them as follows: "Your father is the devil. He has induced you to believe in secularization so that he might reign all the more securely without anyone believing in him. He has invented the notion of atheism and the death of all deities so that his cult might pass unnoticed. His temples today are the supermarkets, the banks, the stock exchanges, the financial transactions, and the offices of politicians, military men, and businessmen whose power dominates the world."

Modern Europe and its present age calls itself Christian. In fact, however, it denies divine otherness in denying anthropological otherness (by exerting imperial domination over Asians, Africans, and other native peoples). De facto denial of a creator God, the negative side of atheism with respect to divine creation, comes down to affirming the divinity of the system as a whole. In short, it comes down to fetishism and idolatry, which is its positive side.

Creationism, on the other hand, is in direct opposition to idolatry and fetishism, as can be seen in Diagram 5. Prophets, Jesus, and real Christians are "atheists" with respect to fetishes. The early Christian martyrs were dragged into the Roman circuses because they were atheists with respect to the system's gods. Their attitude can be seen in Elijah's dealings with the devotees of Baal: "Call louder, for he is a god and may be meditat-

---

DIAGRAM 5

Creationism: "Atheism" with respect to fetishes and the divinized system

1. Negative side: negation of the negation of otherness (atheism with respect to idols).
2. Positive side: affirmation of otherness (anthropological justice and the cult of *latria* vis-à-vis a creator God who is love).

---

ing, or may have retired, or may be on a journey. Perhaps he is asleep and must be awakened" (1 Kings 18:27).

The issue, then, is not whether one is an atheist or not but what sort of an atheist one is. We all are atheists with respect to one God or another. The question is: with respect to which God or what sort of God? Do we deny a creator God and divinize the system? Or do we deny the divinity of the system and worship a creator God?

What deserves notice is the fact that the atheist with respect to a divinized system actually negates a negation. If the system is to be divinized, one must deny otherness: the otherness of fellow human beings, of the poor and those oppressed by colonialism. Fratricide destroys epiphany, removing the point where the creator God might be able to reveal himself to us. Injustice is the way people can go about denying absolute Otherness.Thus fratricide is also deicide, and it is not without reason that Jesus dies as a poor human being, a brother, and God. To negate this negation of our brother is to do justice on the pedagogical, political, and erotic level.

Through justice God reveals himself anew. The ancient prophets, speaking in god's name, asked for justice and mercy, not sacrifice. Today Latin American prophets ask the same thing of Europe, Russia, and North America: Justice in the price of raw materials and manufactured goods should come before ecumenical liturgies in the affluent countries!

This scandalizes some people, of course. They claim that it is turning the gospel upside down and attributing too much importance to politics. But hasn't a false spiritualization of Christianity allowed affluent Christians to feed off the hunger of the poor nations? Between bites of food they call for patience and nonviolence. Christianity, after all, has nothing to do with politics, economics, pedagogy, and erotic relationships. If that is true, however, does it have to do with anything at all? Aren't people "flesh" (Hebrew *basar* and Greek *sarx*), and isn't all flesh to be redeemed and saved? False spiritualizations simply enable Christians to live as oppressive dominators without feeling pangs of conscience over their sinful injustice. God still lies hidden from their eyes under the trappings of liturgical celebrations. It is justice and mercy he seeks, not sacrifice!

God manifests himself in Latin America in the face of the native Indian, the mestizo, the black, the zambo, the exploited peasant, the alienated laborer, and those who are giving their lives for their fellows. When we hear and heed the voice of our creating and redeeming God in the plaints of the poor, we then have *the criterion for an authentic faith*. Any other criterion begins there: "I was hungry and you gave me food . . . " (Matt. 25:35). Those who do not serve the poor are "atheists" with respect to the creating and redeeming God because they think that the poor should serve them and that "god" (their fetish) is with them. Those who serve the poor are "atheists" with respect to themselves and the system because they know that they are supposed to serve the poor. They can believe in a God who is "Other," denying the divinity of the system and proclaiming that the future can be better.

The Judeo-Christian approach to the living God of Israel and Christ represents the *ethical* approach or access to God, as opposed to physical or ontological access. Thanks to it, one can see the "ideological" or "fetishistic" character of any theology that serves as the official teaching of a dominating, oppressive system. One can become suspicious of papal bulls that justified the conquest of the Americas, of doctrines of "Manifest Destiny" that rationalized the takeover of Texas and California, and of talk about "the Christian civilization of the West" that subjects whole peoples to bondage and tyranny.

Unmasking Ideological Pedagogy

The creator God is a Father, father of his child. The father-child relationship is a pedagogical one, paternal or filial as the case may be. God reveals himself primarily in a pedagogical relationship, revealing his mystery to us and leading us toward his pristine exteriority.

Because God is our Father, we come to see that we are *children*. The Word is the Son or Child of God par excellence; in and through him we are established in a filial relationship with God. In the previous section we noted that the theological sin with respect to God or divinity as such was idolatry or fetishism (the "fetishism of money" as one author has put it). Here we can say that the theologal sin on the pedagogical level is *filicide:* the "killing of the child." Filicide is the constant practice of gerontocracies (governments ruled by the old), bureaucracies (habitual administrative structures), and ideological systems of all sorts. In our age of collective communication that would apply in particular to educational institutions, to what Ivan Illich labels "schooling." It is the same murderers who slay young people, innovativeness, and popular culture in general: the father, the state, and authoritarian institutions of an oppressive, castrating sort.

Christianity is the breakup of this authoritarian paternal domination and the oppression of the child: "I have come to set a man at odds with his father, a daughter with her mother, a daughter-in-law with her mother-in-law. . . . Whoever loves father or mother, son or daughter, more than me is not worthy of me" (Matt. 10:35–37). Christianity is the liberation of the child, freeing children to follow the *wishes* of their Father in heaven. They are to learn to love exteriority, even that of their enemies: "This will prove you are sons of your heavenly Father" (Matt. 5:45).

By contrast the *wishes* of the other "father," of an imperialist cultural system or a neocolonial school system or an oppressive communications system, come down to the killing of its child. That "father" is the "father of lies" (i.e., ideology), the violent father of military rule and the police state. Jesus, the Son, died in the sinful meshes of a system promoting filicide. The prehispanic culture of America bears witness to this sinful mechanism of pedagogical domination as filicide: "Four days went by and the Sun in heaven was still. The gods came together in council. Why was he not moving? The Sun (Huitzilopochtli of the Aztecs) was a wounded god turned into the Sun. . . . The hawk approached him and said that the gods wanted to know why he was not moving. The Sun replied: 'Do you know why? Because I want human blood! Because I want them to give me *their children,* their offspring.' "[10]

That pre-hispanic and pre-oedipal tradition bears witness to the filicide that would be repeated when the Europeans arrived here in the sixteenth century. In the *Destruction of the Indies* (1552), Bartolomé de Las Casas tells us that in wars the Spaniards usually spared only *little children* and women. The European conqueror would rape the native women and *educate* the children of the Indian, the African, and the Asian. Whether it be the Spaniard and Portuguese in an earlier day or the Russian and North

American today, the European would come to "extend his power over the *orphans*" of the native mother and father.[11]

The culture of the "power center" saw the colonial child of the periphery as a crude and illiterate barbarian, as a non-entity. Why? Because that culture denied the distinctive exteriority of the "other," whether that "other" was a newborn child or a different culture. This colonial child was left an *orphan:* without father or mother, without its own tradition, culture, and state. Like Pestalozzi and Montessori, Rousseau needed an *orphan* Emile so that he could impress all his bourgeois European ideology on her *tabula rasa.* And all that was done in the name of "naturalness" and a human "nature" that was nothing more than a projection of the imperialist, capitalist world of Europe in the age of French and English liberal revolutions. The prophets of old cried out: "Hear the orphan's plea! " (Isa. 1:17). In his day Hegel proclaimed: "We are the missionaries of civilization of the whole world."[12]

As cultural imperialism, sin destroys the cultures of the periphery. As the enlightened culture of a neocolonial national oligarchy, it represses popular culture. As an educating and "schooling" state, it oppresses children and adolescents. As father and citizen of an affluent society, it alienates the child by separating it from its mother. Is it not evident by now that Freud simply described this basically *sinful* situation in our culture, the *pathology* of its pedagogy as a totality?

Back in 1918 university students in Argentina issued this proclamation: "Young people no longer ask, they demand that people recognize their right to express openly their own thinking" (Córdoba Manifesto). Worldwide student dissent fifty years later, in 1968, thereby takes on distinctive features of its own in peripheral areas. If the second oedipal stage—identification with the state as father—is impossible at the center, it is doubly so at the periphery. It is not just that government is in crisis. Here the crisis is compounded by the fact that we glimpse the *possibility* of being an affluent society and know we are prevented by the *oppression* that we suffer from the imperial centers around us. That is why the child, the young person, and the people live and breathe in the great *fiestas* of history: "The Mexican revolution is an event that breaks in upon our history as an *authentic revelation of our being* (i.e., as children). . . . The absence of a prior program gave it originality and populist authenticity. . . . The populist traditionalism of Zapata bears witness to his profound awareness, insulated in his people and his race."[13]

The *rebellion of the child* is necessary if the child is to be able to freely adore the Father in heaven. The children must revolt against gerontocracies, even though they may be ecclesiastical; against bureaucracies, even though they may be curial; against the imperialism of manipulative propaganda, even though it may be presented as preaching; and against neocolonial bourgeoisies. Jesus tells us: "I no longer speak of you as slaves. . . . Instead I call you friends" (John 15:15). That is why he chose to become the *Son* of man as well as the *Son* of God, experiencing in his own flesh the workings of pedagogical sinfulness without ever having done it in his own teaching. One who hates the Son also hates the Father because such a one is the "father" of sinful pedagogy, the authoritarian teacher backed by repression who cannot help but reject the Father of love: "To hate me is to hate my Father" (John 15:23).

Jesus, the Son, came to worship the *Father* and to liberate the orphans, turning them into free children. Pedagogical sinfulness, whose father is Satan, exerts domination once more over the child, the adolescent, and the common people in the name of the prevailing imperial ideology and culture. At the same time it negates the mother, popular culture, and all the revolutionary symbols that might raise the consciousness of the poor. The pedagogical redemption offered by the heavenly Father liberates every child and people in and through his Son. Dying in the *filicide* of sinfulness, he destroys the ideological system: "Father, forgive them; they do not know what they are doing" (Luke 23:34). We have here cultural revolution as the pedagogical liberation of the child and the orphan (as opposed to what happens to *Emile*).

(Mafalda, "Quino," Mendoza, Argentina)

Unmasking Exploitative Politics

God the Son, then, is also *brother*. Politics is the brother-to-brother relationship. Pedagogical filicide is the wellspring of political fratricide: "Cain attacked his *brother* Abel and killed him" (Gen. 4:8). In terms of exteriority this brother is the alien and stranger to whom we owe the sacred obligation of hospitality. But instead of receiving and welcoming him, we subject him to domination, oppression, and alienation: "Redress the wronged" (Isa. 1:17). The "death of the brother" is brought about by the great lords, the masters and bosses, and the ruling oligarchies in both the centers of power and the periphery. The people who are oppressed and subjected to neocolonial domination of whatever sort are the political "others" who are slain; they are the Abels of current history.

Christians came to the peripheral areas of Latin America, Africa, and Asia as conquerors, warriors, and men of commerce. A Quiché manuscript from Guatemala has this to say about their arrival: "Alas, heavy is the weight one must bear when one has to endure a meeting with Christianity! What will happen then is enslavement, reaching as far as the chiefs enthroned at the time. . . . "[14] And it goes on to describe the resulting situation: "the age of war, the reign of war, war as food and drink, war as an everyday affair, war as the watchword. It will be a time of war for old men and women, for babes and stouthearted men, and for young people. . . . "[15]

It is easy enough for people in the power centers of Europe, Russia, and the United States to talk about nonviolence today, thereby disarming the poor's struggle for liberation. But they have consistently violated and done violence to the poor of the earth. Now that their power grows more shaky, it is suddenly time to talk about nonviolence in the name of the gospel message. What hypocrisy from people who never defended the weak from the conquering arms of Europe and who now are trying to block the revolution of those on the periphery!

To be sure, Christ was neither a politician nor a soldier; his mission was quite different. But he did not condemn the Zealots, and he himself was condemned to death for the same reasons they were: "They started his prosecution by saying, 'We found this man *subverting our nation.... He stirs up the people!*' ... Pilate ... said to them: 'You have brought this man before me as one who subverts the people' . . . "(Luke 23). In 1552 Bartolomé de Las Casas, that great Latin American prophet, had this to say: "I am convinced that *everything* done to the Indians here is unjust and tyrannical."[16] The same would apply to what the British did to the Hindus, the Chinese, and others; to what the French did in Africa; and to what the Germans and Italians did there too, insofar as they had such power. Las Casas condemned the colonial system as a whole and predicted dire consequences for colonial Europe: "God's fury and wrath will be unleashed against all of Spain because the whole country has shared in the blood-stained wealth that has been torn from the hands of its rightful owners and misused."[17]

As early as 1562 we see him formulating what we today would call "liberation theology" on the level of international policy: In his *Testament* he says: "God deigned to choose me as his minister so that I might help all the peoples of the Indies to become the possessors and owners of those lands once again. . . . They have fallen into the hands of the Spaniards against all reason and justice. . . . I must help them to regain the *pristine liberty* of which they have been despoiled. I must *liberate them* from the violent death which they now suffer." Las Casas realized that the Indians were originally free, that they had been alienated from that freedom, and that as a Christian prophet he has been summoned to commit himself to their *liberation*.

Sketch in an Aztec manuscript depicting the European conquest of the "periphery." The "other," the poor human brother, is torn to pieces with a *violence* long since forgotten. That violence has been covered up by the ideological efforts of Christians.

The sin of Cain (fratricide) paves the way for the sin of Adam (idolatry as deicide). The killing of the poor person is the murder of one's human brother in whom one might have seen the epiphany of God, the creator and redeemer. When Europe came to dominate the "periphery," to be followed later by the United States and Russia, its people were left alone at the center in the trammels of their fetishistic creation. They were the humane, the cultivated, the civilized people. They were "being," or Hegel's self-conscious Spirit in history. From their divinized center they oppressed all the other peoples on earth. Isolated in their own narcissism, they felt self-sufficient in their own greatness, wisdom, goodness, and grandeur. Their own hallowed image looked out at them from the mirror, and it was reflected in those colonials who were educated by them (as Sartre brings out in his Preface to Fanon's *Wretched of the Earth*).

Today "fat cat" Europe, another "sacred cow" according to Ivan Illich, is glimpsing the limitations facing its own growth. In typically neurotic fashion it is trying to get over the crisis by placing the blame everywhere except where it belongs: on its own exploitation of the earth's oppressed peoples. What Europe needs today is another great figure like Bartolomé de Las Casas to utter words of prophecy, to tell Europe what is really wrong: "Your own sinfulness is the cause of your present crisis. Now that you see you cannot exploit others endlessly and keep on eating off the fat of their land, you must begin thinking about living justly and humbly. You must begin to respect poor peoples, poor individuals, and poor Jesus! "

But instead of prophets Europe has functionalist sociologists who are interested only in keeping the system operative. It has philosophers of language whose speech is so disjointed that they themselves cannot hear anyone else, cannot hear the cries of hunger and thirst coming from others. Yet Wittgenstein pointed out that we must be silent in the face of that which cannot be spoken. Instead of prophets Europe has narcissistic theologians who think only of internal church reform, who forget that all such reform should be designed to serve the poor outside. And the saddest thing of all is that the world's poor see the great figures of the church consorting with the great ones of this world. The leaders of the church bless their arms, attend their banquets, and carefully avoid creating diplomatic crises:

By the shores of Babylon's rivers
we sit and weep together
thinking back on Zion.
We gaze at Babylon's skyscrapers
and the lights reflected in the river
the lights of nightclubs and bars
and hear their strains of music
and weep.
How I prefer Jerusalem
to all your joys and feasting,
Babel,
garbed in bombs and destruction!
Blessed be he who grabs your children
the creatures of your laboratories
and dashes them against a rock.[18]

Sin is nothing else but the domination of the "other." Political sinfulness is nothing else but the domination and alienation of one's fellow human being and brother, of the "other" embodied in a colonized country, an oppressed class, an impoverished people. The political sin is fratricide. Salvation (or redemption) means liberation from that oppression. Its historical embodiment will be found in concrete socio-political systems, its eschatological embodiment in Christ and his kingdom.

But we will never be able to signify the kingdom in our missionary efforts if we do not offer a concrete, intelligible sign of it: i.e., our concrete involvement in the historical process designed to effect the liberation of the poor in this world. Time and again people try to confuse the issue. Some suggest that the gospel offers a "spiritual" liberation, not a "political" one. It is as much as to say that the liberation of the Holy Spirit is not in fact liberation of the "flesh" from sin. And "flesh" means the whole person: including political, social, economic, and cultural aspects. To propose "spiritual" liberation that is not also "political" is to confirm the status quo. Such a liberation may indeed be "spiritual," but the "spirit" in this case would be Lucifer—the "evil spirit," the "prince of this world": "The father you spring from is the devil, and willingly you carry out his wishes" (John 8:44).

Unmasking Narcissistic Eroticism

What is the wish of our heavenly Father? His "wish" (Freud would use *Wunsch*) is *agape* rather that *eros* or *filia*. It is for face-to-face encounter with any and every "other." On the pedagogical level of face-to-face encounter he manifests himself to us as *Father*. On the political level of face-to-face encounter he manifests himself in the Son as *brother*. And on the level of loving face-to-face encounter he manifests himself to us as the *Holy Spirit*: "God is Love" (1 John 4:16). The triune God is the lover of his beloved: "I also saw a new Jerusalem, the holy city, coming down out of heaven from God, beautiful as a bride prepared to meet her husband" (Rev. 21:2).

This bride or betrothed has prostituted herself often enough, as we know from the sinfulness of the church. Hosea is told to "go and take a harlot wife" (Hos. 1:2). God thus symbolically takes on the man-woman relationship; we get a theologal eroticism, a theologal version of agape. "Let him kiss me with kisses of his mouth" (Song of Sol. 1:2). That is the start of an erotic face-to-face encounter, of a fecund and procreative love that is willing to confer being on a new creature gratuitously. And the new creature is the child *in* Mary the mother, in the church.

By contrast the erotic sin of the modern age (from the fifteenth century on) has been *phallocracy*; and it has taken on concrete shape in *uxoricide*, the slaying of the woman and the assertion of cultural *machismo*. Instead of defending the widow as Isaiah bade his people do, the widowed women of the Third World were violated by the European conquerors. It is another form of violence that has been conveniently ignored by Europeans:

Force and violence such as has never been experienced or practiced elsewhere is commonplace here. Indian women are subjected to force against their will. Married women are taken against their husband's will. Maidens and young girls are violated against their parents' will. By order of the *alcaldes* and *corregidores* they are taken out of their homes, where they might be of use to their families, and forced to work as servants for *encomenderos* and others miles away. They are also transported to ranches and work-sites, where they are often forced into concubinage with the masters, with mestizos, mulattos, and Negroes, and with pitiless men of all sorts [Letter of the Bishop of Guatemala, Juan Ramírez, March 10, 1603].

The Indian woman of America is the mother of Latin America, a mother violated by the male European conqueror. The Latin American child often does not want to acknowledge its mother, who was forced into prostitution. Thus its pedagogical situation comes down to denying both its father (because he was the European imperialist) and its mother (because she betrayed her people). The killing of the mother (uxoricide) is the cause of the killing of the child (filicide). The wishful desire of the male conqueror for the Indian woman as nothing more than a sex object comes down to the very same desire that leads him to dominate his child and his fellow human brother: It is the desire of his father, the devil. This wish or desire is in opposition to *agape* and charity. It is *libido*, the yearning for "totalization" that Augustine described as a primeval "turning away from God."[19] Put in other words, it is male self-love concretized in the deliberate alienation of woman: i.e., in phallocracy. Erotic sinfulness also produces the alienation of the poor person—the woman in this case: "And my poor wife, God knows how much she has suffered! They tell me she took off with some hawk, almost certainly to find the food that I could not give her."[20]

The woman and wife of the poor male in an oppressed colonial country must be liberated. Remember that Mary, a poor girl from the ranks of Israel's common people, accepted the condition of a woman and wife in a nation oppressed by the power of Rome.

It is the liberation of the mother that will effect the liberation of eroticism and allow love to burst forth. The Spirit of love can inhabit only the child of a mother who has not been denied by its father, as was the case in the oedipal situation. The father must respect the exteriority and positive sexuality of the mother. He must not step between mother and child, popular culture and the people. He must allow the mother to attain freedom and sexual fulfillment in the erotic face-to-face relationship which starts with a kiss and culminates in the liturgical rhythm of the sex act itself. Coitus thus becomes a hallowed act in the service of justice, since it serves the fulfillment and realization of "the Other" as "other" (*caritas*). It renders the mother free, as we said above, and it also frees the child—educating the child for freedom.

Love can flourish only in freedom, gratuitousness, justice, poverty vis-à-vis the comforts of the affluent society, and courage to face death for the sake of those who are weakest. The Son of God came "to *destroy* the devil's works" (1 John 3:8), to oppose the idolatrous and imperialistic wishes of Satan with human yearnings for justice and the adoration of God as Other, God as the God of Love. God first loved us, teaching us how to offer gratuitous love and to fulfill the desires of the other person in generous, self-giving love: "Thus do we distinguish the spirit of truth from the spirit of deception" (1 John 4:6).

Conclusions

The discourse proposed here by way of example is designed to be at once trinitarian and anthropological, eschatological and historical, catholic and concrete, spiritual and fleshly (in line with basic Judeo-Christian categories). Salvation, redemption, and liberation are meant to apply to the whole human being. One-sided "spiritualization" is as idolatrous as one-sided "historification." Exclusivist verticalism is as fetishistic as absolutist horizontalism. People are "flesh," bound up with history, politics, economics, culture, and sexuality; by nature people are not "the Spirit." The spiritual person, the *sarx pneumatikos* of which Paul speaks, is the person participating in the kingdom and inhabited by the Spirit. The Spirit of grace inhabits the whole person and everything associated with humankind: history, politics, economics, culture, sexuality, and so forth. To say that salvation or liberation is "spiritual" and should not be mixed with politics or ideology is to empty Christianity of meaning. Refusing to criticize real-life sin means identifying with the status quo and adoring a fetish.

Equally idolatrous is an exclusive emphasis on "historical" salvation. If we say that concern for a utopian kingdom of heaven causes people to forget their current responsibilities and drugs both the revolutionary and the people, then we fall into idolizing some allegedly perfect "system" that has no inherent flaws or contradictions. Ultimately that will allow some class of bureaucrats to claim they are the final authority for some immediate political solution that will brook no opposition. We end up with total oppression and unlimited tyranny: i.e., hell.

Christian salvation and liberation, by contrast, is historical in its witness and preparatory stages, but eschatological in its ultimate fulfillment. Through history, politics, and other such factors Christians fight against the sinfulness of this world and its ruler. Their fight is the "sign" of the eschatological kingdom—*semeion* in John's Gospel. Because they are fighting for a heavenly kingdom, they cannot accept any earthly system as being totally just—neither imperialist capitalism nor Russian bureaucratism. They are atheists with respect to every historical system. But only by fighting for a more just *historical* system can they show that the existing system is the product of sinfulness and that they do believe in a future kingdom that will be more just. Their fight in the areas of pedagogy, politics, economics, and sexuality is their prophetic and sign-giving mediation of the kingdom of heaven.

Christians do not constitute a state through the church, nor are they politicians by "profession," as Max Weber might put it. But if their conduct evades the whole level of politics, then they have made a pact with the devil. For then they are merely *following the line of the prevailing politics*, which is the most anti-Christian type of *political* attitude. Absolutizing a political project is equally anti-Christian. Christians absolutize only the kingdom of heaven. From the standpoint of that eschatological goal they then criticize *every* historical system *both in their theory and their practice:* "He who has ears to hear, let him hear."

NOTES

1. E. Dussel, "Domination—Liberation: A New Approach," *Concilium* 96 (New York: Herder and Herder, 1974), pp. 34–56.

2. *Cláusula del testamento*, B.A.E., 5:539b.

3. See Julio César Chaves, *Tupac Amaru* (Buenos Aires, 1973), p. 145.

4. Octavio Paz, *El laberinto de la soledad*, 1973, p. 108; Eng. trans.: *The Labyrinth of Solitude* (New York: Grove Press, 1961).

5. Ibid., p. 122.

6. *Los obispos hispanoamericanos defensores del indio (1504-1620);* see the author entry in Appendix I for most of the works mentioned.

7. Expression used by Cardinal Cordeiro, October 4.

8. For the contrast between ontic or ontological "difference" and metaphysical "distinction" or "distinctiveness," see my work entitled *Para una ética de la liberación* (Buenos Aires: Siglo XXI, 1973), 1:97–128 and 2:156–74.

9. Being in the Hegelian or Heideggerian sense as expressed by Schelling in his *Philosophie der Offenbarung;* see my book *Método para una filosofía de la liberación* (Salamanca: Sígueme, 1974), Chapter 4.

10. "El quinto sol," Nahua-Mexican tradition.

11. *El libro de los libros del Chilam Balam*, "11 Ahau".

12. *Philosphie der Geschichte*, Theorie Werkausgabe, 1970, 12:538.

13. Octavio Paz, *Laberinto*, p. 122ff.

14. *Chilam Balam*, II, "11 Ahau."

15. Ibid.

16. *Historia de las Indias*, 3:79.

17. *Cláusula del Testamento*.

18. Ernesto Cardenal, *Salmo 136*.

19. *De libero arbitrio*, III, 1.

20. José Hernández, *Martín Fierro*, 1: 1051–56.

10

Theology, Popular Culture, and Discernment

Juan Carlos Scannone
(San Miguel/Buenos Aires, Argentina)

MAJOR SHIFTS IN RECENT LATIN AMERICAN THEOLOGY

Latin American theology has taken several major steps forward in the last few years. The first step really goes back to Vatican II. As was the case in other sectors of the church, it served to create a distinction between preconciliar and postconciliar theology in the Latin American church. At first, however, both versions of Latin American theology continued to look to Europe and European theological trends rather than to the situation and culture of Latin America itself. One side sought to "apply" the Council to our context while the other resisted any such application. But there was no real rereading and reinterpretation of church tradition and the conciliar position from the standpoint of our own history and culture.

The use of the adjective *popular* in this article *(cultura popular)* is very much that of Spanish-language writers in general. While it may be translated "popular" for convenience' sake, the reader should remember that its basic meaning in Spanish is "of the people"—very much in the same sense that Lincoln talked about "government of the people, by the people, and for the people."—TRANS.

The updating of the Council did have one initial effect. It forced us to pay heed to the "day of the Lord," or *kairos* of salvation through which our peoples might be living now. Greater openness to the world, which was very much encouraged by Vatican II, prompted our theology to pay ever increasing attention to our concrete world here. It thus came to an acute awareness of our world's structured injustice and institutionalized violence, along with the conflict that riddles it. The council's focus on salvation history was the product of trends in biblical research and biblical theology. It led our theology to focus on salvation in terms of the concrete happenings in our own contemporary history. Once the Council had attempted to discern the "signs of the times" on a more universal level, we were encouraged to look for them as specific signs of God at work here, as "first indications of the painful birth of a new civilization."[1]

This second major step is embodied in the Medellín Episcopal Conference itself (1968). As was the case with Vatican II, the Medellín Conference synthesized already existing theological trends and also provoked new ones. The latter constitute the post-Medellín theology that is now widespread. And just as Vatican II provoked reactions both for and against it, so did the Medellín Conference—a clear indication that it had touched upon problems that go right to the heart of the church's life on this continent.

So it was that postconciliar theology in Latin America splintered into two predominant trends. Some continued to elaborate a seemingly universal theology on the basis of cultural patterns imported from postconciliar European theology. Others took a very different tack, without rejecting the universality of theology or refusing to dialogue with European theology. They now began to theologize in terms of the distinctive historical and socio-cultural situation of Latin America and its corresponding way of living the faith. Using that situation as its starting point, Latin American theology now sought to offer an appropriate theological response.

A shift in emphasis went along with that shift in basic outlook. Whereas earlier the emphasis had been placed on development (e.g., at the CELAM conference in Mar del Plata), it now came to be placed on liberation. The latter term, with deep roots in the Bible, managed to express the present-day situation, the yearnings of our peoples, and the consciousness-raising that was going on among them. Their situation was no longer viewed from the standpoint of the centers of power outside. They were no longer viewed as underdeveloped countries going through a process of development akin to that of the now affluent countries. Instead they were now seen in terms of their own intrinsic situation, which was and is one of structural dependence on the way toward liberation. Viewed in the light of faith, the liberation would have to be not just social, political, and economic but total and integral.

So just as earlier distress, like that felt in Europe, had given rise to an incipient "theology of development," the new change in outlook gave rise to a "theology of liberation" in Latin America. It has been called "the first major current in modern theology to develop outside of Europe."[2] At the very least it is the first major contribution to world theology that is truly original to Latin American theology. For the first time a theological movement consciously assumed a standpoint of its own on a continent that had already been Christian for some centuries.

Liberation theology, then, is nothing else but the theological side of the experience encountered by Christian faith when it consciously elected to undertake the transformation of a dependent part of the world on the basis of the gospel message. Historically theology had tended to view itself as a science or a form of wisdom. Now it began to view itself as "critical reflection on Christian praxis in the light of the Word."[3] This is not to say that it ceased to view itself as a science or a form of wisdom. It merely means that it had to take note of the real nature of current Latin American praxis. And since that praxis is one of liberation, the resultant theological reflection on it would necessarily take shape as a "theology of liberation."

It would not be merely a new chapter in theology based on the same old theological methodology. It would not be like a "theology of politics," a "theology of revolution," or a "theology of temporal realities." Instead it would be a completely new reworking and formulation of theological activity as a whole from a completely new standpoint: i.e., the *kairos* of salvation history now being lived on our continent. Its reflection in the light of God's word would not just be *about* liberation praxis; it would actually *start from that praxis* to reinterpret the riches of the faith, which itself is praxis.

CONTRASTING EMPHASES

In my opinion, two main lines of thinking can be discerned in this theological trend that has developed since the Medellín Conference. I do not mean to suggest at all that all the varied strands and byways can be reduced to two. But since I cannot treat them all, I will focus here on the main lines of thinking rather than on all the theological currents that one might be able to discern. One of these post-Medellín lines of thought has been adopting Marxist methodology more or less consciously, along with its peculiar categories for analyzing and transforming reality. The other major line of thinking has led theology to take note of the culture and religiosity of the various peoples of Latin America.

From my own standpoint as an Argentinian at least, I think we can point to a new and further step that has been taken beyond that symbolized by the Medellín Conference. It is not a totally new step in that respect, but rather a further explicitation of certain tendencies and a lesser emphasis on others. As a result we find differences in focus and emphasis with the broad current of theology that has been worked out on the basis of the concrete situation of Latin America and its corresponding praxis of liberation. Viewed from my home country, the difference in focus under consideration here is not out of line with the distinctive experience of the Argentinian people in the last few decades. Nor is it out of line with the different assessment that might be made of nationalist and populist movements in Latin America (e.g., Peronism) insofar as their significance for liberation is concerned. And that is true whether the assessment is based on political analysis, philosophic interpretation, or theological hermeneutics.

In order to bring out the nature of the two main lines of thinking alluded to above, I shall focus on a few points and themes where they seem to show some difference in emphasis. Certain questions will help us to see this more clearly.

1. If we start off from the assumption that theology is critical reflection on historical praxis "in the light of the Word," then the first difference between the two lines of thought might be seen in their different understanding of "historical praxis." Are we dealing here primarily with the historical praxis of *the Latin American peoples* or with that of *avant-garde groups* whose political consciousness has been raised? Are we dealing primarily with the *faith praxis* of the people of God—which would include but go beyond political praxis— or are we dealing with *historical praxis pure and simple?* In the latter case we should not be considering anything specific or peculiar to the praxis of the faith; we would not be considering the theologal aspect or impulse that accompanies any action transformed by the faith. In short, we would be

concentrating on what unites Christian avant-garde groups with non-Christian avant-garde groups more than on what unites Christian avant-garde groups with the praxis of the People of God as a whole.[4]

Finally, are we dealing with a praxis that is *rooted* in our past history and even in prior Christian tradition, or are we dealing with a praxis so *new and original* that it is determined almost exclusively by our present heightened awareness of our structural dependence?

Obviously different answers to those questions will give rise to very different theologies. At bottom those questions are asking who is the *subject* of the theological wisdom made explicit reflectively and critically by the theologian, and who is the main *addressee* of any such theology: avant-garde Christians or the people of faith?

2. Connected with all that is one's understanding of the term "people,"[5] and its subsequent relationship to the "People of God" in theological reflection.

On the one hand "people" may be used as an historico-cultural category (a kind of "symbolic category") that designates all those who share in the historical project of liberation, whatever place they may occupy in the production process. In this case it is a cultural category because it alludes to the creation, defense, and liberation of a cultural ethos or human lifestyle. It is a historical category because only through the use of history can we determine who can really be called the "people" and in what way, and who cannot (the "anti-people"). And it is a "symbolic category" because of its convocative richness and its ambiguity (or significatory overdetermination), the latter being removed only in a specific historical context.

On the other hand one may tend to have a socio-economic or classist idea of the "people," identifying the people with the proletariat or the peasantry. Instead of using it as a historical and symbolic category, some use the term "people" as a scientific and dialectical category, usually based on a specific conception of dialectics. In such a case the "awareness" or "consciousness" of the people is usually understood to apply only to various avant-garde groups whose consciousness has been raised.

In the first instance, then, the category "people" is predominantly historical and political, operating in terms of an opposition between "power elites" on the one hand and the "oppressed people" on the other. In the second instance it is predominantly socio-economic, operating in terms of the opposition between "bourgeoisie" on the one hand and "proletariat" on the other.

3. Also closely related to the point discussed in our first section above is the different role assigned to various mediating factors in trying to take a theological reading of praxis in the light of God's word. Some might stress the mediating role of one or another kind of social science, using Marxist categories or Marxist methodology for example. Without denying the mediating role of the social sciences and the real contribution that might be made by Marxist methodology and its categories, others might stress the mediating role of history and choose a historical hermeneutics to explore the national experience of a given people. This choice implies acceptance of the fact that our people's liberation praxis and culture has deep roots in history; it means that their history will not be interpreted solely in terms of the dialectical schema of dependence.

4. Those who accept rootedness in history tend not to ponder history in terms of a dialectics of opposites. Instead they tend to use a dialectics of "already and not yet." In the history of the Latin American peoples they see a process of liberation and a people's liberation praxis that did not begin in the last decade. This was "already" real and present in the history of our *caudillos* and *montoneras*,[6] though it has "not yet" been fleshed out in any total or definitive form. What is more, the roots of this process can be found even in the mother country, Spain, in such movements as the *comuneros*.

Those who tend to bypass history and liberation events in the past are rightfully critical of many pseudo-liberation events and of romantic interpretations of history. The danger is that exclusive emphasis on dependence may tend to make them feel that our whole history was one of oppression until the socialist revolution appeared on the scene.

5. The first group, then, feels that in the past history of our people one can *already* see a distinctive popular culture and a brand of popular wisdom based on faith which can be spelled out somehow in theology. That culture and faith was spurned as "barbarism" by the Enlightenment "civilization" of Bourbon Spain, France, and England,[7] which was imported into Latin America by the native elite. In reality it is the original fruit of Ibero-American cultural intermingling and the baptism that was conferred on it. The *logos* or sapiential rationality of this popular culture is not the

logos of the modern Enlightenment; nor does it correspond with the canons of modern technological and instrumental reasoning. But that does not make it any less human, rational, and logical, nor any less usable for theo*logy*.

6. Depending on the stance one adopts towards the issues cited above, one will then have a differing evaluation of popular Catholicism in Latin America. Without denying its ambiguities, some will find in it an expression of authentic Christian faith inherited from the past and received from the preaching of the first missionaries. It should continue to be evangelized, but in terms of its own proper cultural values.

Others will tend to be more critical of the syncretist forms of popular religion. Influenced to some extent by Protestantism here, they will tend to make a distinction between religion and faith and to see the religion of the people as a socio-cultural by-product of socio-economic alienation. Thus they will tend to contrast the purified faith of avant-garde Christians to the people's traditional forms of religion.

Since the basic approach of pastoral activity as a whole plays a great role here, the basic stances have many more shadings than I have just suggested. But I think it is correct to say that the main currents of theological thinking and pastoral activity would tend to stress one basic option or the other.

7. In general both positions reject the "sacralizing" tendency that dominated the Christendom mentality of an earlier day. It was also rejected by the very first postconciliar reaction noted at the start. The sacralizing tendency was inclined to confuse or identify one particular culture or social structure with Christianity, as if they were the only real Christian culture or society.

Here again we find differences among those who reject "sacralization." Some stress secularization, as that term is understood by European and North American theology. In line with what I said in point 6 above, they will advocate criticism and demythification of popular religiosity, finding inspiration in "suspicion" and the "masters of suspicion" discussed by Ricoeur (Marx and Freud in particular).

This critical attitude may go back to very different roots. In the case of some (e.g., the intellectual elites of a neoliberal or developmentalist stamp) its roots lie in the enlightened reasoning of progressivism. In the case of others its roots lie in Marxist critico-dialectical reasoning, which is equally enlightened but in a dialectical relationship with revolutionary praxis. In both cases we are dealing with a heritage of the modern age, an age which we have experienced here in a basic state of dependence.

Still others, however, are disturbed by both of these brands of criticism. Admitting their value, they will object that such criticism often conceals a "scientistic" or Enlightenment conception of rationality that fails to regard the human value of sapiential and symbolic reasoning. These people are more ready to acknowledge the liberative import of religious symbols. They also stress the distinctive contribution that faith can and does make to both the religious and the secular praxis of our people and their historico-cultural project. This is a contribution that is transcendent and in some sense contemplative. Without denying the critico-prophetical function of the church and its obligation to commit itself to praxis, these people prefer to define the specific quality of ecclesial activity in terms of its religious mission and transcendence; at the same time, however, they see the promotion of human justice as an integral component of evangelization.

Needless to say, these people do not view religion in liberal terms. It is not a water-tight compartment in the midst of life but a transcendent aspect of all human activities, even those that may not be specifically religious. They do not lapse back into any sort of "sacralism" because they have no intention of proposing some alternative or parallel historical project of a sacral character. They respect the autonomy of history as a secular project, but they also want to recognize its transcendent aspect as brought out by the Christian faith.

8. Closely bound up with all the above are the different emphases that these pastoral and theological options may display in their strategy for change and liberation. Some may stress ethical and prophetic criticism, thereby tending to intensify conflict and even class struggle both within and outside the church. Without rejecting prophetic criticism and ethical denunciation, others will stress unity over struggle and conflict. On the one hand they will admit perfect unity does "not yet" exist in the church or among the people, and so they will denounce any pseudounity that serves to disguise existing injustices. On the other hand they will also recognize the reality of the unity that is "already" present here and now, refusing to disregard or snuff out the spark that has already been lit. Thus they have more of a feel for pastoral patience, historical viability, and the time needed for liberation to become a complete reality.

9. The differing points of view are thus open to different tempta-

tions. Those who propound ethical and prophetic criticism may be in danger of falling into "ethicism," classism, violence, and an excessive stress on conflict. The others are prey to a populist romanticism that might easily be taken over by those opposed to liberation; they might also fall prey to an ineffective reformism that would identify viability with compromise.

From all that has been said above I think we can now distinguish four main strands of thought in current Latin America that are based on the varying historical approaches indicated:

a. A conservative, preconciliar theology that is more and more on the wane;
b. A postconciliar theology based on European or progressivist North American models;
c. A liberation theology predominantly influenced by Marxist categories and methodology in its concern to analyze and transform reality;
d. A liberation theology predominantly concerned with being a theology of popular pastoral activity in the sense just described. Here the term "pastoral" should not be taken in a restricted sense. It implies an option for popular culture as the praxis of the People of God in *all* their dimensions.

A perfect example of the last option in Argentina is the chapter on popular pastoral activity in the 1969 San Miguel statement of the Argentinian episcopate. Their statement was designed to adapt the conclusions of the Medellín Conference "to the present-day reality of our country."[8] As Lucio Gera notes, the Argentinian statement does not identify the world or the temporal dimension with the state, as we were wont to do in our preconciliar theology; nor does it describe that dimension in the rather abstract terms that can be found even in postconciliar brands of theology. Instead that dimension is concretized in "the Argentinian people."[9] The church must "involve and incarnate itself in the national experience of the Argentinian people." To do this, it must draw closer to them, particularly "to the poor, the oppressed, and those in need." Here, Gera notes, we find an understanding of the people that is not framed in class terms. The focus is not on ownership of the means of production and the place people occupy in the production process. The important thing is that the people be active agents of their own history and have a place in the decision-making process, though of course the decisions will be fleshed out in material terms.

The pastoral, ecclesiological, and theological focus of the document becomes truly original when it affirms that "the activity of the church should not only be oriented toward the people but also derive *from* the people primarily." Hence "the church must exercise discernment about its liberative or salvific activity from the viewpoint of the people and their interests." It is the people who are the active subject and agent of human history, which is intimately bound up with salvation history. The signs of the times, then, "are rendered present and decipherable in the happenings which the people perform or which affect them." The place where one can discern the real outlook of the people, and hence the proper outlook for church activity, is the history of the people, the national experience in history and the events contained in it. The aim is definitely not to give a nationalistic focus to theology and pastoral activity, however. It is to give them the universality and transcendence that is properly theirs, but by situating them concretely in history and pointing up their salvific embodiment.

POPULAR CULTURE AS A HERMENEUTIC LOCALE

Each of the four main positions summarized above defends real values. The first position accentuates the values of tradition, the institutional and sacral aspect of the church, and hierarchical authority. The second highlights the critical spirit of the Enlightenment, the autonomy of the world and science, technical development, and progress. The third stresses social criticism of injustice, ethico-prophetical denunciation, and identification with the poor and oppressed. The fourth underlines the values of popular culture, the "already" existing unity of the church as the People of God, the Christian sense of our people and their religiosity, the historical roots of the current liberation process, and openness of this process to a qualitatively new society that would be neither capitalist nor Marxist. Each view is in danger of absolutizing its own particular focus and making it the exclusive one.

This does not mean, however, that they all have the same truth value. It is not enough to discern the positive values of each and the dangers of one-sidedness. We must also exercise discernment in trying to figure out *which way* salvation actually travels through history. Our work of theological discernment must therefore try to focus primarily, though not exclusively, on the *starting point* and the *final goal* of the journey and decide the true route.

Two gospel criteria can help us with this work of discernment in the midst of our situation in history. First, we should give preference to the theological and pastoral option that best serves the cause of unity in justice. In other words, we should prefer the option which, being more radical and comprehensive, allows for the most thorough dialectical integration of the other options and their values. Unity is to be preferred over divisiveness and conflict, though we would still respect differences and accept the need for a critical fight against injustice and any ahistorical absolutization. Included under the latter heading would be any ahistorical absolutization of our own theological focus, even though it might be the most comprehensive one. Authentic unity is nothing else but the fruit of human passage through the paschal mystery in every historical "already" and in the eschatological "not yet." Second, the hermeneutic locale of historical discernment is given, in every situation, by the poor and oppressed—which is to say, by those who suffer whatever form of injustice seems to be the most crucial in a given situation.

This means that poverty, injustice, and oppression must always be defined historically. In a given historical instance it may be discrimination of one sort or another—racial, political, socioeconomic, religious, or cultural. The point is that some particular form of injustice will embody the main concrete sin of a given age and society, serving more or less as its "sign." Precisely because it involves the poor, it is also here that the gratuitousness of both historical salvation and definitive salvation is signified. This sign is "efficacious" because it affects and moves people ethically as a summons in which the eye of faith can discern the word of God. This summoning word is to be incarnated into the material structures of history so that they become symbols of the gratuitous possibility of historical novelty. It then symbolizes the real possibility of salvation as both a gift and a task to be taken on by human beings in their historical praxis.

As I noted earlier, our feeling is that the main symbolic poverty (though certainly not the only one) is to be found in the alienation of the people from their right to be the active subjects of their own message and their own historico-cultural project. Here "culture" means a cultural *ethos*, a particular way of living one's freedom, and it naturally has many different features. It would include economic, political, and religious aspects, for example, but the term "culture" itself is not to be restricted to any one of its aspects.

My judgment, then, is that the fourth theological option described earlier is the one which best responds to our concrete situation of sin and to our concrete possibility of salvation. On the one hand, it seems to me, it is the most comprehensive one that best serves to foster unity. It is framed in terms of the "people" and Latin America seems to be an indivisible and indubitable combination of both "the people" and "the People of God" journeying in communion with the universal church through one faith and one baptism. That unity, however, can result only from a conscious decision to renounce elitism in the areas of power, knowledge, and possessions. This holds true for the subject and addressee of any attempt to understand historical liberation and the historical project; and it also holds true for both the subject and addressee of the church's theology and pastoral activity.

Renouncing elitism in the area of possession and ownership is not enough. We must also renounce the elitism in the area of knowledge that we now find among the enlightened elites of both the left and the right. We should not confuse or identify the biblical "remnant," who are the repository of the sapiential loyalty of God's faithful people, with any elites at all.

Moreover, the fourth theological standpoint also adopts the oppressed Latin American of today as its focus. As I see it, Latin Americans today are oppressed primarily in their *being* (i.e., their lifestyle or cultural *ethos*) precisely because they are oppressed in their *capacity to be* (i.e., their power to make decisions concerning their own history and their mission therein).

The hermeneutic locale, then, is the people as they are concretely embodied in their popular culture (in all its manifestations) and as they are interpreted by those in whom they really see themselves interpreted (whatever sort of interpretation it may be). Here the category "people" is taken in a historico-cultural sense as the word was described above. It is not viewed in terms of classes or in terms of some ambiguous populism (a vacuum which anything can fill). As a category-symbol, it is open, convocative, and historically defined. Thus understood, the "people" effectively symbolizes the oppression that is suffered by all, even by the power elite, though in varying degrees and forms according to their social status. It also effectively symbolizes the gratuitousness of the liberation that all can contribute, even the power elite, though here again the form and degree of liberative power will depend on the type of oppression from which one suffers. The values of the power elite, too, must be salvaged so that they can contribute to the salvation of all; but the power elite must "die" to their exclusivism and their absolutization, becoming assimilated into the overall culture of the people.[10]

The subject of theologal wisdom is the concrete people of God here and now, though of course they are in communion with the universal people of God and tradition. Since Latin American theologians usually have been formed in the culture of the Enlightenment, however, this means that they must undergo a real *cultural conversion* without denying the values of the tradition and the critique they got from their training. They will assume those values but they will now radicalize them.

THE MISSION OF THEOLOGY IN LATIN AMERICA TODAY

Aside from what I said above, the fourth theological option seems to correspond best to the Latin American and postmodern situation of any *logos* that would purport to voice the word of God in human and historical terms on the basis of our present salvific situation.

I use the term "postmodern" deliberately.[11] It is not enough to get beyond the premodern scheme of cultural Christendom, which theology has not always done in the modern age and which is still evident in various sectors of our present life. We must also get beyond modernity itself and its Enlightenment reasoning that serves as a mask for "the will to power and profit." This Enlightenment *logos* takes different forms. It is evident both in the one-dimensional nature of technological reasoning and in the reductive, levelling circularity of Marxist dialectical reasoning and its conception of historical praxis.

There are clear signs everywhere that modernity is in crisis. In our case it is our dependent brand of modernity that is in crisis. Adopting what Ricoeur might call a state of "second innocence," we certainly should assume prior historical phases of our tradition and criticism as we try to get beyond modernity. Trying to start all over from zero would be as ahistorical as thinking that history and its salvation are to be found in some earlier phase.

I would also stress the distinctive situation of Latin America because our historical situation is in fact unique. We are the only group of nations in the Third World that is generally Christian and culturally mixed. We are certainly Christian in socio-cultural terms, and, in my opinion, in faith as well. Moreover, by virtue of our cultural mix, and to a large extent by virtue of our ethnic mix as well, we constitute the only continent that is really living through a post-Christian and postmodern period as the developed world is, while at the same time suffering from dependence and longing for liberation. On the one hand we have lived through the cultural regimen known as Christendom (as the "New Christendom of the Indies"); on the other hand our urban centers and other places have gone through the phase of modernity as well. But both realities were experienced from a basic situation of dependency.

When it comes to theo-*logy*, then, we must salvage the *logos* of Christian wisdom that is to be found among the Latin American people and in their historical praxis—the latter being concerned both with liberation and with the creation of their own culture. This particular *logos* has gradually developed as the result of a fruitful cultural blending that was eventually baptized; and it is sapiential, of the people, and historically new. Like the Latin American people, this *logos* was shunted aside and oppressed by the culture of the enlightened elites. They saw it as "barbarism" inherited from Iberian backwardness and Amerindian savagery. The "civilization" of the Enlightenment is not something that we have lived as our very own, assimilating it in the process of fruitful intercultural dialogue. Instead we merely imported and imitated it, thus bearing still further witness to our dependent way of living through the modern age.

This fact of cultural intermixture seems to suggest that Latin America and Latin American theology has a specific and special mediating role to play between two other parties. One would be occidental tradition, which has its roots in Greco-Roman and Judeo-Christian sources, was spread worldwide and suffered inner crises in the modern age, and is now living in the postmodern age. The other party would be the other peoples of the Third World, which are non-Christian for the most part.

The worldwide spread of occidental culture led to the universalization of its particular features: e.g., its science, its technology, its philosophy, its socialist or liberal-democratic forms, and its particular way of understanding and living Christianity. This process of universalization, which took place in the modern age for the most part, clearly implied and signified domination according to the prevailing cultural *ethos* of that period. Now the secret logic of history seems to suggest that there is some connection between the growing crisis of modernity in the northern hemisphere and the reawakened quest for justice and liberation in the Third World, particularly in Latin America. We sense the growing possibility for an authentic universalization of cultures within a community of the world's peoples, though that does not mean there would be only one universal culture.

As Vatican II points out, the church shares in the life of this particular moment in history. As the people of God hierarchically institutionalized, the church has the mission of *accompanying* today's world in and through this historical process. It must contribute the specific thing that only faith can give to the historical project aimed at justice and liberation. What faith offers to us is a theologal aspect: i.e., openness to God's transcendence, and hence to all the dimensions of the human realm. This strongly suggests that it has some "conception of the person and society," but it is not a univocal ideology set up in advance. Instead it comes down to certain ways of understanding the human realm that are to be fleshed out analogously in history, with due respect for the peculiarities of a given age and for the values of a given cultural milieu. At the same time it will criticize the inhuman elements they contain.

Both the church as the community of institutionalized faith and theology as reflection on that faith must place themselves in the service of the faith held by the Latin American people of God. The mission of Latin American theology is to serve our people by offering them the reflective and critical work it has done, in the light of God's word, on the element of transcendence which their faith contributes to their historical experience.

Theology, then, must renounce any desire to inaugurate a historical project or a new world from within its own closed boundaries. It must respect the autonomy of our people in their rightful efforts to fashion their own history. At the same time, however, theology cannot refuse to articulate the saving contribution of eschatological transformation and liberative criticism that stems from the gospel message. It cannot refuse to proclaim the "sacramental" aspect of historical initiatives and achievements. In a critical and articulate way it must point out, in the light of God's word, how they are an anticipatory foretaste and sign of God's definitive salvation, a sign of his saving action being manifested in history. By the very same token theology cannot fail to denounce everything in those human achievements that goes against humankind and God, due to the sinfulness of human individuals, classes, and peoples. Sin turns those potential "signs" of salvation into disfigured caricatures of it, so that they become illusory embodiments of some pseudo-salvation.

That is why theology must provide the function of discernment as it seeks to accompany people through the crucial throes of transition from one historical epoch to the next. All are responsible for making sure that the new epoch will be more humane than the previous one.[12] Theology does not bear the chief responsibility here, but it certainly bears some share of responsibility. That share is greater in the case of a people like ours, who are Christian for the most part. For their cultural *ethos*, the wellspring of their historical project, is deeply imbued with Christianity. Unlike other peoples, Latin Americans have not gone through the secularization process to the extent that is typical of the modern age.

THE UNITY OF HISTORY AND SALVATION HISTORY

If we want to appreciate how theology might accompany our people as it should at this critical historical juncture, we would do well to consider the relationship that exists between history and historical praxis as such on the one hand and salvation history and its praxis on the other.

The mystery of history and its structure is not satisfactorily handled by either dualism (e.g., distinguishing between the spiritual and the temporal as two different planes) or monism (whether it be of the sacralizing or the dialectical type). History is at once profane history and salvation history in some unconfused and indivisible way, just as Christ himself (and humankind in and through him) is at once a Son of man and Son of God. Neither does monism or dualism correspond to the concrete way in which our people live out their existence as a people and as Christians. Both dualism and monism are not genuinely Christian, not authentically liberative, and not truly Latin American.

As Christian faith sees it, history has an incarnational structure thanks to grace. It thus is in the nature of a sign, a mystery, and a sacrament. That grace was already granted unreservedly by God in Christ though human beings, both as individuals and as a people, can accept it, reject it, or even fail to come to know it.

At bottom the problem is that both dualistic and monistic views betray a deficient understanding of transcendence.[13] In dualistic schemes transcendence is viewed as an abstract reduplication of the temporal plane or a projection of it into the infinite; and the temporal plane is viewed in the same atemporal and supratemporal terms as its duplicate. We get the other-worldliness so rightly criticized by Nietzsche and the opiate of the people so pointedly noted by Marx. The distinctions between the two planes are fixed and frozen as substantives dwelling in a world apart, so that the two realms are not seen to be "indivisibly and unconfusedly" intermingled. Viewed in a bit more up-to-date terms, the temporal realm will rightly be accorded its autonomy; but both the temporal realm and its autonomy will still be interpreted in terms of platonic dualism and the liberal view of autonomy espoused by the modern mind.

In monistic schemes we find several alternatives. Transcendence may be viewed in monophysite terms, so that it is confused and identified with certain immanent sectors that are taken to be "sacred." Here one type of civilization or political ideology, etc., is taken to be the *only* valid Christian one. Or transcendence may be viewed in secularist terms as a mere dialectical aspect of historical praxis. In this case the transcendence of faith is reduced by depriving it of any specificity of its own. Relying on some dialectics of identity and totality, such as that of Hegel or Marx, people then tend to equate the surrender of *kenosis* with mere emptying.

Suppose the oneness and sameness of the only human history and historical vocation is interpreted in terms of the logic of totality, a heritage from Greek philosophy that reached its ultimate expression in the modern age. How will one then view the relationship between history and salvation history, historical praxis and the praxis of salvation history, people and People of God? On the one hand one may see it as a relationship between *two* totalities, thus falling back into the dualism evident in the distinction between two different planes. Or else one will see it all as *one* totality, though the relationship may be dialectical, and thus fall back into a brand of monism. Using the logic of totality, one cannot really think in historical terms and contemplate historical realities: e.g., creation, incarnation, and grace. Yet the distinctive character of Christian thinking is precisely that it is historical. In its view history involves the interplay between the transcendent gratuitousness of God's liberative intervention and the freedom of human response to it; even God respects that freedom, and the resultant sphere of freedom is the locale where human beings exercise discernment concerning God's freely proffered and liberative will for human salvation.

The unity involved here is not that of each plane in isolation, nor is it something that is levelled down and treated reductively through dialectics. It is an indivisible oneness that is both historical and gratuitous, that is in the order of liberty rather than in the order of nature. That oneness is given in a dialectical process which is determined concretely but which is also open to the unpredictable novelty of the future, the distinctive otherness of every people and culture, and the transcendence of God. What is involved here is a dialectics of "already" and "not yet." Historical, political, and social liberations are *already* realizations of salvation in history; but they are also anticipatory signs and foretastes of the total and definitive liberation that has *not yet* been consummated and implies some new gratuitousness.

We would be stopping halfway if we were to assume that we need only refer to the dialectics of "already" and "not yet" in order to characterize the transcendence of definitive salvation vis-à-vis liberations in history. We cannot rest content with viewing the historical process in terms of a somewhat revised dialectics of totality where the "already" and the "not yet" are merely reduced to dialectical poles. To do that would be to place transcendence solely in the future. The oneness and distinctiveness of the two aspects is not that of a dialectical totality. Rather it is the fruit of the *gratuitously* unconfused and indivisible oneness of a history that is simultaneously profane and salvific. As we noted earlier, this oneness has an incarnational structure; it is both symbolic and sacramental. It cannot be articulated conceptually with a logic of totality. It requires a symbolic and ana-*logic* logic of liberty and otherness.[14] The transcendent is made present in the symbol, but it is made present precisely *as* transcendent. It remains free in all its gratuitousness, and it leaves people free for the work of recognition, discernment, and interpretation.

THEOLOGICAL DISCERNMENT OF THE
HISTORICAL MEDIATIONS OF THE FAITH

This view of the relationship between history and salvation history will help us to outline how theology might be able to meet its task of accompanying the peoples of Latin America in their history, respecting their secular autonomy while not losing its own theological specificity. I am not going to implement its task of accompaniment here, however. I am simply going to show *how* it is possible, though even that injects some concrete content into the response. My treatment here explores what is involved in any authentic "accompaniment."

It seems to me that "accompaniment" entails three aspects that are nothing more than the three faces of the same process of discernment. The first is a service of criticism designed to foster liberation from, or discernment of, sin and illusion. The second is a service of discerning salvation in history through a theological reading of the signs of God's presence in historical happenings. Here theology will try to point out how and where salvation is operative in them. As I noted earlier, theology denounces sin through its prophetic proclamation of salvation in history; and both the denunciation and the proclamation are uttered in the light of God's word.

That brings us to the third aspect of accompaniment. Theology assumes historical worldliness both in its reflective discourse, which makes explicit its discernment, and in its committed involvement with the resultant historical options. Its assumption of this worldliness has two sides. On the one hand it criticizes it insofar as it is disfigured by sin. On the other hand it acknowledges the autonomy of this worldliness as a symbol and figure of the saving God made history. It does not incorporate historical worldliness into some unitary and absolute discourse. Rather it assumes it because the word of the saving God must be incarnated in human speech, speech drawn from the people, if it is to accompany them salvifically in their history.

The subjects of this discernment are not primarily the theologian, but the people of God as a whole. It is the theologians' function, however, to articulate the sapiential discernment of the people of God, of whom they are members and whom they serve with their theological charism. Needless to say, their function is meant to be in the service of church authority and its specific function, charism, and service.

Now if theology does wish to accompany our people in history, discerning the signs of God in their history, life, and praxis from its own theological vantage point, then it obviously must confront the various socio-cultural mediations of the faith. Consciously rejecting all forms of dualism (which continue to perform an ideological function), theology stresses the *historical* incarnation and the effective realization *in practice* of God's revealed word. This means that among the mediations to be confronted by theology are: the pre-reflective or scientific *interpretations* through which the faith of the people or of different groups reads the signs of the times; the *projects and utopias* that articulate hope in the eschatological kingdom before it arrives; and the *political mediations* through which charity works.[15]

All those mediations imply a choice, which is made now by

people or received from somewhere else. Neither scientific analysis nor philosophical reflection alone can determine the ethical "plus" that is found in human decision-making when people assume concrete responsibility for history. This ethical "plus" corresponds with the "plus" of sapiential sense and truth that is found in every concrete free act and that cannot be reduced to analytical reasons or dialectical totalizations.

Because the choice or option here is an ethical one, salvation and condemnation are at stake in it insofar as life is concerned. This simply means that the work of liberative grace or of sinfulness in history takes concrete shape through our ethical option. So this option is obviously of deep concern to a theology that purports to do its reflection on the historical praxis of the people and from that historical praxis.

The point is that the historical option of human beings and peoples, as well as history itself, has an incarnational and "sacramental" structure. When it opens itself to the activity of God, there shines through it some glimmer of transcendence and the gratuitous presence of the Lord's summons. This permits it to have a contemplative phase or aspect: (*"in actione—etiam saeculari et communitaria—contemplativus"*).[16] Even when our historical option closes itself off from God's action, his summons does not cease to be present; but in this case it is present in the form of a judgment.

This theologal summons to meaningfulness respects the temporal autonomy of the historical mediations in which it is incarnated. It is not reducible to them, not even dialectically; it is absolute. But it does leave them in all their historical contingency. It also liberates them from absolutization, disfigurement, and manipulation by sin. In the modern age that sort of absolutization has shown up as an absolute "will to power and profit." Insofar as sin does lay hold of them in this way, it transforms them into illusions that mask reality. They become idols instead of symbols.

Interacting hermeneutically with the word of God as it is read in church tradition and the ecclesial community, theology has the task of articulating the historical experience and practice of the faith. It must do this in a discourse that is reflective and critical while still remaining analogical, symbolic, and historical. It does this by starting out from the historical praxis of our people. Borrowing their symbols and language and entering into fruitful dialogue with the symbols and language of tradition, it seeks to express the faith in those symbols and language which, in our case, have arisen from the fruitful union of the gospel message and the culture of the people.

That is how theology can perform its prophetic service of interpreting the faith. It cannot perform that service without involving itself in history on the practical level. To do this, it must exercise discernment concerning the historical mediations that it has been using to voice its message of salvation, for they may be infected with sinfulness, illusion, and ideology in the pejorative sense. It must take the risk of defilement because it cannot take refuge outside of history and its options in some allegedly antiseptic world beyond. At the same time, however, it is not trapped in the ideological play of historical and cultural mediations and their ambiguous status as sin or grace. Theology can transcend all that through discernment. For transcendence is incarnated in history, and history, thanks to grace, is structured as a sign and sacrament.

The service of discernment is a reciprocal one. Any given theology is born at a given historical moment and in a socio-cultural milieu motivated by certain interests. It must allow itself to be judged by the word of God for those potential ideologizations that it may have assumed uncritically. This process of criticism may be mediated through the methods of "suspicion" and "unmasking." At the same time, however, theology will operate in the light of God's word to criticize the ideologies underlying those methods as well as the other historico-cultural mediations it uses to articulate God's word and exercise discernment about historical praxis. For in those mediating factors we find a mixture of grace and sin, of the theologal summons to justice and liberation and the illusions stemming from bastard interests.

There is still more to be said here. If a theology is really trying to accompany the people of Latin America in the historical process of liberation, then it will read the word of God and exercise discernment with regard to praxis from a specific hermeneutic locale: i.e., from the culture and praxis of the people. But even its option for that locale must be subjected to the judgment of God's word, which is a two-edged sword. By placing the mediations in question within the theologal orbit of gratuitousness, respect, and freedom—the proper orbit of faith itself—it does them the service of freeing them from any potential absolutization, exclusivism, and univocalness.[17]

For this very reason theology must be the first to de-absolutize itself. It must give up any claim to impose itself without showing any respect for the proper autonomy of temporal mediations. It must also refuse to regard itself as the supreme or absolute discourse on reality that nullifies all other discourse (scientific, poetic, philosophical, and so forth). In addition, it must give up any desire to be the exclusive or only orthodox interpretation of the faith. At the same time, however, it will not give up the judgment that the word of God brings to bear on itself or historical mediations. By making it possible for those mediations to de-absolutize themselves, it opens them up to the freedom of discernment, the novelty of new situations, respect for the otherness of other situations, and the transcendence and gratuitousness of God's activity.

But one should not think that this puts all the different interpretations, historical projects, and practical mediations on the same level. One should not conclude that they all have exactly the same value for faith in a given historical situation. While they all can be saved insofar as they die to their own absolutization and rise to their liberation, discernment is a historical rather than an abstract process. It must *situate* those liberated values and coordinate them with each other *from the context* of the here-and-now historical situation. Operating in discontinuous continuity with a salvific tradition, it must judge them in accordance with the way that God's liberative action in history manifests itself in this particular situation.

Discernment locates and integrates the human and salvific truths and values of the various stances vis-à-vis history and its mediations. But it does *not* do this in some abstract or dialectical theological system. Rather it does it through the historical and open-ended comprehensiveness of a theological doctrine which is critically accompanying our people in their here-and-now historical project, and which is corresponding to their cultural *ethos* from the standpoint of the gospel message. This doctrine might be called a "situated theological universal." Situated in a history and a praxis, it is a universal that corresponds only analogically with other historico-cultural situations. But it does not thereby lose its truth value or cease to be a contribution to universal theology.

We must try to discern the historical interrelationship between different truths and values. But we can only discern that, as well as the internal structure of such a theological discourse, by working a posteriori in and from the historical situation. Here theology goes about its work of discernment in "fear and trembling." Motivated by the evangelical spirit of poverty, it seeks to explore the shadows and bright spots of history and its mediations in the light of the prototypes of salvation history provided by the Old and New Testament. It works with the analogy of faith.

In the case of individual human beings, salvific discernment of one's personal history and vocation results from the convergence of two paschal structures: that of the mysteries of salvation history which are being contemplated on the one hand, and that of the affective attitude of the one who is discerning and being discerned. Something similar takes place in discerning the history and vocation of whole peoples as well as their yearnings and motivating factors. Theology can articulate this discernment reflectively and justify it critically in accordance with the analogy of faith. Working in the light of the biblical prototypes, it can discover the same paschal structure of salvation in history and historical praxis. Although theology does not construct a system, it can at least reread the Scriptures in the concrete tradition of the church here and now. It does this through the use of a doctrine focused on the sapiential *logos* reflected in the praxis of God's people in Latin America, and which then proceeds to make that *logos* reflective and critical.

Discernment makes clear the temporal nature of Christian experience, which theology must then make explicit in its discourse. The Latin American people here and now are sensing and judging in the light of the signs of the times confronting them. Working in the light of faith and God's word, we must discern how much of that sensing and feeling is a proper attitude and response to the liberative summons of the Lord and where it is distorted by sin. We may use the human sciences as a mediating factor in trying to explore our people's sensing and judging, provided that the mediating factor itself is immersed in the rhythm of the discernment process.

The sensing and feeling of the people will take in yearnings and frustrations, hopes and fears, joys and sorrows, peaceable agreements and conflicts. Out of all that will emerge the real possibilities for the future that are open to the people in their freedom. The social sciences can certainly help to determine what the real possibilities are. It can study their material structures, the structures in which the transcendent summons of the future is fleshed out, thus helping us to distinguish truth from illusion. But in doing this the social sciences must not reduce the possibilities in any univocal way, closing them off to the unforeseen originality of history or to the freedom wherewith people take on history.

The historical memory of a people must be a mediating factor in this process of discernment. It is the memory of a concrete past in which a tradition of liberation is "already" taking shape (the history of salvation in the Bible and salvation in one's own history). What is happening now can be discerned as an aspect of salvific liberation or as an oppressive illusion only insofar as it is inserted into an ongoing historical experience of liberation. That past experience will define the present happening without closing it off to the novelty of ever fresh meanings. This memory (and its mediation through the science of history) does not predetermine the future that is already arriving in the present. But it does help us to discern that future, even as it itself is discerned and reinterpreted by the future.

Theology's articulation of discernment cannot help but be analogical and symbolic. It is articulating a people's sapiential sensing and judging as well as their sapiential memory. It is interpreting the symbolic value of happenings that are "overdetermined" insofar as their import is concerned, and which are also open to the future. But this does not mean that it can set aside the mediation of the sciences in its sapiential reading of historical praxis. In doing that reading it uses the analogy of faith to show that such discernment is possible and how. I myself began to do that above when I brought in references to the Incarnation, the paschal event, and sacramental signs.

Thus the symbols and categories of the Bible and Christian tradition, which are historical, can be of service to us in trying to offer a theological hermeneutics of our own continental or national history, of our historical project and what we are doing right now. But the symbols and categories of our own culture and history can also be of service in trying to articulate the faith. This is possible because the analogy of faith finds one and the same rhythm and structure in both. It is triune, incarnational, and paschal. It is the rhythm and structure of the economy of salvation.[18]

A TWOFOLD TASK FOR LATIN AMERICAN THEOLOGY

In conclusion, then, we can say that a twofold task awaits any theology seeking to accompany the peoples of Latin America in their present-day process of liberation and historical creation. On the one hand it must try to discern, interpret, and criticize the present-day situation in salvific terms. It must explore the possibilities and the ambiguities of the present, the historico-cultural project that is emerging from our people, and the historical roots that sustain the whole process.

On the other hand it must also reread and reinterpret the riches of our faith, using the praxis and culture of the Latin American people as its hermeneutic locale. This would mean criticizing certain ways of theologizing, needless to say.

The task is difficult but not impossible, especially since the Lord himself seems to be prompting us to it. It may seem to be of lesser importance right now insofar as service to our people is concerned. But if theology does not take up this task, no one else will do it for theology—to the detriment of our people's faith and its salvific incarnation in their culture and historical project. This pastoral and political responsibility of theology is all the greater insofar as the faith played a predominant role in the growth and subsequent history of our cultural *ethos* and insofar as we hope that our faith will continue to light up the path leading our peoples to liberation.

NOTES

1. Medellín Conference Documents, vol. 2, "Introduction to the Final Documents," no. 4; see Appendix II in this volume.

2. The words are those of Vincent Cosmao and François Malley, "Foi chrétienne et changement social en Amérique Latine," in *Foi et Développement* 1 (September 1972):3.

3. Gustavo Gutiérrez, *A Theology of Liberation*, Eng. trans. (Maryknoll, New York: Orbis Books, 1973), p. 13.

4. I have treated the difference between these two formulations in an article entitled "Situación de la problemática 'Fe y política' entre nosotros," in *Fe y política* (Buenos Aires: Ed. Guadalupe, 1973), pp. 15–47. There I brought out the contrast by comparing the *theological* documents of the movement known as Priests for the Third World with the final document issued by the first convention of the Christians for Socialism (see Appendix II, anthologies, for a collection of documents concerned with the latter movement).

In the article I distinguished four different theological positions on our continent with regard to the whole issue of faith and politics. For a fuller treatment of the issue of faith praxis and politics see my article entitled "Teología y política—El actual desafío planteado al lenguage teológico latinoamericano de liberación," in *Fe cristiana y cambio social en América Latina* (Salamanca: Sígueme, 1973), pp. 247–64.

5. On the categories "people," "culture," and "popular culture" see the works of Lucio Gera: in collaboration with Guillermo Rodríguez Melgarejo, "Apuntes para una interpretación de la Iglesia Argentina," in *Víspera*, no. 15 (February 1970), pp. 59–88; "Dependencia cultural y creación de cultura a la luz de la reflexión teológica," in *Stromata* 30 (1974), nos. 1-2. See also the proceedings of the *Seminario sobre Pastoral Popular*, San Miguel, September 6–9, 1973 (Buenos Aires: Instituto de Cultura Pastoral Popular, 1974).

6. In the political and military actions the *caudillos* acted as popular leaders who interpreted the thinking and feeling and aspirations of their people: e.g., the Uruguayan José Gervasio Artigas (1764–1850), the Paraguayan Francisco Solano López (1827–1870), and the Argentinian Juan Manuel de Rosas (1793–1877). The *montoneras* were armed bands of *gauchos* who fought in the wars of independence or against centralist governments that they felt represented the interests of British commerce and the power elites. Loyalty to their *caudillos* was one of their chief characteristics.

Insofar as the dialectics of "already" and "not yet" is concerned, my feeling is that the Christian experience finds better expression in Blondel's dialectics than in that of Hegel. See my work, *Sein und Inkarnation. Zum ontologischen Hintergrund der Frühschriften Maurice Blondels* (Freiburg-Munich: Alber Verlag, 1968).

7. In 1845 Domingo F. Sarmiento published a book on the *caudillo* Juan Facundo Quiroga, which was entitled *Facundo*. The book's subtitle was *Civilización y barbarie*, and that expression came to characterize the dialectics of "enlightened culture" versus "popular culture."

8. *Declaración del Episcopado Argentino sobre la adaptación a la realidad actual del país, de las Conclusiones de la II Conferencia General del Episcopado Latinoamericano* (Buenos Aires: Ed. Paulinas, 1969), Document VI.

9. See my article, "Apuntes para una interpretación de la Iglesia argentina," pp. 70–73.

10. I outlined the various mediations needed in any liberation dialectics in my article, "La liberación latinoamericana—Ontología del proceso auténticamente liberador," in *Stromata* 28 (1972): 107–50. There I offered an ontological critique of various historico-cultural projects now being proposed in Latin America. By virtue of their presuppositions, many of them tend to match up with the different theological and pastoral positions that I have brought up in this article.

11. On the whole notion of "postmodernity" as treated from a philosophical standpoint, see my article entitled "Transcendencia, praxis liberadora y lenguaje—Hacia una filosofía de la religión post-moderna y latinoamericanamente situada," in *Hacia una filosofía de la liberación latinoamericana* (Buenos Aires: Ed. Bonum, 1973), pp. 245–69. There I pointed out that a "shift" to historicity and historical praxis is not enough to overcome the *logos* of the modern age, that there must also be a shift to popular culture and popular wisdom.

12. The various features of a "new humanism" were discussed at an interdisciplinary seminar chaired by Bernhard Welte in 1973. The proceedings are to be published soon as *Hacia un nuevo humanismo* (Buenos Aires, Ed. Bonum). In that volume see my article entitled "Hacia un nuevo humanismo. Comentario personal de las discusiones desde la perspectiva latinoamericana."

13. I discuss this issue in *Fe y política*. Elsewhere I have presented a philosophical elaboration of the concept of transcendence, taking due account of modern and postmodern philosophy: "La liberación latinoamericana—Ontología del proceso auténticamente liberador" ; and "El itinerario filosófico hacia el Dios vivo—Reflexiones sobre su historia, su planteo actual y su relectura desde la situación latinoamericana," in *Stromata* 30 (1974).

14. The contrast between "totality" and "otherness" (*alteridad*) was inspired by Emmanuel Levinas, *Totalité et infini—Essai sur l'extériorité* (The Hague: Martinus Nijhoff, 1961; Eng. trans.: *Totality and Infinity: An Essay on Exteriority* [Pittsburgh: Duquesne University Press, 1969]). Levinas drew his inspiration from the Bible. Besides my own writing, Enrique Dussel often discusses the contrast between an "ontology of totality" and a "metaphysics of otherness." See article 9 in this volume.

15. I have treated the relationship between faith and ideology in greater detail in my article entitled "The Theology of Liberation—Evangelical or Ideological? " in *Concilium* 93 (1974), pp. 147–56.

16. The Ignatian adage *"in actione contemplativus"* really goes back to Jerónimo Nadal. Gustavo Gutiérrez applies it to political activity in his article entitled "Evangelio y praxis de liberación," in *Fe cristiana y cambio social en América Latina*, pp. 231–45.

17. I have dealt with such a liberation, and particularly with reference to the theological language of liberation, in the works cited in notes 13 and 15. In the first of them I also try to show that de-absolutization and de-univocation does not empty the language of liberation of all content, that instead it opens it up to historical novelty without stripping it of historical concreteness and practical efficacy. The danger of total emptying is of particular concern to Hugo Assmann: *Theology for a Nomad Church* (see author entry for Assmann in Appendix I). In my article cited in note 11, I have discussed the nature of an analogical language that would be defined in historical and practical terms while still remaining open to historical novelty and transcendence.

18. In this article I have not spelled out the triune structure of discernment, which is also found on the socio-historical level. Orlando Yorio has written suggestive comments about it, with particular reference to the Argentinian situation in 1970. See his article entitled "Dios y los valores humanos," in *Teología* 9 (1971):23–60. See also my article entitled "La situación actual de la Iglesia argentina y la imagen de Dios Trino y Uno," in *Estudios* 60 (1970):20–23. In collaboration with José Ignacio Vicentini and this author, Yorio is undertaking a theological reading of Argentina's history and present historical situation. The first results will soon be published. On the matter of a theological reading of the signs of the times, see Paul VI's allocution to a general audience, April 16, 1969, in *L'Osservatore Romano*, April 17, 1969.

11

Capitalism Versus Socialism: Crux Theologica

Juan Luis Segundo (Montevideo, Uruguay)

Latin American theology, particularly that strain which deals with such themes as liberation, is taken to be somewhat of a passing fad in more advanced circles of European theology. Seen as a burst of momentary enthusiasm, it does not deserve to be taken too seriously in their eyes.

Needless to say, that view disturbs us. For one thing it calls us and our work into question. For another, with very few exceptions we find that Latin American seminarians are still being educated in and by a theology that at best is merely a copy of the best and most up-to-date European theology. Thus in the academic education of our future priests and pastors of souls the whole theme of liberation comes across as political and kerygmatic rather than theological in the strict sense. Added to this is the fact that the whole focus on liberation and related themes was introduced primarily by pastoral praxis. So we find that the "theology of liberation," however good or bad that designation may be, is more the subject of talk and conversation than of serious writing in Latin America.

The reader of this volume will by now have noted one point

repeatedly stressed by the contributors. What is designated as "liberation theology" does not purport to be merely one sector of theology, like the "theology of work" or the "theology of death." Liberation is meant to designate and cover theology as a whole. What is more, it does not purport to view theology from *one* of many possible standpoints. Instead it claims to view theology from *the* standpoint which the Christian fonts point up as the only authentic and privileged standpoint for arriving at a full and complete understanding of God's revelation in Jesus Christ.[1]

For all the reasons just noted, I am of the opinion that the whole debate about the seriousness of liberation theology cannot really get anywhere now unless we take some concrete problem as a *test case*. I therefore invite the reader to join me in a concrete theological experiment. Let us confront theology with one of the most urgent human problems facing the Latin American continent: i.e., that of making a choice between a capitalist society on the one hand or a socialist society on the other.

Before we begin, however, I would ask the reader to keep one decisive fact in mind. The choice in our case is not between the possibilities of an already well developed capitalism on the one hand or of an equally developed socialism on the other. For us in Latin America it is not a matter of choosing between the society existing in the United States and that existing in the Soviet Union. Our option must be made from the oppressed periphery of the great economic empires. We must choose some socio-political scheme from our own context as an underdeveloped continent. Which choice, then, will be both effective and consistent with the kind of society we desire for the Latin American people we know?

That is the question, a vital one for us today, that I pose to theology here. Unfortunately it immediately gives rise to another question: Does it really make any sense to pose that kind of question to theology specifically? It is not easy to answer this. Here I am not going to linger over one classic theological opinion which answers in the affirmative, and which is much heard in Catholic circles. It answers "yes" to the question; but it does so on the basis of theological presuppositions that are very debatable and, in my opinion, ultimately unacceptable.

This classic opinion begins by saying that the question is very much in line because the choice in question falls in the area of *moral* theology, which operates on its own particular track. It then usually goes on to say that the option for socialism is morally inadmissible because socialism fails to recognize the natural right of human beings to private ownership, even of the means of production. In my opinion, however, the principles underlying this position are not solid enough to merit any special attention at all. Those principles are: that an unbridgeable gap is to separate dogmatic theology from moral theology; that there is a "natural right" involved here; and, most importantly, that this natural right can be invoked to defend the proposition that the means of production might be owned privately by *only a few people.*[2]

The two negative replies to the same question seem to me to be much more subtle, profound, and worthy of attention. They deny the right or the suitability of posing the option between capitalism and socialism *to theology* at all. One of these negative replies, the more influential in Latin America, is pragmatic in origin. The other, more influential in European theological circles, is theoretical in origin.

I

As one might readily imagine, the pragmatic refusal to deal with our question is based on the task that the Christian churches see as their own proper one. And since it is a pragmatic refusal, it is particularly interesting *for what it does not say*, for its hidden reasons or motives: i.e., for the theory that underlies it.

This negative answer to our question above is perfectly exemplified in the answer of Chile's Catholic bishops to the vital question under consideration. Here is what they said: "The church opts for the risen Jesus. . . . Politically the church does not opt at all; it belongs to all the people of Chile."

Now what is the logical presupposition underlying that practical response? The presupposition is that it would be senseless to make an *absolute* value (a religious value having to do with salvation) dependent on a relative value (preference for one particular system of political coexistence, all of them being imperfect always).

Among intellectuals we find a strong reaction against this sort of pastoral practice and its theological implications; it can go so far as outright contempt. Nevertheless it is quite certain that the vast majority of Christian churches continue to be structured officially as autonomous centers of salvation. They sincerely believe in that. If they do in fact adopt progressivist positions on historical issues, they do so only to add attractiveness to the absolute value of salvation that they claim to communicate to their faithful members.

But would it not be possible, and quite evangelical, to invert that hierarchy of values; to declare, as the gospel does, that the Sabbath is made for man, not man for the Sabbath? Couldn't we then translate that declaration into concrete terms, there really being only one possible interpretation: i.e., that a human societal life liberated as much as possible from all alienation constitutes the *absolute* value, whereas all religious institutions, dogmas, sacraments, and ecclesiastical authorities have only a *relative* (i.e., functional) value?

In Christian circles capable of *theoretical* reflection, this inversion of values in line with the gospel message is relatively easy and is going on in Latin America. But what is the result? The result is that there is ever increasing disagreement and antipathy, and an ever widening gap, between those Christians and the official churches. For the churches continue to be structured around the very opposite principles.

Now we could drop the issue at this point and summarize the situation as follows: So long as the church goes on attributing absolute value to those words, objects, gestures, and authorities that seem to link up the faithful vertically with God, and only relative value to the historical functionalism of all that, then one cannot seriously ask ecclesiastical theology to tell the faithful how they should view the option between capitalism and socialism. We could drop the issue there, leaving it up to pastoral activity to convince the hierarchy of the Christian churches of the authentic scale of values, and hence of the necessity of involving their pastoral activity in a human problem as basic as the one under consideration here. More and more, however, we are pushing the matter a bit further in Latin America. While still remaining within the framework of this pragmatic refusal, we are more and more interested in launching a theoretical attack on such mistaken pastoral motivations to the fullest extent possible.

Now to do that we could follow the approach of European theology. We could make full use of the arsenal of tradition to show from *past* history that the authentic attitude of the church toward such issues was completely different. We could point out when the whole process of deviation began and how the church slowly forgot that the ecclesiastical realm was supposed to maintain a functional relationship with human history. That approach is what is known as the "return to the sources." It is exemplified by Hans Küng, for example, in his work on papal infallibility and the structures of the church.

As I see it, however, there is now a marked tendency in Latin America to tackle pragmatic church problems of that sort with a different approach. Instead of resorting to the past, we are offering *here-and-now* explanations based on the psycho-social sciences. We might ask this kind of question, for example: What might be the underlying psycho-social motivations that would explain the pragmatic attitudes we find generalized in ecclesiastical circles today? Here Latin American theology moves towards an interdisciplinary effort involving the aid of what are called the human sciences. With that aid I think that theology is able to posit and verify the following hypothesis about ecclesiastical attitudes: When gestures, formulas, rites, and authority centers are related directly to salvation and the absolute, when they are situated or located outside and beyond the finalistic system in which everything else operates, it is a clear indication that those who employ them know very well those things would lose not only their absolute but also their relative value if they were introduced into the finalistic system.

That is the danger facing the absolute. Either it is absolute or it is nothing. So when the churches make absolutes out of things that are not absolute, they are really trying to preserve some relative value for them by linking them up with human insecurity. Thorstein Veblen put it this way: "Only individuals with an aberrant temperament can in the long run retain their self-esteem in the face of the disesteem of their fellows. Apparent exceptions to the rule are met with, especially among people with strong religious convictions. But these apparent exceptions are scarcely real exceptions, since such persons commonly fall back on the putative approbation of some supernatural witness of their deeds."[3]

Many people in scientific and scholarly disciplines would of course be inclined to draw up arguments against Christianity in general from such a statement. But when we Latin Americans propose to work with the human sciences for the sake of an interdisciplinary approach, we are proposing to theologize in the strict sense. We are trying to get back to the inner and often unconscious mechanisms that are operative when we think about God, his message, and his church. Our feeling is that it is there, in the realm of those motivating mechanisms which are not just theological, that we will find the roots of the passionate differences now evident on the interconfessional Christian level. In an earlier day, when other mental factors were operative, those passionate differences were framed in terms of christological and trinitarian controversies.

If we turn the proper evangelical hierarchy of values upside down, as in fact the official churches are now doing, is that not heterodoxy? If interdisciplinary study does verify our aforementioned hypothesis, will it not also prove that the heteropraxis of the absolutized churches is grounded on a radical heterodoxy: i.e., a steady, ongoing loss of faith in the gospel message of Jesus Christ? To put it another way, will it not verify a steady, ongoing loss of faith in the gospel's functional use for human beings?[4]

Here theology faces an enormous task. It must pinpoint the frustrated evangelical experiences that lie at the roots of this ecclesiastical insecurity. It must try to discover the criteria governing the authentic historical functionality of the gospel message. It must also try to determine the limits of any such functionality, since every incarnation has limits. We are led once again to the same conclusion. If people decide that the gospel message has nothing to say about such a critical human issue as the choice between capitalism and socialism, then it is obvious that the gospel message can only have an absolute value, a non-functional value. In other words, its value is nil.

II

Aside from the pragmatic objection that we just considered for the sake of example, I said there was a theoretical objection to the view that theology could or should get involved in the political option under examination here.

After all, what currents among the many to be found in theology would seem to be the most likely ones to offer us guidance on this issue? Would it not be that of "political theology" and that of the "theology of revolution," two currents of thought that arose in German-speaking circles of Protestant and Catholic theology? I think so, and yet here we run into something very curious. We find that both political theology and the theology of revolution leave us disoriented when we are confronted with the political and revolutionary option par excellence.

I said above that Latin America is anxious to plan out and construct its own future. Hence it is confronted with an emotion-laden choice between two different systems and their respective logics regarding the person and society. But what does political theology have to tell us? Metz makes this observation: "What differentiates 'Christian eschatology' from Western and Eastern ideologies about the future is not that it knows *more* but that it knows *less* about that future, . . . and that it persists in that poverty of knowledge."[5] According to Metz, then, an eschatological theology should know less about capitalism and socialism than the theoreticians of the two systems.

What this means, then, is that the church is much more reticent than any political program. According to Metz, the church "should institutionalize this eschatological reserve by setting itself up as a court or instance of critical liberty vis-à-vis social development, so that it can stand up against the tendency of the latter to present itself as *absolute*."[6]

Once again, then, we run into the distinction between *relative* and *absolute*. And once again the political option is ranged on the *relative* side. Only this time the absolute factor is not the church, but something which the church itself must serve: i.e., the eschatological kingdom of God, the ultimate future, the future that comes down from God himself to humanity.

Here the church does fully recognize its functional nature with respect to the eschatological kingdom. It is the triumph of the kingdom, not its own success, that is the important thing. Moltmann, for example, puts it this way: "Only through the dialectics of taking sides is the universalism of the crucified one realized in the world. By contrast the false universalism of the church [the first pragmatic objection discussed above] is a premature and untimely anticipation of the kingdom of God."[7]

According to Moltmann, then, the real and proper function of the church is to preclude "premature and untimely" anticipations of the kingdom of God. In this passage he refers explicitly to one of them: the false universalism of the church, the church turned into an absolute. But when we examine this position in the broader context of his work as a whole, we find that *every historical project* tends toward the very same universalism and absolutization. The critical space created by political theology will attack absolutism from whatever direction it comes—from the past or the future, from East or West. It will deabsolutize both the existing order and any projected order.

It is for this very reason that one gets a very definite impression when one reads discussions centered around the "theology of revolution." The revolution envisioned by that theology seems much more akin to the Cartesian theoretical revolution based on methodic doubt than to a real practical revolution. If you like the term, it does revolutionize our way of focusing on socio-political systems from our secure installment within them; but it does not choose between one system and another. If there is any tendency to take sides in the theology of revolution, it is a tendency to opt against whatever system is existing *today*. That is to say, one rejects the capitalist system where it now prevails, and the socialist system where it now prevails. But since both systems now coexist in today's world, all forms of "eschatological" criticism tend to relativize all that exists. The relativization is revolutionary in name only.

Exploring a more profoundly theological track, we arrive at the same conclusion discussed earlier. The conclusion is that it is not proper to question theology about the relationship between God's revealed message and the political choice between capitalism and socialism. As we noted above, the point seems to be that it is not right to encumber the absolute (here the kingdom of God) with the weight of the relative (here perishable political systems). And the underlying reason is that relative values are not even fragments of the absolute value; they remain completely and definitively in their sphere of relativity.

German political theology is meticulously cautious in choosing the words it uses to describe the relationship between any relative political order and the absolute eschatological order. The former order is an anticipation (Moltmann), an analogy or analogical image (Weth), an outline (Metz). All of their terms expressly and systematically reject any idea of *causality* in the relationship.

But who dedicates their life to an "analogy"? Who dies for an "outline"? Who motivates a human mass or a people in the name of an "anticipation"?

Now we know that in Latin America there is a theological tendency that has come to call itself the "theology of liberation." For the moment we can prescind from the question as to how apt that designation is. We can also disregard the differences between various theologians who are included under that head. The point here is that there is something basic shared by all of them. They all maintain that human beings, both as individuals and as political beings, are already building up the kingdom of God here and now in history.[8] Obviously we cannot minimize the basic and radical difference between this position and one which in principle denies any *causality* to political options insofar as the definitive kingdom of God is concerned.

What argument is used by German political theology to deny

such causality? Interestingly enough the argument used is the one which lay at the very roots of Reformation theology: i.e., *Paul's doctrine concerning justification by faith alone, and not by works.* Here is how Rudolf Weth succinctly puts it: "God *himself* performs the revolutionary action that is decisive for the coming of his kingdom. His action cannot be carried out or replaced by any human action."[9] Weth goes on to support his argument by citing a crucial passage from Luther's writings in which he applies the principle of justification by faith alone to the matter of the universal kingdom. Here Luther is commenting on a passage in Mattew's Gospel (25:34) where the world's judge invites the good people to take possession of the kingdom prepared for them from the beginning: "How could they possibly merit what already belongs to them and what was prepared for them long before they were created? Indeed it would be more accurate to say that it is the kingdom of God which merits us as its possessors. . . . The kingdom of God has already been prepared. But the children of God must be prepared in view of the kingdom. So it is the kingdom that merits the children of God, not they that merit the kingdom."[10]

Obviously that exegesis completely rules out any choosing between socio-political systems that would purport to pave the way for the kingdom of God in "causal" terms. Here the reader might be inclined to say that this view represents only that branch of political theology that stems from the Protestant Reformation. But another fact is of great relevance here. The fact is that Roman Catholic theology in Europe, especially since Vatican II, has been drawing closer and closer to Luther's position on justification. In the point at issue here, then, one cannot detect any noticeable difference between the two camps.

In current Latin American usage, the terms "right" and "left" are *broadly* identified with the capitalist option and the socialist option respectively. Accepting that broad equation for the moment, I think it would be interesting to offer a bit of proof for what I have just been saying. Let us take as our example here a comment made by a French Catholic theologian, Henri de Lavalette. He is talking about the "ambiguity" of German political theology:

What possibilities does it open up? Does it tend to divide the church more and more into leftist Christians and rightist Christians? Does it permit a leftist current to exist in a church that is centrist for the most part? Or is it capable of getting Christians to confront their political divisiveness and to see them in terms of reconciliation in Christ? When Paul affirms that in Christ Jesus there is no longer male nor female, the point is that being male or female is no longer an *absolute* that divides people, that means only one or the other can be Christian. In like manner, the division between left and right, which is a political division and a political judgment, is not privileged to provide any exclusivist claim to the label "Christian"; it cannot be presented as the judgment of God. The church is open to males and females, *to the right and the left.*[11]

As this passage clearly indicates, the whole weight of theology as a science comes down on one side. Whether it is speaking in terms of ecclesiastical functioning or in terms of the eschatological kingdom, it tends to rule out the possibility that it might enlighten us on the practical political option which, on our continent, is the focal point for the most profound and total commitments.

And so we are left with a negative conclusion which to me seems unacceptable. There is only one thing left for me to do in the final section of this article. I will try to spell out the conditions that would make possible a theology capable of saying something decisive about the equally decisive options facing society. In the process I will offer a critical reconsideration of the negative arguments that were presented above.

III

If we are going to explore the possible relationship between theology on the one hand and a political choice between capitalism and socialism on the other, we must first be clear on two preliminary points.

The *first* point has to do with what I mean by "socialism" and "capitalism" here. By "socialism" I do not mean a complete, long-term social project—hence one that is endowed with a particular ideology or philosophy. I simply mean a political regime in which the ownership of the means of production is taken away from individuals and handed over to higher institutions whose main concern is the common good. By "capitalism" I mean a political regime in which the ownership of the goods of production is left open to economic competition.

Some might ask here: Why not spell out the socialist model more fully? Or why not talk about the possibility of a moderated, renovated capitalism? For a very simple reason, I would reply. We are not seers, nor are we capable of controlling the world of the future. The only real and possible option open to us lies within our own countries. Right now today the only thing we can do is to decide whether or not we are going to give individuals or private groups the right to own the means of production that exist in our countries. And that decision is what I call the option between capitalism and socialism.

The *second* point has to do with what we mean by theology here. By "theology" here I do not mean simply the scientific investigation of dogmas: how they came to be formulated and how, in the light of changes in language and mentality, they are to be formulated today in order to maintain authentic continuity with the past. I indicated earlier my own opinion about that scientific discipline that is the relatively autonomous sphere of professionals. For some centuries now, in my opinion, it has been emptying out much of its own content to serve the needs of a conservative ideology. It is not so much that it always proposes "conservative" dogmas. It is rather that its own vaunted autonomy vis-à-vis concrete Christian praxis leaves the latter on a secondary plane where it is open and subject to criteria that are independent of the faith. This has given rise to a moral theology behind dogma's back, as it were: and it is a nontemporal moral theology remarkably similar to the civic morality required by the established society. The dogmatic theologian, in turn, has been turned into one of the many purveyors of abstract culture which the consumer society accepts and even protects.

By "theology," then, I mean here *fides quaerens intellectum* in a much more direct sense. I mean "faith seeking understanding" in order to give guidance and direction to historical praxis.[12] I maintain that not one single dogma can be studied with any other final criterion than its impact on praxis.[13]

Having set up those basic definitions of socialism and capitalism on the one hand, and of theology on the other, we can now consider the whole matter of the relationship between the two. Right at the start we reject the notion that the task of resolving the question is to be handed over to some "moral theology." What we are looking for here is a positive or negative relationship between *dogma* and socialism.

When, therefore, was dogma applied to political events? To begin with, there is no doubt that it was so applied in the preaching of the great prophets of Israel. And if I am not mistaken, we will find that prophetic proclamation—or the theology of the prophets, if you will—has precious little to do with the ecclesiological presuppositions prevailing today or with the criteria set forth by current European political theology.[14]

The *prophets*, of course, are not the seers of the future whom we envision today when we use that word. First and foremost they are simply seers, ones who look below the surface of events and discover a will, a plan, an evaluation—God's. But if that were all, then the seers would become legislators rather than prophets. They are prophets because in some way or other they project into the future the historical consequences of God's design or evaluation of events. With their vision of the divine present, they construct a project of the historical future.

Such was the project of Jeremiah, for example, when he gave advice to those remaining in Jerusalem after the exile had begun. He told them it was Yahweh's will that they remain there rather than emigrate to Egypt. He linked that proposal or project so closely to God's will that he made a prediction about all those who would choose to emigrate to Egypt instead: Not one of them would survive.

How exactly did his theological thinking operate? First of all, a more penetrating vision than the normal one showed him God operating in concrete happenings and judging them in terms of their authentic value. Being who he was (theo-logy), the God of Israel could not see what was happening any other way. He could not evaluate the historical data in any other terms. Convinced of that, the prophet imagines a future that is in line with that divine evaluation and endows it with the same degree of certainty. This projected view was a "political" one, and yet the prophet did not submit it to any "eschatologization." He did not try to make his listeners equally critical about the relativity of that historical alternative as compared with the absoluteness of God's kingdom.

What is more, later events gave the lie to his prophecy insofar as it purported to be a vision of the future. Henri Cazelles has this to say about this political fallibility of the prophets: "One extraordinary fact about the political activity of the prophets must be pointed out. As a rule it ended in political failure. Yet, despite that failure, the disciples of the prophets would collect their oracles and recognize their validity as the *word of God.*"[15] To this we might add: that has always been the case where a prophetic theology is being exercised, and it always will be.

What are we to say, then, about any theology that refuses to pass theological judgment, to invoke the word of God, on a political reality, on the pretext that a scholarly science cannot *demonstrate* that the future will be undoubtedly better? Any such theology is clearly moving far away from its prophetic function.

There is no doubt that one could claim that the classic stage of prophecy in the Old Testament had, at best, a very rudimentary eschatological vision of God's kingdom—if it had any eschatological view of it at all. For this reason I think we would do well to jump ahead somewhat and focus on the debate between Jesus and the theology of his time as it is recorded in the Synoptic Gospels. It is very important, I think, and too little attention has been paid to the major feature of that whole debate. The radical difference between the two contending parties is not to be found in the theological content under dispute. Far more important is the way each party does theology or "theologizes," and the tools that each side uses in that effort.

It is this difference that will occupy us here. I am going to leave aside the whole issue of Jesus' involvement or noninvolvement in the politics of his day, which is such a controversial issue right now. But I would like to digress for a moment and make one point about that particular issue. My feeling is that there is something very anachronistic about the way some people try to prove that Jesus had some interest in politics and political liberation. To do this, they resort to the meager data provided by the Synoptic Gospels on Jesus' relations with the Roman Empire. Many exegetes see the Empire as the political structure of that era. To determine Jesus' attitude, therefore, they point out that his followers included Zealots: political rebels against Rome who were condemned to death as political subversives. That is the sort of argument they use.

Such an approach is anachronistic, in my opinion, because they equate the "political" sphere of Jesus' day with the "political" sphere in our own day. And since the structures of the Roman Empire are the closest thing to a modern political empire or regime, they focus on Jesus' relationship to those structures. What they seem to forget is that the "political" life of Jesus' day in Israel depended much more on the "theology" prevalent among such groups as the scribes and Pharisees than it did on the Roman Empire and its structures. It was primarily that "theology" that organized the life of the Jewish citizenry, determined their place and position, fixed their obligations, and subjected them to oppression. It was the scribes and Pharisees, not the Roman Empire, which imposed "intolerable burdens" on the little people or dispensed people from them. It was they who were responsible for the real socio-political structure of Israel. For that very reason Jesus' counter-theology was much more political than any statements or actions directly against Rome would have been at that time.

But let us get back to our point and consider the confrontation between Jesus' theology and that of his Jewish opponents. Right at the start we note that the two theologies share one thing in common: Both attempt to find the presence and guidance of God in the historical events that are taking place. The theology opposed to that of Jesus is one which, according to the Synoptic Gospels, looks for "heavenly signs," or better, "signs from heaven." Relying on the immediate context (and recalling the "sign from heaven" which Satan proposes to Jesus when he tempts him in the desert), we are perfectly justified in describing these "signs from heaven" as anticipations, outlines, and analogies of some properly divine action, of something which by its very nature cannot be attributed to human beings, much less the devil. How else could one possibly look at a historical happening and discern a "sign from heaven" in it?

What sort of "signs" does Jesus set over against those "signs from heaven"? He points to "sign of the times," to concrete transformations effected by himself in the historical present and then entrusted to his disciples both for the present and the future. Remember what Jesus says when the disciples of John the Baptist ask him that "eschatological" question about "he who is to come." Jesus responds to their question by pointing to signs in history that are relative, terribly ambiguous, and a far cry from anything definitive or absolute. The deaf hear, but why? The lame walk, but where to? The sick are cured, but won't they fall prey later to new and even more critical illnesses? The dead are raised to life, but is it worth the trouble if they must succumb to further troubles and eventually death once again? The poor have the good news preached to them, but who is going to change their plight and when?

It is here that we begin to glimpse the different understanding of signs that underlies the two different theologies. The theology that requires "signs from heaven" is interested in knowing whether the concrete happenings in question, the very same ones to which Jesus alludes, proceed from God without any doubt at all or could possibly proceed from the devil. Jesus' theology of signs replies with a boldness that scientific Christian theology has lost completely. For all practical purposes it says that the sign in itself is so clear-cut that even if it is the devil who is liberating these people from their afflictions, it is because the kingdom of heaven has already arrived and is in your midst. Thus Jesus' theology completely rules out applying any theological criterion to history *except the direct and present evaluation of happenings here and now.*

Now in trying to judge historical happenings in themselves, from the standpoint of their human value, theology obviously needs a cognitive instrument that is being equally minimized or disregarded by scientific theology. To use a modern term, we might call it *historical sensitivity.* In the Synoptic Gospels the critical term, used constantly, is the "heart." They contrast the hard and closed heart to the open, sensitive heart.

This is evident when Jesus is engaging in a theological debate over what is a commandment of God and what is merely human tradition. Paradoxically enough, Jesus associates real commandments of God with a heart that is spontaneous and open to other people whereas he associates purely human traditions with calculated reasoning that stems from a closed heart. The fact he points out to his listeners is that an event cannot be judged in itself if it does not correspond with the expectations of a sensitive heart. Reason will remain paralyzed by the ambiguity surrounding the event, and the arguments derived from that event will merely serve people's egotism.

We can thus understand what Jesus has to say about the unpardonable sin after he has cured a mute and provoked a serious debate. Jesus points out that the unpardonable sin is not the theological judgment one may form about the divine or satanic origin of his work. The blasphemy resulting from bad apologetics will always be pardonable. What is not pardonable is one's refusal to recognize something as real liberation when in fact it is real liberation. What is not pardonable is using theology to turn real human liberation into something odious. The real sin against the Holy Spirit is refusing to recognize, with "theological" joy, some concrete liberation that is taking place before one's very eyes.

I say "liberation" quite deliberately because of Luke's Gospel. It is the only Gospel that indicates the broader context of that cure, and it is also the only one that adds a decisive trait to the picture. It presents a parable wherein Jesus describes the cosmic dimension of his work, and one feature of that parable serves as the only theological sign that can precede recognition and acknowledgment of Jesus' person. With the coming of Jesus, the "strong one" who had been dominating humanity and keeping it enslaved up to now is finally disarmed and overcome. But according to Luke's Gospel, the spoils of victory do not go to a new master; instead they are restored to their natural recipients. Speech is restored to the mute.

To complete this brief characterization of Jesus' theology, I must call the reader's attention to the name that Jesus gives to the concrete acts of liberation that he performs. As we have already seen, human reason is here faced with ambiguous events, particularly insofar as the future is concerned. Despite this fact, Jesus gives them the most absolute name in the theology of his own time. He calls them "salvation." Instead of de-absolutizing them, we would be inclined to say that he imprudently absolutizes them. Cures with an uncertain future are called the "coming of the kingdom." Zaccheus's ambiguous decision, made on the spur of the moment and not yet carried out, is considered to be "salvation coming to this house." Time and again he tells people who have obtained favors or cures from him that "your faith has saved you," though it is apparent that the favors and cures ever remain uncertain and fleeting.

Why, then, do we find this seemingly invincible repugnance of modern scientific theology, of European theology in particular to do the same thing? Why is it unwilling to make pronouncements on political alternatives which are exactly parallel to the alternatives that were the object of Jesus' theology throughout his preaching career?

The European advocates of political theology demand that we Latin Americans present them with a proposal for a socialist society that is guaranteed in advance to avoid the defects evident in existing brands of socialism. Why do they not demand the same thing of Jesus? Why do they not demand that Jesus, before telling someone that his faith has saved him and curing him, provide some guarantee that the cure will definitely not be followed by worse illnesses?

To give an example here, historical sensitivity in the face of starvation and illiteracy would seem to demand a society that was not ruled by competition and the quest for profit. Such sensitivity would regard the fact that an underdeveloped nation got basic sustenance and education as a form of liberation. Viewed in the light of potential problems in the future, this particular matter might not seem to be of overriding importance in affluent countries. But in our countries we cannot avoid facing the issue because we live with it twenty-four hours every day. When and if those ills are eliminated in our nations, what scientific exigencies or strictures would prevent theology from saying: "Your faith has saved you"? It is simply a matter of giving theological status to a historical happening in all its absolute and elemental simplicity: "Is it permitted to do good or to do evil on the Sabbath, to save life or to kill? " (Mark 3:1–5).

My remarks in the last section might seem to be some sort of gospel proclamation rather than a serious study of theological methodology. It is certainly true, moreover, that for some time now theological methodology has been looking to other scientific disciplines rather than to gospel proclamation to find analogies for its own underlying criteria. It prefers the categories and certitudes of the other human sciences to the seeming simplicity of the thinking of Jesus and the primitive church. For that reason I think a bit of translation is in order. The original requirements involved in a theological effort to really comprehend the faith in terms of ongoing history must be translated into modern methodological terms. I propose the following points:

1. Far from *relativizing* any given present, the eschatological aspect of any Christian theology *links that present to the absolute*. Absolutization is necessary for all effective human mobilization. What the Christian eschatological aspect does, then, is prevent that mobilization from degenerating into human rigidity, petrification, and a sacralization of the existing situation merely because it does exist.

2. It follows, then, that the eschatological aspect does not define the *content* of Christian theology vis-à-vis secular ideologies nor the function of the ecclesial community in the midst of society as a whole, contrary to what seems to be the implicit or explicit view of European political theology. The eschatological aspect is simply Christian theology's *way* or manner of accepting absolute commitments. The stress placed on the eschatological aspect depends on a proper, constantly reconsidered evaluation of the *kairos*, of the opportunity for liberation at a given moment. The critical space cleared by eschatology is not rectilinear but dialectic.

3. We are making an improper extrapolation when we take Luther's rediscovery of personal justification by faith without works and make it the key to all biblical exegesis, particularly insofar as cosmic and ecclesiological themes are concerned. In other words, we cannot move logically from Paul's demand that we avoid a paralyzing preoccupation with our own personal justification to the communitarian demand involved in the construc-

tion of the kingdom. To do that is to throw Scripture as a whole out of balance. What is it that effectively and definitively builds up disinterested love in the cosmos? What exactly is involved in the practical violence that snatches the kingdom from utopia and plants it in the very midst of human beings? Those questions, biblical questions par excellence, make no sense at all if we start from the a priori assumption that the kingdom is already completely fashioned and is simply waiting for everyone to enter it through faith.

4. Christian theology will have to be grounded much more on sensitivity to what liberates concrete human beings *here and now*. This of course would be in marked contrast to a science that starts out from the assumption that it can foresee and preclude any future dangers or errors with the help of an adequate model, or which presumes to criticize and relativize every historical step that does not provide such guarantees. Theology has sought to be the science of the immutable in the midst of human vicissitudes. Like the theology of the gospel message, it must get back to being the theology of *fidelity*. Grounded on the Immutable, such a theology offers guidance to the venture of history that is subject to all the corrections dictated by real facts and events.

5. Consequently the eschatological horizon does not offer theology the possibility of soaring aloft and maintaining its distance equally from the political right and the political left. The right and the left are not simply two sources of social projects that are subject to the evaluation and judgment of some reason located right in the center between them. As Martin Lotz points out: "The objective of leftist radicalism is to open up society permanently to its future. In the sixteenth edition of the Brockhaus one can find the following definition of the left: 'domain of that which has not yet found form or realization, of that which is still in a state of utopia.' "[16] Thus the sensitivity of the left is an intrinsic element of any authentic theology. It must be the form of any reflection in which historical sensitivity has become the key.

6. What about the relationship between a liberative event in history and the definitive kingdom of God? By virtue of the power of God who lies behind it every such happening, however ambiguous and provisional it may be, stands in a causal relationship to the definitive kingdom. The causality is partial, fragile, often distorted and in need of reworking; but it is a far cry from being nothing more than an anticipation, outline, or analogy of the kingdom. We definitely are not talking about the latter when we

are talking about such option as racial segregation versus full community of rights, laissez-faire supply and demand in international trade versus a truly balanced marketing process, and capitalism versus socialism. In however fragmentary a way, what is involved is the eschatological kingdom itself, whose revelation and realization is anxiously awaited by the whole universe.

By way of conclusion, then, my feeling is that Latin American theologizing is moving in the direction that I have just described. I fully realize that anyone who carefully examines the above guidelines will conclude that I have just delivered a radical criticism of all European theology, even its most progressive currents. I do not deny that, though I grant there are exceptions. It seems to me that over the course of centuries theology struck out on its own paths; that, like the church itself in many instances, theology did not allow itself to be judged by the word of God. The hope of many of us Latin Americans is that theology will draw close to that word once again, becoming a form of human thought deeply committed to human history.

NOTES

1. See Gustavo Gutiérrez, *A Theology of Liberation*, Eng. trans. (Maryknoll, New York: Orbis Books, 1973), passim. To my mind that book and Assmann's *Theology for a Nomad Church* (see author entry for Assmann in Appendix I of this volume) are the only ones that represent a scholarly, well documented debate with European theology.

2. See J. L. Segundo, *De la sociedad a la teología* (Buenos Aires: Ed. Carlos Lohlé, 1970), Part 3, Chapter 2.

3. Thorstein Veblen, *The Theory of the Leisure Class* (New York: Huebsch, 1919), p. 30.

4. See J. L. Segundo, *The Hidden Motives of Pastoral Action*, Eng. trans. (Maryknoll, New York: Orbis Books, 1977), Chapter 5.

5. J. B. Metz, *L'Homme: Anthropocentrique chrétienne*, French trans. (Paris: Ed. du Cerf, 1971), p. 111.

6. Ibid., p. 136.

7. J. Moltmann, "Dieu dans la révolution," in *Discussion sur la 'théologie de la révolution'* (Paris: du Cerf-Mame, 1972), p. 72; in English see "God in Revolution," in Moltmann's *Religion, Revolution and the Future* (New York: Scribner's, 1969).

8. See the works of Gutiérrez and Assmann, also C. Eggers Lan, *Cristianismo y nueva ideología* (Buenos Aires: Ed. J. Alvarez, 1968), p. 46f.

9. R. Weth, "La 'Théologie de la révolution' dans la perspective de la justification et du royaume," in *Discussion*, p. 86.

10. Cited by Weth, ibid.

11. H. de Lavalette, "Ambiguités de la théologie politique," in *Recherches de Sciences Religieuses* 59 (October-December 1971): 559.

12. See G. Gutiérrez, *Theology of Liberation*, all of Chapter 1.

13. See H. Assmann, *Theology for a Nomad Church*.

14. See Gerhard von Rad, *Old Testament Theology*, Eng. trans. (New York: Harper & Row, 1965), Volume 2, passim.

15. Henri Cazelles, "Bible et politique," in *Recherches de Sciences Religieuses* 59 (October-December 1971): 512.

16. Martin Lotz, "Le concept de révolution dans la discussion oecuménique," in *Discussion*, p. 32. Although the term "left" is not used, the following remarks of Michel de Certeau are in the same vein: "A fellowship of faith unites them [i.e., Christians] with the *stranger* who is always 'estranged' as well. . . . Christians have always accorded a privileged place to the prisoner, the refugee, the poor, and the alien" (*L'Etranger ou l'union dans la différence* [Paris: Desclée de Brower, 1969], pp. 12–13). In any case it is clear which of the two sides, left or right, offers continuing evidence of feeling such solidarity and fellowship.

12

Historical Praxis and Christian Identity

José Míguez Bonino (Buenos Aires, Argentina)

The new current of theological reflection in Latin America has not yet gotten beyond *prolegomena*. It is altogether fitting and necessary that it should not be in a great hurry to do so. The meaning and importance of this new current lies precisely in its reformulation of the preconditions, presuppositions, and methods of doing theology at all. This reformulation of basic issues can be seen readily in the pages of this volume. I shall not repeat what they say, nor shall I try to offer an original contribution of my own. In our present situation, it seems to me, what is needed is not so much originality as collaborative effort in a joint undertaking.

From my own background as a Latin American Protestant, I shall try to spell out the problematic issues posed to someone who approaches the new current of theologizing from that backdrop and tradition. I shall consider whether my tradition raises certain problems about participating in the new joint effort, and then I shall explore the matter a bit more deeply in connection with a specific theological issue.

ENCOUNTER AND CHALLENGE

The journey of Protestant theologians toward "liberation theology" both resembles and differs from that of their Catholic colleagues.[1] The points of resemblance would include a gradually growing and deepening awareness that leads one from one step to the next: from a rather vague and charitable concern with social issues to works of social service, then to an awareness of structural conditioning factors, and then to a realization of the priority of the political realm and the inevitable association of theological reflection with socio-political analyses and options. The points of difference would include: membership in a minority religious community with a tradition of avoiding explicit politics while maintaining de facto ties with the system of liberal capitalism and the "neocolonial" setup, and a theological tradition going back to the Reformation.

Be that as it may, in our time Latin America has become ever increasingly aware of its distinctive status as a dependent continent and the implications of the condition in which it finds itself. This has led people to draw up a project of liberation. Growing numbers of Christians, both Catholic and Protestant, have committed themselves personally to it. All this has forced some Protestant theologians to view this new *locus communis* as the one that should take priority in their theological reflection and hence relativize all their distinctively Protestant features. That, at least, is the starting point for the reflections which follow.

In 1971 I was invited to give a talk on "New Theological Perspectives" at an ecumenical conference held in Peru. The best contribution I could make, it seemed to me, was to present the basic lines of the new brand of theologizing that was going on in Latin America and that went by the name of "liberation theology." In my talk I also posed certain critical questions of my own to that new theology. I could not help but be surprised by the strong critical reaction my talk evoked from some foreign theologians. The thing that they found "unacceptable" was obviously the very thing that I myself had gradually come to accept, despite certain objections that I wanted to be answered. It was the "new positioning of theology" involved in liberation theology. I never felt that I had pledged myself to a new theological school or current. I simply was convinced that I could not do theology at all except from the standpoint of the new perspective which many aware Christians on our continent had been seeking and which was now slowly being articulated.

What was involved in this new "positioning" of theology as far as I was concerned? I don't want to repeat what others have already said in this volume, but I would like to summarize briefly how it all came across to me:

There is no direct route from divine revelation to theology; the mediation of some praxis is inevitable. This simple affirmation immediately disqualifies all "idealist" efforts at theologizing. It can be elaborated further on the epistemological level, in terms of the sociology of knowledge; on the historical level, by showing the various relations existing between theological thinking and the life of the community that does that thinking; and on the level of biblical theology, which may be of more interest to us at the moment, by exploring such biblical concepts as faith/obedience and truth/knowledge. In any case it marks the end of any theology that claims to be self-nurturing and self-sufficient or to operate in some autonomous sphere detached from historical praxis.

The area that defines this praxis, and hence the critical plane on which reflection is projected, is the socio-political one. This affirmation, too, can be supported by starting from the witness of the Bible and showing how it has been wrongly directed into excessively individualistic and spiritualistic channels. Or one can also bring out the primacy of the political realm as the sphere in which people take responsibility for the world and history. This entails several things: *(a)* recognizing that theology operates under the conditioning of the political realm with its conflicts and its own kind of rationality; *(b)* incorporating socio-political instruments and categories in our theological reflection, realizing that the political sphere is the realm of structures, ideologies, and power; *(c)* abandoning the assumption that theology can prescind from politics and be nontemporal while at the same time taking on and articulating some concrete option: in our case, the struggle for liberation.

Starting from this basic outlook, we must critically reread and repossess biblical and theological tradition and also the Christian community to which we belong. Without going too deeply into this point, I might well mention the following tasks involved: *(a)* engaging in a critical examination of tradition on the basis of the diagnostic criteria and the suspicions mentioned above; *(b)* rediscovering the liberative thrust present in that tradition in order to make it available to our Christian praxis in the present;

(c) looking to our own religious history in Latin America specifically in order to find the root causes of the factors which both impede and encourage the dynamics of liberation that are operative in present-day Christianity. In this way we can overcome the impediments and give expression to the supporting factors through a critical recovery of our history.

In the above description the reader will readily notice themes developed by other authors in this volume. At the same time it might seem a bit too formal and abstract. So perhaps I might rephrase the whole matter in a bit more concrete terms. A certain number of Latin Americans have decided to do their theological reflection from the standpoint of the existing neocolonial and capitalist order and its state of crisis, with their eyes on a concrete historical project of liberation. This project would be socialist in its political, social, and economic aspects. In their reflection these theologians accept and assume the analytical, ideological, and political mediations that seem to be imposed on us by the situation itself, though they do not necessarily agree on exactly what those mediating factors are. There is a welter of varying opinions and disputed questions, but they also share a common horizon. This shows up most clearly when their theology is compared with that of the North Atlantic region.

This new theology was originally brought up in Latin America from a basically Catholic perspective. That fact, as I noted earlier, is of secondary importance here. Our common situation and project takes first place, relativizing differences in background and tradition. At the same time, however, it does not eliminate those differences entirely. In other words, Protestant theologians who are involved in this project have certain responsibilities of their own. They must face up to them from their own distinctive theological horizon, pondering how their tradition must be revised and how it raises certain questions and demands in the light of the new project. Therein lies their potential contribution to the whole effort, and that is what I propose to do briefly in the following pages.

The central problem posed by all this is the radical "monism" of the new liberation theology being articulated now. It poses a radical challenge to certain classic Protestant formulations: *sola fides, sola gratia, sola Scriptura, solus Christus.* Do such formulations make any sense in a theology that starts off from the integration of the Christian message into the struggle for liberation, the historical praxis of the faith, and socio-political analysis as an

integral part of theological reflection? Are they nothing more
than a theological embodiment of the "distinction of planes"
theory, designed to offer ideological justification for exempting
the liberal, capitalist, bourgeois setup from all prophetic criticism? Are those battle cries of the Reformation nothing more than
a manifestation of the extrinsic outlook in the religion of the
bourgeois world (i.e., Protestantism), whereby the "kingdom of
the world" is abandoned to the rule of capitalism and the profit
motive, protected by the bourgeois state accordingly, and hence
bound to end up in the repressive, fascist state we now experience
in Latin America?

My Latin American colleagues in the new currrent of reflection
have begun to make a credible case that suspicion is in order, that
there is something to the questions I have just raised. Their case
is not the result of any debate with Protestantism. Their case has
developed from a debate with theological tendencies in contemporary Catholicism, European for the most part, and with certain
formulations of Vatican II. At the same time there is no doubt that
those tendencies and formulations are the direct result of the
Catholic rehabilitation of Reformation theses in Europe.
Catholics in Europe have recently been reconsidering and rein-
terpreting Trent's definitions of such things as Scripture and
tradition, faith and works, and justification. Our suspicion is bol-
stered by the fact that many European theological criticisms of
liberation theology do in fact look to the rehabilitated formulations for their support. In this sense, then liberation theology is a
radical and justified critique of the classic Protestant tradition,
and it must be taken as such.

Let me try to clarify this point with an example that will introduce us to an issue that we shall explore more deeply in the second
section of this article. It has to do with the way theologians apply
the notion of "eschatological reserve" to the struggle for liberation. As Juan Luis Segundo has pointedly remarked, European
theologians describe the relationship between action in history
and eschatological transformation in terms that rule out any
causal connection between the former and the latter.[2] One can
never say there is a direct link between the two because the
eschatological kingdom is "totally other." The relevance and re-
latedness of historical effort is situated on another plane and is, at
best, indirect. All historical activity is relativized, and eschatology stands as a *caveat* against all political commitment. As a
result we seem to get some "religious" or at least "suprahistori-

cal" sphere that takes primacy. The *real* eschatological kingdom of God and his message stands over and above the contingent, secondary, and perhaps partially inauthentic realm of historical liberation. While we may use such terms as "liberation" and "salvation" for the latter, our use is at best analogical and at worst equivocal. Salvation in the real and strict sense applies to a spiritual, eternal kingdom; only in an emasculated sense does salvation apply to the temporal realm of history. The ideological functionalism of such a scheme is readily apparent.

I think the above remarks are enough to indicate the seriousness of the questions faced by Protestant theologians. It is not simply a matter of adapting or reformulating. They must radically reconsider the whole theological perspective in which they have been brought up, and the matter is of more than merely academic urgency. The Protestant communities have been nurtured in the above tradition, primarily in its pietistic formulations, and it constitutes one of the biggest stumbling blocks to active, committed participation in the struggle for liberation. If Protestant theologians do move toward the new theological perspective in Latin America, they are immediately faced with the task of unmasking the ideological function of this theologumenon and its variance from the biblical message.

At the same time, however, I don't think it is right or beneficial to simply jettison the questions and preoccupations that Protestant theology has sought to articulate, as if they were useless and excess baggage. While the ideological context should not be camouflaged or disregarded, my feeling is that a central theme of Christian faith did surface in the sixteenth-century Reformation, particularly in its earliest formulations. That central theme was, and is, *the priority of grace.* Put another way, it is the specific nature and quality of the "good news" in Christ's message. This theme seems crucial to me for our theological work and, even more importantly, for any authentic Christian presence in the struggle for liberation. I say "presence" rather than "contribution" because it is more a question of considering the preconditions of its authenticity than of determining in advance the meaning of that presence. This is a legitimate theme, I think, and it is posed to us by the praxis of Christians involved in the liberation struggle. They cannot help but take seriously the task of expressing their faith-view in the struggle: "If the salt loses its savor, of what use is it? "

Bearing witness to the gratuitousness of the gospel message

seems to me to be central to this whole question. This gratuitousness stems from an "exteriority," to use a term dear to Enrique Dussel, which cannot be comprehended in any human ideology, analysis, or praxis on the one hand or set over on the other side as some new element to be manipulated ideologically, analytically, or politically (which would be simply a new form of totalization). My feeling in other words, is that we must make theological reflection even more radically dialectical in the liberation struggle. We must be inflexible in accepting the reality of a God who ever remains gratuitously "himself" in the very process of being totally "for us" and "in us."

ESCHATOLOGY AND HISTORICAL ACTIVITY

I want to be more concrete in discussing a critical recovery of the whole Protestant theological issue in terms of liberation theology. So I would like to go back to the point mentioned above and discuss in more detail the relationship between the kingdom of God and activity in history. I am not proposing to offer an answer for this basic and complex issue. Rather, I should like to spell out the methodological approach and process which I feel might lead us toward such a solution. In short, I shall merely sketch out some of the theological landmarks along the way.

The issue is not abstract at all, of course, except insofar as all theoretical reflection abstracts from some concrete and crucial question for the Christian. Here the issue is *how we are to understand the active and dynamic presence of God's kingdom in our history so that we can adapt our witness and activity to it, particularly at this concrete moment in world history when we must profess our faith and serve the Lord in Latin America.*

1. When we consult the witness of the Bible on the relationship we find that the two are inseparable. In the Bible there is no divine activity that does not have some bearing on human history; and human history is never recounted except in relation to God's sovereignty. Even Yahweh's activity in nature is always framed in a historical context. This would apply to the flood, the division of the waters during the Exodus, and even creation. So right from the start the possibility of dealing with the two as if they were independent or separable quantities is ruled out completely.

This does not mean any equation of identity is set up between "God's sovereignty" and human "history," so that the former justifies and hallows everything that happens in the latter (as

Voltaire's Pangloss would have it) or the latter automatically and unequivocally carries out the former. It would be more accurate to say that God's sovereignty is realized *polemically* in history. To put it even more pointedly: God's sovereignty is an efficacious word that makes history and is itself historicized by summoning and rejecting human beings and peoples on the basis of God's own proposed design. According to the Bible, then, God's sovereignty does not show up in history as some abstract interpretation or action but as proclamation and summons. It is a proclamation that summons, a promise and a judgment which both invites and demands some response. In the Bible, history is this very conflict between God and his people living in the midst of other peoples and in relationship to them.

The eminently political character of this conflict comes across forcefully in the Old Testament. Here I use the term "political" both in the broad sense and the stricter sense, the former referring to the overall life of peoples as collective entities and the latter referring to the control and use of power. Every attempt to separate the religious element and the political element in the Old Testament proves to be artificial. Even the seemingly most personal incidents are inextricably bound up with the activity of other peoples and the people of God: e.g., the call of Moses or Isaiah, the touching story of Ruth and Naomi, and the laments of the Psalms. God engages in polemics with peoples and in their very midst. It is through this conflict that he seals the covenant and establishes a people of his own. Yahweh polemically affirms his sovereignty in their judges and kings, their laws and cultic worship, their commerce and art, their domestic and foreign relations. Through his summons and his rejection, his pardon and his punishment, he offers signposts of his sovereignty and paves the way for his ultimate victory yet to come.

We undoubtedly encounter a change when we enter the New Testament, particularly in the Johannine and Pauline body of writings. To deny that would be to shut one's eyes to the obvious. We are clearly in a different "atmosphere." My feeling is that more recent theological currents in Latin America are often in danger of overlooking that change or bypassing it too quickly. This would jeopardize their ability to discern the distinctive and specific quality of the Christian message.

The real problem, of course, is determining *what exactly* is the difference between the Old and the New Testaments. Some of theology's traditional answers seem to me to derive from Hellenic intellectualism and to bear vestiges of old gnostic and Marcionite heresies. They suggest that the New Testament is "more spiritual" or "more religious" than the Old Testament: While the Old Testament has more to do with history, the New Testament has more to do with eternity. On the basis of that misunderstanding liberal theology has managed to construct its famous theory of the "distinction of planes" which, as we noted above, is a very effective ideological tool. Of much the same stripe is the view that opposes the "individualism" of the New Testament to the "collectivism" of the Old.

It is not enough to reject wrong explanations, however. How exactly do the Old and New Testaments differ in their expectation of the kingdom as it relates to human history? I would propose the following hypotheses: In the New Testament the history of God's action acquires a certain consistency and solidity of its own, a certain "distance" vis-à-vis human history as a whole. Don't mistake my meaning here. I am not talking about a separate or divorced history. It ever remains the history of Herod, Pilate, Nero, and the merchants of Ephesus. But once we get a mission that is inextricably bound up with a particular historical nucleus (the history of Israel and Jesus Christ), the faith of converted pagans becomes subject to a twofold historical reference: their own history on the one hand, and this other history that now becomes constitutive of their faith.

Let me put the same point in slightly different terms. The salvific "recollection" or "memory" of Israel is completely interwoven with its own historical memory as a people, with its own project in history. On the other hand the salvific memory of the Gentile church, while not dissociating itself from its own human history, also incorporates into itself another "alien" history: that of Israel and Jesus Christ. When we Gentile Christians profess the kingdom, we are not simply immersing ourselves in the heritage of our own history. We are simultaneously distancing ourselves from it by linking ourselves up with that other history and making it our own. We thus adopt as our own the Exodus from Egypt, the exile in Babylon, and the events in Bethlehem, Nazareth, and so forth. What is more, we do not simply take over their import or their exemplarity as an idealist theology might; we take them over in all their specific and irrepeatable historicity. Hence we get a twofold history. We Gentiles, unlike the Israelites, cannot "believe" without this twofold reference; hence we cannot have faith without asking ourselves how to relate God's activity with the twofold point of reference in which we are inescapably involved by the gospel message.

2. It is in that situation, it seems to me, that many of the problems faced by current Latin American Christianity and theology are rooted. For the most part we Latin Americans, both Catholics and Protestants, have lived our lives without conscious reference to history. I would be further inclined to say that we have lived our lives without reference to either side of that twofold history. Detached from our own world, we have not really adverted to our general history as a people; caught up in a religious and otherworldly version of the faith, we have not really adverted to the special history of Israel and Christ.[3] Now that we are beginning to take cognizance of those historical dimensions, we do not know how to integrate them. The various theologies now appearing on our continent are attempts to meet this situation.

The problem itself is of course a very old one. One attempt at a solution might be called "dualistic." With due reservations, it can be traced back to Augustine's *City of God*. Essentially it links the kingdom of God with only one of the historical referents, the history of the faith. This becomes a univocal, sacred, and distinct line of history while the other history becomes little more than a general framework of episodic events without any eschatological significance. It is debatable to what extent Augustine himself identified the meaningful history of faith, the *civitas Dei*, with the church. The central point is that the history of the *civitas Dei* is the history of God's kingdom, whether one then identifies the former with the hierarchical church, the church of the faithful, or doctrinal orthodoxy.

This solution, however, runs into unsurmountable difficulties. The alleged continuity between the church and the kingdom of God breaks off because of the undeniable failings of the church. How can anyone deny the obvious fact that the "history of faith" shares all too many of the features of "secular" history and very much seems to be all of one piece with it when viewed empirically? This gives rise to all the theories about the invisible church, the *coetus electorum*, and sectarian views. We are still faced with the whole problem of trying to identify the presence of the kingdom in the particular history of the faith.

Though less noticed up to now, a "dualistic" solution is equally untenable from the standpoint of the Bible. One can hardly read Scripture and continue to maintain that general human history is merely an episodic venture, having no connection with the kingdom or, more specifically, with its eschatological dimension. The whole question came up quite early when people began to wonder about the salvation of pagans who had not come to know Jesus Christ. It is not precisely clear to what extent the New Testament writings were consciously aware of the issue. That debate centers around such passages as 1 Corinthians 15:29, 1 Peter 3:18–19, and the Pauline references to a divine "law" known to pagans or the human conscience.

The issue certainly was raised as early as the second century, and countless theological formulas in both Catholicism and Protestantism have tried to explore the presence of salvation and God's redeeming sovereignty in the general history of humankind. They range from explications of the credal statement, "He descended into hell," to certain aspects of the doctrine of predestination that can be found in Barth's alleged "universalism." I do not think this is a matter of mere abstract speculation either, though some of the theological formulas employed here might give that impression. Jesus' many references to the element of "surprise" in the final judgment and to the upsetting and overturning of the last days seem to raise the issue forcibly. Though his remarks applied first and foremost to Israel, they do forcefully suggest some continuity between general human history and the kingdom. To put it in more straightforward terms, they do seem to affirm the eschatological import of human actions based on love.[4]

Thus it should not surprise us to find that various forms of what I would call a "monist" solution have arisen. In different versions it can be found in such theologians as Irenaeus and Origen and throughout the history of Christian doctrine. The most direct and meaningful version for us here, however, is that which is prevalent in liberation theology.[5] One of the central assertions of Gutiérrez, often reiterated in his classic book, is that there is "only one history." God is in the process of fashioning his kingdom in and from human history in its totality; his activity is a constant summons and challenge to human beings. Their response takes place in the concrete arena of history with its economic, political, and ideological options. Faith does not constitute a distinct history but rather a dynamism, a motivating factor and, in terms of its eschatological horizon, a transforming invitation.

I personally do not think that these solutions are satisfactory in themselves. The dualistic solution tends to cite a whole slew of biblical texts. In addition, it tends to come very close to the prevalent tendency in world religions; that in itself should make it highly suspect! But even worse, it seems to me, is the fact that it rests on a hermeneutic vision that is deeply antibiblical. In my opinion its conception of redemption is borrowed from that of gnostic and mystery religions. The God of the prophets and of Jesus Christ can hardly be equated with the *soter* ("savior") of such sects, for the latter is busy trying to populate his Olympus with a few select souls who have been rescued from the tumultuous sea of matter and human history. The Gospel of Luke and the Acts of the Apostles depict a divine mission that takes on Israel's hope (Luke 1–2) and launches it out toward the limits of this earth and history through the power of the Spirit. The seer of Patmos envisions all the peoples of the world bringing their offerings to the heavenly Zion. Paul describes all creation waiting in expectation for the manifestation of God's children; he proclaims the collapse of all barriers, the creation of a new humanity, and the recapitulation of all things in Christ. All of these notes in the New Testament would seem to be incompatible with the straitening religious view that would make the history of human beings and nations irrelevant.[6] Thus the "dualistic" situation would seem to involve us in grave difficulties from the standpoint of biblical theology and its ethical and ideological functionalism.

The unity of God's work and human history constitutes the inescapable starting point for any theological reflection. However, we must acknowledge that the ways in which we have formulated this point in the past have created serious difficulties for both Christian reflection and Christian praxis. If we are to give concrete significance to this *one* history, we must find some way to transcribe the gospel message so that it can be seen to be operating meaningfully on the level of general human history. In other words, we must "name" the kingdom in terms that fit the idiom of current history.

There are plenty of ways to do this. In general we talk about "love," the "new person," and "liberation" as terms that will allow us to identify God's active sovereignty in history, the redeeming presence of Jesus Christ, and the consequent call and summons to obedience in faith. That seems quite legitimate to me, and I shall return to this point in a moment. But here I should like to point out that these very transcriptions indicate the dangers facing us. For once we do historicize these terms in the general history of humankind, there is a danger that they will be uprooted from the particular history of the faith and hence dehistoricized with respect to it. We may soon be talking about some "love" or "new person" or "liberation" in which reference to the history of divine revelation is secondary, merely exemplary, and even dispensable. If that happens, then we must say that the reference to God has ceased to be meaningful insofar as we are trying to speak in Christian terms. Of what God are we speaking, and of what kingdom? If we carry that tendency to its ultimate conclusion, we will end up wittingly or unwittingly deifying history or humanity itself. In that case we would do better to call things by their right name and profess to total immanentism.

There is no doubt that contemporary Latin American theology has no such intention. But we must ask ourselves whether the formulations we have worked out so far do enough to rule out that possibility.

3. How are we to deal with this problem in our theology? Without suggesting that this in itself is an adequate solution, I do think we would do well to view the issue in terms of the continuity-discontinuity existing between the kingdom of God and human history in its totality. Do historical events and human activity in history in all its various dimensions have any meaningfulness with respect to the kingdom that God is fashioning now and will establish in glory at the second coming of the Lord? Or is the latter the complete and total negation of the former? If there is some positive relationship between the two, how are we to understand it and how does it cut into our own activity?

We should realize that the New Testament offers us very little bearing directly on these questions. That fact is due to its own historical circumstances, it seems to me. But if we keep the overall biblical message in mind, I think we can legitimately pose the issue and then consider it in terms of the analogy evident in the eschatological concepts of "body" (or "flesh") and "resurrection."[7] It is obvious that the concept of "body" does enable Paul to point up both the continuity and the discontinuity between present life in history and the life of the resurrected. He stresses a continuity that affirms the recognizable identity of both, and a transformation that inaugurates the resurrected life. The transformation does not "disfigure" or "denaturalize" bodily life; instead it fulfills and perfects it, eliminating its frailty and corruptibility. It is in resurrection that bodily life attains its true shape and full meaningfulness as communication, love, and praise.[8]

This concept is complemented by another Pauline concept: that of "works." Do the human works performed in this life have any eschatological import? Now that the furor of the old polemics has died down, I find it difficult to say that they do not. But certainly the theme must be explored and deepened. As Paul sees it, the works performed "in this body" have a future insofar as they belong to a new order. The latter is the order of the resurrected world; specifically, it is the order of love. Works done here have that future, not by virtue of any merit assigned to them but simply by virtue of the fact that they do belong to the new order. At the same time, however, there are indeed works carried out in the structures of history as master or slave, husband or wife, parent or child, and so forth.[9]

Needless to say, much deeper probing would be in order here. It must be pointed out, it seems to me, that the distinction between works of the flesh and works of faith in Paul's writings is not equivalent to any later distinction between sacred works and profane works, or "human" works and "Christian" works. The Pauline distinction has to do with their relationship to the new era inaugurated by Christ, a relationship that is embodied in love. For a variety of reasons that we need not go into here, Christian theology and Christian ethics have tended to separate human actions from their historical context, and hence to restrict them to their connotations on the level of the individual. Thus they have obscured the relevance of Paul's whole line of thought for the problem which concerns us here. The later restrictiveness, in my opinion, has nothing to do with Paul's thinking at all, which was grounded in the Jewish conception of the "eons" in which the divine proposal would be fulfilled.

If we free ourselves from those later restrictions, I think we can posit a continuity-discontinuity between history and the kingdom of God which is of the same order as that between the earthly body and the resurrected body. Thus the kingdom of God is not the negation of history but rather the elimination of its frailty, corruptibility, and ambiguity. Going a bit more deeply, we can say it is the elimination of history's sinfulness so that the authentic import of communitarian life may be realized. In the same way, then, historical "works" take on permanence insofar as they anticipate this full realization. But in both cases all possibility of confusion is ruled out because the reality of judgment intervenes to divide and separate.

Here we must deepen our understanding of the apocalyptic literature. The kingdom is not the natural outcome of history. Conflict and judgment intervene. Yet the kingdom does salvage, transform, and fulfill the "corporeality" of history and the dynamism of love and fellowship at work in it. This means that the eschatological reality, in turn, is fashioned, nurtured, and raised in history.[10]

If we look at the matter in this light, then it seems to me that the most important question ceases to be: Where is the kingdom rendered present or visible in present history? It now becomes: How do I, both as an individual and part of a community of faith immersed in a concrete history, share in the world that is coming, in the promised kingdom? The main question, in other words, is not so much noetic as existential and ethical. Or perhaps it might be better to say that the noetic question is resolved ethically. The real questions are: What ought I do? What ought I say? How do I do it? How do I say it?

In relation to the kingdom, history is not an enigma to be deciphered but a mission to be carried out. This mission, be it noted immediately, is not a mere ensemble of actions but the manifestation of a new reality—of the new life that is offered and communicated in Christ and his Spirit. The first fruits of the Spirit are the *anticipation* of the kingdom. They are the quality of personal and collective existence that has a future, an eschatological reality, and that concentrates authentic history around its center.

The questions as to what I am to say and do, and how, are not easy to answer of course. It is here that we are once again confronted with the irreducibility of the two historical referents, which maintain their own proper consistency despite their unity. Activity that is associated with the kingdom, that has a permanent reality, must be an activity that *names* the future and *corresponds* to its character. That is why it is impossible to reduce proclamation to the efficacious action of love, and vice versa. There has been much debate about this whole matter recently, and it has often been framed poorly. We cannot eliminate the tension involved here without falling into error. *Both* proclamation and action are eschatologically meaningful, and that is why we are way off-target when we try to contrast "horizontal" with "vertical," or "secular" with "evangelical." The unity of these two elements lies beyond our grasp right now. Indeed there often seems to be tension and conflict between them. Only in the fullness of the kingdom are proclamation and action fully rescued from the ambiguity and isolation, united and brought to perfection, and *made manifest* in the biblical sense of the word.

In my view, it is to this eschatological unity of what is named

and what is done that the Bible is referring when it talks repeatedly of the element of surprise in the Last Judgment. Right
now, however, we live in the tension created by these two referents. They are one in Jesus Christ and the final kingdom, but they
are never completely one in our present experience.[11]

The question, then, is our *discernment of the kingdom in obedience*. The importance of this expression cannot possibly be exag-
gerated. The kingdom can be discerned only through obedience.
Seeking the presence of the kingdom in history means asking the
Lord to show us our task and to deign to accept our obedience into
his kingdom. That brings into the picture the whole ethical question of how we are to know the will of the Lord and make out the
pathway of obedience (or of good works).

My reply may not seem to be very original or inspiring, but on
the theological level I do not see any other answer except the
careful and meticulous work involved in a theological ethics. We
must reconstruct such an ethics, leaving aside the idealist perspective once and for all. But this must be done on the theological
level, I would insist, because we cannot denigrate the discernment
that the Lord gives to a simple, straightforward faith. The
theologian simply reflects critically on a "spiritual" obedience
that is already present among God's people; that is the
theologian's "theoretical" work.

In this connection some theologians have sought to provide an
ethical interpretation by starting off from this question: What is
God doing in history today? They then try to link up our actions
with that. Without overlooking the fruitfulness of that question, I
must say that I do not find it to be completely adequate because it
can give rise to the fanaticism of the Crusader. Once people think
they have discovered "what God is doing," they quite logically
tend to absolutize it and their own actions; they are led to sacralize their own ideology.

For this reason I think it is of fundamental importance that
ethical reflection accept those things that *mediate* between the
kingdom and our obedience. Every action purporting to be an
obedient response to the gospel message must also see itself as an
action mediated through human criteria, decisions, and analyses.
Purporting to have some unmediated access to the will of God is
the very essence of fanaticism. The mediations may be conscious
or unconscious, explicit or implicit, but they are inevitable in any
case. Our advantage at present, it seems to me, is that we now
possess a set of instruments—psychological, sociological, and

theologico-critical—that permit us to be more clearly aware of those mediations and to correct or neutralize them to some extent.

We must consider this matter again in connection with the unity and distinctiveness of the historical referents of Christian praxis. Here the mediations are of two kinds, I think. On the one hand we have our understanding of Scripture and the gospel message and the theologico-hermeneutic reasoning or instrument that we are using. On the other hand we have our understanding of the historical context. Both our personal and our collective actions—be they political, economic, or simple face-to-face interpersonal relations —express some understanding of humanity, reality, and the future. In short, they constitute an ideology. And insofar as they are the actions of a professed Christian, they also express some understanding of the gospel message. The two are not isolated from one another, but they should not be completely equated with each other either. Today I think it is particularly urgent that we take due note of this fact. We must disentangle those mediations in our analysis of "Christian" lines of conduct, confronting them critically and accepting them consciously; for without them there is no authentic obedience.

4. My argument so far might be summed up in three propositions: (*a*) We can discern the kingdom in history only through the obedience of faith; (*b*) this obedience cannot and should not try to evade the tension involved in its twofold historical reference—i.e., both naming and making manifest the eschatological reality that it awaits; (*c*) this obedience takes place historically in doctrinal and ideological mediations that we must recognize, analyze, and accept critically. For this reason there is no real need to try to formulate some general, nontemporal Christian ethics. We need only try to formulate concrete, temporal positions.

To conclude, then, I should like to engage in a concrete exercise pertinent to the present moment in history and unavoidable for us Latin Americans. It has to do with the relationship between the kingdom and the social, economic, and political dilemma of Latin America. In tracing out the general lines of a reflective approach to this matter, I think the reader will come to see the importance that I attach to two facts: (1) the critical tension amid which Christians live their historical involvement; and (2) the specific option that must be made if we are to get away from idealism. In my opinion, European political theologies have not managed to make the second step.

We cannot start from some allegedly neutral situation or abstract schema. We find ourselves in a history with its own particular tensions and dilemmas, which I shall not attempt to describe here. Living in that particular situation, Christians of different denominations have played different roles in the past and still do. It is not a matter of working up some theoretical alternative to see how we might then historicize it. Instead we start from the present-day historicizations of the faith and confront them critically with the mediations mentioned above.

To spell out my own composition of place in somewhat overly simplistic terms, I would say that the historicizations of the faith in Latin America tend to move in two directions that are becoming increasingly polarized. One group tends to opt for a more or less modified continuation of the existing economic and political structures; this would include conservatives and developmentalists. The other group feels that the time has come to switch to a noncapitalist economic structure, with all the cultural and sociopolitical modifications that would entail. While I would readily admit that this formulation itself might be based on a questionable analysis, I think it is satisfactory here insofar as it is a possible analysis. For the thing I want to stress here is that Christians on both sides profess a common loyalty to God's kingdom, so that we do have a potential starting point for dialogue. We begin then with the fact that Christians have opposing historical options but profess the same hope in God's kingdom.

That brings us to a first point for discussion. Is it possible for us to say something about the quality of human life—both personal and communitarian—that really does correspond with God's kingdom and therefore has eschatological significance? If it were possible, then we could say that our active efforts to historicize that particular quality of life, however ambiguous and incomplete they might be, would move in the direction of the kingdom and its dynamism. Some of my Latin American colleagues, fearful of reintroducing idealist criteria here, have flatly rejected the above question; but my feeling is that they are not justified in doing so. There is no question of idealist norms here, nor of "parabolic" extrapolations of revelation history. It is a matter of discerning a historical thrust or direction at the core of the events that prompt our faith.

It seems to me that the whole message of the prophets, the ministry of Jesus, and Paul's description of the "new life in Christ" point in the same direction. I do not want to argue that issue in detail here since I have treated it in another book.[12] Here I would simply be bold enough to say that it is their shared direction that justifies our use of the concept of liberation as an ethico-theological one. If we accept that basic hypothesis, then we can start out on a process composed of two basic lines. The two lines are very much interlaced but they are also distinguishable from one another. They are bound up with a critique of the present-day praxis of Latin American Christians.

The first line has to do with comparing our praxis with what the Bible has to say about the quality of life that we call "liberation." Avoiding both exegetical naiveté and overly critical cavilling, we can describe that mode of life with such heuristic terms as justice, solidarity, the real possibility of accepting responsibility for oneself and others, access to the creation that God has given us, freedom to establish one's own community through one's own effort and love, and space for worshipping God.

Admittedly those things are a bit abstract, but when taken together they do describe a particular texture of human life. They are certainly concrete enough to frame a general critique of the concrete conditions facing human beings on our continent!

The second line of our critical process has to do with the conditions that structure our lives in Latin America. It includes the way in which people relate to each other and the surrounding milieu, the way culture is transmitted, the way goods are produced and consumed, the way basic needs are determined and met, the way conflicts are resolved, and the way life is arranged in general. We have scientific instruments to help us with this process; and though the instruments may be relative and eventually surmountable, they are indispensable for making an evaluation here and now.

Exploring the two lines of this critical process, some Christians on this continent have become convinced that liberal capitalism, framed in the context of the monopolist international system that now prevails, is not a viable structure for historicizing the kind and quality of human life that has a future in God's kingdom. In terms of its concrete reality, the only one on which we can pass judgment and in which we can participate, we are forced to conclude that its way of defining human conditions and relationships is a denial of the quality of life suited to the kingdom. It is the direct opposite of liberation; in terms of the kingdom, it is oppression and slavery. Thus the term "liberation" links us up historically with those who are fighting for the elimination of that bondage, however tense our relationship with them may be.

It is not enough to make that assertion, however. Because it is a question of active obedience rather than just speculative construction, we must make a concrete, historical option which will enable us to obtain conditions more in line with the kingdom's quality of life. More recently some Christians have opted for a historical alternative that is generally labelled "socialist." Here again much greater precision would be in order. But to state the matter in somewhat polemical terms, I would say that for us Latin Americans today socialism, as a socio-economic structure and a historical project, is viewed as our active correlation with the presence of the kingdom insofar as the structure of human society is concerned. On that level it represents our obedience in faith and it is the matrix of theological reflection.

Once we have formulated the matter in the above terms, a few final observations are very much in order. First of all, we are not proposing to sacralize any one particular social order. Though it might be correct in some sense, I would not say that God is fashioning a socialist society in place of the existing capitalist one. It is we human beings who are doing that in the clearing for thought and action that God has allotted to us so that we might carry out a rational, human task. Thus it is a human effort replete with all the precariousness and promise of every human effort. It is likewise an order to be transcended both historically and eschatologically. Its present value for the Christian lies in the fact that it offers conditions for a style of life and a quality of existence more in accord with the kingdom than the existing system.

Since Christians fully realize that the new order will also have to be transcended eschatologically, they will be motivated now to transcend it in history as well. Working from *within it*, they will engage in immanent criticism of the order that they are fashioning. Focusing on those elements that highlight the humanizing character of the new order and honing their instruments of analysis and projection, they will be motivated to move beyond that order in history itself. Finally, bearing witness to that "history" in which the kingdom has *already* revealed to faith its eschatological fullness still to come, Christians invite all human beings to faith. In doing this, they *simultaneously and inevitably* summon them to receive in faith the liberation of the coming kingdom: Christ's forgiveness of sins, the new life in Christ, and hopeful expectation of his coming. They also summon them to accept in their own lives the concrete obedience that the kingdom signifies.

Other Christians have made other options. What are we to make of that? Is it permissible for us to dissociate the two reference points of our faith? I don't think so. As we saw above, these options entail mediating factors: theological interpretation, scientific analysis, and ideological synthesis. All such mediating factors are human and fallible, and so I cannot absolutize my option eschatologically. But neither can I take refuge in mere relativity. Either one or the other option is in error on this continent, at this point in history; or else there is some third option, not an abstract one but a concrete, viable one in real life. The erroneous option is, in reality, disobedience. It is as much a "work of iniquity" as lying, adultery, and homicide. Only in a polemical context, then, can I recognize the existence of other options. I must invite my fellow human beings to join with me in analyzing our theological and socio-political mediations, so that we may be able to join together in professing the kingdom in word and deed. To do anything else would be to denigrate either one's fellow human beings or one's witness to the kingdom.

Perhaps the most distressing feature in all this is the fragmentary character of the whole process. We simply cannot reduce the mediating factors to direct, immediate revelations or to the univocalness of a single horizon. If some absolute orthodoxy or direct revelation enabled us to do that, then we could avoid risk and the eschatological transcendence of our actions would be assured. The effort to make such a reduction is what Paul would call "salvation by works," in my opinion. Here again the last word is "salvation by grace" through faith. Working in and from a concrete historical commitment, we cannot hope for the kingdom and our activity to coincide in any way except through the gratuitous mercy of God! I think this note also has a legitimate place in liberation theology.

NOTES

1. I attempted to describe the ongoing process of social awareness in Latin American Protestantism at the El Escorial meeting: see my article, "Visión del cambio social y sus tareas desde las iglesias cristianas no-católicas," in *Fe cristiana y cambio social en América Latina* (Salamanca: Sígueme, 1973), pp. 179–202. For a more autobiographical treatment see my article, "El camino del teólogo latinoamericano," in *Cuadernos de Marcha* (Montevideo).

2. See Article 11 in this volume.

3. This statement may sound strange on first reading. In Latin America there seems to be a persistent Catholic identification with the realm of political power, while Protestantism seems to be marked by biblical and christological concerns. One might even be inclined to propose that the Roman Catholic church has tended to identify itself with the "general" history of the people, the Protestant camp with the "particular" history of Israel and Christ. But such an interpretation would be erroneous, in my opinion. While the Catholic church has indeed maintained close ties with the political power structure ever since it arrived in Latin America, it has done so with an ecclesiocentric view in mind. In trying to make a *tabula rasa* of the native Indian's outlook, religion, and culture, it completely disregarded the eschatological import of the history into which it was immersing itself. It made use of the whole colonial apparatus (be it conservative or neocolonial) to propagate a church that was completely alien to the new historical reality; with few exceptions, then, it alienated itself from the Latin American population and denied its concrete humanity. The human history of Latin America was not of any theological significance to the Roman Catholic church in Latin America.

We Protestants, in turn, have talked a great deal about Jesus Christ and the Bible, but in a "docetist" manner for the most part. We reduced the Bible to a doctrinal schema: the "plan of salvation" or certain "spiritual norms." We presented Christ with hardly any concrete humanity at all. He was someone who was hung on the cross and raised from the tomb in accordance with some mechanical plan; neither his own ministry nor the Old Testament had much to do with it at all. Moreover, we turned Jesus Christ into little more than a cipher or a mechanism for triggering certain subjective, individualist experiences. Thus the ecclesiastical structure of the Catholic church and the individualist subjectivity of the Protestant church has tended to absorb both biblical history and the overall human history of Latin America.

4. This formulation brings us right to the ethical aspect of the issue. Both in apologetics and in Christian daily life we are faced with a problem that can be phrased in two complementary questions: If being and doing good in the eyes of Christians comes down to the will of God as revealed in Jesus Christ, how do we explain the fact that other human beings have achieved a certain knowledge and practice of the good apart from that revelation? Where can we find a meeting point that will make possible cooperation between believers and nonbelievers in the tasks that have to do with their life in common?

The "natural law" theory, backed up by that of some "natural revelation," seemed to be adequate for several centuries. Although the Protestants of the Reformation rejected the Aristotelian-Thomistic theology on which that theory was founded, they still managed to retain some elements of the theory itself. Using the theory of "the order of creation," they sought to reformulate the same issue on different theological grounds and ended up with the same problems. Though those two lines of thought may indeed be inadequate, I think the underlying issues behind them are indispensable to any Christian ethics. I shall return to this in my final section.

5. Two major treatments of the theme can be found in: G. Gutiérrez, *A Theology of Liberation*, Chapters 5 and 9 (see author entry under Gutiérrez in Appendix I); and J. L. Segundo, *The Community Called Church* (Maryknoll, New York: Orbis Books, 1973), especially Chapter 1.

6. The dilemma might seem to be solvable by celebrating some transforming activity of God in the history *mediated through the church*. That seems to be the thrust of a few young Protestant theologians in Latin America. One of them, René Padilla, does not hesitate to proclaim: "Christ has been enthroned as King, and his sovereignty extends to the whole universe." The church, in turn, is the messianic community, "the sphere in which we find operative the life of the new age unleashed by Jesus Christ." In what sense, then, are the church and the world historical correlates of the kingdom? Padilla concludes: "The Church has cosmic significance because it is the affirmation of Christ's universal authority. In and *through* the church, the powers of the new era unleashed by the Messiah are present in the midst of human beings. The correlate of God's kingdom is the world, but the world which is redeemed *in and through* the church."

We do not have room here for a detailed examination of this important theme, which finds corresponding versions in Catholic theology. But three observations do seem to be in order. (1) In the New Testament there is undoubtedly a close unity between the Lord and his church, by virtue of which the church shares in his prophetic and sacerdotal ministry. (If I am right in my recollection, a participation in his royal ministry is mentioned only in eschatological terms!) So there is an authentic mediation of the powers of the "new age" through the church. (2) Despite that fact, we must side with the Protestants of the sixteenth-century Reformation in saying that the Lord is not limited to or by the mediation of the church. As was the case in the Old Testament, he manifests his sovereignty in the world even through people who do not profess his name; and he also carries out his work through them. Moreover, despite what some authors maintain, I think we must say that the New Testament does not limit the work of the Holy Spirit to the community of believers. (3) We must complete the work which the Protestants of the sixteenth century did not complete. We must relate the two manifestations of the kingdom not only formally but in terms of their intrinsic connection and content. Our ability to see this relationship is obscured, in my opinion, by a certain "docetism" that quickly found its way into Christian theology. It has obscured our view of the life and teaching of Jesus as well as of the prophetic content of the Old Testament. It is precisely the message of the kingdom, embodied in its prophetic content and in the concrete humanity of Jesus, that makes it possible for us to recognize and tie together that action of the Spirit (i.e., the risen Lord) in the world and its priestly-prophetic mediation in the church. Study of this correlation is one of the most urgent tasks facing theology in our area today. As I see it, it is the operation and use of this prophetic criterion that will enable us to view critically, and eventually get beyond, the adoption of some criterion based on "natural theology" alone and viewed autonomously. Such a criterion might be proposed in classic terms, in Teilhardian terms, or in terms of some populist or Marxist ideology.

Needless to say, I am not proposing any form of philosophical or ideological asepsis in which options would be smuggled in without acknowledgment. What I am saying is that we must make our instruments even more dialectical by using a "hermeneutic circle" which starts from a central focus: the message mediated by the text.

7. We are no longer surprised to see the notions of body and resurrection applied not only to the realm of the individual and the person but also to the realm of history and the community. We now know that such a schism is no part of the biblical view. Both concepts have connotations that are both personal and communitarian throughout the whole Bible.

8. The depth of the transformation is taken in Jesus' famous remark in Mark 12:25ff. That remark does not eschatologically cancel the male-female distinction, it seems to me. Instead it suggests a radical transformation of its meaning, particularly with respect to the historico-biological necessity of descendants.

9. Two passages deserving serious consideration in this connection are the two classic parallel texts having to do with "resurrected life" in this world: Colossians 3 and Ephesians 4:17–6:20.

10. Two questions might be raised regarding these assertions. One has to do with New Testament statements that the world is "in the power of evil." Here the problem lies in the fact that often the "world" is viewed in spatial terms rather than in temporal terms. The world is not "what is happening on the planet Earth." It is what is in the "orbit" of the "old eon characterized by sin." A new era or "eon" has burst upon this very planet that we sometimes call "the world." A new age has broken into our very history. It is already at work, breaking down the power of evil and darkness.

That brings us to the second question: Are we not talking solely and exclusively about the "works" of the church that are realized through "faith in Christ"? The issue deserves more careful exegetical study. But it is my view that in principle the faith-love dialectics calls for, and opens up the possibility of, works of love: works that perdure, works that faith names in terms of their connection with the particular historical manifestation of Jesus Christ but that can sometimes be carried out by love without this explicit reference. In some mysterious way, as divine works whose meaning has been revealed in Christ, these works make Christ's work present in the midst of the old humanity. To claim that the church has exclusive rights over the domain of love is, in my view, to go against the clear evidence as well as the explicit testimony of Scripture. And we would be contradicting the explicit statements of Jesus if we were to maintain that the love we perceive in the world is somehow less "divine" and less "eschatological" than that practiced by the Christian.

11. The quest for this unity is, I think, the fundamental ecclesiological criterion. The "true church" is defined in relation to the kingdom. Hence its "mark" is the unity of proclamation and action. It must strive to strip proclamation of its ambiguity and its ideological risks, defining it and verifying it in historical praxis. It must equally strive to strip its action of ambiguity and the danger of absolutization, linking it up with the promise of Jesus Christ and the proclamation of God's gratuitous future. The infidelity of the church, then, can be measured in terms of the extent to which it is willing to divorce the two elements. This divorce may take the form of an idealist form of proclamation ("speech without power," to use Paul's term). Or it may take the form of some line of action that purports to have meaning and permanence in itself: e.g., pharisaical works, clericalism, ecclesiocracy, and even some forms of "revolutionary emptying" which are no less spurious for being generous. This ecclesiological criterion has been well noted, from a somewhat different standpoint, by B. Dumas in *Los dos rostros alienados de la Iglesia una* (Buenos Aires: Latinoamerica Libros, 1971).

12. J. Míguez Bonino, *Doing Theology in a Revolutionary Situation* (Philadelphia: Fortress Press, 1975), Chapters 6–8.

13

From Paradise to the Desert: Autobiographical Musings

Rubem Alves (Campinas, Brazil)

Neither in the Paradise of Genesis nor the Holy City of the Apocalypse are there any temples. In Paradise religion is not yet necessary, and in the Holy City it is no longer necessary. Religion is the memory of a lost unity and the nostalgia for a future reconciliation. Under the surface layers of happiness and peace which it proclaims, religion always presupposes an I unreconciled with its destiny.

The oldest memories of my own religious nostalgia go back to my early childhood. I was eleven years old. It was not a matter of a precocious theological vocation. It was rather a precocious experience of fear. That was the first time that I personally experienced what is known as "anxiety."

Up to that time I had lived in a small town. Everything in it had been friendly and familiar to me: the streets, the trees, the streams, the people. The "other" people who were "relevant" for me were my mother, my father, my brothers and sisters, and my friends; and I looked on them with calmness and respect. They were part of my universe. I scarcely was aware of myself as such, because I and my world were fused into one single whole. Waking up in the morning, going to school, playing outside, and going to bed at night were part of a liturgy that was picked up again every day and that celebrated a world that made sense.

Suddenly, without realizing it, I was driven out of Paradise. They transferred me to a big city. My "relevant others" were dissolved in the incomprehensible complexity of city life. They remained "others" but they were no longer "relevant." They were no longer the emotional center of my world, from which I drew my sense of identity and the meaning of my future. They were not to blame for what had happened to me because they, too, were lost.

For the first time I experienced the uneasiness of being different. I became self-conscious. My accent revealed who I was: a country bumpkin. My schoolmates would not pardon me for that. How cruel children can be! I found myself alone, without friends, without knowing what to do. I was different and ridiculous. I did not possess the human resources needed to sustain myself in that abysmal solitude. Sociologists call that situation "anomie." How much suffering is buried in that little word! Primitive cosmogonies always talk about a primordial conflict between the dry land and the sea. Dry land is the place where human beings can walk with security. The waters of the sea symbolize the horrendous possibilities that menace human beings unceasingly. "Chaos" and the "void" ever threaten to engulf the world of human beings. My dry land had been invaded by those waters, my universe had been engulfed by their waves.

But human consciousness cannot survive indefinitely in a state of anomie. Inevitably we must resolve the problem of loneliness and impotence in a hostile world, and consciousness makes use of a trick to solve the problem. By means of a magic trick it tries to make the real unreal, organizing its perception of reality as if its own desires and aspirations were the ultimate reality. Its own desires and aspirations are ontologized and reified. Thanks to the magic power, the "omnipotence" of thought, human beings weave together a verbal world out of the depths of their impotence and the heights of their passion. It is a verbal world that affirms and confirms their own values. The new world constructed in this fashion becomes their "vicarious gratification," their new world of happiness that compensates for the frustration and suffering encountered in the real world. And frequently, though not always, this "vicarious gratification" is religion.

That was the route I unwittingly followed. I became religious. After all, it did not matter that the world mocked us. True religion is above and beyond all that. Even if our "relevant others" are reduced to impotence and insignificance, there is a Relevant Other who knows and loves us and who has infinite power at its disposal. I do not mean to reduce religion to this type of experience at all, but neither can I conceal what really happened to me.

I became a fundamentalist, a pious fundamentalist. Fundamentalism is an attitude which attributes a definitive character to one's own beliefs. The really important feature is not *what* the fundamentalists say but *how* they say it. Fundamentalists are characterized by a dogmatic and authoritarian attitude with respect to their own system of thought and by an attitude of intolerance (the Inquisition) toward every "heretic" or "revisionist."

You can have revolutionary fundamentalists, be they devotees of Marxism, women's liberation, or black power. You can have scholarly and scientific fundamentalists, especially when they forget that they are working with models, as Kuhn points out,[1] or with simple "opinions," as Popper suggests.[2] You can have counterculture fundamentalists who absolutize their own personal experiences. And you can even have liberal fundamentalists. The fundamentalist is a person full of self, a person incapable of the slightest *humor* where self is concerned, a person whom Kolakowski characterizes as "the priest" as opposed to "the clown."

The important feature in fundamentalism is not the ideas that are affirmed but the spirit in which they are affirmed. You cannot just shift the bottles around on the shelves. If the shelves stay exactly as they were, then the system itself remains the same. To put it a bit more abstractly: It is the *structure* that defines the fundamentalist mentality, not the elements that go to make up its content.

Fundamentalism may well be the great temptation facing us. As the serpent tells Adam: "You shall be like God, knowing good and evil." And don't we all long to trade in our opinions for images of reality, our doubts for certainties, our provisional status for eternity, our distress and incompleteness for peace and self-fulfillment? The fundamentalist solution frees us from our painful encounter with a reality that ever remains incomplete, changing, upsetting, and distressing.

Convert to fundamentalism—the type doesn't matter. You will find yourself liberated from the endless process of building up and then tearing down only to begin again. Fundamentalists are those who have already finished the job. Nietzsche rightly described them as the enemy of the future because the fundamentalists *already* know who and what is good. That is very useful and functional from the emotional standpoint. From that standpoint religion provides us with certainty and security. And when one has discovered a religion of that sort, the logical next step is to become an apostle of one's truth. So it was that I entered the seminary.

But language is unpredictable, and remember that it is language that sustains our world and the structure of our personality. Language is a tool, as it were. It is created, used, and preserved so that it may adequately serve us for the solution of our existential problem. But suppose now that this basic problem, this emotional matrix around which we have structured our existence, suddenly alters. The old language suddenly becomes superfluous and no longer has any function. The function of my fundamentalist language had been to resolve the anomie that arose out of my loneliness. Meanwhile in the seminary I had found a group of companions like myself who shared the very same problems; the scripts of our biographies were very much alike. We became friends and formed a community; and in sharing our problems we found a solution. The anomie was overcome, along with the fundamentalist language. That language was no longer needed.

Wittgenstein once observed that language has a "magic" power.[3] Linguistic structures tend to situate us in an enchanted realm where we can see the world only in the way that language itself allows. So when we "forget" some language, we somehow begin to see the world in a completely different way. We experience *astonishment* at suddenly seeing things that were always there but that we had not noticed before. We cannot help but ask ourselves: Why am I incapable of seeing so many things? How could I have failed to notice so many features of reality that were right before my eyes?

So it was that I discovered the social roots of our religion—and also its neurotic origins. Its negation of the world, its absolutization of eternity, its rejection of liberty, its discomfort in the face of human, sensuous reality, and its rejection of all that was provisional: Didn't all these things represent a conspiracy against life?

Our perspective on reality changes according to the standpoint from which we examine it. My new vision of our space, our time, and our existence revealed a Bible that had been hidden from my eyes up to that point. What a surprise it was to discover that the human beings in the Bible felt at home in the world! From beginning to end the Bible celebrates life and its goodness. It is good to be alive, to be flesh and blood, to exist in the world. Suddenly the Calvinist obsession with the glory of God seemed to me to be profoundly inhuman and antibiblical. Isn't God's only concern the happiness of human beings? Isn't that the very epitome of God's will? Isn't God a humanist, in the sense that humanity is the one and only object of his love?

Bonhoeffer became our friend. We read him passionately:

> It is only when one loves life and the world so much that without them everything would be gone, that one can believe in the resurrection and a new world. . . . To long for the transcendent when you are in your wife's arms is, to put it mildly, a lack of taste, and it is certainly not what God expects of us. We ought to find God and love him in the blessings he sends us. If he pleases to grant us some overwhelming earthly bliss, we ought not to try and be more religious than God himself. . . . It is not with the next world that we are concerned, but with this world as created and preserved and set subject to laws and atoned for and made new. What is above the world is, in the Gospel, intended to exist *for* this world.[4]

Salvation *from* the world, that touchstone dogma of Brazilian Protestantism—was it not in direct opposition to the Bible itself? Personal salvation cannot take place to the detriment of the world because humanity and the world belong to each other. It is first and foremost in our struggle for the redemption of the world that we achieve our personal totality. Thus saviors of souls were transformed into rebuilders of earth. One thing seemed certain to us: The church would have to free itself from the spell of fundamentalist language that had kept it prisoner. Once this was realized, the church would take the lead in the battle to transform the world, or so we hoped.

In our minds the reform of the church and the redemption of the world were one single task. We left the seminary with the assurance that we had settled that question. Wasn't our idea intoxicating? Who could help but fall under its spell?

But reality made a mockery of our naive aspirations. We were not ready for the reality of institutional life. To the ears of ecclesiastical officials our new reading of the gospel sounded like apostasy. Their experience had been different. They could not comprehend or love what had been felt so immediately by us. We were accused of being heretics, pointed out as people with dangerous political ideas, and rejected as apostates because we committed the sin of accepting Catholics as our brothers and sisters. We were forced into exile: "Love it or leave it, but do not try to transform the church."

Two things became clear. The first thing was that the institutional church was not the church we loved. Reading the prophets, we found that Hosea had the same experience. God's exclamation, "You are not my people," became the name of one of his children. The church for which we yearned, the community of liberty and love, was not to be found in the confines of the ecclesial organization. We would have to give up the ideal of reforming it. You cannot sew patches of new material on old cloth. You cannot pour new wine into old bottles. It is impossible. More to the point, it is stupid.

But how is one to survive in solitude, far from any community? If values are not shared, they tend to be forgotten. To the extent that values are not hard facts, they are absent entities. Not yet born, they persist as a possibility, a promise, a hope. Their presence in the present depends on a language proclaiming their realization. Hence our disillusionment with the ecclesiastical organization did not mean that we had given up hope of finding a community. On the contrary, we began to look for it in places where we had never looked before. New questions confronted us: "Was it possible that today the church was dispersed, hidden, unrecognized in the world? " Was it not possible that those who are truly living in expectation of the kingdom did not know its name?

To our surprise we found more signs of the Spirit outside the restricted bounds of our ecclesial communities than inside. A new type of ecumenism emerged, completely different from the institutionalized ecumenism that is found on the upper levels of ecclesiastical hierarchies and that is based on agreements over doctrine or ecclesiastical discipline. We discovered a new unity on a different front, where people were preoccupied with human beings and the renovation of the world. Indeed it seems to me that the more the church closes in on itself, even if its intent is to find some lost unity, the more it sinks down into its own contradictions. On the other hand when it gives itself up totally to the cause of redemption in a concrete, experiential way, it then discovers something that it had not even been looking for: its own unity.

The second thing that seemed clear was a byproduct of the first. The patronizing guardians of God, those who allege to hold some monopoly on the divine, use his name in a way that bears strong resemblances to the Inquisition. "God" becomes an ideological weapon designed to preserve the power structure, justify the status quo, and assassinate dissidents. Thus the word "God" suddenly ceased to make any sense. Or, to put it better, it was stripped of meaning in its institutional and traditional theological context. God's name was no longer the symbol of liberty and love. For many this meant that God was dead. They suddenly found themselves faced with the task of reconstructing the world. Out of ecclesiastical frustration was born a secular humanism. Theology was traded in for sociology, the church for the world, God for human beings.

Others, however, did not take that path. From their hopes and frustrations, from their reading of the Bible and the daily newspaper, there arose a new way of talking about God and a new way of envisioning the community of faith. This new approach was given the name "liberation theology." Essentially it comes down to a dialectical hermeneutics in which people read the Bible from the standpoint of the hopes and anxieties of the present, and read the present from the standpoint of the hopes and anxieties of which the Bible speaks.

Quite logically then, an act of faith is present in this procedure. With Paul it assumes that "all creation groans and is in agony even until now," awaiting "the revelation of the sons of God." The pangs of childbirth entail both tears and smiles. They point to an emerging reality. The Spirit has impregnated creation. Its womb filled with new life, creation waits and anxiously hopes for the advent of the new, even as we, groaning inwardly, look for the same thing (see Rom. 8:22–23).

The theology of liberation cannot rest content with remaining indifferent to life and the world. Isn't the gospel message an account of the good news of the Incarnation? Doesn't Christ's life bear witness to God's solidarity with human beings? There is no question of reducing faith to sociology. The primary assertion is that transcendence is concretely revealed both in the groaning cries for liberty and in the struggle against everything that oppresses people.

Many years have now gone by. Our age-old hopes have not been fulfilled. We live amid the ruins of our religious expectations. One form of captivity was abolished only to be replaced by another. Now, in trying to find meaning in our biographies, we find that we have been steadily beating a retreat. Our backs are to the wall, and there is no escape. The exodus of which we dreamed earlier has miscarried. Instead we now find ourselves in a situation of exile and captivity.

Let me explain. We were born in a world illuminated by transcendental certitudes and absolute values. Our hopes were indestructible. Our world was a universe that drew meaningfulness from a vision of the heavenly Jerusalem. God was in heaven, all would go well on earth.

But our gods are dead. Or, if not dead, they are hushed and still. They were sent into exile, even as we were. In their place came our heroes, and politics was transformed into religion. With the help of politics, all that had been mere expectant groaning would find concrete fulfillment in reality.

But now even our heroes are dead. We were not able to carry out the task we proposed to ourselves. The universe was invaded by chaos. What else could we do but beat a retreat once more? Lacking gods and heroes, we still had our day-to-day values. It is almost incredible to find how our horizons have narrowed. In the beginning, with religion, our horizon stretched to the very boundaries of time and space. With politics it became a bit more restricted; we were bounded within the confines of history. Now our universe is confined to the narrow walls of our own house and the brief span of our own life. Lacking gods and heroes, we still have a wife or husband, children, friends, our work, music, and the contemplation of nature.

I was told that after the 1968 student uprising in France there was a great increase in vocations to the agrarian way of life. That is very interesting. At least farming is an activity where we can be fairly certain that we won't reap thorns if we plant grapes. If we cannot control history, we resign ourselves to a more restricted world. But even this retreat is condemned to failure. We cannot preserve rural values in a technocratic world. Once upon a time peasants could resolve the problem of anomie that arose when they moved to the big city by going back to their original world. Today, however, the problem is no longer a spatial one. Something has happened to our space. It has been engulfed by the new time that bureaucratic and technological society has created. We cannot win out over anomie by going back to our lost Paradise because it no longer exists. Chaos has invaded every sector of our civilization.

One day we saw our gods die. The next day we embraced heroes, only to see them die. Then we were restricted to our domestic confines. Now we suddenly discover that unless we ourselves succeed in generating new gods, we will be left with no alternative except to go mad. Even Nietzsche, who proclaimed the death of God, pointed out that a universe in which God is dead is dark and cold.

Biography and history go together. As Marx saw so well: "Man is not abstract being squatting outside the world. Man is *the world of man*, the state, society."[5] Even if we mark off our own space with the signposts of private property, even if we refuse to look at the world that is assaulting us, even if we cherish the illusion that we are living our own individual lives, the fact remains that our personal destiny is rooted deeply in the destiny of civilizations. In one way or another, our biography is always a symptom of the conditions prevailing in our world. That is the reason behind the discovery we all frequently make. Despite the fact that we live in different places, posts, and political contexts, our biographies strongly resemble slight variations of one and the same script. They have the same structure. They go through the same sequence of hopes and frustrations.

It is this personal history that drives me into theological research. I have lost my points of reference. I find no concrete signs to give me hope. What we find in our present historical situation allows us no trace of optimism. But I know very well that we cannot live without hope. It is hope that gives us what Prescott Lecky describes as "self-consistency."[6] Psychotherapy has discovered that objectively there is no hope for those who subjectively do not possess hope.[7] Hope is a *wager*. We bet on the possibility of our values being fulfilled. And it is this wager that gives us the emotional energy to live through feelings of frustration and impotence. And so I myself feel caught painfully between the anthropological necessity of hope on the one hand and its historical impossibility on the other. I do not know how to associate my biography with history, the personal with the structural, the existential with the material. I do not have at my disposal any paradigm that will enable me to reconstruct my universe.

That is the problem which lies at the roots of my theology. Theology is a science for people who have lost the pristine unity of Paradise or who have not yet found it. It is a search for points of reference, for new horizons that will enable us to find meaning amid the chaos that engulfs us. It is an attempt to piece back together the shattered fragments of a whole that has been destroyed. At its origin lies the problem of hope, the plausibility of the human values we cherish in a world that conspires against them.

Thus theology and biography go together. Religion, noted Feuerbach, is "the solemn unveiling of a man's hidden treasures, the revelation of his intimate thoughts, the open confession of his love-secrets."[8] Religion is the proclamation of the axiological priority of the heart over the raw facts of reality. It is a refusal to be gobbled up and digested by the surrounding world, an appeal to a vision, a passion, a love. When the heart constructs some utopia, is it not translating into words a world that just might be divine? Does it not embody a nostalgia for the kingdom? When I evince a passionate desire for peace and justice despite the fact that I do not see any concrete possibility for them in this world, am I not saying in my heart something like the following—even though I may claim to be an atheist: "How wonderful it would be if there were a God to confirm my values. Though I cannot come to believe in such a God, how I wish he did exist"? When, in the midst of misery and oppression, I feel overwhelmed with sentiments too deep to be expressed, may I not be unwittingly praying?

We must recognize and acknowledge the human origins of religion. Even if it were possible for some religion to exist that did not arise out of our existential situation, how could I comprehend it? How could it be the object of my love? We must agree with Nietzsche: "The belly of being does not speak to humans at all, except as a human."[9] If that remark sounds a bit too human to pious ears, those people would do well to reread a bit of Luther. Human beings can assume a religious attitude only toward something that they sense to be a value, something that has to do with life and death. It is completely wrong to say that religion is mere anthropology. We would be closer to the mark if we said that anthropology is religion. As Feuerbach puts it: "If the plants had eyes, taste, and judgment, each plant would declare its own flower the most beautiful." Hence "the Absolute to man is his own nature."[10]

Theology is our effort to bring together the petals of our flower that is continuously torn apart by a world that does not love flowers. It is "the sigh of the oppressed creature" (Marx) who is incapable of resurrecting his dead flower yet dares to hope that his seeds will germinate once the winter is over. Theology is the expression of that unconscious and unending project that is the very heart of human beings: the creation of a world with human meaningfulness.

Norman O. Brown remarks: "It is the human ego that carries the search for a world to love."[11] The ego, in other words, does not remain closed up in itself. It yearns to flow out over nature and fecundate it with its seed. The human ego seeks to humanize nature, to impregnate it with the future, to transform the physical universe into an *ordo amoris* (Max Scheler). What is coarse and lifeless and incapable of feeling must become an extension of the human body, an instrument for human hands and an expression of the human heart: "Human existence is, *ab initio*, an ongoing externalization. As man externalizes himself, he constructs the world *into* which he externalizes himself. In the process of externalization, he projects his own meanings into reality. Symbolic universes, which proclaim that *all* reality is humanly meaningful and call upon the *entire* cosmos to signify the validity of human existence, constitute the farthest reaches of this projection."[12]

This is the origin, function, and meaning of theology. I appeal to the words of an antitheologian, Nietzsche, to express what lies behind the folly of theology: "Let the future and the farthest be for you the cause of your today."[13] Theology is contemplation of today in the light of the future. It looks facts in the face in order to effect their abolition and fulfillment (*Aufhebung*). It dissolves objectivity magically in the name of a utopian order that becomes one's prospect and final destination.

Here the reader might well interpose an objection: "If that is the case, if theology is a projection of human desires, then it has no objective validity. It is nothing more than an evasion, an illusion, a vicarious gratification invented to evade the harsh facts of reality." To clear up that problem we must for a moment drop the line of thought we have been pursuing and start over from a different perspective.

Our way of thinking is conditioned by a whole set of unconscious presuppositions[14] that we accept as our point of departure in the process of knowing. They are the "silent adjustments" of which Wittgenstein speaks,[15] the "God-terms" noted by Philip Rieff.[16] These silent adjustments are our eyes, as it were. We see *through* them but we do not see *them*. They fashion our reality, but we do not advert to the fact that they themselves have been fashioned too. All together, they constitute a kind of collective unconscious underlying our mental processes. They are unconscious and we do not see them; that is why in most cases they are inaccessible to our criticism and exert such strange "magical" power over us. They make it impossible for us to contemplate the world in any way different from the way we have programed it.

Our ability to see reality and the faculties used by us are conditioned by a whole set of "silent adjustments" that have been codified by science. First of all, we assume that knowing is duplicating. Underlying the scientific ideal of objectivity we find the assumption that knowledge is nothing more nor less than a simple copy or reflection of what is given. In this respect academic western sociology does not differ one whit from what is called Marxist science. I recall Engels's observation: "Modern Socialism is nothing but the reflex, in thought, of this conflict in fact."[17] Whether we admit it or not, we are empiricists; we assume that thought must be a copy of the datum in reality. Consequently we also assume that propositions have meaning only when they can be verified through a confrontation with the data of experience.

The second dogma of our collective unconscious derives logically from the first. If knowing is duplicating, then people are considered normal to the extent that their mental processes do not contradict the rules of the "copying" process. It is worth noting that Freud sees neurotics as people who attribute "excessive value to their own desires" in their behavior. In other words, behavior that takes values as its point of reference is regarded as unhealthy. Freud puts it very succinctly: "One thing only do I know for certain and that is that man's judgments of value follow directly his wishes for happiness—that, accordingly, they are an attempt to support his illusions with arguments."[18] The conclusion is inescapable: To the scientific ideal of objectivity there corresponds, on the epistemological level, a psychosocial understanding of normality in terms of adaptation.

This unconscious metaphysics of ours further maintains that historical and social processes are independent of human beings. The essence of Marxist science, notes Lukács, is the realization that the forces that really move history are completely independent of any psychic awareness that human beings might have of them.[19] Even Marx himself remarked that what the proletariat imagined directly was completely irrelevant. The important thing is what *really* is and what that obliges us to do.[20]

What are the causes and explanations for human behavior? The intentions and aspirations of human beings, perhaps? Definitely not. The content of consciousness is a secondary phenomenon. It is an effect, not a cause, of social processes. It is the social structure that explains consciousness, not vice versa.

Academic sociology in the West accepts the same axiom. Social structures are independent and autonomous; hence they are self-explanatory. As Peter Blau puts it: "Once firmly organized, an organization tends to assume an identity of its own which makes it independent of the people who have founded it or of those who constitute its membership."[21] What Althusser says of Marxist science can be applied here too. To know the human world, the scholarly scientist must put humanity itself in parenthesis. Concrete human beings contribute nothing to our knowledge and comprehension of the institutions to which they belong: "Strictly in respect to theory. . . one can and must speak openly of Marx's *theoretical anti-humanism,* and see in this *theoretical anti-humanism* the absolute (negative) precondition of the (positive) knowledge of the human world itself and of its practical transformation."[22]

This presupposition is not peculiar to just the social sciences. Psychological behaviorism, especially that influenced by B. F. Skinner, also takes it for its point of departure. Human behavior is to be understood as a simple response to stimuli. Human action, is, in reality, re-action. As behaviorism sees the matter, the whole complex of stimuli perform the same function that social structures perform in the view of the social sciences. In the last analysis, human beings are not *factors* at all. They do not make history. Their activity does not flow from their freedom but from the complex web of concrete determinisms surrounding them.

The last axiom I should like to consider here is implicit in the third just mentioned. The imagination does not make history. Freud's fight against the neurotic is the same fight Marx waged against the utopian socialist. Both the neurotic and the utopian refuse to accept the verdict of reality. They act as if their values were in a position to alter the inevitable course of objective reality. They think that imagination is capable of creating new conditions. But since imagination represents a refusal to accept and duplicate what is given and implies a magical transformation of the objective world (Sartre),[23] it must be abandoned as false consciousness and a form of illness.

It is this last axiom that is of most interest to us here. After all, what is religion but a form of imagination? Religion is imagination and, by the same token, imagination always has a religious function. It is obvious that religion does not seek to describe what is given in experience. As Feuerbach observed: "Religion is the dream of the human mind. . . . We only see real things in the entrancing splendour of imagination and caprice, instead of in the simple daylight of reality and necessity."[24] According to the logic of the scientific mentality, then, religion along with imagination must be classified as a form of illness or false consciousness.

Thus when we reject religion as *mere* imagination, we are unconsciously accepting the hidden metaphysics that governs the scientific mentality. We are assuming that knowledge is duplication and that normality is adaptation. Consciousness is taken to be like a camera that takes photographs of the world. And since religion does not take photographs, since it transfigures the data according to the logic of the heart, we reject it as meaningless.

But the world as a concrete way of existing is not the objective world of scientific abstraction. As Dewey put it: "Empirically, things are poignant, tragic, beautiful, humorous, settled, disturbed, comfortable, annoying, barren, harsh, consoling, splendid, fearful. . . . "[25] Our experience of the world is primarily emotional. To this the objective scientist might reply: "True, but that is because we are *not yet* used to true, pure, and disinterested knowledge." That is wrong. Things are that way because human beings, in their relationship with their surroundings, are always faced with the imperative of survival. It is precisely because they wish to live that they never perceive their milieu as neutral. Their surroundings promise life and death, pleasure and pain. Hence anyone really enmeshed in the struggle for survival is forced to perceive the world in emotional terms. It is this immediate and emotion-laden experience, which in most instances is not and cannot be verbalized, that determines our way of existing in the world. This emotional matrix constitutes the structure of the world in which we live.

What I am saying here is that consciousness is not pure. The mind does not exist as an entity independent of matter, as Cartesian philosophy would have it. It is not pure, free reason existing beyond interference from the vital and emotional components of the subject, as Kant believed. Consciousness is a function of the body. It exists to help the body solve the problem of its survival. And since survival is always the ultimate human value, even when one commits suicide, consciousness is structured around an emotional matrix. As Nietzsche put it, the body is our "Great Reason." What we call "reason" is really a little reason, a tool and plaything of our Great Reason.

If the core of consciousness is emotion and value, then consciousness is radically religious. As we have already noted, it is not a mechanism for duplicating an order that is given empirically. Piaget tells us that consciousness is not a copy but an organization of the real.[26] And since the real is devoid of human significance, it becomes a human world only after we give it structure by attuning it to our own needs and values. In other words, what we call reality is the construction of the religious matrix of consciousness. As Emile Durkheim has pointed out, religion is the origin and foundation of the categories of reason.[27]

The reason why we tend to downgrade religion as mere imagination is that we are caught in the snares of our collective unconscious. We are inclined to know things solely through the logic of the subject-object relationship, or what Martin Buber calls the "I-it" relationship.[28] What does the scientific criterion of verification mean except that every sign stands for some object? But life exists prior to any such artificial fragmentation, since life is relationship. An organism and its milieu must be immersed in a process of dialectical relationships if life is to manifest itself. Once that process terminates, life is overcome by death. Insofar as religious thinking has to do with life rather than with dead abstraction, its point of reference is the set of relationships that precede the dichotomy between subject and object.

It is precisely for that reason that religion makes use of symbols rather than signs. The function of a symbol is to represent a living relationship. Relationships are not perceived; they are not objects. First and foremost they make up the milieu in which life exists.

One of the great contributions of psychoanalysis was the discovery that dreams have meaning. The apparent absurdity of dreams is a veiled way of revealing some truth. The problem is that their meaning lies hidden. If we try to decipher them with the logic of the subject-object relationship, then we will end up with absurdities. Why? Because in dreams serpents are not serpents, rivers are not rivers, and mountains are not mountains. They are symbols, revealing and hiding at the same time. If we think that in dreams we are dealing with *signs* that point to certain objects, if we forget that we are dealing with *symbols* that express relationships, then the meaning of dreams will remain forever hidden from our understanding.

But what is religion except the dream of whole groups of human beings? Religion is for society what the dream is for the individual. If that is true, then we are making a great mistake if we classify it as a form of false consciousness. *Religion reveals the logic of the heart, the dynamism of the "pleasure principle," insofar as it struggles to transform a nonhuman chaos around it into "ordo amoris" (an order of love).*

At this point the reader might rightly make a complaint: "You are offering an apology for religion. But even suppose we accept it. You still have not offered us any convincing reason why we should dedicate ourselves to theology. You have not made it clear why we should go beyond the fantastic variety of religious experiences that arise naturally even today in order to immerse ourselves in things that happened long ago in biblical times."

You would be perfectly right, but let me try to explain myself. You know that all of us are neurotics to a greater or lesser degree. We are not free. We live our daily lives under the power of an infinite number of "evil spirits" that our past has bequeathed to us. Our personal histories, which have molded us, are fraught with frustrations, aggressive feelings, sado-masochistic tendencies, guilt-feelings, and fears. It makes no difference that we struggle against them with all our strength. We are defeated day after day. So long as we remain within the boundaries of our own biographies, we simply shuffle and reshuffle our gods and our evil spirits between us. We may indeed live through different emotional experiences, but the actors of our script remain the same. In desperation we realize that there is no substantive change.

The great discovery of Luther in going through his own personal conflicts was the realization that there is no hope for us if we try to solve our contradictions without going outside ourselves. You know that we become a person only to the extent that the Other rises before us. We are what we are by virtue of the "relevant others" with whom we speak. The I takes shape to the extent that it responds to a Thou. If we remain imprisoned within our selves, at the mercy of an anonymous "self" (Heidegger's *Das Man*[29]), then our only possible way out is to find a new set of "relevant others."

That is theology as I understand it. It is an effort to overcome biography through history, to expand the circle of "relevant others" with whom we are in contact in order to overcome the straitened boundaries in which our life has imprisoned us. Evaluating my own personal experience, I came to see that I scarcely engage in any serious discourse with the people who are in a strictly spatial relationship with me. Our talk ranges from the functional-bureaucratic realm to the other extreme of polite banalities and habitual remarks. My serious conversations, the ones which are a matter of life and death, have almost exclusively been with absent people who are no longer alive: Jeremiah, Jesus, Luther, Nietzsche, Kierkegaard, Berdyaev, and Buber—not to mention such artists as Bach, Scarlatti, Mozart, and Vivaldi. So it is true for theology too: First and foremost theology has to do with the "relevant others" whom we include in our dialogue concerning the problem of our day-to-day life.

What is involved is not an article to publish or a book to write. They are secondary byproducts of the ultimate question: how to survive as a human being in a cold world that has sent our values into exile. It is not a neutral problem that can be broached objectively or dispassionately. What is at stake is my destiny, and so infinite passion is demanded of those who take part in the dialogue. "Doing theology" is making a decision about the battles that ought to be fought. In that sense I find myself fighting those battles all the time. Even if I do not use theological jargon or religious symbols, I am always caught up in religion and theology.

In any case there is more to be said here. If you want to play a certain game, you must know the rules. Discussion and debate is a game. If we do not agree on the implicit rules, there will never be any communication. We can still talk, but at the end we will be exactly where we were when we started. The boundaries and structures of our personality will remain unchanged. So before we begin the discussion called "theology," we must realize who and what it is that establishes the rules of the game. We can decide to be in charge of the game. Indeed that is what happens in most cases. It is *my* experience that is absolute. What matters is what I *think.* I am the very navel of the world. My own ego becomes the ultimate criterion for understanding the whole world. Insofar as I take that tack, I affirm that reality must be subjected to the criteria of my own personal experience.

The problem is that all our ingenuity and optimism about ourselves, and even all our mental gymnastics, will not save us. If we adopt our own neurotic ego as the criterion for understanding ourselves, we cannot possibly get away from the snares of our own neurosis. The point I am trying to make here is somewhat in line with the wise gospel remark: "He who would save his life must lose it." Luther noted that the human being, in his inmost depths, is a *cor incurvatum in se ipsum,* "a heart curved in upon itself." We start off from our personal experiences, we absolutize them, and then we try every which way to get a new vision of reality. We do discover some new facet and then we exclaim: "I see, I see. I have seen the face of God." And we do not notice that we have seen nothing more than our own fears, frustrations, fantasies, good intentions, and naiveté: i.e., the gods and devils that populate our own unconscious. Our hope of salvation is nothing more than our condition of damnation. We are not saved; we are simply bedazzled by our own illusions.

That is the reason why I myself, in trying to find new horizons, identify myself emotionally with the experience of "captivity": "By the streams of Babylon we sat and wept when we remembered Zion" (Ps. 137:1). Captivity is characterized by the sorrowful juxtaposition of yearnings for freedom and a conscious awareness of impotence. Only dreamers and visionaries feel impotent. Those who do not have dreams and visions drown in a settled world. They adapt to it, become functional, and are content.

That is one of the reasons why I have serious suspicions about psychoanalysis. It alleges and seeks to solve the problem of neurosis not by transforming the objective pole of experience but by altering the subjective pole and making it adapt to established reality. But adaptation always implies passive acceptance of a world that has not been redeemed.

To feel oneself a captive, on the other hand, is to refuse to accept the world as it is. It is a sad and painful refusal, however, because it is not accompanied by the optimism of those who feel strong enough to complete the transformation demanded by consciousness. Captives are condemned to sadness, and the sadness is not transformed into desperation or accommodation if, in the midst of captivity, one glimpses a hope of liberty. But this hope of liberty is not fashioned by our own strength. We are impotent. To hope for liberation in captivity is to hope for the impossible: the unexpected. In the old idiom of religion it is to have trust in a God who summons things that do not exist into existence and makes the barren fruitful.

But why choose this particular way of seeing things rather than another way? I don't know. In the last analysis it is a matter of love, of hope. But that is true for all the dimensions of our life. Even in science, as Kuhn has pointed out, there can be no advance without the risk of faith and a vision of hope.[30] Perhaps our choice is mistaken, but we have no alternative except to make some choice. Even not choosing is making a choice.

We are condemned to gods and demons. We are condemned to religion. It is even possible that we may be ashamed of this and that we will cloak our values and dreams in the respectable dress of science. Of one thing I am certain: Life is not accompanied by inescapable certitudes but by visions, risks, and passions. As Nietzsche put it: "Whoever had to create also had his prophetic dreams and astral signs—and had faith in faith."[31]

NOTES

1. Thomas S. Kuhn, *The Structure of Scientific Revolutions* (Chicago: University of Chicago Press, 1962).
2. Karl Popper, *The Logic of Scientific Discovery* (New York: Harper & Row, 1968), p. 278: "We do not know: we can only guess. And our guesses are guided by the unscientific, the metaphysical . . . faith in laws."
3. Ludwig Wittgenstein, *The Blue and Brown Books* (New York: Harper & Row, 1958), p. 27.
4. Dietrich Bonhoeffer, *Letters and Papers from Prison* (New York: Macmillan Paperback, 1962), pp. 103, 113, 168.
5. Marx-Engels, *On Religion* (New York: Schocken Books, 1964), p. 41.
6. Prescott Lecky, *Self-Consistency: A Theory of Personality* (New York: Doubleday, 1961).
7. Ezra Stotland, *The Psychology of Hope* (San Francisco: Jessy-Bass, 1969).
8. L. Feuerbach, *The Essence of Christianity* (New York: Harper Torchbooks, 1957), p. 13.
9. F. Nietzsche, *Thus Spoke Zarathustra*, Eng. trans., Walter Kaufmann, *The Portable Nietzsche* (New York: Viking Press, 1968), p. 144.
10. Feuerbach, *Essence of Christianity*, pp. 5 and 8.
11. Norman O. Brown, *Life Against Death* (Middletown, Conn.: Wesleyan University Press, 1959), p. 46.
12. P. Berger and T. Luckmann, *The Social Construction of Reality* (New York: Doubleday, 1966), p. 96.
13. *Portable Nietzsche*, p. 174.
14. A. Gouldner, *The Coming Crisis of Western Sociology* (New York: Basic Books, 1970), p. 29.
15. L. Wittgenstein, *Tractatus Logico-Philosophicus* (London: Routledge & Kegan Paul, 1922), section 4.002.
16. Philip Rieff, *The Mind of the Moralist* (New York: Doubleday, 1961), p. 35.
17. F. Engels,*Socialism: Utopian and Scientific* (New York: Scribner's, 1892), pp. 47-48.
18. S. Freud, *Civilization and Its Discontents*, Eng. trans. (New York: Norton, 1962), p. 92.
19. G. Lukács,*History and Class Consciousness* (Cambridge: M.I.T. Press, 1971).

20. Ibid.

21. A. Gouldner, *Coming Crisis*, p. 51, citing Blau, "The Study of Formal Organization," in Parsons, *American Sociology*, p. 54.

22. L. Althusser, *For Marx* (New York: Vintage Books, 1970), p. 229.

23. J.P. Sartre, *The Psychology of Imagination*, Eng. trans. (New York: Washington Square Press, 1968), p. 159.

24. Feuerbach, *Essence of Christianity*, p. xxxix.

25. John Dewey, *Experience and Nature* (Chicago: Open Court, 1925), p. 96.

26. Jean Piaget, *Biologie et Connaissance* (Paris: Gallimard, 1967), p. 414: "Le vrai n'est pas copie, il est alors une organization du réel."

27. Emile Durkeim, *The Elementary Forms of the Religious Life*, Eng. trans. (New York: The Free Press, 1969), p. 466: "We have established the fact that the fundamental categories of thought, and consequently of science, are of religious origin."

28. Martin Buber, *I and Thou*, Eng. trans. (Edinburgh: T. & T. Clark, 1955).

29. Martin Heidegger, *Being and Time*, Eng. trans. (New York: Harper & Row, 1962), pp. 167–68.

30. See Kuhn, *Structure of Scientific Revolutions*.

31. *Portable Nietzsche*, p. 232.

Appendix I

Biographical and Bibliographic Data on the Contributors

RUBEM ALVES was born in Brazil in 1933. He was educated at the Campinas Presbyterian Seminary (State of São Paulo, Brazil), Union Theological Seminary (New York), and Princeton Theological Seminary (New Jersey). Recently he withdrew from the Presbyterian church in protest against its theological, social, and ecumenical conservatism. He now teaches at the Campinas State University in the department of social sciences.

His two major works will occupy our attention here. The first was his doctoral thesis at Princeton Theological Seminary, which was published with an introduction by Harvey Cox: *A Theology of Human Hope* (Washington, D.C.: Corpus Books, 1969). It represents his attempt to restructure Christian theology in terms of "messianic humanism," a humanism that is willing to accept the difficult work involved in authentic humanization. According to Alves, we are witnessing the emergence of a new type of human awareness and its accompanying idiom. It is a new kind of humanism focusing on people's freedom to re-create themselves rather than on some abstract human essence. It is, in short, a political humanism. But although Christians would readily join in this effort at liberation, they cannot rest content with this "political humanism" alone. Their passionate struggle for human liberation can be expressed better in terms of a "messianic humanism," a humanism that accepts the same historical task and struggle but is also open to God and the liberation experience described in the Bible. The Christian hopes against hope, knowing that liberation is not only a human struggle but also a divine gift. The future is created by God and human beings working in collaboration.

His second major book appeared several years later: *Tomorrow's Child: Imagination, Creativity and Rebirth of Culture* (New York: Harper and Row, 1972). It is concerned with the conditions required to establish a future society that is truly worthy of human beings. Borrowing an expression from Rollo May, he says that our present society operates on the "logic of the dinosaur." It is obsessed with unlimited growth, hence it neglects the role of creative acts. Forgetting that the human being is supposed to be a creator, it makes society the measure of all things. Alves champions a utopian humanism based on creative imagination and rooted in a community of faith that really knows how to speak the language of liberty. His utopian humanism is the humanism of prophets, saints, and revolutionaries. While we may not be around to see the birth of this new society, we can participate in its conception.

Alves's initial work was based on a theology of hope. In his later writings the theological theme of captivity has begun to come to the fore. It is nowhere more evident than in the moving autobiographical reflections that he has contributed to this volume.

HUGO ASSMANN was born in Brazil in 1933. He pursued his study of philosophy and sociology in Brazil, and his study of theology in Rome; he has also studied his own specialties at various universities in Latin America. He has a licentiate in the social sciences, a doctorate in theology, and a special diploma in the study of the mass communications media.

From 1962 to 1965 he taught courses in theology at the Jesuit theologate in São Leopoldo (Brazil) and at the pontifical Catholic University of Porto Alegre (Brazil). From 1966 to 1968 he was coordinator of studies at the São Paulo Institute of Philosophy and Theology (Brazil). In 1969 he served as a visiting professor on the theology faculty of the University of Münster (West Germany). In 1971 he was a member of the CEDI research and study group (Oruro, Bolivia), dealing with the specific issue of the political awareness of Bolivian miners. From 1971 to 1975 he served as secretary for the ISAL study group (*Iglesia y Sociedad en América Latina*). In this post he acted as the coordinator for various international theology seminars on the communications media and socio-political issues. Since 1974 he has been in San José (Costa Rica), serving as a professor in the school of journalism at the University of Costa Rica. He is also a member of that university's research institute dealing with the social sciences, and a professor in the ecumenical department of the national university's faculty of religious studies.

Between 1962 and 1969 various pastoral studies of his were published in Brazil. A work published in 1971 presented a critical analysis of the Christian presence in the Teoponte (Bolivia) guerrilla movement: *Teoponte: una experiencia guerrillera* (Oruro, Bolivia, CEDI). The book was withdrawn from circulation by the Bolivian police after the coup of August 1971; it was reissued in Caracas in 1971 (Editorial Nueva Izquierda). His *Teología de la liberación* was published in Montevideo in 1970 (MIEC-JECI). Those thoughts, further developed and expanded, were reissued in the volume entitled *Opresión-liberación: Desafío a los cristianos* (Montevideo: Tierra Nueva, 1971). With further elaborations, the content of those two earlier volumes was reissued as *Teología desde la praxis de la liberación* (Salamanca: Sígueme, 1973; Eng. trans. of Part 1: *Theology for a Nomad Church* [Maryknoll, New York: Orbis Books, 1976]). Divided into two basic sections, the book deals with theoretical and practical aspects of a theological reflection framed in a liberation context.

Assmann is also the editor of several important anthologies, including *Habla Fidel Castro sobre los cristianos revolucionarios* (Montevideo: Tierra Nueva, 1973). At present he is collaborating with Reyes Mate on an important trilogy that will anthologize the most important and basic Marxist texts on the religious question.

His own contributions to various anthologies include: "Die situation der unterentwickelt gehaltnnen Länder als Ort Einer Theologie der Revolution," in E. Feil and R. Weth, eds., *Diskussion zur "Theologie der Revolution"* (Mainz and Munich: Kaiser and Matthias Grünewald, 1969), pp. 218–48; "Aspetti fondamentali della riflessione teologica nell' America Latina e valutazione critica della 'teologia della liberazione,' " in *Teologie dal Terzo Mondo: teologia nera e teologia latino-americana della liberazione* (Brescia: Queriniana, 1974), pp. 37–53.

LEONARDO BOFF is a Franciscan who was born of Italian stock in Brazil (Concordia, State of Santa Catarina) on December 14, 1938. He pursued his philosophical and theological studies in Curitiba (State of Paraná) and Petrópolis (State of Rio de Janeiro), under the direction of such professors as Boaventura Kloppenburg and Constantino Koser. The latter is now Superior General of the Franciscan Order. Boff then pursued specialized study in Europe at Ludwig-Maximilian Universität in Munich under the direction of K. Rahner, L. Scheffczyk, and H. Fries. He also took courses at Würzburg, Louvain, and Oxford.

At present he is professor of systematic theology at the Petrópolis Institute for Philosophy and Theology. He is also the editor of the *Revista Eclesiástica Brasileira* and the Portuguese-language edition of *Concilium*. He is a member of the theological commission for the Brazilian National Episcopal Conference (CNBB), the Brazilian Religious Conference (CRB), and the Latin American Confederation of Religious (CLAR). In addition, he is the director of the religious division of Vozes, the Brazilian publishing house in Petrópolis.

Boff gained his doctorate in theology in Munich with a thesis on the church as a sacrament in the context of events in this world: *Die Kirche als Sakrament im Horizont der Welterfahrung: Versuch einer strukturfunktionalistischen Grundlegung im Hinblick auf das II. Vatikanische*

Konzil (Paderborn: Verlag Bonifacious, 1972). In one of his major works he presents an interpretation of Christology in terms of cosmic evolution, along the lines of Teilhard de Chardin: *O Evangelho do Cristo cósmico. A realidade de um mito e o mito de uma realidade* (Petrópolis: Vozes, 1970).

His best known work is *Jesus Cristo Libertador. Ensaio de cristologia crítica para o nosso tempo* (Petrópolis: Vozes, 1972). Eng. trans., *Jesus Christ Liberator* (Maryknoll, N.Y.: Orbis Books, 1978). Starting out from the general context of current Christologies, he traces the main lines of a Christology based on the situation of oppression in Latin America. This Christology is characterized by the following main features: the primacy of the anthropological element over the ecclesiological element; the primacy of the utopian element over the de facto element; the primacy of the critical elements over the dogmatic element; the primacy of the social element over the individual element; and the primacy of orthopraxis over orthodoxy. His article for this volume moves in very much the same direction.

Boff has written many other works ranging from spiritual to dogmatic theology. They include: *A oração no mundo secular. Desafio e chance* (Petrópolis: Vozes, 1971); *A ressurreição de Cristo. A nossa ressurreição na morte* (on the anthropological dimensions of Christian hope) (Petrópolis: Vozes, 1972); *Vida para além da morte. O presente—seu futuro, sua festa, sua contestação* (Petrópolis: Vozes, 1973); *O Destino do homen e do mondo. Ensaio sobre a vocação humana* (Petrópolis, 1974); *Experimentar Deus hoje* (Petrópolis: Vozes, 1974); *Ensaio de teologia narrativa* (Petrópolis: Vozes, 1975).

Among his many articles we should mention the series of ten articles on the theology of liberation and captivity which he wrote for the periodical *Grande Sinal* in 1974. He is currently engaged in a reconsideration of all the tracts of traditional dogmatic theology from the standpoint of liberation theology and the situation of alienation and dependence that characterizes Latin America.

JOSEPH COMBLIN was born in Brussels in 1923. He pursued his studies at Louvain and Malines and was ordained to the priesthood in 1947. From 1950 to 1958 he was a parish curate in Brussels. From 1958 on he has taught in many different institutes and universities in Latin America: the Campinas Catholic University in the State of São Paulo, Brazil (1958–1962); the Santiago theology department in Chile (1962–1964); the regional seminary and subsequently the theological institute in Recife, Brazil (1965–1972). On March 25, 1972, he was expelled from Brazil. Since then he has been teaching primarily at the Talca campus of the Catholic University of Chile. From 1968 to 1973 he was also a professor at IPLA (the Latin American Pastoral Institute) in Quito, until that organism closed down. Since 1970 he has also been on the theology faculty of the University of Louvain.

He has produced a vast body of work covering many different theological disciplines. In the field of biblical theology he has written *La résurrection de Jésus-Christ* (Paris: Ed. Universitaires, 1959); *Le Christ dans l'Apocalipse* (Tournai-Paris: Desclée, 1965); and a series of gospel meditations published by Vozes in Petrópolis, Brazil (in English see his *Jesus of Nazareth: Meditations on His Humanity* [Maryknoll, New York: Orbis Books, 1976]). He has taken stock of the current situation of theology in such works as: *Hacia una teología de la acción* (Barcelona: Herder, 1964); and *Mitos e realidades da secularização* (São Paulo: Herder, 1968). In the field of political philosophy he has written *Nação e nacionalismo* (São Paulo: Duas Cidades, 1965); and *O provisorio e o definitivo* (São Paulo: Herder, 1968). His articles on pastoral activity in Brazil have been collected in the volume entitled *Os sinais dos tempos e a evangelização* (São Paulo: Duas Cidades, 1968).

Of particular note are his writings on various contemporary themes and topics: *Théologie de la paix* (Paris: Ed. Universitaires, 1960 and 1963); *Théologie de la ville* (Paris: Ed. Universitaires, 1968); and in particular his two recent volumes on the theology of revolution, which will be discussed in more detail here. Comblin has written two articles on the themes of liberation: "El tema de la liberación en el pensamiento latinoamericano," in *Perspectivas de Diálogo*, 7, 64, pp. 105–14; "Freedom and Liberation as Theological Concepts," *Concilium* 96 (1974), pp. 92–104. But his principal works in this area are two recent volumes published by Universitaires press in Paris: *Théologie de la révolution*, 1970, and *Théologie de la pratique révolutionnaire*, 1974. They represent the fullest treatment so far of the theology of revolution, which made its first appearance in 1966 at the Geneva Conference of the World Council of Churches on "church and society." Selections from that meeting can be found in *The Church amid Revolution*, edited by Harvey Cox (New York: Association Press, 1967). The basic topic was pursued at another international conference which produced the volume entitled *Diskussion zur "Theologie der Revolution"* (Mainz and Munich: Kaiser and Matthias Grünewald, 1969).

On its first appearance the topic of revolution was overly affected by the whole issue of violence and its use. When liberation theology began to appear in 1970, it formulated the theme of revolution in the broader context of liberation praxis and revolutionary praxis. Comblin's two volumes deal with these issues in a structure and formulation that becomes very much his own as his thought develops. This is particularly true of the second volume, which is presented as a continuation of the first. Comblin picks up the issue of revolution theology and frames it within the broader context of liberation theology and liberation praxis. He is led to a radical questioning of theological methodology, as is evident in the article that he contributed to this present volume.

ENRIQUE DUSSEL was born in Mendoza (Argentina) on December 24, 1934. A Catholic layman, he is the father of three children. His scholastic degrees include a licentiate in philosophy from the University of Mendoza, a doctorate in philosophy from the University of Madrid, a doctorate in history from the Sorbonne, and a licentiate in theology from the Catholic Institute of Paris. He also pursued courses of study in Mainz and Münster (West Germany) and spent two years in Israel working as a laborer in Paul Gauthier's group. Formerly a professor on the faculty of Cuyo University in Mendoza, he lost his post because of his dedicated commitment to the cause of liberation and transferred to the University of Mexico City. He has given courses at Lumen Vitae (Brussels), CIDOC (Cuernavaca), and the institute for pastoral work among young people in Bogotá. He is president of the study commission concerned with the history of the church in Latin America (CEHILA).

One of his first works was concerned with church history: *Hipótesis para una historia de la Iglesia en América Latina* (Barcelona: Ed. Estela, 1967). After his sojourn in Israel he wrote *El humanismo semita* (Buenos Aires: Eudeba, 1969). It was the first effort in an ambitious attempt to sketch the history of peoples and civilizations. It has been followed by *El humanismo helénico* (Buenos Aires: Eudeba, 1974); *El dualismo en la antropología de la Cristiandad* (Buenos Aires: Guadalupe, 1974); and his magnum opus on Latin American church history, *Historia de la Iglesia en América Latina: Coloniaje y liberación (1492–1973)*, a revised and updated third edition appearing in 1974 (Barcelona, Nova Terra).

In a series of six lectures he offered his basic historical and theological interpretation of the Latin American continent: *Caminos de liberación latinoamericana I* (Eng. trans.: *History and the Theology of Liberation*, Maryknoll, New York: Orbis Books, 1976). In a second series of similar lectures, he offers a theological and ethical interpretation of the present situation in Latin America: *Caminos de liberación latinoamericana II* (Eng. trans.: *Ethics and the Theology of Liberation*, Maryknoll, N.Y.: Orbis Books, 1978).

In another major work he presents the broad outlines of a Latin American philosophy: *Para una ética de la liberación latinoamericana*, 3 vols. (Buenos Aires: Siglo XXI, 1973–1975). Reacting against the cultural domination of Latin America by power centers in Europe and North America, Dussel seeks to destroy the imported philosophical categories which hide the real situation rather than explaining it. A truly Latin American philosophy would offer a metaphysics centered around "otherness" and respect for "the other," and an ethics centered around the liberation of the oppressed. In the third volume Dussel spells out its concrete applications in several different areas. Liberation must produce new relationships between man and woman (the erotic aspect), parent and child (the pedagogical aspect), human beings in their societal life and fraternal relationships (the political aspect), and human beings in relationship to God (the theological aspect). His most recent book in this same vein is *Método para una filosofía de la liberación* (Salamanca: Sígueme, 1974).

In addition to the article prepared for this volume, he has outlined his thinking in two articles for *Concilium* (47, 1969; 96, 1974; both available in English). Another article, "The Political and Ecclesial Context of Liberation Theology," is included in *The Emergent Gospel*, ed. Sergio Torres and Virgina Fabella, M.M. (Maryknoll, N. Y.: Orbis Books, 1978).

SEGUNDO GALILEA was born in Santiago (Chile) in 1928. Ordained a priest in 1956, he spent the first few years of his ministry there and also served as the editorial director of the periodical *Pastoral Popular*. In 1962 he left his native country to serve the Latin American Episcopal Conference (CELAM) and other continent-wide organizations. In courses, lectures, and writings he has specialized in the area of pastoral theology, residing in Cuernavaca (Mexico), Quito (Ecuador), and Medellín (Colombia). Currently living in Medellín, he is in charge of fundamental pastoral study and research at the Pastoral Institute sponsored by CELAM.

Some of his many publications on pastoral theology are *Hacia una pastoral vernácula* (Santiago: Dilapsa, 1966); *Para una pastoral latinoamericana* (1968); *Evangelización en América Latina* (1970); *Reflexiones sobre la evangelización* (Quito: Ed. IPLA, 1970); *¿A los pobres se les anuncia el Evangelio?* (Bogotá: CELAM-IPLA, 1972); *Contemplación y apostolado* (Bogotá: CELAM-IPLA, 1973); *¿A dónde va la Pastoral?* (Bogotá: Paulinas, 1974).

Galilea has tried to spell out the basic lineaments of a liberation spirituality in the work entitled *Espiritualidad de la liberación* (Santiago: Ed. ISPLAJ, 1973). Such a spirituality would be based on five basic intuitions: (1) Conversion to God is actualized through conversion to one's fellow human beings; (2) the history of salvation is intimately bound up with the history of the liberation of the poor; (3) the tasks and commitments involved in the liberation process are anticipations of the kingdom of God; (4) liberation praxis is the historical shape taken by the exercise of charity; (5) it is possible to have a "Latin American reading" of the beatitudes, a reading done by the poor on a continent of poor people.

The basic lines of this spirituality are also indicated in his article for *Concilium* 96 ("Liberation as an Encounter with Politics and Contemplation," 1974; see Appendix II, anthologies). And they can be seen in his article for this volume.

GUSTAVO GUTIÉRREZ was born in Lima (Peru) in 1928. He finished his high school studies in his native city and then enrolled in the school of medicine at the National University in Lima. After five years of university study, during which time he was active in political groups at the university, he broke off his medical studies and enrolled in a course of philosophical and theological studies in order to prepare himself for the priesthood. After a semester of study in Santiago (Chile), he went to Europe. From 1951 to 1955 he studied philosophy and psychology at the University of Louvain. It was at this time that he began his close friendship with Camilo Torres, who arrived at that university in 1953 to pursue studies in the social sciences. From 1955 to 1959 Gutiérrez studied in the theology department at Lyon (France). In 1959 he was ordained a priest in Lima. During 1959 and 1960 he spent one semester at the Gregorian University in Rome. Since then he has lived in Lima, where he is a professor of theology in the Catholic University and a national adviser for the National Union of Catholic Students (UNEC).

His chief work is *Teología de la liberación, Perspectivas* (Lima: CEP, 1971; Eng. trans.: *A Theology of Liberation* [Maryknoll, New York: Orbis, 1973]). It is now the classic presentation of what is called the "theology of liberation," and it has been translated into many languages.

The formulation embodied in that work developed in three stages. The first stage goes back to 1964, when Ivan Illich organized a meeting in Petrópolis (Brazil) to discuss the pastoral activity of the church in Latin America. At that meeting Gutiérrez developed the epistemological theme of theology as critical reflection on praxis. The same theme would reappear in *La pastoral de la Iglesia latinoamericana: análisis teológico* (Montevideo: Ed. Centro de Documentación MIEC-JECI, 1968) and Chapter 1 of *A Theology of Liberation*. The second stage began in 1965, when armed groups began to fight actively in Latin America to liberate the continent from its dependent status. The new political awareness and the new concrete situation posed new problems for the theologian, and the theology learned in Europe proved incapable of solving them. There thus developed an interest in the underlying social and political backdrop, and this interest has continued to mark the theology of liberation. The third stage dates from July 1967, when Gutiérrez presented a course on poverty in Montreal (Canada). Now the poor were viewed from a new standpoint: both as a social class and as the bearers of God's word. This new turn of thought would be developed in the concluding chapter of *A Theology of Liberation*.

Gutiérrez presented the first rough sketch of a liberation theology at a conference held in Chimbote (Peru) in July 1968. It was published the next year as *Hacia una teología de la liberación* (Montevideo: Ed. Centro de Documentación MIEC-JECI, 1969). The same theme was further elaborated at a meeting organized by Sodepax on "theology and development," which was held in Cartigny (Switzerland) in November 1969. It is not correct, however, to view liberation theology as a direct outcome of concern for a theology of development (as does Eduardo Ibarra, in *Teologie della liberazione in America Latina* [Rome: Città Nuova, 1975], pp. 64–67). Gutiérrez simply presented his own fresh view at a conference that had been organized by others from a somewhat different perspective. His paper was later published in several languages, and there is an English edition of it (*Notes on a Theology of Liberation* [Lausanne: Sodepax; 1970]).

Two further articles appeared in 1974: "Praxis de liberación, teología y anuncio," in *Concilium* 96, published by Herder and Herder in the United

States; and *Praxis of Liberation and Christian Faith*, based on a course given at the Mexican American Cultural Center in San Antonio (Texas) and published by that Center. His contribution to the Ecumenical Dialogue of Third World Theologians (Dar es Salaam, August 1976) can be found in *The Emergent Gospel*, ed. Sergio Torres and Virginia Fabella, M.M. (Maryknoll, N.Y.; Orbis Books, 1978).

The selection used here is his Prologue to *Signos de Liberación* (Lima: Ed. CEP, 1973). Where possible, footnote entries have been brought up to date.

JOSE MIGUEZ BONINO was born in Santa Fe (Argentina) in 1924. Married, he is the father of three children. After his initial studies in Rosario (Argentina), he attended the Evangelical theologate in Buenos Aires, Emory University in the United States, and Union Theological Seminary in New York. In 1948 he was ordained a Methodist minister in Argentina, after which he was assigned to pastoral duties in both Bolivia and Argentina.

Since 1954 he has been on the faculty of the Evangelical theologate, holding a chair in theology and ethics. He served as rector from 1960 to 1969. Besides teaching there, he is now in charge of postgraduate studies at the Evangelical Institute of Advanced Theological Studies in Buenos Aires.

Míguez Bonino was an observer of the Methodist church at Vatican II, and he has served on various boards of the World Council of Churches. He has been a visiting professor at Union Theological Seminary in New York, the Waldensian theologate in Rome, and the Selly Colleges in Birmingham, England.

His books include an evaluation of Vatican II (*Concilio abierto* [Buenos Aires: Aurora, 1968]), a discussion of the problems facing Christian ecumenism in Latin America (*Integración humana y unidad cristiana* [Río Piedras, Puerto Rico: La Reforma, 1968]), and a presentation of Christian ethics based on love (*Ama y haz lo que quieras* [Buenos Aires: La Aurora, 1972]). He also edited an anthology dealing with ecumenical relationships between Catholics and Protestants in Latin America (*Polémica, diálogo y misión* [Buenos Aires: Centro de Estudios, 1967]). Liberation theology and the problem of violence have come under consideration in such articles as: "Teología de la liberación," in *Actualidad Pastoral* 3 (1970):83–85; and "La violencia: una reflexión teológica," *Cristianismo y Sociedad* 10 (1972) 28: 5-12.

An important and elaborate contribution to liberation theology is his book entitled *Doing Theology in a Revolutionary Situation* (Philadelphia: Fortress Press, 1975). Exploring the impact of both Catholicism and Protestantism on Latin American society and its history, he considers the views of other liberation theologians and tries to spell out the historical effort it will entail. This book prompted Jürgen Moltmann to write his "Open Letter to José Míguez Bonino" (*Christianity and Crisis*, March 29,

1976), that being the first reply of a European political theologian to a Latin American theologian of liberation.

RONALDO MUÑOZ was born in Santiago (Chile) in 1933. After pursuing studies in architecture, he joined the Picpus Fathers in 1954. He pursued his philosophical and theological studies at their seminary in Los Perales (Chile), where he was ordained a priest in 1961.

On his first tour of study in Europe, he obtained a licentiate in theology at the Gregorian University in Rome and pursued doctoral studies at the Catholic Institute of Paris (1963). Since 1964 he has divided his time between teaching fundamental and dogmatic theology, doing pastoral work among urban workers, and serving as a theology adviser for various community and ecclesial organizations in Chile and elsewhere in Latin America. Since 1966 he has been on the theology faculty of the Catholic University of Chile in Santiago. He has been deeply involved in the postconciliar updating of the Chilean church, participating in seminars, programs, and diocesan synods. After serving as a theological adviser for the lay commission of the Latin American Episcopal Conference (CELAM), he became the theology adviser for the Latin American Confederation of Religious (CLAR).

On a second tour of study in Europe (1970–1971), he worked with the interdisciplinary group headed by Professor Norbert Schiffers, who holds a chair in fundamental theology at the University of Regensburg (West Germany). There he devoted himself to a theological analysis of the many research and study documents being produced by the Latin American church. The result was his imposing monograph, *Nueva conciencia de la Iglesia en América Latina*, which brought him his doctorate in theology from that university in 1972. That work has been published in Chile (Santiago: Nueva Universidad, 1973) and in Spain (Salamanca: Sígueme, 1974).

Returning to Chile in 1972, he has divided his time between research and active works of service to a church caught in the midst of social convulsions. In 1974 he was invited to teach in Spain, and from November 1974 to January 1975 he gave courses under the auspices of the theology departments of Comillas (Madrid) and Salamanca.

He has published numerous articles on current theological thought and research for the periodical *Mensaje* in Santiago and for other periodicals in Chile and Latin America. One such article is "La teología de la liberación en el último Sínodo Romano," which appeared in *Mensaje* in 1972 (21, 208, pp. 735–746). More recently he contributed to the anthology entitled *Nuestra Iglesia Latinoamericana: tensiones y quehacer de los cristianos* (Bogotá, 1975).

Here we shall conclude by considering his major work, which has placed him in the forefront of ecclesiological studies dealing with Latin America. In *Nueva conciencia de la Iglesia en América Latina*, Muñoz examined approximately three hundred documents produced by various Christian groups and spokespeople in Latin America between 1965 and 1970. His aim was to discern the new awareness of the Latin American church as it was exemplified by more avant-garde Christian groups. The first part of the study examined the new awareness of Christians with regard to society and its structures. The second division examines this new awareness with regard to the established church. Thus the book makes clear that the basic polarization is not between church on the one hand and society on the other, but between groups of Christians whose consciousness has been raised on the one hand and the established church of less aware Christians on the other. The ecclesiological emphasis and concern of the author is also evident in the article he has submitted to this volume.

JUAN CARLOS SCANNONE was born in Buenos Aires (Argentina) in 1931. He entered the Society of Jesus in 1949 and was ordained a priest in 1962. He received a doctorate in philosophy from the University of Munich (West Germany) and a licentiate in theology from the University of Innsbruck (Austria). At present he is dean of the philosophy department at the Universidad del Salvador (Buenos Aires/San Miguel), where he teaches philosophical theology. He also teaches in the theology department of that university. He is the vice-president of the Argentinian Theological Society and an adviser to the periodical *Stromata*.

Some of his many publications deal with philosophical issues and the work of such philosophers as Hegel, Heidegger, Blondel, and Lonergan. One such publication was *Sein und Inkarnation—Zum ontologischen Hintergrund der Frühschriften M. Blondels* (Freiburg and Munich: Alber, 1968), which dealt with the ontological background of Blondel's early writings.

Scannone has also dealt with various God-related issues from the Latin American standpoint: "Hacia una filosofía de la religión posmoderna y latinoamericanamente situada," in *Hacia una filosofía de la liberación latinoamericana* (Buenos Aires, 1973); and "El itinerario filosófico hacia el Dios vivo—Reflexiones sobre su historia, su planteo actual y su relectura desde la situación latinoamericana," in *Stromata* 3 (1974).

He has contributed important articles on the theology of liberation: e.g., "Hacia una dialéctica de la liberación, tarea del pensar practicante en Latino-América," *Stromata*, 1–2 (1971) 27:23-60; "El lenguaje teológico de la liberación," in *Víspera*, 7 (1973):41–47; and "The Theology of Liberation: Evangelical or Ideological? " in *Concilium* 93 (1974). He has also written articles to present the whole topic of liberation theology to the German- and French-reading public: "La théologie de la liberation en Amérique Latine," in *Christus*, no. 75; "Die Theologie der Befreiung in Lateinamerika," in *Orientierung* 1 (1973).

Several of the articles mentioned above are included in his *Teología de la liberación y praxis popular: Aportes críticos para una teología de la liberación* (Salamanca: Sígueme, 1976).

JUAN LUIS SEGUNDO, a Jesuit priest, was born in Montevideo (Uruguay) in 1925. He completed his philosophical studies in Argentina and his theological studies at the Louvain in Belgium, obtaining a licentiate in theology in 1956. In 1963 the University of Paris conferred on him the degree of Doctor of Letters, for which he had prepared two theses on the philosophy of religion: *Berdiaeff, une réflexion chrétienne sur la personne* (Paris: Aubier, 1963); and *La cristiandad ¿una utopía?* (Montevideo: Cursos de Complementación Cristiana, 1964). Presently he is associated with the Peter Faber Center in Montevideo, specializing in research concerned with the sociology of religion. He has published numerous articles in various Latin American periodicals as well as in *Perspectivas de Diálogo*, the official review of the Peter Faber Center.

In collaboration with others he is the author of a major course in theology for adult lay people. Instead of exploring all the details of theology as a scholarly science, this five-volume work takes the present crisis of faith as its concrete starting point. Operating out of the real world of contemporary human beings, it concentrates on some of the more fundamental mysteries of faith and divine revelation. This major work has been translated into English under the general title, *A Theology for Artisans of a New Humanity* (Maryknoll, New York: Orbis Books, 1973–1974). Each volume can be read as an independent work, but the whole series is the outgrowth of reflection and discussion in which lay people were active participants. Volume Five (*Evolution and Guilt*) complements Volume Two (*Grace and the Human Condition*), providing the broad outlines of a Christian moral theology that gives serious consideration to the political implications of grace.

Segundo has produced two other works of major importance. *De la sociedad a la teología* (Buenos Aires: Ed. Carlos Lohlé, 1970) spells out the tasks incumbent on a Latin American theology that seeks to proclaim salvation truths in a general context of social transformation and liberation. *Liberación de la teología* (Buenos Aires: Ed. Carlos Lohlé, 1975; Eng. trans., *The Liberation of Theology* [Maryknoll, New York: Orbis Books, 1976]) is an expanded version of a course given at Harvard University in the Spring of 1974. It subjects the methodology of academic theology to a thoroughgoing critique, offering major contributions to the development of a new theological methodology.

Segundo has also discussed these varied issues in articles such as the following: "Instrumentos de la teología latinoamericana," in *Liberación en América Latina* (Bogotá: Ed. América Latina, 1972), pp. 37–54; and "Liberación: fe e ideología," in *Mensaje* 208 (1972):248–54. For this volume he has asked us to reprint an earlier article of his which appeared in *Concilium* 96. Exploring one of the crucial issues on the frontier of present-day theology, it was widely quoted and discussed when it first appeared.

LUIS G. DEL VALLE was born in Mexico City on May 29, 1927. After completing his studies in the humanities, philosophy, and theology, he was ordained a Jesuit priest in 1957. He subsequently majored in dogmatic theology, studying in Germany and in Rome. He received his doctorate from the Pontifical Gregorian University in Rome in 1963, and since then he has been a professor of dogmatic theology in his native country. He has also been active in pastoral activities and ecumenical studies in Mexico City. He is one of the most typical representatives and spokesmen of liberation theology among the theologians of Mexico.

Most of his thinking has appeared in the form of articles and papers. They include the following: "Fe y Desarrollo," in *Reflexión Episcopal Pastoral* 3 (1969):49–57; "Hechos significativos y significatividad de los hechos," in *Memoria del primer Congreso Nacional de Teología* (Mexico City: Ed. Alianza, 1970-71), 2:19–25; "Crítica profética de la Iglesia y en la Iglesia," in *Christus* 426 (1971): 11–16; "El papel de la teología en América Latina," in *Liberación en América Latina* (Bogotá: Ed. América Latina, 1971), pp. 17–33, also published in *Christus* in 1972, p. 439ff.; "Identidad del cristiano revolucionario," in *Contacto* 9, nos. 3–4 (1972):42–50; "Fe y compromiso temporal," in *Contacto* 11, no. 2 (1974):22–35, also published in *Christus* in 1974.

RAÚL VIDALES was born in Monterrey (Mexico) on February 28, 1943, and was ordained to the priesthood in 1967. He holds a licentiate in both theology and sociology, and he has been very active in grassroots organizations and church organisms in Latin America.

For a time he was a professor at the Latin American Pastoral Institute (IPLA) in Quito, where he worked with Segundo Galilea, Joseph Comblin, Enrique Dussel, and Leonidas Proaño. There he was involved in pastoral reflection based on the many and varied concrete pastoral experiences to be found in Latin America. He subsequently worked with different institutes engaged in reflection on pastoral theology: the Regional Institute of Higher Theological Studies in Mexico, the Missionary Training Institute in Guatemala, and the Latin American Catechetical Institute in Colombia. He has also taught courses in many parts of Latin America under the auspices of various universities: e.g., the Catholic University of Quito, the University of Monterrey, and the Catholic University of Lima. He has been particularly interested in working with pastoral-action groups, trying to move them toward the practice of liberative evangelization.

In recent years he has written articles for various theological periodicals in Latin America: e.g., *Servir* (Mexico), *Christus* (Mexico), and *Actualidad Pastoral* (Argentina). He has also contributed to the MIEC-JECI documentary service in Lima.

At present he is working with Gustavo Gutiérrez at the Bartolomé de las Casas Research Center in Lima. He is in charge of the division dealing with "liberative evangelization and popular religiosity," which was the subject of his first published work. He directs groups of theology students who are working on liberation theology and also does research in close contact with other research centers in Latin America.

One of the younger theologians involved with liberation theology, his name and work are well known in Latin America. He has studied various questions of Christology and ecclesiology from the standpoint of active involvement with the common people. His publications mark him as a specialist in the methodology of liberation theology, as the article contributed to this volume indicates.

His principal works include: *La Iglesia latinoamericana y la política después de Medellín* (Bogotá, 1972); with Segundo Galilea, *Cristología y pastoral popular* (Bogotá: Paulinas, 1974); with the IPLA-CELAM study group, *Pastoral y lenguage;* and with Tokihiro Kudo, *Práctica religiosa y proyecto histórico* (Lima, 1975).

Among his most important articles are the following: "Tareas y proyecciones en la teología de la liberación," in *Servir* 9 (1973):185–202; "El método en la teología de la liberación," in *Christus* 38 (1974): 28–33; "Sacramentos y liberación," in *Servir* 10 (1974): 67–77; "¿Cómo hablar de Cristo hoy? " MIEC-JECI documentation service, Lima, nos. 22–23, pp. 4–15; and "Some Recent Publications in Latin America on the Theology of Liberation," in *Concilium* 96.

Appendix II

Supplementary Bibliography
of Authors and Anthologies

AUTHORS

Gonzalo Arroyo

1972 "La larga marcha hacia el socialismo," *Hechos y Dichos*, 432.

1972 *Significado y sentido de Cristianos por el Socialismo*, published by the National Secretariat of the Christians for Socialism movement, Santiago, Chile. Arroyo was a leader in this movement in Chile before the 1973 coup. For a fuller discussion see the anthology entitled *Christians and Socialism* below.

1974 *Coup d'Etat au Chili*, Paris, Ed. du Cerf.

Ignacio Ellacuría

1974 *Teología Política*, San Salvador, Interdiocesan Social Secretariat; Eng. trans.: *Freedom Made Flesh*, Maryknoll, New York: Orbis Books, 1976.

1974 *Carácter político de la misión de Jesús*, Lima, MIEC-JECI Documentation Service, 13–14.

1975 "Posibilidad, necesidad y sentido de una teología Latino-americana" (Parts I and II), Mexico City, *Christus* 40:12–16, 17–23.

Dom Antonio Fragoso

1969   *Evangile et révolution sociale*, Paris, Ed. du Cerf.
1971   "Lutter pour la liberation de l'homme," *Communion*, 25, 97, pp. 52–55.
1974   "Résurrection et libération," *Communion*, 25, 100, pp. 46–50.

Lucio Gera

1970   *Apuntes para una interpretación de la Iglesia argentina*, Montevideo, MIEC-JECI Documentation Center.
1973   "Liberación del pecado y liberación histórico-secular," *Perspectivas de Diálogo*, 8, 77, pp. 198–207.
1973   "Teología de la liberación," *Perspectivas de Diálogo*, 8, 72, pp. 38–50.

José Porfirio Miranda

1971   *Marx y la Biblia: crítica a la filosofía de la opresión*, Salamanca, Sígueme; Eng. trans.: *Marx and the Bible*, Maryknoll, New York: Orbis Books, 1974.
1973   *El ser y el Mesías*, Salamanca, Sígueme; Eng. trans.: *Being and the Messiah*, Maryknoll, New York: Orbis Books, 1977.

Alex Morelli

1971   *Libera a mi pueblo*, Mexico City and Buenos Aires, Ed. Carlos Lohlé.

Bishop Eduardo Pironio

1970   *La Iglesia que nace entre nosotros*, Bogotá, issued by CELAM.
1970   *La Iglesia, Pueblo de Dios*, Bogotá, issued by CELAM.

Bishop Leónidas Proaño

1972   "A Church and Politics in Ecuador," *Concilium* 71, pp. 99–105.
1973   *Pour une Eglise Liberatrice*, Paris, Ed. du Cerf.

Bishop Samuel Ruiz

1973   *Los cristianos y la justicia en América Latina*, Lima, MIEC-JECI Documentation Service.

ANTHOLOGIES

1968   Medellín Conference Documents. Second General Conference of Latin American Bishops (Medellín, Colombia, 1968). Official English edition edited by Louis Michael Colonnese, Latin American Division of the United States Catholic Conference, Washington, D.C.: *The Church in the Present-Day Transfor-*

mation of Latin America in the Light of the Council; Vol. 1: *Position Papers;* Vol. 2: *Conclusions.*

1969   *Signos de renovación,* Lima, Ed. Universitaria, postconciliar documents from and about the Church in Latin America; Eng. trans.: *Between Honesty and Hope,* Maryknoll, New York: Maryknoll Publications, 1970.

1969   *Iglesia Latinoamericana: ¿protesta o profecía?,* anthology edited by J. Rossi and introduced by J. L. Segundo, Avellaneda, Ed. Búsqueda.

1970   *Teología de la liberación,* a two-volume symposium, Bogotá, Ed. Presencia; Vol. 1: *Aportes para la liberación;* Vol. 2: *Opción de la Iglesia latinoamericana en la década del 70.*

1972   *Liberación latinoamericana.* A special issue of *Stromata* (1–2, 193) devoted entirely to the subject of Latin American liberation, Buenos Aires.

1973   *Signos de liberación,* an anthology of the church's witness in Latin America from 1969 to 1973, Lima, Ed. CEP.

1973   *Fe cristiana y cambio social en América Latina,* Salamanca, Sígueme; the 1972 El Escorial theology convention on the situation and theology of Latin America.

1974   *Concilium 96: The Mystical and Political Dimension of the Christian Faith,* edited by Claude Geffré and Gustavo Gutiérrez; Eng. trans., New York, Herder and Herder/ Seabury; devoted entirely to current Latin American theology.

1975   *Christians and Socialism,* Eng. trans., Maryknoll, New York, Orbis Books; a major anthology of documents dealing with the Christians for Socialism movement centered in Chile before the military coup.

OTHER ORBIS TITLES

THE COMING
OF THE THIRD CHURCH
An Analysis of the Present and Future of the Church

Walbert Buhlmann

"Not a systematic treatment of contemporary ecclesiology but a popular narrative analogous to Alvin Toffler's Future Shock." America

ISBN 0-88344-069-5 CIP   *Cloth $12.95*

ISBN 0-88344-070-9   *Paper $6.95*

FREEDOM MADE FLESH

Ignacio Ellacuría

"Ellacuría's main thesis is that God's saving message and revelation are historical, that is, that the proclamation of the gospel message must possess the same historical character that revelation and salvation history do and that, for this reason, it must be carried out in history and in a historical way." Cross and Crown

ISBN 0-88344-140-3   *Cloth $8.95*

ISBN 0-88344-141-1   *Paper $4.95*

CHRISTIAN POLITICAL THEOLOGY
A MARXIAN GUIDE

Joseph Petulla

"Petulla presents a fresh look at Marxian thought for the benefit of Catholic theologians in the light of the interest in this subject which was spurred by Vatican II, which saw the need for new relationships with men of all political positions." Journal of Economic Literature

ISBN 0-88344-060-1   *Paper $4.95*

THE NEW CREATION:
MARXIST AND CHRISTIAN?

José María González-Ruiz

"A worthy book for lively discussion." The New Review of Books and Religion

ISBN 0-88344-327-9 CIP   *Cloth $6.95*

CHRISTIANS AND SOCIALISM
Documentation of the Christians for
Socialism Movement in Latin America

edited by John Eagleson

"Compelling in its clear presentation of the issue of Christian commitment in a revolutionary world." The Review of Books and Religion

ISBN 0-88344-058-X   *Paper $4.95*

THE CHURCH AND
THIRD WORLD REVOLUTION

Pierre Bigo

"Heavily documented, provocative yet reasonable, this is a testament, demanding but impressive." Publishers Weekly

ISBN 0-88344-071-7 CIP   *Cloth $8.95*
ISBN 0-88344-072-5   *Paper $4.95*

THE GOSPEL IN SOLENTINAME

Ernesto Cardenal

"Upon reading this book, I want to do so many things—burn all my other books which at best seem like hay, soggy with mildew. I now know who (not what) is the church and how to celebrate church in the eucharist..The dialogues are intense, profound, radical. The Gospel in Solentiname calls us home." Carroll Stuhlmueller, National Catholic Reporter

ISBN 0-88344-168-3 CIP   *Cloth $6.95*